Praise for Philip L. Fradkin's
Wallace Stegner and the American West

"Respectful of his subject but never worshipful, Fradkin has given us our first full critical portrait of the man and his protean career. A widely published author on wilderness and the West, the Pulitzer Prize–winning Fradkin was the first environmental reporter for the *Los Angeles Times*. Which is to say he's thoroughly steeped in the very landscapes and conflicts with which Stegner spent his life grappling." Hampton Sides, *Men's Vogue*

"Author of many books on the American West, western editor of *Audubon* magazine, and a Pulitzer Prize–winning reporter for the *Los Angeles Times*, Philip L. Fradkin has a résumé that seems to suit him perfectly to write the life of that most Western of literary figures, Wallace Stegner. And after reading *Wallace Stegner and the American West*, it is clear that this is an ideal match between biographer and subject." Front page, *San Francisco Chronicle Book Review*

"As Fradkin notes in this astute biography, it was a miracle that [Stegner] didn't write pulp westerns. Instead, Stegner took as his subject the failure of his father's homestead, built on denial of the most fundamental Western reality: drought." *The New Yorker*

"Fradkin's dynamic and probing portrait of Stegner brilliantly combines literary and environmental history, and provides a fresh and telling perspective on the rampant development of the arid West, and Stegner's prophetic warnings of the complex consequences." *Booklist*

"Stegner disliked the epithet 'dean of Western writers,' but many authors, readers, and environmentalists are grateful he earned it. Fradkin's clear-eyed biography is another occasion for their gratitude."
Los Angeles Times Book Review

"Novelist, biographer, and chronicler of the North American West; ardent conservationist and influential teacher of writing: Wallace Stegner retains a loyal constituency of readers. Still, even before his death in 1993, he had begun to fade from view. Philip Fradkin's biography, *Wallace Stegner and the American West*, is nicely timed to set the table for Stegner's centennial in 2009."
The New York Times Book Review

"An engaging, holistic recounting of a rich, rough-and-tumble literary life, anchored in the rugged Western terrain, a fast-vanishing wilderness that Stegner would say we must preserve for our very sanity, a landscape crucial to our human 'geography of hope.'" *BookPage*

"An absorbing biography." *Outside*

"Relentless research and a chronological narrative give way to a balanced biography rich in anecdote." *High Country News*

"Provides the comprehensive story of Stegner's achievements with inclusiveness and grace." *Rocky Mountain News*

"Because Stegner, whatever else, was blessed with the gift for beautiful writing, it is only fair that his biography be equally well-written. With this classy, well-balanced book, Fradkin has outdone himself, presenting Stegner as the eminent scholar and writer he was, but also as a flawed human being who made mistakes." *Deseret News*

"It's easy to fall into the trap of hagiography when writing about a high achiever of exemplary character. Reality is always more complicated and interesting, however, and Philip L. Fradkin is able to push past the plaudits in *Wallace Stegner and the American West* and get closer to the man." *The Oregonian*

"The complexity of this important figure is finally captured in a remarkable new biography by Philip L. Fradkin. . . . Fradkin brings a novelist's eye to this well-told life story." *Seattle Post-Intelligencer*

"Sturdy and fact-packed, Philip L. Fradkin's *Wallace Stegner and the American West* will satisfy anyone who wants to know what Stegner did and when and where he did it." *San Jose Mercury News*

"Fradkin's life of Stegner reveals a man of great determination, broad gifts, generous spirit, and impressive accomplishments." *The Boston Globe*

"A handy field guide to [Stegner's] literary fault lines as well as an astute assessment of Stegner's legacy as both a teacher and a conservationist."
East Bay Express

"Fradkin has given readers a gift that goes beyond what we learn in its pages about Wallace Stegner's life and work, to include the West itself, a unique geography that Stegner once called 'the geography of hope,' a geography whose future is now in our hands." *Bookpaths*

"There are two earlier biographies of Stegner. . . . These were literary biographies, or 'writer as hero tales.' By contrast, Philip Fradkin was interested in the whole man, flaws included. In *Wallace Stegner and the American West*, he has created a variation on biography that I can only call 'writer as hero in the landscape.'" *The Bloomsbury Review*

Wallace Stegner
and the American West

Wallace Stegner and the American West

Philip L. Fradkin

UNIVERSITY OF CALIFORNIA PRESS

Berkeley · Los Angeles · London

University of California Press, one of the most distinguished university presses in the United States, enriches lives around the world by advancing scholarship in the humanities, social sciences, and natural sciences. Its activities are supported by the UC Press Foundation and by philanthropic contributions from individuals and institutions. For more information, visit www.ucpress.edu.

University of California Press
Berkeley and Los Angeles, California

Published by arrangement with Alfred A. Knopf, a division of Random House, Inc.; previously published in 2008 as a Borzoi Book by Alfred A. Knopf.

Grateful acknowledgment is made to the following for permission to reprint previously published and unpublished material:

Alfred A. Knopf: Excerpts from seven letters from Alfred A. Knopf to Wallace Stegner. Reprinted by permission of Alfred A. Knopf, a division of Random House, Inc.

Doubleday: Excerpts from various letters from Ken McCormick and Stewart Richardson to Wallace Stegner and his agent, Carol Brandt. Reprinted by permission of Doubleday, a division of Random House, Inc.

Trinity University Press: Antonya Nelson's definition of "angle of repose" from *Home Ground: Language for an American Landscape* edited by Barry Lopez, © 2006 by Trinity University Press. Reprinted by permission of Trinity University Press.

University of Nevada Press: Excerpt from *Stegner: Conversations on History and Literature* by Wallace Stegner and Richard W. Etulain (revised edition 1990; Reno: University of Nevada Press, 1996). Reprinted courtesy of University of Nevada Press.

Library of Congress Cataloging-in-Publication Data

Fradkin, Philip L.
  Wallace Stegner and the American West / Philip L. Fradkin.
    p.   cm.
  Originally published : New York: Alfred A. Knopf, 2008.
  Includes bibliographical references and index.
  ISBN 978-0-520-25957-7 (pbk. : alk. paper)
    1. Stegner, Wallace Earle, 1909-1993. 2. Authors, American—20th century—Biography. 3. Conservationists—United States—Biography. 4. West (U.S.)—In literature. I. Title.
  PS3537.T316Z64 2009
  813'.52—dc22
  [B]   2008043602

Manufactured in the United States of America

18   17   16   15   14   13   12   11   10   09
10   9   8   7   6   5   4   3   2   1

This book is printed on Natures Book, which contains 30% post-consumer waste and meets the minimum requirements of ANSI/NISO Z39.48-1992 (R 1997) (*Permanence of Paper*).

Again for my father,
Leon Henry Fradkin,
*who was also a gentleman and passed on
his love for the West to me*

I've made a kind of American hegira from essential poverty through the academic world, from real ignorance (my parents never finished the sixth grade) to living in a world where my natural companions are people of real brilliance. As Americans, it seems to me, we are expected to make the whole pilgrimage of civilization in a single lifetime. That's a hell of a thing to ask of anybody.

Wallace Stegner, in David Dillon,
"Time's Prisoner's: An Interview with Wallace Stegner"

The past keeps feeding into the present. It isn't lost and thrown overboard as much as it seems to be. It isn't as useless or as irrelevant as it seems to be. The past controls you a whole lot more than you might want to be controlled.

Wallace Stegner, in Forrest G. Robinson and Margaret G. Robinson,
"An Interview with Wallace Stegner"

Nearly self-explanatory, the oxymoronic-seeming term angle of repose designates the maximum angle at which a slope of loose material (such as soil or sand) remains stable. It is the point at which gravity challenges friction, the tense moment before one succumbs to the other. . . . It's a term begging to be made metaphorical for human relations, as Wallace Stegner demonstrates in his Pulitzer Prize–winning novel by the same name. In the book, the fraught connection of the present to the past, one generation to the next, replicates the peculiar tension between friction and gravity, between hanging on and falling apart. "You were too alert to the figurative possibilities of words not to see the phrase as descriptive of human as well as detrital rest," Stegner writes. "As you said, it was too good for mere dirt; you tried to apply it to your own wandering and uneasy life. It is the angle I am aiming for myself, and I don't mean the rigid angle at which I rest in this chair."

Antonya Nelson, "Angle of Repose,"
in *Home Ground: Language for an American Landscape*

CONTENTS

INTRODUCTION

Past attempts to assess Wallace Stegner have judged him on the terms he preferred, as a writer of novels. Writing novels was really all he wanted to do. But he had another full-time occupation and a part-time avocation. Stegner needed to teach in order to support his family, and the nonfiction words he produced propelled him, somewhat reluctantly, into the ranks of the conservation activists.

Stegner made remarkable contributions as a writer, teacher, and conservationist. What he achieved in any one of those fields would have gained him lasting recognition in the West. The complete Stegner package, however, reached beyond regional boundaries. The uniqueness of Stegner's contributions was also the cause of his diminishment, because scholars and critics were unable to recognize the totality of the man's achievements. They needed to put him into a niche. So they made him a novelist, as he asked them to.

The two previous biographies of Stegner were written by professors of literature who were mainly interested in him as a literary figure. They didn't deal very extensively with the fact that he was human, meaning that, like the rest of us, he was flawed. I am more intrigued by the whole man—or as close as I can get to him—set against the passing backdrops of his life. This is a book about a man and the physical landscapes he inhabited and how they influenced him. Within that framework it is also the story of a quintessential westerner who eventually could not deal with the wrenching changes that are a constant of the American West. sĭ·nĕk·dē·kē

Synecdoche, meaning a specific example used to illustrate a generality, was one of Stegner's favorite words and writing techniques. In a similar fashion, I use the life of Wallace Stegner as the vista from which to gaze upon the panorama of the American West in the twentieth century, for his time spanned the transition from prairie frontier to Silicon Valley. Stegner inhabited all of the West's different landscapes physically, emotionally, and mentally, as well as in his writings. The prairies, mountains, deserts, plateaus, rivers, coast, remote villages, small towns, and cities of the West were intimately known to him.

The man embraced those spaces and that time and gave them meaning. The dense mosaic of human experience within the West that he wrote about, the many gifted writers he unleashed as a teacher, and the lands and water he placed a value upon and actively protected as a conservationist were his lasting gifts to the nation. Those offerings made him far more than a regional presence—they made him unclassifiable.

THE FIRST BIOGRAPHY, titled *Wallace Stegner*, was written by Forrest G. Robinson and Margaret G. Robinson and published in 1977, at the height of Stegner's writing career. Robinson is a professor of literature at the University of California at Santa Cruz, and his wife was a reference librarian at the university. The second biography, *Wallace Stegner: His Life and Work* by Jackson Benson, was published in 1996, three years after Stegner's death. Benson taught American literature at San Diego State University.

The Robinson and the Benson books gave me the basic structure of Stegner's life, to which I could affix the themes and details that I thought were most meaningful. In addition, Benson's many taped and transcribed interviews with Stegner and Stegner's colleagues and friends, which became available in 2005, provided information that would otherwise have vanished. I thank the Robinsons and Benson for breaking the Stegner Trail. Along the way I was able to gather much material that has never before been published.

There was room, I thought, on the eve of the centennial of Stegner's birth, for another biography, one by an environmental historian with no advanced degree. I have been attempting in recent years, through a variety of subjects (the West, California, and earthquakes), to demonstrate the effect of landscape—meaning nature—on human destiny, history, culture, and character. This book allows me to focus that inquiry on one individual.

When I embarked upon this project, in the spring of 2004, Stegner's widow, Mary, was ailing. The Stegners' only child, Page Stegner, and Jo Ann Rogers, a longtime family helper, jointly held the power of attorney of the Stegner estate. Neither Page nor Jo Ann placed any restrictions on my use and interpretations of the material, and both were extremely helpful. In fact, Page and I aided each other: I sent him letters for his projected volume of selected correspondence, and he did the same for my book. Our projects were mutually enriched by this exchange.

A WORD—or rather an image—about the structure. Picture, and remember for the time it takes to read this book, a piece of rope eighty-four inches long. I am suggesting neither a piece of natural hemp nor an artificial Dacron or nylon product but rather a combination—something with a roughened internal texture and an even exterior, like Stegner. Each inch corresponds to a year in his life, and the whole represents most of the twentieth century in the American West.

At the start of the rope ("Unformed Youth") all the strands lie neatly plaited together. A considerable number of pages are devoted to his youth, not only because it was so formative but also because Stegner wrote about it so extensively. I twist the rope in the middle sections just enough to reveal three narrative threads ("Talented Teacher," "Reluctant Conservationist," and "Prominent Author"). Stegner's three principal contributions deserve separate examinations in order for me to portray the uniqueness of this individual and his legacy. Some chronology is involved, however, among those overlapping components of a career. He was a teacher first, a conservationist second, and although he was a writer from the beginning of his adult years, he was a prominent writer only in the last quarter century of his life.

SOME OF THE best biographies are written because the biographer recognizes a part of himself or herself in the subject. This is certainly true of me. Although I'm not a native of the West and have written no fiction, I have traveled to many of the same places in the West and New England that Stegner traveled to and have written about the West in newspapers, magazines, and books. I met Wallace Stegner only once, when I drove from my home north of San Francisco to his home south of that city and interviewed him for an *Audubon* magazine article in 1981. That was shortly after I had received a typewritten postcard stating that he was reviewing my "splendid book," *A River No More: The Colorado River and the West* for *The New Republic*. His note hangs on the wall of my office; it was my first validation as an author.

I corresponded with him briefly after the visit and asked for letters of recommendation and feedback on what I was writing. This busy man always replied in a courteous manner and was generous in fulfilling my requests, just as he was in response to the requests of many other writers. Stegner didn't tell me, and I didn't discover until I read my file at the University of Utah after beginning research on this book, that he had nominated me for a MacArthur fellowship in 1982. I didn't receive that grant, nor did I receive any of the others for which he wrote recommendations on my behalf, but that certainly was not his fault.

In reference to my subject I use the more familiar Wally rather than the formal Wallace not because I was close to the man but because that was how he asked me and others to address him once we passed the initial formal "Mister," "Doctor," or "Professor Stegner" stage. Although I felt uncomfortable using his nickname when corresponding with him, he was not the kind of man you contradicted. Besides, Wallace just sounds wrong. This is the West, where we tend to be less formal.

Wallace Stegner and the American West

Prologue

Los Altos Hills, California, lies just eastward of the San Andreas Fault. Salt Lake City, Utah, at the boundary of the stark Wasatch Range and the desert of the Great Basin, is at the center of the arid West. Greensboro, Vermont, is verdant New England personified. The harsher realities of the geologically newer, arid, more vertically uplifted, and more varied West differ greatly from the stable New England landscape, where the worn hills suggest greater age.

I went looking for Wallace Stegner almost a dozen years after his death and had a difficult time finding him. The search began on the West Coast and ended on the East Coast. It took me through a cross section of Stegner Country, that being California, Utah, and Vermont, where he had lived and about which he had written.

I drove up a narrow driveway, whose fishhook shape led through eucalyptus and oak trees to his hilltop home overlooking Silicon Valley. The shell of the house, but not the essence of the man, had been preserved in the foothills of the Coast Range where he had lived for forty-five years, his longest time in one place.

The ostentatious mansions of the new and very rich that emulate exotic architectural styles surround the modest, one-story home on 2.4 acres of land. My guess was that the home and surrounding preserve would soon disappear unless some nonprofit institution decided to rescue it for altruistic purposes, such as a memorial or a conference center. But that was not to be. Not long after my visit the home, writing studio, guest cottage, and far more valuable property were sold for a price that would have made Stegner's frugal genes quiver with astonishment.

I drove to Salt Lake and the city cemetery on the hillside above the sprawling desert metropolis. It was hot, and the sun was merciless. The cemetery is not far from the University of Utah, the scene of Stegner's first social, athletic, and literary triumphs. The secretary in the office said that no one had ever inquired where the Stegner plot was located. "Who was he?" she asked.

It took time and further help from the secretary, communicating by cell phone with a grounds worker, to locate the three graves in Park Plat, block 37, lot 6. The two granite headstones that had once been flush with the ground cover were overgrown with grass that had partially obscured the markers. I weeded and brushed the grass aside to get a better look at the inscriptions. One grave marker said "Mother" and the other, "Husband."

By carefully reading the dates, I realized that they were mother and son. It wasn't Wallace Stegner who was buried in the city cemetery, however, but rather his older brother, Cecil, a married man who died of pneumonia in 1931—thus the designation of husband. Hilda, their mother, died of cancer two years later. She has a slightly larger and more ornate headstone. Two roses sculpted in bas-relief frame her name.

But where was George Stegner buried? The secretary had said there were three graves. George was Hilda's husband and the father of the two boys. He had killed a girlfriend and then shot himself in 1939. The worker called the office again. Back came the answer: George was buried on the other side of Hilda, in an unmarked grave.

I noticed something else that was unusual, something symbolic of Stegner's early years, a period he had minutely dissected during a lifetime of writing: the lettering on the two headstones of the non-Mormon Stegners faces westward, toward California, whereas the inscriptions on the nearby markers face the east, the direction from which the Mormons had emigrated to Utah. Both directions, as viewed from this crossroads city, suggest wanderings.

Born in Iowa, where he spent the first three weeks of his life and a few years during graduate school, Stegner said that although he retained warm feelings for that place, "I'm probably a good deal more native to Saskatchewan and Utah and California than to the state I was born in."[1] Yet he was buried in none of those places. So where had Wallace Stegner finally found repose?

I flew to Boston and drove to Greensboro. Stegner had spent one winter and many summers in Vermont. I asked my question in Willey's general store, the social and commercial hub of the small village that Stegner had described as resembling "a Hudson School River painting, uniting the philosophical-contemplative with the pastoral-picturesque."[2]

An employee gave me directions to the Four Corners Cemetery, on the northern side of Caspian Lake, around which the summer colony is clustered. Tourists who come seeking Stegner's final resting place are directed to the graveyard. I again had difficulty locating a gravestone. That was because it was a flat, polished piece of Vermont granite raised only a few inches above the grass. Engraved on it are the words "Stegner, Wallace E., 1909–1993, and Mary Page, 1911," with no date of death for his wife. At the age of ninety-three, Mary Stegner was then tenuously holding on to life in a California rest home. The granite marker was a place where Wallace Stegner's devoted readers could pay their final homage. Stegner's remains were not buried there, however. His ashes had been scattered outside his summer cottage on nearby Baker Hill.

I drove to the other side of the lake and ascended a narrow dirt road. The profusion of maples, hemlocks, and white birches choked the once-clear view of the hourglass-shaped lake. A thick ground cover of ferns and mosses, goldenrod, and joe-pye weed covered the spot where this archetypal westerner's ashes had enriched the already luxuriant growth.

Unformed Youth

Seattle

> He was a strange child. Now he clung to her skirts so closely that he hampered her walking, and she laid her hand on his head and kept it there because she knew that somewhere deep down in his prematurely old mind he lived with fear.
>
> Wallace Stegner, *The Big Rock Candy Mountain*

WALLACE STEGNER'S LIFE could be described as a continual search for the angle of repose.

Stegner was a man of many different and seemingly contradictory components. He was a gentleman. His consideration was legendary; his anger was implacable. He lived according to an inflexible code forged on the frontier, tempered during the Depression years, and never bent or broken to fit the changing times. Stegner was a good man, but he was not the perfect man he was eulogized as being.

He came from nowhere culturally and became a writer whose books were translated into numerous foreign languages. He was a barefoot frontier youth who would later consort with the intellectual elite in this and other countries. He worked exceedingly hard and lived a full, rich life. His transgressions were minor. Although he spent a lifetime seeking knowledge of himself on paper, he never felt as secure within himself as he seemed to be on the surface. He was captive to the guilt and anger that had its roots in childhood.

As a student working toward a master's degree in an innovative writing program and as a professor with a doctorate in a recognized academic specialty (both degrees from the University of Iowa); as a teacher in the top writing programs in the country (Iowa, Bread Loaf, Harvard, and Stanford); and as a writer of volumes of commercially published fiction and nonfiction, Stegner not only bridged the gap between professor and professional writer but also constructed by example and teaching the tenuous structure that allowed many others to cross that same chasm.

Wallace Stegner taught writing students whose names have come to constitute a virtual hall of fame of American letters (Edward Abbey, Wendell Berry, Ken Kesey, Larry McMurtry, Robert Stone, and Scott Turow, to name just a few); he had a decided impact on national conservation issues (dams, wilderness areas, and national parks); and he was a versatile and prolific writer of novels, histories and biographies, journalism and essays, and short stories.

A nearly complete list of his works—many of which remain in print—includes 13 novels, 9 nonfiction books (one written with his son, Page), 242 nonfiction articles, and 57 short stories in magazines and newspapers. His books and short stories have been translated into French, German, Greek, Italian, Japanese, Polish, Portuguese, Spanish, and Swedish. Stegner edited seven collections of his own short nonfiction and fiction (his wife, son, and daughter-in-law edited other works), and he edited numerous collections of writings by other authors. Stegner also contributed many introductions and forewords to books. In addition, Nancy Colberg's 1990 *Wallace Stegner: A Descriptive Bibliography* includes a miscellaneous category.

In his lifetime he garnered almost all the literary awards and honors available (Pulitzer Prize, National Book Award, two Guggenheim fellowships, PEN USA Body of Work and Freedom to Write awards, the Robert Kirsch Award for lifetime achievement from the *Los Angeles Times*, eight honorary degrees, and endowed chairs named after him at two western universities, among other more prosaic forms of recognition).[1] One of his students, Wendell Berry, caught the totality of the man when he wrote, "He was perhaps his region's greatest teacher: its greatest storyteller, historian, critic, conservator and loyal citizen."[2]

Stegner defined place in words and actions, the latter activity being a rare characteristic for a writer. He stressed the realities of the West in classroom lectures, speeches, his writings, and his environmental activism. He was a slayer of myths about this outsize land. Rapacious economic booms followed by inevitable busts, the need for wilderness and national parks to renew the spirit, and the concept of aridity as it defined the West were topics Stegner introduced to national audiences through his writings and conservation activities. He made the subject of the West respectable for other writers back at "headquarters," his term for the Boston–New York publishing axis.

Stegner reluctantly acted as the spokesperson for the region. No single person has filled that position since he died. Through his multiple legacies, Wallace Stegner remains the emeritus authority on the American West.

He was of the region, but he also ventured beyond its borders. He dealt with racism as a national subject long before civil rights became a fashionable issue. During the early months of the Kennedy administration, he participated in discussions about the formation of a national arts policy—talks that resulted in the National Endowment for the Arts and the National Endowment for the Humanities. The differences between East, West, and Midwest that he had absorbed from living on both coasts and in the interior of America constituted another theme that this man, mistakenly labeled a regionalist, explored. Of the West, Stegner once explained to a correspondent: "You are right in thinking that I see it as a little America, a late (and by aridity modified and intensified) variant of the American experience."[3]

Many of the students he taught or writers he advised informally (the latter included Ivan Doig, Barry Lopez, and Terry Tempest Williams) pushed his ideas further in different styles and from diverse perspectives and are still producing works of great value.

That there was more than one side to Stegner is typified by this jotting from one of his notebooks: "I have a trouble that until now I always knew myself too well, and I was never what I knew I publicly seemed. One lived with a mask until one thought the face fitted it. Then suddenly one day another face looks out of the mirror and the mirror cracks."[4] Regardless of which mask he wore and what face emerged from the cracked mirror, he was nothing but extremely and obsessively honest with himself and ultimately—insofar as he was able to be—with his readers.

Immensely attractive, articulate, and intelligent, Stegner was described by friends and co-workers who knew him well as reserved. His wife, Mary, said that in his earlier years he had been more outgoing and the life of numerous parties, but the Stanford bureaucracy and students dampened his spirit in the late 1960s, when the threat of change pervaded the campus, the West, and the nation.

Wally and Mary came from the sparsely inhabited regions of the interior of the country and found themselves among the elite on both coasts. The couple inhabited two worlds during their lifetimes. They were *in* by dint of hard work and talent—not breeding, great wealth, or elite schools. As one of Stegner's close friends and a Stanford Nobel laureate remarked about his patterns of speech, "You are getting two voices out of Wally, the rhythms of the country and the diction of the university."[5]

The multiple achievements that were accompanied by the requisite awards were not enough. Stegner wanted acceptance by all. He was repeatedly vilified in the 1970s by that paragon of eastern bookishness, *The New York Times Book Review*, and there was the nagging question of his use of sources for his greatest work of fiction, the Pulitzer Prize–winning novel *Angle of Repose*. Some have termed it plagiarism. Anger marked his reaction to negative criticism and to anyone who crossed him personally or professionally. He never forgot, and he rarely forgave.

Stegner made a mighty effort, but he never came to terms with his fractured youth. From his early years to the end of his life he was burdened by self-doubt. Wally was haunted by guilt for his mother's unhappiness, illness, and death. The anger his father directed toward him—which Wally reciprocated as hatred—never dissipated, although he attempted to exorcise it in his books.

The periodic, intense anger directed by fathers toward their sons was almost biblical, or genetic, in its passage through four generations of Stegners. It may have preceded George Stegner, but since nothing is known about his forebears, what can be said with certainty is that it spread insidiously from George to his son, his grandson, and his great-grandson. Wallace Stegner testified to the force of his anger. He said a few years before his death that his rages "sort of scare me now and then."[6]

Wally was personally involved in societal shifts of seismic proportions during the twentieth century. His major flaw was that ultimately he could not adapt to the region that had formed him and that he had defined and represented so eloquently. Stegner despaired of his homeland and what he once called "the geography of hope."

Change bred insecurity in this outwardly assured individual. He first experienced change in one of the last frontier settlements during the early 1900s and again at the end of his life, during the frantic 1990s in Silicon Valley. There was no escaping change, not even in his beloved Salt Lake City. For along with its close relative, transience, rapid change and the physical manifestations it caused were the defining cultural characteristics of the West.

The irony was that Stegner knew this and had documented it in many words. In the end he sought to escape change by having his ashes deposited in a seemingly more enduring place. Stegner's fictional doppelgänger, Bruce Mason, inquires in *The Big Rock Candy Mountain*, "But going home where . . . Where do I belong in this?"[7] It is a question that is more endemic to the West than to any other section of the country.

. . .

STEGNER'S FIRST DIM memory was of huddling in a tent in Redmond, Washington, after a tramp had told the family there were mountain lions in the surrounding forest.[8] His first clear memory was of an orphanage in Seattle. Wally could recall the rain and the dappled sunshine that fell upon the family tent in the rain forest near the Puget Sound logging town of Redmond and eating crusts of stale bread in the orphanage.

It was boom times shortly after the start of the century for nearly everyone except the Stegner family. The forests of the East and the South had been cut. Now it was the turn of the Pacific Northwest. Here the trees were taller and straighter and yielded more board feet: Sitka spruce, cedar, western hemlock, Douglas fir, and Jeffrey pine. Puget Sound offered a huge, safe harbor from which the lumber could be exported to Pacific Rim markets. Firms like Pope & Talbot, people like Frederick Weyerhaeuser, modern technology like the double-bit ax and the longer two-man saw with raker teeth, and new railroads and steamships fueled the boom that had begun with the Klondike gold rush of 1897 and didn't end until the Great Depression of the 1930s.

The city of Seattle, "buoyantly speculative in spirit" from its start as a small mill town, did not question the efficacy of booms. Its citizens, like others in the West, accepted them as their due, promoted them beyond the sustainability of the particular resource, and then wrote off the subsequent busts as aberrant and best-forgotten history.

The cheerleader mantra of "the Seattle spirit" prevailed. Hills were leveled, canals dug, and wetlands filled to create a waterfront. Labor problems were dealt with in time to capitalize on the demand for lumber in the early World War I years, when timber production was extremely profitable. The price of lumber peaked in 1912 and 1913, shortly after the Stegners arrived in town from North Dakota.

Wallace Stegner was too young to appreciate the economic vicissitudes of the Northwest, but he would soon be cognizant of the wheat boom on the northern prairie and all the subsequent booms and busts in the twentieth-century American West. His father had a habit of missing the main chance, leaving, and then appearing elsewhere when the next opportunity seemed imminent. Then the cycle was repeated.

From Redmond, George took off. "Then there was a bad time," Wallace Stegner wrote years later in an imagined letter to his dead mother. "You left my father, or he you; nobody ever told me."[9]

An aunt provided Wally with a sketch. George was joined in Redmond by a professional gambler he had known before he met his wife.

The married couple opened a café, where Hilda Stegner did the cooking and took care of Wally and Cecil. Neither George nor the good-looking, well-groomed gambler was a typical restaurateur. The money came in too slowly for them. The pair departed for British Columbia, leaving Hilda to run the café, make the installment payments on the restaurant equipment, and care for the children. The café failed, and Hilda and the two young boys moved to Seattle. She got a job in the Bon Marché department store, where her sister, Mina Paulson, also worked.[10]

Hilda found it impossible to hold the job and adequately care for her children in the fall of 1913. The desperate mother deposited them in what their aunt euphemistically called "a private home" but in reality was the Sacred Heart Orphanage on Beacon Hill. To Wally, "it was a dump. It was literally an asylum of the old-fashioned kind."[11]

The memory of the orphanage lodged permanently in young Stegner's mind and was subsequently incorporated into his books and speeches. Homelessness had a great impact on him, as it would on any sensitive child. Hilda visited her children on Sundays, but the reunions did not lessen the traumatic experience for her sickly, scared four-year-old son. Cecil, who looked after his brother, was a six-year-old and more robust.

Wally recalled "the musty, buttery odor" of the stale bread crusts, some already half-eaten and resembling "bits of old shoe soles," that were served as a midmorning snack. Hungry kids ran from all directions of the yard "like ravens." The bread pan "was practically torn out of the woman's hands. I never got any because I was little, and once in a while my brother would take pity on me and give me a bite." He disliked the oatmeal that was served for breakfast and the tomato sandwiches at lunch. His appetite was deemed finicky, and the obdurate child was punished by the nuns for not eating. He was spanked with a ruler or with bare hands. Skinny Wally cried a lot.

The orphanage was also the product of boom times. It had been founded by Mother Francesca Xavier Cabrini in 1903 on Beacon Hill, from where there was a view of Lake Washington and the eastern half of the city. By 1913 it housed more than one hundred children, and the property had become valuable. The city wanted to level the hill. Through a miracle, as it has been described, Mother Cabrini found another property on the shore of Lake Washington. After the Stegner brothers departed, the remaining orphans moved to Sacred Heart Villa in 1914, and Mother Cabrini went on to found sixty-seven institutions—schools, orphanages, hospitals, and the like—throughout the world and became the first American saint and the patron saint of immigrants.[12]

Hilda wrote to her father, asking whether she should divorce George. Her father replied that unless she had the one reason for which the Lutheran Church would sanction a divorce—that being adultery— she would have to remain married. Hilda took her children out of the orphanage after a few months and returned to the home of her parents on a farm near Lake Mills, Iowa. They lived in the house where a girl-friend of Hilda's had taken Hilda's deceased mother's place as her father's second wife. Wally remembered being praised by his step-grandmother and the neighborhood women for being able to sing "Whistling Rufus."

GEORGE, THE WANDERING boomer, and Hilda, the nester—as Stegner described them and as they appeared in his autobiographical writings under other names—first met in 1906 in Osnabrock, North Dakota, where Hilda Paulson had moved to care for a widowed uncle following her father's second marriage. George operated a pool hall and speakeasy, also known as a blind pig.[13]

When she met George on his first visit to Lake Mills after marrying Hilda, Mina liked him. He gave the impression of being a man of the midwestern world. "He had coal black hair, gray eyes, and although inclined to be stout," Paulson said, "he was very nice and could be charming." George knew how to tell funny stories. But he didn't win over Hilda's father, who disliked this man who ran a blind pig, belonged to no church, and had no family background. He said nothing to Hilda because she didn't ask him if he approved of her handsome, rakish choice.

When Hilda returned home from Osnabrock to give birth to Wally, George visited a second time. Mina now noticed his "bad spots." A few nights before Wally was born, they were playing cards. "Sis and George were partners, and she did not play to suit him. He got so angry, he swore at her and bawled her out something terrible." This was the first time the family witnessed his violent temper.

Wally was born on February 18, 1909 and was baptized in a Lake Mills Lutheran church three weeks later. The Stegner family returned to Osnabrock. Mina soon followed to help care for the new baby, who had pneumonia. George had "some trouble" with his speakeasy and had to leave town hastily. He returned and took his family to Seattle.[14]

There was a history of movement in the Stegner family. George's family came from Germany and Hilda's from Norway in the nineteenth century. Iowa, North Dakota, Washington, Iowa, Saskatchewan, Montana, Utah: these were the way stations during the first dozen years of Wally's life. "I was born on wheels," Stegner said. "I know the excitement of newness and the relief when responsibility has been left behind. But I also know the dissatisfaction and hunger that result from placelessness."[15]

Asked years later if, in writing the autobiographical novel *The Big Rock Candy Mountain*, he had been seeking his own "angle of repose," Stegner replied:

> Only with regard to my father. That obviously is a kind of experience that is central to a child. The dominant figure in your life probably is your father, if you have one, and if he happens himself to be mixed-up, irritable, and frustrated, and to feel himself many times a failure—those things do bounce off a child's head and leave knots. Surely, I was exorcising my father, and in a sense making some kind of recompense to my mother, who led a very rough life with him. Whether that's reaching my angle of repose or not, I don't know. The effect, I'm sure, of such a dominating and hair-trigger kind of father on many kids is to breed a kind of insecurity which may never be healed. I was probably looking for security.[16]

From British Columbia, George heard about the wheat boom in Saskatchewan. He lured his family north from their temporary refuge in Lake Mills. They were reunited in June of 1914 just over the Canadian border in the frontier settlement of Eastend, Saskatchewan.

Eastend

He thought that he knew enough not to want to distinguish himself by heroic deeds: singlehanded walks to the North Pole,
incredible journeys, rescues, what not. Given his way, he did not
think that he would ever want to do anything alone again, not in
this country. Even a trip to the privy was something a man might
want to take in company.

Wallace Stegner, "Genesis"

STEGNER'S MEMORY, FROM which four books and numerous
short stories about his early life were stitched, kicked in full-time
when Hilda and her two boys arrived in a stagecoach in Eastend,
and it never let him go for the rest of his days. "That was the first place
in my life where we lived for more than a few months. I was five when
we arrived, eleven when we left. The years when I watched that town
get born were the shaping years of my life. I have never forgotten a
detail of them," wrote Stegner.[1] Others who have studied Stegner's life
and works have agreed with his assessment. "This place, of all the
places in Stegner country," wrote Forrest and Margaret Robinson, "was
the one that formed him most decisively, that bruised him into an
awareness of himself and his special identity, that loaded his memory
with the landscapes and faces and voices and events that appear in much
of his best writing."[2]

It was a miracle that Stegner did not write pulp westerns. His introduction to the Wild West, as he first described it in unadorned prose to
his New York literary agent, was about as wild as it got:

I grew up on the Frenchman River, one of the headwaters of the
Milk, which is in turn part of the Missouri system, in the years
when this country was first being opened. It was still virgin buffalo grass in 1914, and the town of Eastend did not exist. My

family helped found it; our first house was a derailed dining car on the half-built spur of the CPR [Canadian Pacific Railroad] that came down from Swift Current. The river was full of beaver and muskrat; my first honest dollars were earned trapping muskrat, a few beaver, mink, and ermine along the Frenchman and in the sloughs on the north bench, and my first memory of that town is coming into it on a stagecoach on the lap of a cow-puncher named Buck Murphy, who a few months later was shot off the seat of a democrat wagon and killed by a trigger happy Mounty. This was, in other words, practically the last real frontier; the town started from scratch, as a thousand American and Canadian towns have started, and developed its institutions and its local history, personalities, lore, from nothing.[3]

In terms of what Stegner would become and the company he would keep, it is hard to imagine how he got there from where he began. "I was charged with getting in a single lifetime from scratch," Stegner said, "what some people inherit as naturally as they breathe air."[4] He meant not only culture and acceptable social behavior but also the rudiments of a civilized life, like how to use a bathtub and a flush toilet, conveniences he didn't encounter until he was nearly twelve years old. There was an instant bond when, in later years, he met people who had also grown up on the prairie. "We recognized the same things. One of the things I recognize most commonly is that same cultural hunger. Growing up in deprivation like that must be sort of like growing up in Siberia—the whole world, any part of it, looks exciting."[5]

EASTEND WAS JUST as typical of the American frontier as it was of the Canadian frontier. The border existed in name only. The flat horizon of the mixed-grass prairie could not be limited by an imagined line running between black iron obelisks. There was an easy interchange between the inhabitants of both countries. "A border so unwatched that it might have been unmapped," wrote Stegner, recalling his family's homestead directly on the forty-ninth parallel.[6] The Northern Plains Indians who crossed and recrossed the border called it the medicine line. For the Native Americans the magical political power of the international border conferred safety, just as it would for George Stegner's bootlegging activities.

The vastness of the prairie landscape was unmatched anywhere else in North America. Only buffalo and wheat in their separate times intruded upon the empty spaces. The wind blew over, around, and through whatever structures were erected to block it. As those deserted structures weathered into prairie ghost towns and solitary, exposed reminders of past failures, the wind remained triumphant in the end. "Nowhere else in the west," wrote a Canadian author, "does the stranger feel himself more exposed to the wrath of the gods and the fury of the elements than in the middle of the Saskatchewan prairie."[7]

Water, or the lack of it, was the other dominant natural element. As Stegner would make abundantly clear in his later writings, and as he and his family and other homesteaders so painfully experienced first-hand on the Canadian prairie, water shaped the West. A history of the Canadian prairie describes southwestern Saskatchewan thus:

> In the southern plains, on the less fertile brown soils of Palliser's Triangle where precipitation in the growing season (May to September) is lowest, short grasses of six inches to one foot in height provided up to 80 per cent of the vegetation cover although sage and common cactus were also present. Surrounding this district was an arc of "mixed-grass prairie" (short grass as well as mid-grasses which were two to four feet high), where the dark brown soils were more fertile and the precipitation was a little more certain.[8]

Even that added degree of uncertain certainty was no help to the Stegner family and others who settled on the mixed-grass prairie in the early years of the twentieth century. Stegner the writer would come to depend upon the use of specific examples to illustrate a general situation. The Stegner family served as an excellent example of what happened to others on the prairie during that time. That same prairie history noted:

> The next phase in prairie agricultural history, the decade after 1908, was marked by a great error in Canadian domestic policy. In throwing open to settlement the relatively dry regions of southwest Saskatchewan and southeast Alberta . . . where the light brown soils indicated a historic absence of vegetation, the Canadian government was taking a great risk. Settlers in this district suffered the painful consequences of the government's excessive optimism when several thousand of these farms were abandoned during the lengthy drought after 1917.[9]

From the urban bustle of Seattle and settled Iowa, the Stegner family stepped back in time. The idea that there was no frontier remaining in 1914 was erroneous. It arose from the superintendent of the U.S. Census Bureau declaring in 1890: "Up to and including 1880 the country had a frontier of settlement, but at present the unsettled area has been so broken into by isolated bodies of settlement that there can hardly be said to be a frontier line."[10] The same was true of southern Canada.

Three years later Frederick Jackson Turner, a young assistant professor of history at the University of Wisconsin, took that statement and made it the cornerstone of his frontier thesis. The frontier, meaning the push westward by white pioneers that shaped this country's history, was gone, he said. Young Stegner, who would one day also teach at the University of Wisconsin, could have made the case (and eventually did) that Turner was wrong: not only did the frontier still exist but other forces and other peoples had also shaped the West.

SOME OF THOSE others had preceded the Stegners and their fellow settlers. The bones of a forty-foot-long *Tyrannosaurus rex* and other dinosaurs were found nearby and now reside in an Eastend museum. For a time southwestern Saskatchewan was "the melting pot of hell." It was inhabited and fought over by Native Americans, including the Assiniboins, Crees, Crows, Blackfeet, Gros Ventres, North Piegans, Sioux, and Métis.

A few white men, mostly strays from across the nonexistent border, moved in after a British survey by Captain John Palliser in 1859 gave the name Palliser's Triangle to the northern extension of the Great American Desert. Stegner said that Palliser had determined "with some justice" that the triangle was unfit for settlement. In her recent history of the border country, Beth LaDow wrote that the triangle had "all the allure the Bermuda Triangle would exert a hundred years later. Explorers avoided it."[11]

Sitting Bull, his Sioux warriors, and their families fled north across the medicine line after his victory over General George Custer at the Battle of the Little Big Horn. His bedraggled band wandered between Wood Mountain in Saskatchewan and what would become Eastend before crossing the border again in the summer of 1881 and surrendering. They had been treated sympathetically by the North West Mounted Police. The French-speaking Métis, of mixed French and Indian blood, were the last native group to inhabit the triangle.

Fights between marauding whites from across the border and Indians climaxed in the Cypress Hills Massacre. The growing whiskey trade also tended to incite passions; thus the Mounties were brought into what was then the Northwest Territories. Violations of the liquor laws by smugglers, which would be a problem again in the next century, was the single largest category of crime encountered by the police in the 1880s.

Following the disappearance of both the buffalo and the Native Americans, boom times arrived with the coming of the cowboy and the cattle culture, imports from south of the border. The nationalities and subgroups that made their way to the triangle included Scandinavians, English, Scots, Norwegians, French, Ukrainians, Canadians, Texans, and other Americans. The extremes of geography and climate tended to unite these disparate people. They drove vast herds of cattle onto the seemingly limitless plains of Saskatchewan, where they wandered freely on the open range.

Harold S. "Corky" Jones was part of this influx. He came from the Isle of Wight in England. The remainder of the passengers on his train across Canada were on their way to the Klondike gold rush in Alaska. Jones got off in Moose Jaw, Saskatchewan, and sought work as a cowboy. "It was still pretty empty when I arrived here in 1898," he said. "There was no settlement between here and Wood Mountain and the boundary. Maple Creek was the only village between Medicine Hat and Moose Jaw."

Corky Jones was a sticker, remaining long enough to witness wheat booms that resulted in large surpluses. "Dry seasons and tough times, I am afraid, will come again," he predicted. Jones was an anomaly in another way. He was interested in the natural and human history of the triangle. It was Jones who first collected the dinosaur bones, organized a small collection in the basement of the Eastend school, and drew the attention of Canadian museums to his important finds. He was the principal informant for Stegner when in 1953 the author came searching for the town's history, which he later incorporated into *Wolf Willow*.[12]

There had been a Hudson's Bay trading post in nearby Chimney Coulee, and sixty Métis families had lived there at one time, Jones recalled. A detachment of Mounties was stationed in the coulee in the mid-1870s. At an undetermined time in the past one group of Indians had massacred another. The Mounties picked up the bones and buried them. From time to time, Indians gathered in the protected gulch. They decorated trees with blue and yellow streamers. "Packages and plugs of tobacco were left for the departed," wrote Jones. He began his mimeographed history of the town:

> Eastend had its beginning in a coulee about four miles north of the present town. This coulee is now known as Chimney Coulee and was evidently a favorite camping spot of the early pioneers and takes its name from the stone chimneys that were left standing after the abandoned shacks of these pioneers had disintegrated. The last of these chimneys collapsed in 1915.[13]

In Canada the law tended to arrive before any settlements. The opposite was the practice to the south. The police post moved four miles, to what would become the townsite of Eastend but in 1887 was the deserted cabin of Tom Doyle, the first settler to bring cattle into the region, in 1883. The first permanent settlers came in 1895. The Mounties gave the cluster of cabins the name Eastend, it being at the east end of the Cypress Hills.

The invasion of sheep below the border drove Montana cattlemen north with their Texas longhorn steers. The Canadians complained about Montana cattle feeding on their native grasses. It was not an easy life for the ranchers and their hired hands. As one of those hired hands, Jones drove cattle from just south of the border to Eastend in 1903. The horses stampeded one night. The riders and the herd were caught in a May snowstorm for three days, an experience Stegner drew upon for his powerful short story "Genesis," which was later incorporated into *Wolf Willow*.

The summer of 1906 was extremely wet. Beginning on November 5, the blizzards came early, with one following upon the heels of the other through Christmas. "The range cattle were dying in December," said Jones. The corpses formed "grisly mounds of death. . . . Stunned cowboys struggled into camp snowblinded and exhausted," wrote LaDow. Approximately half the herds were lost. Ranchers just quit, sold out for what they could get, or reduced their herds. "Almost as suddenly as the disappearance of the buffalo, it changed the way of life of the region," wrote Stegner. Wheat farmers replaced cattle ranchers, and seven years after the last bust the Stegner family arrived near the end of the wheat boom.[14]

Three quarters of a century later LaDow asked Stegner what had gone wrong. He answered: "As for what we did wrong, that seems to me easy. We plowed up Palliser's Triangle, one of the driest parts of the western plains, and destroyed the native grasses, imported weeds, mined the soil for wheat for a few years, created a dust bowl, and eventually abandoned what we should never have tried to settle."[15]

THE THREE STEGNERS—Hilda and the two boys—landed in Saskatchewan in 1914 unaware of the previous history of the transience of the human populations, the rapid boom-and-bust cycles, and the fact that they were arriving at the end of the land rush that brought more than one million immigrants, one third of whom were from Europe, to the Canadian prairie. The bait, in the form of pamphlets distributed by the Canadian government and the Canadian Pacific Railroad, was free land and reduced transportation costs.

During their half-hour wait in the customhouse at Weyburn young Wally was cowed into silence by the portraits of grim-faced mounted policemen staring down from the walls. At the end of the dust-encrusted stagecoach journey from Gull Lake, Saskatchewan, to Eastend, the family of three alighted amid the late-May dirt and detritus of an instant frontier settlement and were greeted by George.

Two years before, the townsite had been a hayfield. Now it was a frontier settlement. Mud puddles, lumber piles, and discarded farm equipment silently welcomed them. From a shack with the initials RNWMP carved over the door stepped a Mountie, a vision of rectitude and order dressed in a scarlet tunic, blue breeches with a yellow stripe on the outside of each leg, glistening boots, a wide-brimmed campaign hat, and a holstered revolver to which a white lanyard was attached. The vision was so startling that Wally, who had not seen his father for some time, could not later remember greeting him. But the memory of the policeman remained with him for a lifetime.

The family arrived in the same month that the cemetery was established in Eastend to house the settlement's first recorded death, a man struck in the head by a baseball during a game. Eastend consisted of the Z-X Ranch, a rickety dam and irrigation system, one muddy or dusty main street, a few shacks, a general store, a wood-frame hotel, and a boardinghouse for the railroad crews constructing a branch line from Moose Jaw. When the rails were laid and the trains arrived a few weeks later, the settlement grew by a few old railroad cars.

The family lived that first winter in the faded glory of an old railroad dining car, after which they moved to a rented shack. One year after Eastend's founding, in 1914, the three-story Cypress Hotel and a grain elevator stuck out on the flat, treeless plain. In 1916, George built a small two-story wood-frame house and a barn at the west end of town. The property backed on the Frenchman River, known locally as the Whitemud River because of an exposed deposit of white clay.

The smallness of Eastend and the freedom to roam the surrounding wild lands were a small boy's dream come true. It was a barefoot-in-the-summer, berry-picking, Huck Finn type of existence. The small community at the east end of the Cypress Hills and at the edge of the vast, rolling prairie clung—as did the wolf willow trees, with their pungent, talismanic smell—to the meanderings of the Frenchman River. "I loved that dam and the main ditch. Almost as much as the river they defined my world of town," Stegner wrote.[16]

The river, in the midst of all that surrounding aridity and howling wind, was a sheltering place. Stegner described the bottomlands in *Wolf Willow:* "What I remember are low bars overgrown with wild roses, cutbank bends, secret paths through the willows, fords across the shallows, swallows in the clay banks, days of indolence and adventure where space was as flexible as the mind's cunning and where time did not exist. That was at the heart of it, the sunken and sanctuary river valley."[17]

Wally learned to swim in the irrigation ditch. He hunted with a .22-caliber rifle. At the age of eight he rested the muzzle of his .22 on the toe of his right boot, accidentally pulled the trigger, and suffered a slight flesh wound. The junglelike terrain was a place for hideouts, forts, and play entrenchments during the World War I years. When the weather turned frigid and it snowed, there were sledding, ice-skating, curling, and bonfires.

The family went on outings to Chimney Coulee, where they picked fruit. The chokeberries, raspberries, gooseberries, and Saskatoon berries were preserved and used in winter desserts. George, who could be creative in his recitation of invented songs and tall tales, told the boys that the ruined chimneys were used by the Indians to send smoke signals.

Back in town the brothers hung out with the cowboys at the Z-X corrals and absorbed their behavior patterns. They copied their way of walking, swearing, spitting, and playing practical jokes. They took part in what they called shit fights—throwing snowball-shaped globs of fresh green manure at each other. Wally wanted desperately to belong. He aped the way the cowboys mocked and tormented the others, meaning, in the argot of the time, the Chinks, Jews, half-breeds, and haughty English.

MORE OR LESS A SECRET VOCABULARY & IDIOM PARTICULAR TO A GROUP

The two American boys got a taste of their own medicine shortly after Canada, as part of the British Empire, declared war on Germany in August of 1914, whereas the United States remained neutral for nearly three more years. The Canadian boys taunted the brothers.

> *Here's to the American eagle*
> *He flies over mountain and ditch*
> *But we don't want the turd of your goddam bird*
> *You American son of a bitch.*[18]

They were caught between two cultures and each responded differently. Cecil fought back, usually successfully; Wally was ashamed and slunk away.

Then there were the pranks. The brothers found a box of percussion caps in the town dump and placed them on the railroad tracks, almost derailing gandy dancers on a handcar and earning an anonymous mention in the local newspaper. Wally and his friends, whom he described inclusively as "sensuous little savages," stole a .44-caliber pistol and dynamite caps from a shack owned by an unsavory character and tried to burn the structure. They were, in short, footloose frontier boys. "We swam without lifeguards, hiked without scoutmasters, carried deadly weapons before we had reached the age of discretion, came and went as we pleased except when school kept us hobbled."[19]

When Stegner arrived in Eastend, the school was in Anderson's Hall, above a poolroom. Nine grades of "scholars," as the students were called, were taught by one teacher in one room that was heated by a single stove. The school then moved to a vacant shop next to the town butcher. With the town growing and acquiring such luxuries as plank sidewalks, a two-room brick schoolhouse was constructed in 1915; two more rooms were added in 1917.

School was eight hours a day, five days a week, ten months a year of reading, writing, arithmetic, geography, and history, all presented with a bias toward eastern Canadian English and European experiences. The battle for Quebec on the Plains of Abraham, English poetry, and the War of 1812 presented from an anti-American perspective were examples of Wally's lessons. "I don't remember any subject that was oriented to western Canada," said Stegner.[20] There was no hint, except for what the boys uncovered in their wanderings, that Eastend had any history. The instantaneous frontier, its accompanying success story, and the values that supposedly made it possible—even if they were mostly absent from everyday life—were the lessons absorbed by the children, nearly 60 percent of whose families would soon experience failure as the homestead boom collapsed.

A crude justice was dispensed for the infraction of rules in school. Because he took a drink from the water cooler and was late to class, young Stegner had to remain draped over the fountain for an exhausting hour and a half.[21] The frontier code drilled into the youngsters was that you didn't complain, you kept a stiff upper lip, and you never abandoned anything. In other words, you were a sticker, a favorite Stegner expression of approval in later years.

Young Stegner excelled in school. "He was most talented and had a gift of memory that impressed me greatly," a classmate recalled. "He could remember a whole story word for word once read and indeed could make up poetry at will." Wally would walk to the blackboard, take up a piece of chalk, and write verse after verse of memorized poetry or, with the same ease, create a poem from scratch. Learning meant memorization, and he got excellent grades. A shy boy, said his friend, but a good playmate.[22]

His skill at memorization later paid social dividends at parties at the staid universities where he taught. From Eastend cowboys, gandy dancers, and his father he picked up the words to such western classics as Robert Service's "The Cremation of Sam McGee" and such songs as "The Ballad of Old Sy Hubbard," "Blood on the Saddle," and "The Cowboy's Lament." Wally recited or sang the lyrics to lusty cheers and clapping at the polite gatherings of intellectuals. "The Cowboy's Lament," also known as "Streets of Laredo," was his favorite. It contains the following verse:

> *Oh, beat the drum slowly and play the fife lowly,*
> *Play the dead march as you carry me along;*
> *Take me to the green valley, there lay the sod o'er me,*
> *For I'm a young cowboy and I know I've done wrong.*

WALLY WAS AN admitted "mamma's boy."[23] Like his mother, he was bookish. He was also slight and cried a lot, sometimes with good reason in the frigid winters. His hands were always cold. Later it was discovered that he had what was called Raynaud's disease then and is known more commonly as Raynaud's phenomenon now. The blood vessels in the extremities constrict, and they become cold. When his hands became white up to his wrists, his father would yell: "Put on your goddamn mittens and shut up."[24] Such advice was unreasonably abrupt, Stegner thought at the time, but in the long run he believed it was good for him. It taught him not to complain.

Unworthiness was bred into Wallace Stegner at an early age. "I was what I was," he later wrote, "and because the town went by the code it went by, I was never quite out of sight of self-contempt or the contempt of my father and others. School, and success therein, never fully compensated for the lacks I felt in myself."[25]

The combative Cecil was his husky father's favorite; the bookish Wally favored his mother, who tried to serve as a buffer between father and son. George Stegner's thoughtlessness and his lightninglike attacks of anger, which were sometimes followed by contriteness—whether real or feigned—eventually alienated both sons. But Wally took the brunt of it. He was hit by his father with a piece of stove wood that broke his collarbone. Another time he was given a severe beating for playing with his father's loaded rifle. Wally's revenge was to secretly aim an empty cartridge case at George Stegner and fantasize murder.

What was particularly hurtful were the two or three times George Stegner invited his son to take a ride with him in the car. "I am sure he did not take me for my company, for he was never very fond of it. Probably he took me to open gates," said Stegner, referring to the rural custom that the passenger gets out and opens and closes livestock gates while the driver guides the vehicle through them.[26]

As family life unfolded in Eastend and, later, in Great Falls, Montana, and Salt Lake City, Stegner's hate for his father grew in direct proportion to his excessive love for his mother. He later recognized his "Oedipal conflict," which "is not a comfortable situation for anybody." But, he insisted, "it's absolutely routine, standard Oedipal: there isn't anything funny about it, or odd." Stegner was riddled with remorse that shaded into guilt that he hadn't loved his mother enough. Near the end of his life he wrote her an imagined letter: "You are at once a lasting presence and an unhealed wound."[27]

Stegner handwrote some notes near the end of his life, titling them "Autobiography." They showed that the family ghosts he had sought to exorcise, both internally and publicly, through his writings, had still not entirely dissipated:

> Letter to my mother—as written.
> Letter to my father—not self-justifying. Inquiring. Wonder-

ing who failed worse. Acknowledging the good, deploring the impatient and violent. Generalizing the consequences.

Address to myself—serious effort to assay what their genes and their influence, and the influence of our surreptitious antisocial life, did to me or for me, for good or ill. What I was capable of, what I managed, what I missed, what I failed. An American life from the bottom upward.[28]

Familial issues were at the core of his fiction. Stegner told his close friend and Stanford colleague Richard Scowcroft the following story. A friend had made the remark to Stegner that she liked his books and added, Scowcroft recalled, "But for Christ's sake why didn't he get himself psychoanalyzed so he would stop writing about himself." When Wally told the story to Scowcroft, he laughed and said, "If I got psychoanalyzed I wouldn't be writing any books." Stegner summed up his work: "Most of us have one overbearing story to tell and tell it in many ways, over and over, often without being aware that we are repeating."[29] Wallace Stegner was constantly seeking his identity through his written words. From the vantage point of middle age he wrote: "I may not know who I am, but I know where I am from. . . . However anachronistic I may be, I am a product of the American earth." At the age of eighty he wrote, "I had always known, not always happily, who I was." Referring to his first extended stay outside the West, in his early twenties, he added: "Now I began to understand what I was. I was a westerner." That primal identity had begun to seep into Stegner's consciousness on the Canadian prairie.[30]

WHEN THE FAMILY left the security of the town and was exposed to the elements that buffeted the prairie homestead during the hot summer months, their dysfunction intensified as failure piled upon failure. They had no idea that they were part of a history of failure that had yet to be recorded, nor that it would be written for the first time by this whiny son.

The land they claimed as a homestead had a stark record. The 160 acres of southwest section 3, township 1, range 24, west third meridian, were filed on first by a Percy Kurtz or Kuntz on May 12, 1913, and then canceled. The property was next filed on by George Stegner on August 3, 1915. Both men had also laid claim to the adjoining 160 acres, designated northwest section 3. The land was farmed for four years by

George Stegner and then abandoned in 1920 during a drought. Fifteen years later the bleak property was once again filed on, by a Paul Bouchard, just as the devastating drought of the mid-1930s was getting under way.

The past and future, however, were unknowns when the Stegners set out for their new homestead with hope for a new and profitable start. They were not the only ones. Another Eastend child, a contemporary of Stegner's, later recalled that time: "So many settlers came out, with hopes high and little capital, and in a very short time both were lost. . . . I remember quite well the glowing stories of the money to be made in growing wheat that my father heard and retold to us. The men would get together and talk about it and finally the morning came and the cars were loaded and they were off to the new Mecca."[31]

It took the Stegners two days by lumber wagon with the cow tied behind, one very long day by the lighter and less burdened democrat wagon, and "seven or eight excruciating hours" by Model T Ford over a graded dirt road and a rutted track to navigate the fifty miles from town to homestead. Then the reality of life on the open prairie began. The "improvements" consisted of a tent that almost blew away in a tornado and then a wood-frame tar-paper shack with a chicken coop and outhouse.

The beauty, wildness, and loneliness of the northern plains were acute. Some of Stegner's most powerful descriptions of place evoked the prairie, such as this passage from his famous Wilderness Letter of 1961:

> On our Saskatchewan prairie, the nearest neighbor was four miles away, and at night we saw only two lights on all the dark rounding earth. The earth was full of animals—field mice, ground squirrels, weasels, ferrets, badgers, coyotes, burrowing owls, snakes. I knew them as my little brothers, as fellow creatures, and I have never been able to look upon animals in any other way since. The sky in that country came clear down to the ground on every side, and it was full of great weathers, and clouds, and winds, and hawks. I hope I learned something from knowing intimately the creatures of the earth; I hope I learned something from looking a long way, from looking up, from being much alone. A prairie like that, one big enough to carry the eye clear to the sinking, rounding horizon, can be as lonely and grand and simple in its forms as the sea.[32]

Stegner did not mention gophers. He shot, poisoned, trapped, and bludgeoned gophers to death with the abandon of a frontier child engaging in animal genocide in order to protect a crop and earn a few dollars. As the tender shoots of wheat grew under ideal conditions that first summer of 1915, the gophers began their work, as did the Stegner brothers. "We went up and down the mile-long field with traps and .22's and buckets of sweet-smelling strychnine-soaked wheat."[33] The brothers were given a prize for collecting more gopher tails than anyone else. Prairie dogs, badgers, and black-footed ferrets, the latter known as big weasels and now extremely rare, were also victims of that "murderous summer season."

The bumper wheat crop of 1915 was the Stegners' "last triumph." Too much rain the next summer brought on the rust. But potatoes raised in town by a Chinese man for the family in their absence thrived. Their potato crop was stored in the basement of the hotel, which burned to the ground. "My father did not grow discouraged: he grew furious."[34] George Stegner remained angry as droughts claimed his wheat and flax crops in the summers of 1917, 1918, and 1919.

The elder Stegner turned to gambling and bootlegging. He had the temperament and the background and was ideally situated for both occupations. Rube ranchers came into town for a game of poker with marked cards. One lost his ranch to Stegner, and those earnings fed the family that bleak winter of 1916. Because of the location of his homestead on the border, he knew intimately the location of the rough tracks that crossed the medicine line.

Governments obliged Stegner by fitting their enforcement and liquor laws to his needs. The U.S. Customs station was a portable tent, and the few patrols were conducted by horseback in winter and by a single Model T Ford in summer. Saskatchewan went dry on the last day of 1916. Liquor flowed north from Montana and then reversed direction two years later. There was no law against exporting liquor south from Canada in 1918 when Prohibition went into effect in Montana.

The Bronfman brothers, who would later create the Seagram empire, opened a large warehouse in nearby Govenlock, Saskatchewan. Cloth-top touring cars pulled into the warehouse in the early evening hours, were loaded with liquor, and the Fords, Packards, Hudsons, and Studebakers with heavy-duty springs to cushion the heavy loads sped south across dirt roads, open fields, ditches, and creeks. The bootleggers were regarded as a romantic breed of smugglers. They were financed by local banks and aided by local farmers.

George Stegner (and his fictional counterpart, Bo Mason, in *The Big Rock Candy Mountain*) added his personal touch to the illicit trade. He found a dummy, Hilda dressed it in her old clothes, and George propped it up in the passenger seat of the fast automobile. " 'This is camouflage,' he said. 'It's too easy to spot a car with one man in it, traveling fast. Henriette here is coming along to look after me,' " wrote Stegner.[35] The family could hear the bootleggers' cars at night as they crossed the fields. With the passage of the Volstead Act in 1919, which made Prohibition the law across the entire United States, all kinds of new business opportunities opened up for George Stegner.

BESIDES THE ARTIFICIALITY of political boundaries, there was one other lesson to be learned on the homestead, and that was the lack of value placed on a human life when land and water rights were disputed in the West. A brutal murder on the prairie brought western priorities to the attention of young Stegner.

The Stegners received their mail and bought basic supplies in the summer at a small combination store, post office, and home just across the border in Hydro, Montana. Hydro had been settled in the same land rush that had taken place across the border in Saskatchewan. Mennonites who had emigrated from Russia to Oklahoma, Kansas, and Canada had arrived in Hydro in 1914. Besides the small general store, there was a school with thirty-seven pupils and a church. The nearest town was Chinook, thirty miles to the south.

Jacob and Elizabeth Krause, along with their three children, Arnold, Betty, and Carl, arrived in April 1914 and filed a homestead claim on 160 acres with a creek running from north to south through the property. Krause expanded the house he built in early 1917 to accommodate the post office and general store. He stocked shoes, overalls, sugar, flour, oatmeal, and other staples. Wally and Cecil were acquainted with the Krause children.

Jacob was a dark-haired, fully mustached Russian Mennonite. On the night of November 12, 1917, Elizabeth was at church and Jacob was home helping Carl with his reading at the kitchen table. A kerosene lamp illuminated the domestic scene. Carl heard a noise outside and looked out the window. He saw three men. There was a single shot. The .45-caliber bullet grazed Carl and hit his father in the back. Jacob slumped to the floor, dead. The children blew out the lamp and huddled under the table until their mother returned home.

Dr. Carl Foss, who practiced dentistry in Harlem, Montana, had moved from that town, where he was not liked, to Hydro after filing a homestead claim in 1913. Foss had a quick temper and was the head of a gang that threatened other homesteaders. He had eight brothers and sisters. The creek that ran through Krause's property was also a water source for Foss and the land claimed by his siblings, which encircled the Krause property. The application of one of Foss's family members for 320 acres of land under the Desert Land Act had been contested by Krause. One of Foss's brothers pushed Krause, Carl Foss threatened "to get him," and they told Krause to leave the country. Krause was shot shortly before he was to appear as a witness against Foss in a hearing to be conducted by a U.S. commissioner.

Two of Foss's brothers were charged with the murder, but the prosecution was unable to obtain convictions in two trials. Foss was convicted on a federal charge of conspiracy in connection with claims on government land near Hydro and sentenced to one year in prison. After serving his sentence, he resumed his dental practice in nearby Havre, a wide-open western town.[36] Wally was aware of the murder, and the killing later formed the core of a short story he titled "Pete and Emil."

AFTER THE SUMMER months there was the journey back to Eastend. The Stegners passed their few neighbors on the dirt track and paused on the south bench before descending into the river valley. The visual relief of green willows and the camaraderie of his friends waiting to take "late shivery swims" in the river and to play hare and hounds in the bottomlands quickly replaced the ache of loneliness on the prairie.

Wally was back in a real house in a real town. He could sneak a kiss from Eileen Huffman on the piano bench, get a treat at the Greek's ice-cream parlor, and see a silent Saturday-night movie accompanied by a piano player at the Pastime Theatre. The Stegner family was in the news in 1918. George Stegner went swimming "and found it wet," the local newspaper reported. Wally posted the best score of eighteen students in the promotion exams for fourth-graders.

DEATH STALKED THE prairie—as it did the continent—in the fall and winter of 1918–1919. Influenza, first called *la grippe* and then the Spanish flu, struck Eastend. One tenth of the population died during the epidemic. There was an incredible emotional toll in the frontier community, where families were tight and neighbors knew and helped one another out of necessity and liking.

The newspaper described how to tell the difference between a cold and the flu. *La grippe* struck suddenly, "as if by an unseen hand." Chills and fever quickly followed. The first victim was hauled into town on a buckboard on Halloween night, two weeks before the end of World War I. Eileen Huffman's father was one of the sixty deaths.

The sick were taken to the brick schoolhouse. One room became known as the Death Room because it housed the most critically ill patients. Wally and his mother shared a bed in the third- and fourth-grade room, which was set aside for mothers and children. Wally was delirious most of the time, and his nose bled on the sheets and on his mother. He was sure that his illness had compounded hers.

The men, including George, were in an adjoining room. "Because everyone was in it together," said Stegner, "there was a good deal of yelling back and forth between wards, and jokes, and songs, and efforts to make everything into a sort of picnic."[37] The treatments were soup and Epsom salts inside the school and chewing tobacco and whiskey outside. There was one doctor, and the nurses were healthy house-wives. The school janitor hauled the dead to the town cemetery in a horse-drawn bobsled.

The newspaper reported that the school-turned-hospital was full in mid-November: "Few houses have not contained one or more patients. Fortunate, indeed, is the home that has escaped entirely. The Workers have been tireless in their labors toward the sick but gradually first one man and then another of the first voluntary contingent has been laid upon his back until hardly one remains who has kept going from the beginning."[38] Death was referred to as the Grim Reaper, and the news-paper's editor was so frightened of catching the disease that he stayed home, and several editions were not published.

There was a lesson to be learned from the town's response to the flu, one that Stegner would eventually apply to the entire West: the benefits of community versus the futility of individual efforts. That lesson was embedded in his early homestead novel, *On a Darkling Plain*. The World War I hero, patterned on an Eastend homesteader whom Steg-ner knew, doesn't find what he is searching for on the prairie. The flu forces him to town, where he becomes part of the community. "He knew, as he had always known since Ypres," Stegner wrote, "that in the comradeship of ruin there was a tempering of the spirit."[39]

Bad news got short shrift in the weekly newspaper. The news of the flu—except in obituaries, and even there the cause of death was not always specified—disappeared from the *East End Enterprise* after a couple of months. But the epidemic persisted. More than five thousand perished in the province during the first year. What remaining news of the flu there was had to be gleaned from the paid advertisements of the provincial health authorities. News of the third successive year of crop failures was also handled gingerly in the summer of 1919. Subscribers were told that the poor crops were a trial all pioneering settlers had to face. They were a rite of passage. Be a sticker, was the newspaper's message, and "would-be men" would become "real men."[40]

The Stegners recovered from the flu and resumed a normal life. That spring a two-reel comedy featuring the Canadian-born Mack Sennett played at the Pastime Theatre, and it cost Wally fifteen cents to attend. In June he was promoted to the sixth grade, this time placing second in the exam.

The family was remembered years later. Hilda was "a good friend and neighbor" to the grieving Huffman family. She helped with the cooking at the local hospital and was remembered for her frugality. A nurse remarked on it to a friend, who wrote Stegner: "Marion says that she was the most amazing person because she made every bit of food count. Marion told about her canning pears for them and making jelly from the skins."[41]

Compared with the professional men in town, George seemed tame. Three of the doctors died of what appeared to be suicide. A series of lawyers who floated through town were drunk, incompetent, or disbarred. Corky Jones, who bought his own ranch and subsequently operated a garage and the town's electric system, had a photo of George Stegner and a group of men friends on the veranda of the rebuilt hotel. "Your father is quite prominent in it," he wrote Wally, "old felt hat and all. We had quite a few amusing experiences with him down at the old garage."[42]

GEORGE WAS BECOMING restless by the spring of 1920, so the family moved. They left in the early summer, bound for Great Falls, Montana, and greater opportunities in the cross-border liquor trade. On the drive south they spent one night in the musty homestead shack, not bothering to remove the boards that protected the windows from the slashing winter storms. They touched familiar objects, took a few with them, and said good-bye to a place in which they had invested many emotions and much hard work but to which they knew they would not return. It was, as Stegner later observed, "our own special plot of failure," there being many such plots in the frontier West.

Stegner never again journeyed to the prairie site of the abandoned homestead. He couldn't face nonexistence. "To return hunting relics," he wrote, "to go down there armed only with memory and find every trace of our passage wiped away—that would be to reduce my family, myself, the hard effort of years, to solipsism, to make us as fictive as a dream." He thought the reservoir might remain, but that would be all. He was right.

The overloaded green Essex bumped down the field that was full of gopher holes and thick with Russian thistle and crossed the medicine line. They picked up the graded county road at Hydro. "Well," Hilda said, "better luck next time."[43]

Stegner returned to the town of Eastend only once, and that was in late June of 1953. It was a strange episode. He acted like a spy revisiting his past. Wally's undercover name in town was Mr. Page, and the purpose of his one-week stay was to gather material for the book that would eventually become *Wolf Willow*.

While Wally roamed the town, his wife, Mary practiced her violin in their camping trailer, which was parked near the old Stegner house. So that no one would recognize him—meaning postmistresses who "read all the postcards and hold all the envelopes to the light when there's a mysterious stranger in town"—Wally enclosed a note to his son, Page, in a letter to his close friends Phil and Peg Gray in Greensboro.

Why the disguise? He told his Vermont friends, "Simply I don't want to be stared at, spared, or even forgiven for my old man's sake. It is much simpler to be Mr. Page." Stegner then wrote a remarkable description of what it was like to have been a youth in Eastend, to go home again after more than three decades, and to be a witness to the rapid transformation of a frontier settlement into an established town, a phenomenon that was typical of the fast-forward West:

> Revisiting the childhood home, especially incognito, has its interesting points. There is a moment when what—especially since it's never been revisited—has always seemed unreal, or like an especially vivid but unbelieved-in dream, has to be accepted as real, and that's an astonishing thing, almost as astonishing as the

syntax of this sentence. This is earth, like other earth, even though that shadowy progenitor of mine walked it. Here is the river, smaller than I remembered it, but going around the same bends in the same directions and dimpling with the same raindrops and flopping with the same carp and suckers. Right across the street from where we have parked our trailer in a vacant lot is the Presbyterian Church where I recollect spending the bulk of my childhood. There it sits, unchanged, and I heard its bell twice today. Up the street is the old bank of Montreal, now the post office; the old hardware store, the old Chinese restaurant, now a tavern; the old railroad station and the old Pastime Theater where I saw my first movie damn near forty years ago. This is all very strange, because I've written about this town until I think I imagined it. Now I have to imagine it over, because in thirty-five years it has grown a dense crop of trees all over itself, and the bare windswept flats I cut across are dotted with little old cottages and shacks hidden behind lilac and honeysuckle hedges and with cottonwoods sixty feet high all around them. The school where they carried out all the dead ones from the flu epidemic in 1918 is right through the hedge across the alley; I carry water from its well every morning now. The cutbanks and the swimming hole and the footbridge are as specified, only smaller. The picnic ground, though now overgrown with man-planted trees, is much the same, and the sand feels the same underfoot and the chokecherry and wildrose smells the same, and when I went quietly through the willows on the old path and came down to the beaver dam rapids, two mallards took off from the quiet little watery place as if this were 1916 and I were a kid with large bare dirty feet and an air rifle.

The town newspaper is in the same building it used to be in. The editor, whose canoe I used to swipe to run riffles in 1919, is a balding little Englishman who knows me now as Mr. Page and who gives me the run of his shop to look into the files. I can remember when this little man got aboard one of the first trains to go through this town, and went up to Swift Current to become a trooper in the Glengarry Horse. Somehow, remembering that about him makes me feel older than he is, and I feel ashamed to be calling myself by a phony name, and long to throw myself on his mercy and say, "Look, I was the guy that used to sink your canoe and pull it out of your boathouse under water, and use it for an hour or two and put it back before you came back from the newspaper office at five to your tent camp down by the beaver dam. I am the kid that skinned the paint off your rowboat. I am the kid who on a dare jumped off your diving board at the high cutbank and bloody near killed himself, and thereafter looked upon you with awe because every afternoon you used to do swan dives off that thirty foot board with great grace and ease."[44]

On returning home to Los Altos Hills and resuming his teaching at Stanford University, Stegner wrote Corky Jones, "I'm afraid I made some people mad by pulling that fool incognito act. . . . Well—having made a silly mistake, I guess I'm stuck with it." Part of the reason, he said, was because of "my father's probable reputation" in town.[45]

"Your fears were quite groundless as your mother was very well-liked and respected," Jones replied. "Also we are not a people given to visiting the sins of the father upon the child, besides many people have read your writings and have heard your broadcasts which gives you a prestige in your own right."[46]

Four years later, while continuing the research on what would become *Wolf Willow*, Stegner wrote an Eastend friend that everyone with whom he had been in contact was "full of homesickness for the place. And that is a strange thing, isn't it? I remember it better than any place I ever lived."[47]

Down through the years, Wally's secret visit became an Eastend myth that ran something like this: "Everybody was trying to figure out who that man was, and then old Mrs. So-and-So said, 'I know who it is! It's Wallace Stegner.' And the next day he was gone."[48]

Great Falls

And when my mother, learning how to drive, knocked a streetcar off its tracks and threw me against the front seat so hard it loosened my ribs and bent my new Eversharp pencil into a pretzel, even the notice in the paper managed to demean me. Listing the injuries, the reporter concluded that "the little boy, Wallace, was more frightened than hurt."

Wallace Stegner, in "Finding the Place"

G REAT FALLS WAS a brief, unhappy interlude during which the necessary adjustments were made for the more urban life that awaited the family in the city by the Great Salt Lake. In Stegner's own words, "Great Falls, though it taught me things almost faster than I could take them in, was never a comfortable place. It was a place of humiliation, a city of strangers where I was a freak, a runt in funny Canadian clothes thrust into the eighth grade among pupils three years older. Great Falls was something I survived."[1]

As in Saskatchewan, the rainfall in Montana had declined, and wheat production had plunged. But another industry, also based on grain, was gaining ascendancy. Bootlegger trails consisted of many interlocking fragments known only to the locals. Fast cars lined up on the Canadian side and headed south every night. "While some drivers were intercepted," stated a local history book, "prohibition enforcement was a spotty, understaffed effort everywhere, and good whiskey could readily be obtained in Great Falls."[2]

The newspaper that served the city of twenty thousand inhabitants promoted oil production and tourist attractions, which never seemed to pan out, and ignored the thriving trade in liquor. Numerous stills were located inside and outside the city. The Maverick Bar was one of many watering holes, and George Stegner was a principal supplier. Understandably, the Stegner family kept a low profile. They were not mentioned in the local newspaper or listed in the city directory. Nearly ninety years later no federal, state, county, or city historical entity seemed aware that the Stegners had lived there.

It was in Great Falls that an eleven-year-old Wallace Stegner encountered his first bathtub, flush toilet, and green lawn. The used water in the claw-foot bathtub did not need to be carried outside and dumped; rather, it swirled magically down a small hole when the plug was removed. The water in the toilet bowl, however, needed to recover its proper level before the chain was yanked a second time. Of the miracle of a green lawn, Stegner wrote: "I stooped down and touched its cool nap in awe and unbelief. I think I held my breath—I had not known that people anywhere lived with such grace."[3]

The Stegners arrived in June and would remain for just one year. On his first day in town, Wally also discovered cement sidewalks, streetcars, and streets with names and numbers, such as 448 Fourth Avenue North. In the rented home at that address there were other wonders, such as a polished hardwood floor, across which a boy could slide in his stocking feet, and electricity, which nearly ended his life right then and there. As Wally was storing his horde of pennies and nickels in the box housing an electric outlet, "the world exploded in my face, paralysis flashed through me, and I was knocked silly." He picked up his dented and scorched coins, arose, and walked shakily away.[4]

Disaster of a different type struck on his first day at school. His mother hadn't had time to buy proper clothes for a town school. That was okay with Wally. He thought he would impress everyone with his orange sweater with its single wide white stripe, bought from a Canadian mail-order house, and his short pants, long black stockings, and elk-hide moccasins. Young Stegner envisioned himself as an exotic Canadian version of Daniel Boone. Instead, he drew stares and laughter and was the object of his fellow students' cruel tricks and derision. "That day left permanent scars on my self-confidence," said Stegner.[5] Compounding the sartorial mistake and his feeling of being an undersize outsider was the fact that he had skipped two grades. An eleven-year-old, Wally was now competing with thirteen- and fourteen-year-olds, one of whom was six feet tall, needed a shave, and weighed twice as much as him.

This giant, whose name was "Joe Something, something Polish," rescued Wally and walked him home. Stegner helped his new friend with his schoolwork. A symbiosis between the two Steinbeck-type outcasts was formed. Of all the valuable lessons Wally learned that first year in civilization, "the lesson of kindness and human decency, unmotivated by anything but good nature and goodwill is the one I most value," he wrote six decades later.[6]

The youngster composed a theme for his demanding teacher, Miss Grace Temby, about being partially buried in a cave-in above the Frenchman River. She praised it. "I really believe she was the first person who indicated that I might have a literary career." Wally worked hard and by the end of the school year was at the top of the teacher's "praise list," an achievement that did not endear him to his fellow students.[7]

Stegner was too young and too little for organized school sports or a regular job. He did manage a couple of times to mow the lawn of the cowboy artist Charlie Russell, whose romanticized images of the West would be undercut by Stegner's realism in future years. Wally later wrote a description of his brother and himself at this time. The older brother was "husky, stringy with muscle, the younger one thin, puny actually, with staring hungry eyes and spindly legs."[8] The strange, lonely boy reverted to baby talk, which drove his father crazy.

Gradually, Wally adjusted. He joined the Cub Scouts in the spring, and for the first time he participated in organized outdoor activities, such as hiking, swimming, and camping. A neighbor kid, whom Stegner called a sharpie, taught him how to catch carp with his bare hands, charge watermelons to the family's grocery bill, ask for double the price when selling tutti-frutti ice-cream cones in the park, and kill baby owls. He probably would have adapted to Great Falls, but it was time for the family to move again.

Salt Lake City

All his earliest years in Salt Lake had been an effort, much of the time as unconscious as growth itself and yet always there as if willed, to outgrow what he was and become what he was not. A stray, he yearned to belong. An outsider and an isolate, he aspired to friends and family and the community solidarity he saw all around him in that Mormon city.

Wallace Stegner, *Recapitulation*

W ALLACE STEGNER NOT only found social acceptance in Salt Lake City, but he also discovered history, a subject the roots-conscious Mormons incorporated into their religion and daily lives. Regional and family history gave Stegner meaning. He would have to create it for Saskatchewan and the American West; it already existed in Utah when he arrived.

There are three types of Utah histories. When Stegner looked back twenty years after his arrival in Salt Lake City and wrote his anecdotal *Mormon Country*, he trod the thin line between the paeans of the Mormons and the jeremiads of outsiders. Stegner was both an insider, meaning that he had lived there, and an outsider, or a Gentile, as all non-Mormons are called in Utah.

The wandering agnostic who attended Mormon social functions as a youngster wrote about the Latter-day Saints with both compassion and skepticism as an adult. He felt compelled to explain that unusual position: "Since the stance from which I have written will surely strike some as being just as biased as anything in the library of Mormonism and anti-Mormonism, I may as well define it. I write as a non-Mormon but not a Mormon-hater."[1]

The history, as Stegner saw it, was essentially a history of group effort, of a persecuted minority out of necessity forging a religious and secular community and transporting it from the East across the Midwest to what was then Mexican territory. The religious and social cohesion forged on the trail translated into the mind-set that transformed desert lands into a virtual garden. Stegner, whose family failed on its Canadian acreage, later wrote admiringly of the Mormons: "The American Dream as historians define it did not fit these whiskered zealots. Theirs was a group dream, not an individual one; a dream of Millennium, not of quick fortune."[2]

Wally was accepted by the Mormons in Salt Lake City and admitted, insofar as his unbeliever status would allow, as a participant in the Tuesday-night social ritual known as Mutual, held in the local ward house. Mormon and Gentile youngsters alike were welcomed, the former so that they might further their education and the latter so that they might be proselytized in an innocuous setting. An undersize, shy Wally dribbled, passed, and shot a basketball and quickly ascended the scouting ladder that virtually every Utah youth attempted to climb.

Through Boy Scout outings and summers at his family's cabin in southern Utah, Stegner was transported beyond the city to the Uinta Mountains and the Colorado Plateau where he discovered wilderness. Of the fatal beauty and the depth of time inherent in the natural and human histories of the canyonlands, Stegner wrote with great longing from the confines of Harvard University during World War II:

> Its distances were terrifying, its cloudbursts catastrophic, its beauty flamboyant and bizarre and allied with death. Its droughts and its heat were withering. Almost more than the Great Basin deserts, it was a dead land. The ages lay dead in its brilliant strata, and the mud houses of the . . . [Anasazi] rotted dryly in caves and gulches. In the teeth of that—perhaps because of that—it may have seemed close to God. It was Sanctuary, it was Refuge. Nobody else wanted it, nobody but a determined and God-supported people could live in it. Settle it then, in God's name, and build the Kingdom under the very eaves of that geological charnel-house.[3]

From what he absorbed during the years of his unformed youth, which climaxed in his Utah experience, Stegner would spend much of his life attempting to unite humans with the spectacular beauty of that landscape without their destroying it. Although he would roam widely around the world, write of many places, live most of his life in northern California, and have his ashes scattered in Vermont, Salt Lake City and southern Utah remained central to who he was and what he thought about the West. Remembering, he wrote: "It is a good country to look at, and with the hardships out of the way a good country to live in."[4]

Young Stegner had been rough-cut into a western gemstone by East-end. The polishing began in Salt Lake City. He called Salt Lake City home on and off for nearly twelve years between 1921 and 1937. The 1920s for Wally were the age of innocence, as they were for most of the country. The second half of the decade was "that crackpot bohemian pre-Crash wonderful time" when he was in college. Stegner described his undergraduate experience at the University of Utah as "the happiest years I ever knew or will know," and he would come to regard Salt Lake as the closest to a hometown that he had ever experienced.[5]

THE FAMILY MIGRATED to the city because of business opportunities for George. The journey south from Great Falls in Wally's twelfth year was a pleasant awakening. Raised on an arid prairie, he discovered rivers pulsing with spring snowmelt through thick pine forests from glacier-carved mountains. Through river valleys and across high mountain passes from Great Falls to Salt Lake City in his father's brand-new Essex Super Six, Wally soaked up the refreshing scenes. He later wrote in an ode to mountain water that derived from this youthful experience: "By such a river it is impossible to believe that one will ever be tired or old. Every sense applauds it."[6]

When the family arrived in Salt Lake, they found a bustling city of 120,000 inhabitants snuggled up against the backbone of the Wasatch Range, with a view westward toward the Great Salt Lake Desert. The city, Stegner would write later in notes for his autobiographical novel *Recapitulation*, was "a semi-island preserved by church and family piety."[7] That he adapted so well to the prevailing culture, considering that his family lacked both religion and piety, was testimony to his hunger for acceptance and the warm welcome he received when he participated in the more secular activities sponsored by the Church of Jesus Christ of Latter-day Saints.

Salt Lake City and the state that surrounds it were, and still are, an anomaly in the American West. They comprise, for the most part, an ordered society that marches to the beat of its own drum. There were, however, a few breaks in the ranks; George Stegner would exploit one of them when the family arrived four years after Utah became a dry state and shortly after the Volstead Act made Prohibition the law of the land.

The 1920s were the Jazz Age, and although tendrils of frivolity and wealth snaked inward to the heartland of the interior West, Salt Lake City did not share in the prosperity experienced elsewhere in the country. The city was suffering from the stresses of a newly industrialized society.

At the time it was one of the most active mining and smelting centers in North America. Smoke from the many smelters and residential coal-burning stoves contributed to a layer of smog that choked the valley from Murray, Utah, to Salt Lake. Stegner recalled twenty years later, in a letter to a friend who was considering teaching at the University of Utah, that Salt Lake "is extremely smoky; if you go there, try to get a house as high up as possible because the lower town is as smoky as Pittsburgh or St. Louis."[8]

Ash and trash blew across the bleak, wide streets and empty lots. The city's watershed, in the nearby foothills, was polluted by grazing sheep. It was not a healthy place to live. Children contracted diphtheria at excessive rates.

To counter the physical foulness, a nascent City Beautiful movement was organized. Minimal city planning was instituted. Men wanted a golf course, and women called for landscaping. A higher moral tone was sought, with indifferent results. Child-labor laws were not enforced. Juvenile delinquency was on the increase. Cigarettes and liquor were sold despite laws banning them. Gambling was a problem. So was racism, with the appearance of the Ku Klux Klan in a city whose population was predominantly of northern European extraction. There were very few minorities.

The Mormons were far and away the most dominant religious and cultural group. Unwritten social codes with strange twists existed. For instance, David Freed was a star tennis player from an affluent family. His mother was a Mormon, and his father was a Jew, or a "half Jew," as Freed described him. His friend Wallace Stegner was a mediocre tennis player from a poor family. The non-Mormon Stegner, of northern European ancestry, was a member of a fraternity at the University of Utah. But Freed, despite being a prominent athlete and having a Mormon mother, was not. Freed said, "None of the fraternities wanted any Jews belonging to them"—even though the persecuted Mormons felt a theoretical affinity for the Jews.[9]

The Utah historian Thomas G. Alexander called the 1920s "a decade of contradiction and indecision" in Salt Lake City.[10] At the heart of the contradictions was the booming liquor trade, in which George Stegner took a very active part, much to the distress of his wife and sons, who felt that it made them social outcasts. In fact, George was part of a distinct minority of the population who served what many viewed as a useful if not publicly recognized need.

Prohibition did not work in the driest of all dry states. In a study of bootlegging in Utah, Helen Papanikolas concluded: "Legal maneuvers, speakeasies, rum-running, fashionable cocktail parties, gang wars, and hypocrisy fused into the milieu of the dry years. From its inception Prohibition enforcement was a delusion."[11] A contemporary Utah writer called it "the Era of the Big Lie." Liquor poured in from Canada and Los Angeles and points in between via padded suitcases, railroad cars, the rumble seats of automobiles, horses, and airplanes. Various ruses were employed. A Park City, Utah, mortician drove to a supposed mine disaster in Wyoming in a hearse followed by grieving town notables in their cars. They filled the coffin with liquor, and the funeral cortege was waved through a roadblock on its return.

Bootleggers came from all types of professions and jobs: unsuccessful doctors and attorneys, successful druggists, ranchers, railroad workers, miners, businessmen, and operators of shoeshine stands. They connived with the law, through either a wink or hard currency. Papanikolas wrote: "The illegality of liquor and the determination of drinkers to get it by any means led to unprecedented corruption."[12] The Ogden mayor, a county commissioner, the chief of police, a police captain, a patrolman, the sheriff, and two deputy sheriffs were indicted for collaborating with a bootlegger.

It seemed as though madness circulated in the air, along with the smog, and topsy-turvy ruled the times. The Wild West that the sedate city of Salt Lake had seemingly evaded alighted in Zion for a few years. The badly outnumbered and underfinanced federal and state liquor agents, who tended to be either Mormons or Protestants, were harshest in their enforcement activities when dealing with immigrant communities. The 1928 state Republican convention in Ogden was "a big drinking party," said the chairman, who was running for governor. In Salt Lake City a newspaper reported that the nightly war waged by the police and the bootleggers was a "one-sided conflict, in which the rum dealers have the odds."[13]

THE STEGNER FAMILY moved constantly, from rented house to rented house, to avoid a raid. Wally estimated that in ten years they must have had twenty residences. Of one of those homes, he wrote:

"Life in that house was full of tensions. For one thing, they were afraid of the law, and were constantly poised to move, though a move meant losing customers who might never find them again." Hilda, who came from a midwestern Lutheran family, although not particularly religious herself, was the wrong wife for the operator of a speakeasy in the family parlor. She and her sons avoided that room when there was "company." Wally did not bring friends home.[14]

The advantage for Stegner in such moves was that occasionally books had been left behind by previous tenants. Some were of dubious value; others weren't. In this haphazard fashion he read John Locke, George Berkeley, and David Hume in the Harvard Classics series and the works of other philosophers, of which he understood very little. He also read most of Conrad, whom he liked. Captain Cook's adventures in the South Pacific, some Shakespeare, and John Clark Ridpath's histories, including the salacious illustration of the rape of the Sabine women, were perused in a similar manner. Wally became a public-library addict, making two or three visits a week to the public library on State Street and coming home with three or four books each time.

"I found all kinds of consolation in books that I didn't find in my family," Stegner said, "and so all of a sudden I was living another life, and that other life just sucked me away over a long period of time." He felt isolated in this new city where his family moved frequently. There was no continuity of boyhood friendships. "All of that security was cracked open. So I found the public library. . . . Books are a habit, and once you've created a book habit I suppose it lasts."[15]

With George frequently gone on his liquor-collecting or liquor-distributing trips, her younger son reading a book a day or playing basketball with his Mormon friends, and her oldest boy involved in organized sports, Hilda Stegner led a "terribly limited and lonesome life," her son said. A wife's place was with her husband, she thought, regardless of his wanderings and his treatment of the children. She had few friends and no permanent residence, the only home she knew as a married woman having been abandoned in Eastend. Hilda practiced frugality and attempted to keep the family together.

Wally was a self-described "grind." He skipped another grade in East High School, landing in the same class as Cecil. The runt of the family weighed less than one hundred pounds. There is a 1925 photograph of him in the *Eastonia*, the high school yearbook. His hair is parted in the middle and slicked down on either side. His ears stick out.

Stegner played basketball in his junior year, served on the business staff of the school magazine, was a member of the chemistry club and president of the Latin club, and was first lieutenant in Company D of the school's Reserve Officers' Training Corps. He led a platoon down Main Street in the Decoration Day Parade, their uniforms complete with Sam Browne belt, puttees, and sword. His nickname was Wallie. His grades ranged from the mid-80s to the low 90s, quite high for those times. His brother played varsity baseball and basketball and was quarterback on the football team. His nickname was Steg. The brothers got along because they were not competitive in any way.

Gradually, Wally migrated outdoors again, this time through organized activities that differed greatly from his solo wanderings across the prairie. He rose rapidly to the rank of Eagle Scout. As with the military activities in school, he liked the uniformity of uniforms. They made him feel as if he belonged.

One of the more memorable trips was into the Granddaddy Lakes Basin in the Uinta Mountains, where the scouts got sick from beans cooked in a zinc-lined pail. On another trip in 1923 to the same lakes in the High Uintas, Wally's troop would find an ideal campsite, freezing-cold water to swim in after a long, hot hike, and trout galore in this "Eden." It was his first sampling of what would become an officially declared wilderness area, a concept Stegner would one day advance on a national level.

The most significant trips were Wally's first ventures to the Plateau Province in southern Utah and the canyonlands that were already national parks or would be soon. He traveled with his scoutmaster and his son in 1924. The scoutmaster, an Episcopalian minister, lit his pipe while driving, and the embers blew up his sleeve and caught fire in his armpit. The boys "died laughing." There were other trips into canyon country with the scout troop. Stegner described the places they visited:

> At Zion, Mormon farms still extended to the mouth of the canyon. We picked grapes off the roadside fences in Rockville, and walked clear to the Narrows without seeing more than forty people. On the Kaibab the mule deer browsed and grazed in African numbers, only months away from the catastrophic die-off that taught the nation one of its first lessons in ecology. The North Rim of the Grand Canyon dreamed barely-peopled above the great gulf, its blue air owned by hawks. Bryce, still called Utah National Park, was only a year old; Capitol Reef was neither park nor monument, only a little Mormon oasis of alfalfa

fields and fruit trees tucked among the red cliffs along the Fre-
mont River. Arches and Canyonlands were not even conceived.[16]

The Stegners escaped the heat of Salt Lake in the late 1920s and
early 1930s, spending portions of those summers in a small cabin on the
shoreline of Fish Lake in southern Utah. At an elevation of nearly nine
thousand feet, Fish Lake is surrounded by pine and aspen trees. It was a
summer oasis for the middle class. The lake, encased by two parallel
ridges, resembles the dented crown in a hat. The constant water level
maintained by the snowmelt and springs gushing from the parallel fault
lines makes Fish Lake an anomaly in the arid West, where the level of
standing bodies of water varies widely, depending upon runoff, evaporation, damming, and human use.

Perched on the lip of the canyon country, Wally became familiar
with the red-rock landscape and participated actively in the social
scene. There was fishing in the six-mile-long Fish Lake and in the
other lakes scattered throughout the nearby mountains. The family ate
the trout he caught, if mountain lions did not filch them first as they
hung from nails on the unscreened porch where Wally slept. Dances
with a local band were held on Saturday nights, at first in an outdoor
pavilion and then in a giant ballroom in the newly constructed
Skougaard's Lodge, a pine-log behemoth nearly one block long, with
two huge fireplaces, that is still standing. Because of the altitude, a
small amount of liquor went a long way on Saturday nights.

There was drinking elsewhere around the lake. A very religious but
practical Mormon lived in the adjacent cabin. The father came out one
day and stretched in the morning sun. Wally was stacking wood. Not
knowing he was being watched, the neighbor reached under the back
porch and pulled out a jug. He patted it lovingly and then took a long
swig. "When he brought it down again his eyes were clearer and he saw
me. He cackled, 'By golly,' he said, 'that's the way I like to fish.' "[17]

Closer to home were the magic of warm summer nights and the lure
of bright lights on the edge of the Great Salt Lake. Wally got a job selling hot dogs and hamburgers at Saltair, the Coney Island of the interior
West. There was a sign warning against diving off the end of the pier
into the mineral-laden shallow water. An Illinois high school boy disregarded it and broke his neck. Wally helped pull him from the water.
The locals knew better. They sneaked down the ladder at night and
swam and splashed in the sulfurous-smelling brine. Above, in the warm
night air, were the rich smells of frying meat, buttered popcorn, and
spun candy. The ceaseless clamor of the milling crowds, big band music,

screech of metal against metal, and the screams of girls on the pitching and dipping rides rent the air. Near midnight it was time for the long ride home on the trolley.

Then Wally—or his father acting in his behalf—discovered tennis. This sport gained him social and athletic acceptance that lasted through his college years. |At the same time a miracle occurred: he sprouted six inches between the ages of fifteen and sixteen. "Suddenly I was big enough to hold my own in sports. Suddenly I had friends who looked on me as an equal and not as a mascot. Suddenly, as a freshman in the University of Utah, I was playing on the freshman basketball squad and a little later on the tennis team. Suddenly I was being rushed by a fraternity and acquired brothers, and a secret grip, and a book of tong songs. Beatitude."[18]

One of George Stegner's clients was the manager of the Salt Lake Tennis Club, which had five clay courts. George obtained a membership for Wally's birthday, and Hilda found a secondhand racket and had it re-strung. She sent her reluctant son off to the club with two tennis balls. He was met there by Jack Irvine, who taught him the rudiments of the game and became his close friend. Another young player at the club was Dave Freed, who would win a national seniors championship at Forest Hills and coach two Davis Cup teams. Freed thought Stegner was a good doubles player. "He had quite a temper," said Freed, who witnessed Wally erupting and throwing his racket several times. Stegner's memory served him well as he recalled the summer scene at the tennis club in a novel: "Under the arbor, in the weathered, creaky, unraveling wicker chairs, sprawled the figures in white flannels and ducks who were his first idols and friends."[19] He also played on the East High tennis team, which lacked a coach and official status.

While catching a football at the tennis club, Wally injured the ring finger of his left hand in an accident that necessitated his having the entire digit amputated. When asked by his son, Page, how he lost his finger, Stegner would invent a story: he had been testing the sharpness of a buzz saw; he mistook the finger for kindling when chopping wood; or he went to catch a ball and snagged it on the mirror bracket of a passing truck—the version that came closest to the truth. His multiple answers were the product of the "don't complain" attitude inherited from his frontier experience.

The loss ruled out touch-typing and restricted him to typing with his two index fingers. Stegner was both a speedy and a relatively accurate typist. Since he was right-handed, the accident did not hinder his tennis playing.

The University of Utah

Along with growth, friends. There have been no such friends since. If they were more athletes than scholars, I needn't apologize for them. They were hearts of gold, and they accepted *me*.

Wallace Stegner, "It Is the Love of Books I Owe Them"

M OST EAST HIGH graduates went to the nearby university, which looked down upon the center of the smoggy city from the former shoreline of ancient Lake Bonneville. Stegner was no different from the majority, except that he was a skinny, precocious sixteen-year-old when he began his freshman year, in September of 1925.

Tennis continued in college, as did his friendship with Jack Irvine. Jack taught Wally not only tennis but also confidence. He gave him the much-needed gift of close friendship. "Simply by accepting that outcast," Stegner wrote of the Irvine character, Joe Mulder, in *Recapitulation*, "he made him over."[1] In fact, the entire Irvine family adopted Wally, who dated Jack's sister for a time. Jack's father gave him a job in the family business, the I&M Rug and Linoleum Company, at twenty-five cents an hour, with a raise to forty cents after three years. That provided him with money to spend for the first time on girls, clothes, and books. From the Irvine family, with whom he lived for a time, he experienced the warmth of a secure home.

The university's tennis team had a coach who knew nothing about the game but a lot about motivating his players. When Freed, who was the same age as Wally but two grades behind him, joined the team two years later, it won a conference championship. A photograph of the team, with the taller, thinner Stegner and the shorter, stockier Irvine, in letter sweaters and white pants, holding tennis rackets, ran in the 1930 edition of the *Utonian*, the university's yearbook. The doubles partners stood side by side.

Jack and Wally were partners not only on the court but also in the Salt Lake City social scene. They were both members of the Tillicums Club, an informal social organization of male university students whose main purpose seems to have been having a good time. They drank copious amounts of beer and gin. They had their code words for drinking. *Hanging a few shades* meant "going for a drink." The expression derived from their work at the linoleum company, where they sold and installed shades and blinds. *Getting high from bowling* meant they had been or were on their way to the nearby bowling alley, which served beer. They dated feverishly and exhaustively and drove cars and the linoleum company truck madly, damaging the truck once. In other words, they were normal youths.

While Jack was out of town, Wally dated his girlfriend in a brotherly manner. At the same time he was seeing a Mormon girl who never "warmed up" to him and a young woman who smoked and drank and ran with "a hard crowd." He was sure he was in love "this time," but it didn't last. One night Stegner and three friends drank three bottles of beer apiece and a quart of gin. They then drove down the steps of the Utah State Capitol. Wally got sick, passed out, and regained consciousness in time to change the car's tire with a friend. "Neither of us knew how in hell we got there, or when we stopped or a damned thing about it," he wrote Jack. His letters to his close friend were full of sophomoric humor and laced with sexual innuendos, such as this cigarette jingle:

Camels are Brown
Old Golds are Not
Took Edie out Thursday
And was she Hot? Whoee.[2]

Stegner and Irvine parted company when they graduated from the university, and their lives took different turns. Irvine ran an antiques shop on State Street. When the author visited Salt Lake years later, he telephoned his old friend, but there was no answer. Wally then wrote Jack: "I guess I don't want not to recognize you. I don't want you not to recognize me. We ain't the same, and it's been too long since we saw each other." Stegner sent Irvine an inscribed copy of *Recapitulation* when it was published in 1979. After Jack's death, Stegner wrote his widow that he "was the first friend I had, and the longest, and the best."[3]

THE TRANSITION FROM high school to college involved more than tennis and high jinks. Stegner had two recurrent dreams. In his high school dream he was constantly being humiliated, fleeing through mazes of corridors, being in the wrong place at the wrong time, and generally suffering from a "blind panic." His college dream was quite different:

> I am coming along Thirteenth East on my way to an eight o'clock class. It is a marvelous morning—It is always a marvelous morning, whether the air is hazy with autumn and the oakbrush on the Wasatch has gone bronze and gold, or whether the chestnut trees along the street are coned with blossoms. The early sun slants across lawns and throws tree-shadows halfway across the pavement and warms the faces of houses on the other side. Cars pass, people wave, walkers across the street give me greetings— faces that I am glad to see, and that are glad to see me. I am enveloped in universal friendliness. As I turn at the drugstore on Second South and start uphill toward the Park Building at the head of the U drive, I meet Harold, the enthusiastic imbecile who appoints himself cheerleader at all athletic events and wants to be mascot to everybody in the college. . . . Often he watches tennis matches, and he knows me as a hero. We slap each other on the back and exchange pleasantries. His sweet adoring smile hangs on the morning air of the dream, welcoming me into a day placid without threat and rich with possibility, and then I pass and he fades like breath off a mirror, leaving only his warmth behind.[4]

That eight o'clock class could very well have been the freshman composition course taught by Vardis Fisher. From the assistant professor of English Stegner learned not only how to write but also that writing was a possible occupation, albeit a poorly paying one that needed to be supplemented by teaching. It was Fisher who not only pried open his mind but also "planted within it an ambition to write."[5]

Fisher, at that point an unpublished novelist, pushed the promising freshman to think creatively and freely in and outside class. "Fisher felt that I could write," Stegner recalled. "He gave me good grades and patted me on the head and boosted me out of freshman English at the end of the first quarter and into an advanced writing course with him. I got the impression pretty early that writing was something I could do." Of the advanced composition course, Stegner said, "I attended every session with my mouth open."[6]

Additionally, Fisher took the subversive position at the University of Utah of encouraging his students to think for themselves. On the first day of Stegner's class, he announced that he was going to take a can opener to the closed minds of his students. "He sounded a note of intellectual recklessness that contradicted the complacency of the campus," said Stegner.[7]

Fisher was the campus radical, a Mormon apostate who was critical of all religions, including Mormonism. He taught at the church-dominated university, where students and faculty and junior and senior members of the faculty did not mix. An attitude of aloof respectability was cultivated by the professors, none of whom was more aloof than Sherman Brown Neff, chairman of the Department of English. The fact that Fisher's days were numbered at the university gave him an air of excitement, heightened, as Stegner saw it, by his "caustic tongue and great contempt for time wasters." He was "not exactly lovable but was anything but dull," said Wally.[8]

Fisher urged Stegner to join the Radical Club, consisting of intellectually curious students and the more rebellious members of the faculty. They sponsored the talk of a Communist on campus, which drew the ire of *The Deseret News*, the Mormon-owned newspaper in Salt Lake. Usually, they met in Fisher's off-campus apartment and heard papers read on the history of Jesus Christ, discussed the birth-control measures advocated by Margaret Sanger, and listened to a faculty member from an eastern university who had been dismissed because of his dangerous ideas. The books they discussed were radical mostly in their explicit sexual content. It was rich if not always understandable fare for the seventeen-year-old Stegner.[9]

Wally also encountered a different view of Utah in his freshman year. Walking down the hall of the English building, he was startled when a professor yanked a door open and hurled a copy of *The American Mercury* into the corridor. Stegner picked up the magazine. It contained an article on Utah by a disgruntled native named Bernard DeVoto, who had gone east and would later play a key role in Stegner's life. The article, Wally said, was "a calculated piece of mayhem that out-Menckened Mencken."[10]

Salt Lake City and its university were, and are today to a lesser extent, walled off from the outside world. The landscape that sheltered the dominant religion and its squeaky-clean lifestyle formed a barrier. "Isolated, far-off, adrift among our native deserts and mountains," Stegner later wrote in a University of Utah publication, "we heard echoes of intransigence and change and were led to books that in class we could have discussed only gingerly, if at all."[11]

In later years the prickly Fisher, who left the university in 1929 and enjoyed some success as a novelist, tended to denigrate his most successful student. In his book on writing fiction for beginners, he took Oliver La Farge, Sinclair Lewis, and Stegner to task for being unable to find good titles for their books, although he did allow that *Main Street* and *Babbitt* "were happy choices."[12] The character of Paul Latour in Stegner's short story "The View from the Balcony" has more than a passing resemblance to Fisher, indicating that Fisher had an important influence on Stegner.

Between his freshman and sophomore years, Wally's parents moved to Hollywood. So he enrolled in the University of California at Los Angeles. But he was homesick. Before classes began at UCLA, he was back in Salt Lake and took up residence in a boardinghouse, which gave him lots of freedom. Of his sophomore year, Stegner said, "I discovered girls, fraternities, beer, and sports and the frantic pace of intellectual awakening subsided into a sort of slumber, the happiest slumber of my life."[13] Accordingly, his grades suffered. From mainly A's and B's in his freshman year, his grades slipped to B's and one C, the latter being a course in English drama taught by Professor Neff. The only other course in which he received a C was philosophy.

By the time he was a junior, his grades had begun to rise. His first contact with the chores of teaching came with reading the papers of his fellow students for his English professors that year. He took a short story course in 1929 and submitted "Reciprocation" to *The Salt Lake Telegram*, winning the newspaper's short story contest. The prize was publication of the story in the newspaper, a first for Wally.

It was as if he wanted to jam all of life—as he knew it at the time—into one moment, knowing it would never get better. With the hyperactivity came stress. Wally developed ulcers during the last years of college, an affliction that would return to plague him during a similar stressful period in the early 1940s. In fact from this time on, he never stopped running; he slowed down only near the end of his life. Talent, instinct, drive, ambition, and discipline were the reasons he accomplished so much. His wife, Mary, would provide the assistance in a few years that would allow him to accomplish even more.

In addition to reading students' papers, Wally read unassigned books by Hemingway, Fitzgerald, Frost, Yeats, Willa Cather, Anatole France, and Knut Hamsun on the streetcar while shuttling between the job at the linoleum company, his apartment, and the university. He worked from 1 p.m. to 6 p.m. on weekdays and from 8 a.m. to 6 p.m. on Saturdays. He pumped iron at the gym, played on the tennis team, and edited *Pen*, the campus literary magazine. Stegner read assigned texts and studied between midnight and 3 a.m. He still found time to fall in love with one or another young woman. He had to drop out for most of what would have been his junior year in order to earn more money. Wally graduated one year later, with honors.

In January of 1930, with graduation on the horizon and an undetermined future facing him, Stegner wrote a scathing attack on complacency at the university in *Pen*. The Fisher-styled parody was titled "How the Smart People Escaped Annihilation." The geniuses escaped by quitting the rigid institution, where, lured by "the illusion of Learning," they had received irrefutable answers from the professors. Average students remained to graduate and then proceeded "smugly on to Babbittry."[14]

Stegner's decision to remain in academe as a graduate student and professor for the next forty-one years came about by chance. He didn't know what he wanted to do as June approached. On the one hand, he could remain with the linoleum company in comfortable Salt Lake and risk Babbittry; on the other hand, he could venture forth to graduate school, possibly in another state. The head of the psychology department offered Stegner a fellowship. Professor Neff was appalled that he would consider psychology as a career and found Stegner a job as a teaching assistant in the English Department at the University of Iowa.

In a reference to one of Robert Frost's poems, Stegner later wrote: "Two roads diverged in a wood, and I, I took the one I was pushed into." He elaborated: "It appalls me to realize really how much brute accident accounts for what became of me. . . . Every significant movement in my life resulted from a conjunction between a lurking inclination, which was the talent undeveloped and raw, and opportunities that were not merely not taught to me or shown to me, but weren't sought for and often weren't recognized when they opened up."[15]

The Iowa Years

All around her the afternoon was thick, humid, stirring with the slow fecundities of Midwestern summer—locust-shrill and bird-cheep and fly-buzz, child-shout and the distant chime of four o'clock from the university's clock tower.

Wallace Stegner, "The View from the Balcony"

TREE-SHADED IOWA CITY, set in the midst of Grant Wood country, was known as the Athens of the Midwest because of the abundance of arts activities. Wood himself was a professor and artist in residence at the School of Fine Arts at the time Stegner was a graduate student at the university. He typified the regionalist movement, which was prevalent at Iowa and spread, much to the distaste of the classicists, throughout the curriculum and so to the newly emerging writing program.

Iowa City should have been a homecoming for Stegner, who was an Iowan by birth and had spent time in Iowa as a young child. He had relatives living nearby. But it wasn't his real home. He missed Utah most of the time he was in Iowa. Nineteen thirty ushered in a fifteen-year period during which Stegner shuttled back and forth across the country, from Boston to Berkeley, with stops to the north and south and in between, before he settled in northern California for the remainder of his life.

For the first five years he bounced between Salt Lake City and Iowa City and came to know the route well. He traveled it by transcontinental train, bus, and car. He drove it in his Model A Ford in thirty hours before multilane interstate highways had been constructed, and he hitchhiked it in thirty-six hours.

Iowa was a strange place to Wally. The university's tennis courts were surfaced with gravel; the large squirrels resembled foxes or small wolves and scared him; and the heavy, rib-sticking food was cooked by "retired glue factory workers." He was taking courses in French,

Anglo-Saxon, and Middle English. Wally's expertise in the different grades of linoleum and carpets allowed him to judge the status of various university administrators.

It was in Iowa City that Stegner discovered he was a westerner. The identification with place hit him hard. "I grew up Western, and the first time I lived outside the West I realized what that meant to me." He was accustomed to the earth tones of the desert Southwest and was "offended" by the endless green of the Midwest. Bare ground was nonexistent. The underlying geologic strata were hidden. There was no pungent smell of wolf willow or sagebrush. In the intermountain West the sun rose over mountains and set over mountains, not over flatland. Here was a drab landscape whereas out West there was drama. What did he miss? "It was the whole West," he wrote later in life, "and I began to realize how lucky I had been to see so much of it. I also began to realize how much it had had to do in the making of me."[1]

Meanwhile, there was work to do, and in typical Stegnerian fashion he applied himself energetically to the task at hand. He arrived at the university just as the country's oldest creative writing program for graduate students was being put into place. He referred to himself as one of the first guinea pigs.

Stegner was in at the start of a concept that he would advance at Utah, Wisconsin, Harvard, Stanford, and the Bread Loaf Writers' Conference: the idea that writing could be taught. He would be the sower of seeds that would be cast widely and would grow and be harvested in the form of some of the foremost writers in this country.

What Stegner took from the rootstock of Iowa and refined, and what exists to this day, was the basic technique of teaching writing. It went something like this: A writing assignment was made and completed. The professor or a student would read it. Then there was the "tearing apart," in the words of one Iowa student, meaning comments and criticism from the class. A short or long lecture, depending on the professor, would follow. Infrequent one-on-one conferences were held between teacher and student. Other writing assignments followed a similar pattern. The practice of having real writers teach writing, or at least make short visits to the campus, was introduced at Iowa. That was how writers became part of the academic scene, a process that is commonplace today.

NORMAN FOERSTER HAD also arrived at the University of Iowa, as director of the new School of Letters, in 1930. One of Foerster's innovations was to allow students the leeway to write creative works for their doctoral theses rather than footnoted dry academic dissertations. The university already permitted fictional works for a master's thesis in the writing program.

Stegner, a mere teaching assistant in the English Department who fancied himself a writer, wished to be admitted to the writing program. Foerster was not impressed by his Utah writing samples, so Stegner added determination to accident. "I beat my way in, more or less against Foerster's best judgment (I was barely twenty-one, and green as grass)."[2] Stegner and others disagreed with Foerster's new humanism, Wally favoring his prairie- and desert-bred regionalism. New humanism was concerned with ethos and ideas; regionalism was centered in place. Both Foerster and his students, however, agreed on the educational value of creative writing. Together they hammered out a creed that influenced Stegner for the remainder of his life. It was this:

> Revolting against domination by the city (especially New York), against industrial civilization, against cultural nationalism and cosmopolitanism, and against an abstract humanism—all of them conceived as making for an artificial rootless literature— regionalism seeks to direct preponderating attention to the natural landscape, human geography, and cultural life and mark off particular areas of the country from other areas, *in the belief that writers who draw from their own experience and the life they know best are more likely to attain universal value than those who do not*.[3]

Stegner found Foerster "intellectually open," and liked him personally. He thought his course in intellectual criticism was the most stimulating he had encountered in college or graduate school. Wally took three semesters of creative writing courses and wrote his master's thesis for Edwin Ford Piper, a poet. "There was nothing remarkable about the first creative writing classes," Stegner said.[4] Under Piper's permissive guidance, the graduate students wrote, read aloud, and then commented on one another's poems or short stories. In 1932 Stegner received the English Department's second master's degree granted for creative work—three short stories titled collectively *Bloodstain and Other Stories*. The stories, which later appeared in newspapers or magazines and were based on his Saskatchewan experience, were "Pete and Emil," "Dam Builder," and "Bloodstain." Four years leter, the master's degree program was formalized under the name Iowa Writers' Workshop.

It was Foerster who recommended that Stegner pursue a doctorate in American literature, a master's in creative writing not being particularly bankable in those Depression years. American literature was at least recognizable—albeit as an oxymoron—as a proper discipline by the Europeanists who dominated university English departments. Creative writing was not a legitimate subject at the time.

In this manner, Stegner was launched on his bipolar careers of writing and teaching and into the worlds of the imagination and academia, of fiction and fact-based writing, of melding real people and history to meet fictional needs. Of the Greek Muses of epic poetry—the closest the Greeks came to what we recognize as fiction—and of history, Stegner said, "Calliope and Clio are not identical twins, but they *are* sisters."[5]

It was also Foerster, the author of *Nature in American Literature*, who suggested that Stegner pick a western naturalist for his doctoral thesis. Stegner thought—incorrectly, as it turned out—that Foerster wanted to add a chapter to future editions of his book based on the material Stegner gathered. Clarence Edward Dutton, whom Wally selected for his thesis subject, led Stegner to John Wesley Powell and the subject of aridity in the West. Stegner had first encountered the work of the two scientists when a sophomore at the University of Utah.

As MEANINGFUL AS Stegner's relationship was with Foerster, his close friendship with Wilbur Schramm, a fellow graduate student, was even more important. It was Schramm who would introduce Wally to his future wife, give him the news of his father's death, and provide him with the contacts that furthered his career. "Wilbur had an extraordinary and continuing effect on my life," said Stegner.[6]

Schramm had arrived at Iowa via Ohio, a flute scholarship at the New England Conservatory of Music, a position in the Civic Symphony Orchestra of Boston, a stint as a journalist with the Associated Press, and a master's degree in literature from Harvard University. He met the western rube named Stegner, who had a .38-caliber revolver in a gunfighter's holster and a cartridge belt draped over his dresser as decoration and a statement of who he was and where he came from. Schramm set out to civilize Stegner, who later described himself as an "incomparably green and ill-prepared first-year graduate student from the Wild West."[7]

Wally, who had never heard a symphony orchestra, practiced

"Dream a Little Lullaby" on a banjo ukulele; Schramm practiced classical music on the flute for the university symphony. When Stegner's gay roommate departed after he made a move on the faux cowboy and was repulsed, Wilbur moved in. They became so close that Foerster, for whom they sometimes wrote paired papers on the same subject, nicknamed them Simon and Schuster.

Schramm tutored his culturally deprived roommate in classical music and German and introduced him to exotic travel, taking him to such places as Chicago, the farthest east Stegner had ever ventured. In what was an equitable division of interests, the roommates watched the Cubs play in Wrigley Field and visited the Art Institute of Chicago. They hitchhiked to northern Iowa and Minnesota to visit Stegner's relations. It was Schramm's idea to carry their texts of *Beowulf* with them to the University of Minnesota to hear Frederick Klaeber lecture on the subject. Klaeber had edited the canonical text, and he autographed the books for the two awed graduate students.

The Depression hit Iowa in 1931. Schramm and Stegner cooked most of their meals in their room, using a hot plate for a stove and the window ledge as a refrigerator. But they found time for graduate school tomfoolery, using pot lids as Frisbees in their room and wadded paper napkins to shoot baskets into water glasses in the university cafeteria.

The worsening economy, demanding studies, and personal problems bore down upon them. "We lived by loans and barter," said Wally. Schramm was with Stegner when he received the telegram announcing the death of Cecil from pneumonia in January of 1931. Wilbur lent Wally the train fare to Salt Lake and his warm overcoat. Stegner returned to Iowa and then journeyed west again that summer.

He visited his parents in Reno, Nevada, where his father was now part owner of a gambling casino. Reno was bustling at 2 a.m., Wally discovered, but the cops kept a tight lid on the town. He was going to watch the heavyweight Max Baer fight. He asked Jack Irvine to send some Shine-All for the linoleum in his father's casino. His mother gave him a used Model A, which he nicknamed Laura, after the girlfriend of the moment. Hilda was very proud of her remaining son.

Stegner completed the work for his master's degree in January of 1932 and immediately began work on his doctorate. Of that time, he said, "I suppose I learned more, and faster, during two years in Iowa City than in any other two-year period in my life."[8] The roommates separated in June. After a brief interlude, Stegner would return to Iowa and continue his studies, but he would room with someone else.

Schramm continued to play an important role in Wally's life. He was the first director of the Iowa Writers' Workshop, the editor of *American Prefaces*, and one of the intellectual giants in the field of communications. The former roommates were reunited when Schramm became a professor of communications at Stanford University in 1955.

HILDA HAD RETURNED to Salt Lake and was diagnosed with cancer. Her health was deteriorating rapidly. The family drove to the cabin at Fish Lake in the summer of 1932, and Wally attempted to help her mend. Hilda and George then moved back to Los Angeles. To be closer to his mother, Stegner enrolled in the doctoral program in the Department of English at the University of California at Berkeley. His roommate was Milton "Red" Cowan, a friend from Salt Lake City and a German scholar.

The Cowan family had lived across the hall from the Stegners at one point in Salt Lake, and Red had had the time and the mind to assess the family carefully. He remembered Hilda Stegner as "fairly tall with a pleasant, angular face with a million years of misery in the eyes." She was quiet, kind, and not bitter, "given the husband that she had." Cowan added, "I think she forgave him. She loved the guy." To Cowan, George Stegner was full of energy. He made frequent nonstop, round-trip drives in his big, open Buick from Salt Lake to Las Vegas or Los Angeles for liquor. Stocky, round-faced, with thick black hair and physically strong, George served as his own bouncer in the old frame house that was a speakeasy in Salt Lake City. Card games were upstairs, drinking downstairs, and there was a back door for a quick getaway, Cowan said. If people wanted to drink, let them, was George's philosophy. It was George Stegner against the predominant Mormon society. George was a gambler, and the family was frequently broke, but he was good to his family when he took the boys and Hilda to Fish Lake.

Red and Wally lived in an apartment near the Berkeley campus. They cooked in their room and played literary games, Cowan stumping Stegner occasionally with the name of a German poet. Wally was always punning. Cowan gave this example: " 'Red, do you know what a humanist is?' 'No, Wally, what is a humanist?' 'A humanist is a man emeritus.' " They bought an old sailboat for $50, fixed it up, and left it with a man to sell but never received any payment. It was a major financial loss.[9]

The year was the bottom of the Depression. Wally graded freshman exams for twenty-five cents an hour. Their expenses, including bootleg beer and wine, were $60 a month. Their feelings, purposes, and resources were shared. "It was a lovely time, actually," Stegner recalled. "There was no bottom to fall to: you were already on it."[10] Wally found the Berkeley program too steeped in arcane subjects, and Cowan's studies were going nowhere. They remained only one term and returned to the University of Iowa, again as roommates, in time for the spring semester of 1933.

FROM HIS LAST years at the University of Utah to the end of his graduate school years at Iowa, Stegner was involved in three serious love affairs, which generated raw and intense emotions that would never be so visible again. He was a handsome, intelligent, virile man. He liked women, and women were attracted to him. First was Juanita Crawford, then Sara Barnard, and last Mary Page. Thereafter there was only one woman, and that was Mary.

Juanita and Wally were engaged. She jilted him, and he never fully recovered. Being dropped without warning for another man—a friend, in fact—hurt. As he did with his father, Stegner attempted to come to terms with Juanita by writing a book. Nola Gordon in *Recapitulation* is a reasonable facsimile of Juanita Crawford. In the 1970s, Stegner jotted in a notebook some revealing thoughts about the novel and the character of Nola, ending with "How much was Nola ever part of his life? Not of tennis, not of books or ideas, little of family. A compartment. A mismatch, as Holly perceived."[11]

Raised on a farm in central Utah, Crawford attended Brigham Young University and graduated from the University of Utah in 1928. She was known to her close friends, one of whom was Peg Foster (Holly in *Recapitulation*), as Juanie. Crawford was a quiet woman. She had dark curly hair, brown eyes, and light olive-colored skin. She was sultry in a 1920s flapper sort of way when she and Foster posed for a series of photographs in various costumes.

Wally and Juanita were a couple in the late 1920s. "He was very, very smitten with her," said Cowan, who thought Juanita was sexy and attractive. Stegner took her to the family cabin at Fish Lake. Together they visited her family's farm. She was supposed to wait for him to return from his first year at the University of Iowa. Instead she was "swept off her feet"—in her daughter's words—by Marv Broberg, who was in Wally's group of friends.[12]

It wasn't as if Wally had been true to Juanita during that year. He'd had a brief affair with a married woman in Iowa. "Eros is a hard god to abandon," he wrote Jack Irvine, adding, "I'm still trying to figure out the perfect life for a man. So far I have only you and Juanita included." He would not be in Salt Lake for Christmas, so he sent his friend $25 to purchase at wholesale cost through the linoleum company a cedar-lined chest for Juanie. Twenty-five dollars was a considerable sum of money in that Depression year. "God damn being poor," he said.[13]

Stegner heard about the affair between Juanita and Marv. When he arrived home, he immediately went looking for Broberg, who also worked at the Irvine family store. Wally stormed into the store "ready to kill him," in the words of a mutual friend. Irvine hustled Broberg out the back door.[14]

The Brobergs' marriage was troubled. Marv and Juanita married and divorced twice. Juanita was emotionally fragile and suffered from depression. Her daughter would say of Stegner years later, "I think he married the right woman." Wally remained the love of her life. She kept a photo of him and a copy of a typewritten poem titled "Fish Lake" that concluded:

> *Of all this mountain peace without your Face*
> *And all the murdered dreams that haunt the place.*

He also never forgot her.[15]

When Wally wrote Mary in June 1934, shortly after meeting her, it was obvious that Juanita had loomed quite large and traumatically in his life. The letter to the woman he would soon marry was a testimonial to his openness with her and was a powerful, if somewhat jejune, evocation of his love for her and Juanita. In it Mary takes on the saintliness of his mother while Juanita assumes a dark presence. The letter is both a cry for help and a statement by a serious young man attempting to understand himself and life. There is no record of Mary's reaction to this remarkable unburdening, in which Stegner comments on Vardis Fisher's new novel, *Passions Spin the Plot:*

> If Fisher had been trying to write my life he could hardly have come closer to the self-torture and the pride and the vanity and the morbid eroticism that made my boyhood a miserable dark torment. And if he had had Juanita for a model, he couldn't have drawn her portrait any more clearly than he has in Neloa Doole.

And if he had been in my skin for four years he couldn't have dug out the restfulness and peace and freedom from the inner consciousness that happy times with her brought, or the hell that doubt created. She is complete even to the eyes, with the depths in them that meant something or nothing, the thing inside that showed through, and which was never readable. It was simply all life, all love and all woman, all the dark mystery that lies behind and beyond consciousness, and is capable of being seen but never interpreted. It is the eyes, I think, that have made fools like Fisher and me love women like Neloa and Juanita so intensely and so utterly—because our half-mad adolescence is frightened away from actual women, and feeds on the Idea of Woman, on the eternal mother, the life principle, the thing that stands for the opposite of unbeautiful death. And yet the thing we saw in those eyes was not in the woman at all. I have seen the same thing in the eyes of a cow . . . and I think it is in the eyes of all people and all animals, if we look closely enough. But in the eyes of this sort of woman, quiet, primitive, unable to read herself or what she stands for, it is a symbol that haunts me yet. Your eyes don't have it, except at rare moments, because there is intelligence in your eyes. This isn't an intelligent look. It is like quiet water, and you can look through it on and on until you get lost and bewildered in the shadows of it. I can read you in your eyes—I could never read Juanita, because the thing behind her eyes was not thought, was nothing that could be expressed. It was merely life, not even consciousness, but only life. And it was life I was trying to understand, and life I loved. The principle of fertility, of reproduction and continuity, not the woman, was what I wanted to know, and so my love for her was more agonizing than my love for you. I love you as a human being, as a mind, as a woman. I loved her as an abstraction and as a mystery. Looking back at her now, I know that she was not a fine woman; she was not intelligent; she was not a character whom one could love for herself. One loved her for the mystery that looked through her eyes, which she had nothing to do with. And the whole thing, probably, can be explained on the basis of pigmentation and lack of eye strain and lack of thought. Beautiful eyes rarely go with deep thought.[16]

Stegner lost the girl, but he put the experience to good use. *Story* magazine paid Stegner $25 for "Home to Utah," which appeared in the August 1936 issue. In it a young man is hurrying home from the Midwest in his Model A only "to find that the girl he was hurrying back to had located other consolations in his absence."

The lives of Juanie Crawford and Peg Foster, two girls from Utah farm communities, diverged in remarkable ways. Juanita stayed in Salt Lake City for the remainder of her life. Her close friend and roommate moved to China (as does Holly in *Recapitulation*), where she married Edgar Snow, who wrote *Red Star over China*, long considered the classic work on Communist China. The Snows interviewed Mao Zedong in his mountain hideout and had numerous adventures in China before World War II. Peg wrote books using the pen name Nym Wales, divorced Snow in 1949, and as Helen Foster Snow was active in Chinese affairs on the East Coast. After she died, at the age of eighty-nine in 1997, Helen Snow was commemorated in the Great Hall of the People in Beijing, a long way from where she was raised, in Parowan, Utah.

BY THE TIME Stegner attended the University of California, he had a serious girlfriend in Salt Lake. From 1932 to 1934 there would be an exchange of letters between Wally and Sara Barnard that is revealing of not only their relationship but also his activities and thoughts at the time his mother was dying. There is an innocent playfulness in the letters. The literary references are profuse and a bit show-offy. He wrote on his father's fancy "GHS" embossed stationery and signed himself Seneca, Lovelace, Wishfort, or Steinblatz.

It seems that they just missed each other at Berkeley: by the late spring of 1933 Sara was attending the University of California there and he was writing from his parents' address on South Harvard Boulevard in Los Angeles. He identified Los Angeles as "God's Country" despite the recent earthquake in Long Beach. He was mostly relaxing but also reading Dickens, Elizabethan dramas, and Dutton's book on the Grand Canyon.

By June he was at Fish Lake. His mother's health was improving, so he thought the family would remain there for the summer. Red Cowan was visiting. They had just gone fishing, had had no luck, and then had hiked ten miles to Crater Lakes, where they saw an eagle strike a mallard. Wally and his father were working on the cabin, adding a kitchen and screens to the porch to keep predators out. He was reading the Bible for its literary content and the entire works of Shakespeare. Wally had no idea what he would be doing in the near future. It all depended on his mother's health.

Stegner inadvertently described his tangled relationship with his father in one letter: "Went fishing with Pa this morning at four thirty (two bells to you) and got me a mackinaw that weighed just an ounce and a half under five pounds. You should have seen us with our lines tangled, the motor dead, Pa's line off the reel, the boat going in circles and the sun stopping to see what the devil was going on."[17]

He wrote that he would like to visit Salt Lake City and Sara when his father drove to town, but he couldn't leave his mother alone. He might be living in Salt Lake that winter, in which case he and Sara could see more of each other. His mother was urging him to go back to graduate school. Hilda enclosed a note thanking Sara for sending her a book.

The family returned to Salt Lake in September of 1933, and Hilda died in a rented apartment in November, with Wally and a nurse present. His father had conveniently disappeared, and for that and much more Wally never forgave him.

Stegner was bereft. Her last, halting words were "You're a good . . . boy . . . Wallace." That shamed him. "By God," he said years later, "I was not, and am not, but if anything could make me what she thought I was, it would be the memory of herself."[18] When he was nearing eighty, he addressed his mother "too late":

> You had little in your life to judge goodness by. I was not as dense or as selfish as my father, and I got more credit than I deserved. But I was not intelligent enough to comprehend the kind of example you had been setting me, until it was too late to do anything but hold your hand while you died. And here I am, nearly eighty years old, too old to be capable of any significant improvement but not too old for regret.[19]

That fall and winter in Salt Lake was the lowest period in his life. He roomed with his father, toward whom he was feeling a growing hatred.

Red and Wally returned to Iowa in February of 1934. They rolled into town in Wally's Model A, drunk on beer. There was a fair amount in his letters about drinking, studying, girls, and having a good time. Sara brought up the issue of honesty. "What *about* this honesty issue?" he asked defensively. Stegner signed his letter: "All my love—very Platonic." As Sara may have guessed, he had met and fallen in love with another woman.

· · ·

WHILE HE WORKED on his doctorate, Stegner taught in the spring of 1934 at a small Swedish Lutheran college in Rock Island, Illinois, near where his father had grown up, in Annawan. Wilbur Schramm got him the job. Wally was the acting head of the English Department, which consisted of one person—himself. He liked his first full-time teaching job at Augustana College. "I dish out a lot of bromidal tripe and call it lectures, and the funny thing is, so do the students, and we get along fine."[20]

That spring, Schramm had introduced Wally to Mary Stuart Page, a short, slight graduate student with a keen mind who worked in the university library. Wally dated Mary, and Red Cowan took out her roommate, eventually marrying her. Stegner soon began confiding in Mary more than he had in anyone else before. He explained his intense anger directed at his father and his inability to forgive, two characteristics that would be directed at others and would persist throughout his lifetime.

> Had a letter from my father today, and a package containing some shirts and ties. Think that over. The one man on earth that I hate as utterly as I love you sends me presents, writes letters that are almost pathetic in their loneliness. To me, whom he has never liked, and whom he knows has never liked him. I wish to God there wasn't so much of a moping, sick, gnawing Hamletism in me, so that I could hate him whole-heartedly and be done with it. The hell of it is I have the unhappy faculty of seeing things from both sides at once. I can understand how he could crush my mother's life out, and never be conscious of the fact. I can even understand the woman he has picked up with. I suspect that he has married her, and is ashamed to tell me. Either way it is just as bad, and I hate him just the same with a fury that scares me.

He hated his father, Stegner said, for what he had done to his mother, not for what he had done to him "personally." He told Mary he couldn't marry as long as his father was alive because he didn't want to inflict "even the shadow of that past" on anyone. He didn't think his father had long to live.[21]

The more he saw and corresponded with Mary, the more he disengaged from Sara. Sherman Neff had written him that there was no job for him at Utah and that meant staying at Augustana, he told Sara. Actually, Stegner had turned down a job offer from Neff in order to be

closer to Mary. He offered vague excuses to Sara: there were unspeci-
fied health problems, and he was burdened with an "unpleasant past."

Sara's father died in May. Finally, on June 23, Stegner owned up to
being in love with Mary. He had delayed telling her, he said, because of
her father's death. Stegner's letter to Sara was a mixture of melodrama,
excuses, self-loathing, and a rare revelation of his inner turmoil. The
doctors didn't know how much longer he had to live, perhaps two or
three years. "I've no more control over myself than a child," he
lamented. "The whole sickening background of my life comes back on
me, and I simply have to try to make a desperate grab for whatever
there is left in life for me." He felt deeply grateful to her, "but you know
by now that I am as weak as water, and that the thing I am is nowhere
near the thing I'd like to be." Even Mary was not spared as Stegner flag-
ellated himself for loving another. "I compare her to you in some ways
and I loathe what my passions have gotten me into." There was more
news, which might be "worse for you": he would be returning to Utah
after all, thus raising the possibility that they might soon meet.[22]

Augustana College had had a change of administrations, and religious hard-liners had gained power. Stegner was accused of not being a
Lutheran, not believing in the Apostles' Creed, not believing in the
Bible, not believing in the "real objectives" of Christian higher education, and being an agnostic and an atheist. He was also described as
having an excellent character, being morally upright, and being the
"very finest" teacher. On balance it was a damning indictment from
that particular institution, and he was no longer welcome to teach at
Augustana. To Mary he wrote, "I can't get over the impression that
these religious old coots around here are the most colossal hypocrites
that I have ever known."[23]

Wally was homesick and ready to leave the Midwest. He fantasized
in a letter to Mary about his return to Utah with her, proving that when
he dropped his literary pretensions he could write powerful, rhapsodic
prose about the part of the country he loved most:

> Every once in a while I would wake up from . . . [reading] and
> discover that what I was thinking about was Mary, and how we
> would go for long boat rides at Fish Lake before settling
> down . . . in front of the fireplace, and how the wind would be
> rushing or rustling or something in the aspens, and the birds
> would be heading south, and nobody much would be up at the
> lake, and we could get some horses from Elmer the dairy man

and go riding up on top of the plateau by Rock Springs or Crater Lakes, and how the deer would be coming down again now that the fishing season was about over, and how much fun it would be to chop wood again that you could use to fry me a boiled egg. Oh my. We could climb up on top of the rim behind the cabin (two hours of climbing. Are you good and strong?) and look away down south, over Aquarius and Thousand Lake mountains, with the horizon rising in long swells and dropping off at the edges in sharp cliffs, and the sun slanting across red walls, and the aspens beginning to turn on the slopes. Oh my once more. I didn't realize until today how homesick I am, and I am just beginning to become aware of how much fun I'm going to have showing you gods country, and how sad I am going to be if you find it depressing or arid or too sage-brushish, or too lonesome, or too rough.[24]

In this manner Wally wooed Mary with love, passion, and a sense of place.

WALLY BORROWED $50, and they were married on September 1, 1934, in Mary's parents' home in Dubuque, Iowa. With the addition of a son in three years, Stegner's immediate family would be complete. "My wife was the best thing that had happened to me since I first knew my mother," Stegner wrote later in a revealing biographical sketch. "She was a musician, a reader, and an eager and curious searcher of the world."[25] Small-boned but possessed of an iron will, Mary Stuart Page Stegner could be described as pretty or fetching. In one color photograph a young Mary with long hair is beautiful in an all-American way.

To people outside the immediate family the Stegners' fifty-nine years of marriage were a near-perfect mutually supportive union. The photographic image that lingers is of an elderly couple walking arm in arm through a golden field in the California sunshine. Years later Stegner would define love as "the tight wire on which we dance, strung between two shadows."[26] The couple remained devoted to and dependent on each other in a monogamous relationship. Their marriage lasted despite the copious amounts of alcohol consumed at parties and the bohemian lifestyles of many of their writer friends and acquaintances whose personal lives fell apart around them.

Mary had many talents. She was the first reader of all Wally's manuscripts, mainly spotting problems of tone, putting small check marks beside rough spots, reading them aloud to Wally, and then discussing them. "She always irritates me because I don't want her to be right," he said. "I want it to be done." Mary was generally right when she said that a manuscript was ready for submission. She described how he worked. Sometimes there were fragmentary notes. She never saw him write from an outline; he composed as he typed. "He says he doesn't know where he is going until he gets there," she told an interviewer. "I think unconsciously he must know. I think it is worked out somehow." He used parts of her in novels, particularly *All the Little Live Things* and *The Spectator Bird*.[27]

Along with her husband, Mary served as Houghton Mifflin's West Coast editor in the immediate post–World War II years. She also edited a volume of O. Henry short stories. Mary was an accomplished violinist, playing in a local symphony orchestra. A baby grand piano was located prominently in their Los Altos Hills home. She was an interior decorator as well and selected the Scandinavian furniture that the Stegners preferred for the Jones Room in the Stanford Library, where Wally's writing students met.

She was supportive in the manner of a traditional politician's wife, meaning that her public role was subservient to her husband's presence. Mary was always there, hovering in the wings while Wally was center stage. She served as a buffer, filter, cook, hostess, and social secretary, all of which allowed Stegner to work with few distractions. In the many letters to Wally from friends, fellow writers, and former students, there is the obligatory say-hello-to-Mary salutation at the end.

It could be a lonely and boring life, especially on the road when Wally was to receive an honor, give a lecture, or meet with editors and publishers. She visited art museums or tagged along. "I think it was a man's world," she said.[28] Mary dampened Wally's temper when it threatened to erupt. Next to his towering, lanky presence she gave the appearance of being a small appendage. One of Wally's writing students kept wanting to call her Birdie because she was small-boned and fluttery and seemed to peck a lot.[29] She was there for him even after he died, polishing the rough edges of his image with a biographer and a documentary filmmaker.

Mary's family saw her as the ruling presence in Wally's life, outside his work. She controlled him by the guilt he felt for not having loved or cared enough for his beloved, badly treated mother. Mary was constantly ill with real or imagined sicknesses. She kept a detailed medical

journal that indicates <u>extreme hypochondria</u>. There were daily nota-
tions for sleep, diet, alcohol intake, pulse rate, medications, doctors'
visits, and intimate physical details. Wally's correspondents frequently
asked about Mary's health, always near the end of a letter. Stegner
replied to one such inquiry:

> You ask about Mary. She has been having a sort of bad time,
> part anxiety/depression, part neuromas and fairly constant pain,
> and a good part sleeplessness. Sleeping two or three hours a
> night for weeks on end is no good; sleeping pills, for her, are no
> good either. Finally they have put her (after trying everything
> from exercise to acupuncture) on Elavil, and I see signs in the last
> week that the waves are subsiding, the nights are better, the pain
> is less, the hydrotherapy has more effect, the exercise doesn't
> leave her feeling worse than before she started it.[30]

<u>Witnessing his partner's constant discomfort</u> couldn't have been
<u>easy, but Stegner never complained</u>. His work did not diminish despite
frequent trips to doctors and hospitals. He used a light touch to deflect
whatever he truly felt about his wife's health, once beginning a magazine article: "I regard travel as an expensive way to be endangered or
uncomfortable, but my wife, an ardent, unlucky traveler, has a different
view of it. She has a knack for getting hurt or sick in exotic places, and
being rescued by people so poor, simple, unsanitary or otherwise
unlikely that every time it happens I suspect her of staging it, just to get
her faith in humanity restored."[31]

To their closest friends, Peg and Phil Gray, Wally once wrote:
"Mary has been fighting off arthritis and some sort of obscure ailment
of the innards, and living mainly on pills, none of which have the slight-
est effect." The nearest he came to criticism was in a 1979 letter to his
granddaughter Rachel, in which humor shades into irony: "Grandma is
still dragging to doctors, three or four of them. All doctors seem to
know one thing only. If they know hearts, they don't know lungs. If
they know lungs, they don't know lumps. But by going to about three a
week, Grandma is managing to stay afloat."[32]

<u>Page Stegner remembers his father as the nurturer and caregiver</u>—
Wally was the one who tirelessly massaged his infant son's leg, render-
ing it useful after it was broken during the breech birth that nearly
killed Mary. <u>Page thought Mary really hadn't wanted to be a mother. A</u>
<u>child was an intrusion into her and Wally's tight space.</u>

There was love in the family, but it was not openly expressed. Wallace Stegner put his feelings for his son on paper. Knowing that he had produced his masterpiece, he dedicated the Pulitzer Prize–winning 1971 novel, *Angle of Repose*, to Page. His son had to open the book to discover it was inscribed to him. Almost all of Wally's other books honored Mary. The last tribute, for a collection of his essays published one year before his death, read, "For Mary, who, like Dilsey, has seen the first and last, and been indispensable and enspiriting all the way."[33] Dilsey is the African American cook in William Faulkner's *The Sound and the Fury*, who cares devotedly for the Compson family.

WITH HIS YOUTH now past and a matter to be explored in his writings, Stegner had assumed the general size, shape, looks, and condition of health and moral outlook that would carry him through life. He was tall and thin, with slit eyes, the result of epicanthic folds that adapted his eyes to the harsh sunlight of the West before the age of sunglasses. A thick thatch of wavy hair would gradually turn silver. Stegner had a level, appraising gaze: a serious man with a sense of purpose and a lurking sense of humor would be the immediate judgment. A sustained look could wither a person. When he smiled, especially in later years, deep canyons of creases formed at the corners of his eyes, and he radiated a warmth. Those who knew him best said that he was shy underneath that imposing exterior. *Reticent* was another word they used.

Gregory Peck and Gary Cooper, two tall, thin, good-looking men, could have played Wallace Stegner on the screen. Women thought Wally was handsome. One of the coeds he taught during the 1930s at the University of Utah said seventy years later, "We were all in love with him."[34] As a teacher he favored pressed slacks, white shirt, bow tie, and a sport coat. A pair of thick-framed bifocals were settled on a tanned face just below a creased forehead.

Wally's susceptibility to cold remained with him all his life. During the 1930s and through the first half of the next decade it was thought that he had some type of heart ailment, and Mary prevailed upon him to give up tennis, which he did reluctantly. Long walks, cutting wood, and rigorous gardening became his exercises of choice. The diagnoses of two physicians in Palo Alto in 1945 were "a slight manifestation of coronary arteriosclerosis" and "a coronary sinus arrhythmia." He had a history of sinus attacks, infrequent headaches, occasional dizziness, and ulcers. During the 1970s, when Stegner considered himself looking forward to 5 p.m. with too much anticipation, he cut back on his alcohol intake. His consumption of highballs, wine, and beer corresponded to that of his social peers and never constituted a serious drinking problem. In 1983 a Los Altos doctor pronounced him "a very healthy gentleman."[35] Then old age began to take its toll.

Stegner remained a moral man throughout his life, "a square" in his own words. Professional sports were a passion from which he drew moral lessons. He was an ardent San Francisco Giants baseball fan and often listened to radio broadcasts of their games. He thought sports announcers were good indicators of public morality. In unpublished notes for a possible essay, he wrote that a pitcher had been thrown out of a game by the umpire for throwing a spitball. The announcer had joked about the incident, not mentioning that the pitcher had broken the rules and cheated. Stegner found the omission "pernicious, evil, corrupt, and corrupting."[36]

Talented Teacher

Back to Utah and
Forward to Wisconsin

Our years in Salt Lake began as one of those subsidence periods
after turmoil. Ambition did not gnaw me. We had friends. We
enjoyed our life.

Wallace Stegner, in *Contemporary Authors*

I remember little about Madison as a city.... Before and
between and after my classes, I wrote, for despite my limited
one-year appointment I hoped for continuance, and I did not
intend to perish for lack of publications.

Wallace Stegner, *Crossing to Safety*

THE COUPLE DEPARTED shortly after the Dubuque wedding,
in September 1934, for the teaching life in Utah. They drove
west in the Model A through the Black Hills, Yellowstone, and
Jackson Hole, Wyoming. Mary's comments gave Wally "new eyes to
see the West." What he took for granted, she saw with a fresh perspective. Stegner began teaching full-time as an instructor in the Department of English at the University of Utah in the fall of 1934 at a yearly
salary of $1,700.

Arcadian idylls with friends in the surrounding Wasatch Mountains
were mixed with bouts of hard work during Wally's first year of teaching. The intense drive to write and be published was just emerging.
"Pete and Emil" came out in the Sunday, December 9, 1934, edition of
The Salt Lake Tribune under the byline "Wallace Stegner, Salt Lake
City, Free Lance." He was paid $5, his first income from the written
word. The story was one of the three that he had submitted as his master's thesis. Pete and Emil were tar-paper shacks on the Saskatchewan

prairie that had been named by homesteaders after their former occupants. Stegner transformed the shacks into human characters who were
involved in a murder. The shacks symbolized the loneliness of single
men in a harsh environment. From thesis to short story to insertion
into *The Big Rock Candy Mountain* and *Wolf Willow*, the Pete and Emil
material had a long life.

Stegner read about a Little, Brown novella prize—$2,500 and pub-
lication of the work. What could he write? Mary supplied the answer:
"I remembered a family account about my two gaunt aunts who lived
with their son in western Iowa. As a young girl I wasn't sure whether
the child was the son of the older widowed sister or of the younger
spinster sister, but for the purposes of Wally's imagination it didn't
really matter what I knew or recalled in detail."[1]

Stegner made the child the son of the younger spinster sister and
the husband of the older married sister, who would become a widow in
the course of a tightly written small gem of a book about silence and the
repression of feelings. He wrote swiftly for six weeks, working from
eight until a few minutes before ten o'clock each morning. It took seven
minutes to trot the two blocks to his first class of the day. On the afternoon of January 31, 1937, Stegner was notified that he had won the
contest. That evening, Mary went into labor. Page was born after a difficult birth. The novella was first published in *Redbook* magazine and
then as a book, *Remembering Laughter*.

Some basic Stegnerian writing characteristics became evident during this time. Wally was a realist who depended upon his past, or the
past of others, for much of his material. He was as frugal with his stories
as his mother had been with the skins of pears. He was, in fact, the king
of recycling stories. A work might begin as an original short story,
be incorporated into a novel, and wind up in a collection of short stories. He was also frugal with office supplies. Stegner typed on both
sides of a sheet of paper, shunned margins (once boasting to his agent
that his 222 manuscript pages were equivalent to 300 pages with margins), hammered on typewriter ribbons until the small elite typeface
was almost illegible, and used whatever stationery he could put his
hands on.

There were failures and successes while Stegner was teaching at
Utah. He wrote and discarded a novel in the winter of 1935 about the
flu epidemic in Saskatchewan. He published his first two short stories
in literary publications in the next couple of years. "Home to Utah"
introduced Bruce, a name Stegner would use for his alter ego in later

stories and novels. The Eastend-located "Bloodstain," which appeared in *American Prefaces*, edited by his former roommate Wilbur Schramm, was a reworking of another of his master's thesis stories. It contains an echo of the young Stegner aiming an empty cartridge case at his father and imagining murder. A kid who prowls the river bottom, as Stegner once did, mistakes his best friend's father for a rabbit and shoots him. One of Stegner's lesser-known achievements, which appears in no bibliography, is a "home-evening handbook" ghostwritten for a fee paid by "a good Saint," meaning a Mormon. The purpose of the once-a-week home evenings was to bind a family together with religious education.

It was during his Utah teaching stint that Stegner thought he might become a professional writer. Teaching—although he would be very good at it—became secondary to setting words down on paper. It was a means to earn a steady income to support his family while he devoted his remaining time to his true passion. Of this period he later wrote: "Something in me began to wake up. Never having known any writers I thought of them as distant in both time and space, perhaps as mythical as gryphons. Now my psyche began to hint to me that I could be one."[2]

In a remarkable set of bookends that demonstrated the breadth of his divergent careers, Stegner commented on his teaching and writing lives at the start of his professional life and again at the end. The first issue of *Intermountain Review*, published in 1937 in Murray, Utah, contained a front-page essay by Stegner, "Can Teachers Be Writers?" Forty-three years later his views on teaching and writing were solicited from audiences at Dartmouth College while he was a Montgomery Fellow at that Ivy League school in 1980.

A young Stegner argued that the teaching of writing was essentially a negative endeavor, meaning that it focused on pointing out errors and was constrained in an academic setting by theories. Writing fiction was an art form: a personal, subjective, and thus positive exercise. The path to writing as a career led through teaching or journalism, starvation not being an acceptable alternative for most writers. "A strong enough urge" to write was needed to overcome the "deadening routine" of both teaching and journalism. The advantages of teaching, he said, were "steady wages and comparatively long vacations." If the creative writing attempt failed, the teacher could contribute to "the educational reviews, write a rhetoric, and pretend that he can teach what he cannot do."[3]

Stegner's thoughts at Dartmouth on writing and teaching were published after he died, in *On Teaching and Writing Fiction*, edited and with a foreword by his daughter-in-law, Lynn Stegner, who is a novelist. "Wallace Stegner, with less than a handful of others, essentially invented writing as a field of study within the Academy," she wrote, "and from the 1940s on, similar, frequently imitative, programs sprang up all over the country."[4]

By the late 1930s, Stegner had developed a strong work ethic, which, along with talent, gained him admission to the ranks of recognized writers. If there were no conflicts, such as a class to teach, he wrote seven days a week from 8 a.m. to noon. "I was already a confirmed moonlighter," he wrote of that time. "I had a profession which paid me wages, a living wage, and I had an avocation which demanded all my attention and time, which devoured them in fact." Stegner drilled that sense of discipline—of immersion in a "familiar rut"—into his students.[5]

WALLY THOUGHT THAT being famous, at least in Utah, would lead to a promotion to the position of assistant professor. The campus newspaper published a glowing account of Stegner's winning the Little, Brown prize, complete with a photo of the English instructor in rimless eyeglasses and a double-breasted suit, his hair parted just to the left of center; he looks at the check with a smile on his face. However, the university's president, George Thomas, was less than thrilled with the novella's theme of adultery, although he liked the characters and thought "the English is excellent."[6]

Although Stegner had enjoyed his undergraduate years at the University of Utah, his teaching experience at his alma mater was less than satisfactory. The university would later lay claim to him in a big way: it invited him to writers' conferences, to speak at the dedication of its new library; it awarded him an honorary degree and, in the law school, named a center for land, resources, and the environment after him. The library would eventually receive Stegner's personal papers, a gift that was made more out of pique at Stanford than of pleasant memories of his teaching experience at Utah.

Utah was a small, provincial, stiff-necked school in the 1930s and was not known for being liberal with promotions. The chairman of the English Department, Sherman Neff, whom Stegner characterized as a "benevolent despot," was criticized by Stegner and other young instructors for maintaining "too rigid a standard of scholarship and being too conservative in recommending promotions." Stegner and another instructor had the requisite doctorates. That was not what was holding up their promotions, said Neff, who had nudged Stegner into graduate studies in English at Iowa seven years earlier. Other young instructors were available for the same salary or less during the Depression. George Thomas agreed with Neff, stating: "It is impossible to make everybody a professor in this institution."[7]

Stegner was angry, and he let Neff know it. He resigned "for obvious reasons" on May 9 without going through the proper channels. He should have first notified Neff, Thomas pointed out to a regent. Estella K. W. Shields had written Thomas after Stegner had telephoned her: "If he really has the ability to write it would be sound policy for us to cherish that ability." What if he made the same exception for all the instructors in the university? Thomas answered. And besides, someone who has taught for only three years at the university should not be in a position to dictate policy.[8]

That was the end of the matter. Wally had stepped on some important toes. A recent graduate of the university who was working on his master's degree at the University of California was hired to replace Stegner at $100 less a year. Stegner was not someone who forgot a slight. Seven years later he told his close friend Phil Gray, who was considering a teaching position in the Department of English at Utah, "You're likely to find the people both at the university and in the town fairly provincial, and you may find the department somewhat ingrown and jealous of its individual standings." He characterized the university as "a cow college, but not a completely bad one."[9]

WALLY AND MARY celebrated the Little, Brown prize by leaving their months-old son with Mary's parents in Iowa and touring England and France on bicycles for three weeks in 1937. It was the first of their many trips outside the country. The steamship *Berlin* was carrying mostly German passengers back to Europe on the eve of World War II. Mary noted on her typed transcript of Wally's travel diary: "2 important paragraphs a turning point in Wally's writing." Those paragraphs read, in part:

> Third Day Out—July 3
> Just before the concert Mary came into the cabin with news that a boat was in sight. It was dark on deck, and a gray melan-

choly near-dark over the sea. The boat, a Banks fisherman, looked small and very forlorn, a dark ghost on an unfriendly and painfully lonely ocean. Not a light showed. The *Berlin* weaved around her, and the schooner, still dark and silent, tacked off silently and dissolved into the indistinct horizon.

Fourth Day out—July 4

Some talk about the transmutation of real experiences into the images of poetry and prose—The Ancient Mariner, etc. One such moving experience as that simple meeting with a dark and lonely fishing smack might serve as one line, one image. How many lifetimes of living could be packed into one really good novel. Most of what I have written seems to have been false or second-hand experience, or else plain out-and-out padding.[10]

Returning to the States nearly broke, Wally found a job, with Norman Foerster's help, at the University of Wisconsin. That involved more hard work:

> Many years later, writing of those Madison years in *Crossing to Safety*, I toned down the facts for fear readers would not believe them. In two years, besides collaborating on a textbook and writing a dozen essays and book reviews, I wrote four short stories, a novelette called "One Last Wilderness" that killed *Scribner's Magazine*, a novel called *On a Darkling Plain*, another novel, called *Fire and Ice*, and the first few chapters of *The Big Rock Candy Mountain*. This while teaching four undergraduate classes.[11]

At first good things happened in Madison. Page's leg, damaged at birth, was healing, as was Mary from the ordeal. Wally's affectionate nickname for his son at this time was Beetle, for the way Page scrabbled across the floor. Wally and Mary made friends with another young faculty couple, Phil and Peg Gray, who would introduce them to Greensboro, Vermont, and whose enduring friendship Wally celebrated in *Crossing to Safety*.

Phil was Wally's rich friend. His paternal grandfather, John S. Gray, had helped finance Henry Ford and served as the first president of the Ford Motor Company. The Grays were part of the aristocracy of the Greensboro summer community. Their clan was grounded there; the Stegners, ever in search of home, were wanderers until the Grays introduced them to the small Vermont enclave. Phil and Peg respected the rawness, work ethic, and talent that Wally possessed. The Stegners were attracted by the Grays' rootedness. The couples complemented each other.

Stegner got a start on the story that he really wanted to write—about his "orphaned and symbolic family"—when he was given a new portable typewriter for Christmas of 1937. The novel, eventually titled *The Big Rock Candy Mountain*, did not come easily at first. "For one thing, I had too much material. I had to find ways of shortening it." That essential task would take a few more years.[12]

Wisconsin was another step up intellectually and was, for Stegner, an introduction to the international politics that were dividing the globe at the time. Madison was a hotbed of progressivism and its off-shoots. Stegner went to meetings of the Young Communist League, whose membership was swollen by Jews from New York, whom quotas had kept from attending the discriminatory Ivy League universities.

The alternative to the Communists was the Fascists. Neither attracted Stegner. Wally thought that he had been politically neutered while buried deep within the interior of the continent. He was not a coastal person, one who might veer in radical directions. Stegner's political inclinations, which were usually allied to the Democratic Party, were slightly left of center. Later he did not favor the Vietnam War, but neither did he protest against it in a radical manner. That was not his style.

Stegner also occupied the middle ground professionally and was thus considered somewhat suspect by the academic establishment and some freewheeling writers. He was neither an academic nor an author of popular literature; he was both. That dual status, established out of economic necessity and personal preference, was highly unusual at the time. He took stock of what he had done and where he was going at Wisconsin:

> To date, all the short stories which I have written have been, like the novel I burned, frankly practice pieces. I do not need to be told that as a writer I am still in, or at best just coming out of, the pen, paper, and waste-basket stage. *Remembering Laughter* was also an experiment, though it came off better than I had expected. The one thing which I have been aiming at for ten years or more is sufficient skill to write a long novel based partially on the experiences of my own family in wanderings that

took us through Iowa, North Dakota, Washington, Saskatchewan, Montana, and Utah in a futile hunt for the New Jerusalem.
It is that novel which I hope I am ready to write now.[13]

ONE HELPFUL INGREDIENT for a successful writing career was missing at the time, and that was a literary agent: someone who was working
in the same city where most of the major publishers had offices and
could sell his work and negotiate contracts. Stegner had the bona fides
to attract a good agent: magazine stories that would generate sales and
the promise of more in the future. The president of Little, Brown
suggested that he contact Brandt & Brandt Literary Agents in New
York City. Stegner wrote the distinguished firm, and Bernice Baumgarten answered his query. Thus began a lifelong relationship with that
agency.

Stegner was extremely fortunate. Baumgarten was a well-regarded
agent, to whom the publisher Alfred A. Knopf once paid the supreme
compliment of stating, "I will buy the next book you send me."[14]
She was known as "the best agent in New York" during her tenure at
the agency.[15] Baumgarten was married to the novelist James Gould
Cozzens, whose career took off after she began representing him.[16]
Cozzens would win a Pulitzer Prize in 1949 for the novel *Guard of
Honor* and scored great commercial—but not critical—success with *By
Love Possessed*. Another of her clients, the poet Conrad Aiken, had won
a Pulitzer. She also represented Raymond Chandler, Ford Madox Ford,
John Gunther, Thomas Mann, J. P. Marquand, Peter Matthiessen,
Mary McCarthy, John Dos Passos, and other notable authors. Stegner
was a promising young writer whom Baumgarten added to her client
list in 1937.

Citing the enthusiasm of "everyone" at Brandt & Brandt for
Remembering Laughter, Baumgarten said she would like to see some of
Stegner's short stories. At that time the slicks, such as *Collier's, The Saturday Evening Post*, and *Redbook*, were a lucrative market for writers.
Baumgarten's first sale for Wally was "My Great Grandmother's Cow,"
which *Redbook* bought for $600 in December 1937. Baumgarten helped
her client with salable book and story titles, editing suggestions, constant encouragement, and repeated submissions following repeated
rejections. She also shielded him from some of the harsher criticism of
his work by magazine editors.

They liked each other. Bernice mothered him. When Wally was

broke before Christmas of 1940, she sent him an advance against a novel that the agency had not yet received. Wally worried between sales. "I know this long dry spell is very upsetting," she told him in December 1941, "but please believe that I'm doing my honest best."[17] Over the years, Baumgarten submitted countless Stegner stories to *The New Yorker.* Katharine White, the fiction editor, wrote her in 1956: "I know that he has had on the whole bad luck with us—only one story bought in all these years—but the fact remains that I, and others here, admire his short stories and I do hope that he and you have not closed your minds against sending us other stories of his." White had previously rejected one story as being "too flamboyant" for the magazine.[18]

Stegner trusted Baumgarten's judgment. She let him write the stories he wanted to write, and when they had been perfected, she sent them out. "I can remember late in our relationship just before she left the agency," Stegner said, "I wrote her some story or other and she wrote back saying, '*Playboy* wants this, but I really wonder if you want it in *Playboy*?' And I said 'no.' Not many agents will do that."[19]

WHILE AT THE University of Wisconsin and beginning work on *The Big Rock Candy Mountain*, Stegner absorbed the thinking of one of the school's more illustrious former faculty members. Frederick Jackson Turner had died by the time Stegner arrived in Madison, but his theory of American history, based on the westward movement across the continent, gave Stegner the historical framework on which to hang his family's history. Stegner found that the intellectual exchanges with other young Wisconsin faculty members were more stimulating than those at Utah and extremely challenging. While at Wisconsin, in 1938, Wally submitted an application for his first Guggenheim Foundation grant. He applied, again unsuccessfully, in 1939 and 1942, and finally received a grant in 1949 and then in 1959, when he was a known quantity.

Disappointment came in the midst of the Depression. Stegner's appointment was not renewed after his second year at Wisconsin. His publications were viewed by the tenured faculty as too frivolous. In *Crossing to Safety* the Stegner character names possible reasons for his dismissal: " 'No Ivy degree,' I say. 'No defined field. No articles in *PMLA*. No studies of romantic excess in *Comus*.' "[20]

The New England Years

> If I had gone to New York looking for an entry into the literary establishment I could not have done a quarter as well as I did in the intimate atmosphere of Bread Loaf. Publishers, editors, and agents came through the place in twos and tens, looking, it turned out, for just such "promising" young writers as I was.
>
> Wallace Stegner, in *Contemporary Authors*

W ITH WILBUR SCHRAMM's help, Stegner would get his big break in the summer of 1938. He wanted to sample the East, so he wrote the Bread Loaf Writers' Conference in April, asking if any fellowships were available. None were, he was told. He accepted an invitation to spend the month of July working on his big novel at Yaddo, a retreat for writers and artists in Saratoga Springs, New York. Meanwhile, Theodore Morrison, the director of Bread Loaf, near Middlebury, Vermont, was having "unprecedented difficulties" filling all the faculty positions for the August session.

Schramm was teaching at the Bread Loaf School of English, which held its annual session before the writers' conference. Hearing of Morrison's difficulties, Schramm persuaded him to hire Stegner, who, in Wally's own words, "had then published one small book and a few stories." Morrison agreed. Schramm wrote Stegner, told him he would be getting a telegram shortly from Morrison, and outlined the job. He would have to evaluate the manuscripts of "middle-aged school marms," all of whom thought they were writers but few of whom actually were. He continued:

> Your chief occupations will probably be to play tennis in the afternoons—fair courts and some pretty good players, if they stay over for the conference (Morrison himself isn't bad); to drink consistently—I heard that the conference is a pretty liquid

affair; to associate with DeVoto, Morrison and the others on the regular faculty, and to meet the visiting lecturers—Robert Frost, Untermeyer (a snake, if I ever saw one), etc—who will be in Bread Loaf for about a day each.[1]

The chief advantage of teaching at Bread Loaf, Schramm said, would be that Wally would have the opportunity to meet important people and make valuable contacts. The acquaintances and friends that Stegner cultivated at Bread Loaf would lift him out of the boondocks of the Mountain West and the Middle West and launch him into the elevated ranks of East Coast teaching, writing, and publishing.

After arriving at Yaddo, the Grays motored to Saratoga Springs and brought Mary and Page back to Greensboro. At the end of July, Wally drove from the retreat to Vermont, and all the Stegners were the guests of the Grays. They liked northeastern Vermont so much that they purchased a dilapidated Civil War–era farmhouse in North Greensboro, along with a barn and two hundred acres, for $600, money Wally had earned from the sale of magazine articles and *Remembering Laughter.*

Fast-growing vegetation was quickly reclaiming the land, which had been abandoned by a farmer who wanted to escape his hardscrabble existence. The barn collapsed in the 1938 hurricane, but the farmhouse, which the Stegners renovated, stood through the early years of World War II. When they were unable to drive to Greensboro because of gas rationing during the war, someone broke into the house, allowing porcupines to enter and devour the interior woodwork. They were advised by a state forester to shoot the ravaging animals and burn what remained of the farmhouse, and that was done, but not before the usable wood had been salvaged.

From Greensboro, Mary and Wally continued on in mid-August to Bread Loaf. "Out of that Bread Loaf fortnight, for which Wilbur was entirely responsible," Stegner wrote many years later in a tribute to his former roommate, "came a later invitation to teach at Harvard, and out of the Harvard years much that I could not have anticipated."[2]

STEGNER WAS IN on the ground floor of the most prominent efforts to teach writing in this country. Just as the Writers' Workshop at Iowa, in whose beginnings he participated, was the prototype for subsequent graduate writing programs, so Bread Loaf, founded in 1926 by the publisher John Farrar, was the model for the writing conferences that have since proliferated throughout the country. While directors had come and gone, the poet Robert Frost was the dominant presence at Bread Loaf during the early years and never more so than in 1938.

The Stegners were in the celebrity heaven of the eastern literati. Wally would later refer to those annual two weeks as a "combination of Plato's Academy and Walpurgisnacht."[3] They lived on top of a mountain—actually, more of a hill by western standards—with a hard-drinking crew of writers and their student acolytes. In group photographs of the staff, Mary sits slightly apart from the others. As a couple they were young, serious, constrained, and different from the more studiously casual eastern crowd.

Mary wrote to Peg and Phil Gray: "Everyone here seems to suffer from insomnia except Wally and me. The parties rarely break up until the wee small hours of the morning. Robert Frost used to milk his cows at three in the morning and he has never broken the habit of staying up all night and sleeping in the morning."[4] Wally reported to their friends that they were "drinking and gabbing" with the greats of American literature and added: "Frost is undoubtedly one of the few great men in the world—certainly the greatest I ever met, the most integrated, the one who fuses man and poet most fully. And DeVoto is clever as hell, even though a little loud."

As for the students, said Stegner, most were middle-aged "and pathetically agitated at being in the midst of Life and among Celebrities." He thought they would rate grades ranging from C minus to B in second-year English back at Wisconsin. The fellows, who were nominated by editors and publishers and judged to be promising writers, were "pretty generally good." Stegner thought he should trade places with some of them.[5]

The Stegners were cast into a cage of literary lions that first summer at Bread Loaf. That they didn't get devoured was a tribute to their innocence and sense of self-worth. It was one of the most brilliant and contentious sessions in the twelve-year history of the conference. Reverberations of that session's events would be felt for years.

Robert Frost was at the center of most of the controversy. Other characters who were very much part of the scene were Ted and Kay Morrison and Bernard DeVoto. Frost, with his large stature and mane of white hair, was truly leonine in appearance. He was in his mid-sixties and had won his third Pulitzer Prize for poetry the previous year and would receive another in a few years. Yet he was tremendously insecure. Generosity of spirit was mixed with cruelty, especially when he felt slighted or in competition with another poet. He came first in almost all matters, even to the extent that the opposing team would allow his baseball team to win in the annual Bread Loaf game.

In Stegner, Frost found a sympathetic listener who would become a friend over the years. They had some traits in common: both were westerners, albeit from different Wests. Frost was born in San Francisco and spent his first eleven years there. He believed that "locality gives art," and "he sought locality in his life and art," according to one of his biographers, Jay Parini. Frost's western roots were subsumed by his New England persona. Both writers used place as a point of departure.

Ted Morrison, a Harvard graduate of New England stock and a former editor of *The Atlantic Monthly,* was a poet and novelist who would serve as director of Bread Loaf from 1932 to 1955. A senior lecturer at Harvard, he would take over as director of the English A program, the basic freshman writing course. In 1938 he instituted a policy of hiring talented young writers to teach sections of the course. His wife, Kay Morrison, was a graduate of Bryn Mawr College who had first met Frost in 1918, while still an undergraduate. Two years later she brought him to the campus to speak. Kay was "beautiful, charming, and sophisticated in a way that Frost had rarely seen in a woman," wrote Parini, and "strikingly independent as well."[6] Photographs of her show a slim figure on the move or graciously arranged on the clipped grass at Bread Loaf. Whereas Kay was outgoing, the tweedy, pipe-smoking Ted was reserved, even stoic.

Bernard DeVoto, known as Benny to his friends, was a wild card out of Utah by way of Cambridge, Massachusetts. He lacked an advanced degree (as did all the others except Stegner), which helped end his teaching career at Harvard. His unconstrained nature and wide interests encompassed various other careers—novelist, historian, essayist, conservationist, editor, and teacher. He had many publishing contacts. Benny would become Wally's surrogate father, career counselor and enabler, writing consultant, and mentor in the realm of conservation. Years later Stegner recalled: "He had a lot of influence on me. He was very persuasive. He knew a lot. He was from the same part of the country as I was, we had a lot in common. And, I suppose, he looked upon me as a kind of protégé, so he felt justified in kicking and boosting me."[7] Wally repaid the many debts he owed Benny by writing his biography, titled *The Uneasy Chair,* a play on the title of DeVoto's monthly column in *Harper's* magazine, "The Easy Chair."

DeVoto had been one of the judges who selected *Remembering Laughter* for the Little, Brown prize, and Stegner had written to thank him. He received "a very decent and very intelligent response." The two first met at the annual meeting of the Modern Language Association in Chicago in 1937. At Bread Loaf, DeVoto was the informal head of the fiction contingent, and thus Stegner was his immediate responsibility.

There was one other member of the Bread Loaf faculty who would play a key role in Stegner's future. Although not at the 1938 session, Edith Mirrielees, a short story writer from Stanford University, taught at subsequent conferences that Wally attended and brought a sense of decorum to the proceedings. Stegner described her as "a maiden lady as gentle as DeVoto was bumptious" and an acute judge of manuscripts who could "cut away literary gangrene, or put a deformed story out of its misery, so gently that the victim did not even know he bled, and kissed the knife that ventilated him."[8] One of Mirrielees's Stanford writing students of the 1920s, John Steinbeck, wrote a glowing tribute to her in the preface to one of the many editions of her popular book, *Story Writing*.

With DeVoto its titular head, the triumvirate of westerners (Stegner and Mirrielees being the other two) made up the Bread Loaf fiction team for a number of years. The practical goals of the conference were "to advise its members in regard to definite literary problems, and to help them master the techniques of the main forms of writing."[9] Tuition in 1938 was $100. The faculty was paid $200. Advertisements for the conference were placed in publications that circulated mainly in the Northeast. Sixty-five conferees, eight fellows, and fourteen staff members gathered on the mountain to read and critique manuscripts, swim, hike, square-dance, play baseball and tennis, drink, and engage in extracurricular sex. DeVoto lectured on fiction writing, Stegner on regional publishing.

THE 1938 SESSION of the conference, wrote Stegner, was the year of Robert Frost's "disaster." Years later Wally wrote that Frost hadn't been "quite sane."[10] Frost's close friend Kay Morrison said with great restraint, "Never an easy fortnight, this session outdid others in the problems it presented."

Frost's wife of forty-three years had just died, and the poet was distraught. He soon fixated on Kay Morrison, who was happily married and had two children. Frost asked her to marry him. She refused. He persisted. They had an affair—brief, sexually charged, and discreet, but not so discreet that two of Frost's closest friends, DeVoto and the poet Louis Untermeyer, didn't know about the liaison, as did Ted Morrison, who tolerated it.

Frost's erratic behavior continued. Archibald MacLeish came to read his poetry on August 23. Frost sat at the rear of the Little Theater while MacLeish talked and read. He noisily rolled and unrolled the mimeographed notice of the event, raising the batonlike roll of paper or his bushy eyebrows to indicate, in Stegner's words, "an impartial, if skeptical, judiciousness." At one point he leaned over and said to no one in particular, "Archie's poems all have the same *tune.*"

He became more agitated as the reading proceeded. At its climax— a thirty-six-line poem that was a single sentence—Frost struck a match and set fire to the papers he had been fiddling with. Then he made a great fuss of stomping out the small bonfire and dispersed the smoke by wildly waving his arms.

MacLeish, Frost, friends, and the staff adjourned to Treman Cottage, an informal faculty club where the serious drinking took place. Some of them sat on the worn wicker furniture. Some stood on the porch that overlooked a large meadow. MacLeish was asked to read his new radio play. Frost interrupted constantly, belittling the work and humiliating MacLeish with his biting comments. "People sat where they had been trapped," said Stegner, "and looked into their drained glasses and did not quite dare look around." Finally, DeVoto muttered just loud enough for Frost to hear, "For God's sake, Robert, let him read." Not long after the rebuke, Frost retired to his room, and the reading reached its lame ending.

At the end of that summer's session, when DeVoto said good-bye to Frost, they shook hands, and DeVoto said, "You're a good poet, Robert, but you're a bad man."[11] Having made invaluable contacts, the Stegners departed, wondering about the strange behavior of these easterners. Years later Wally would note about Frost: "He had everything but magnanimity."[12]

STEGNER RETURNED EIGHT times to Bread Loaf over the next fifteen years, as a member of the faculty, a speaker, or a visitor. The banner year for fellows at Bread Loaf during his tenure was 1940, when Eudora Welty, Carson McCullers, and the poet John Ciardi were selected to attend. A precocious, flamboyantly dressed twenty-year-old copyboy from *The New Yorker* named Truman Capote was present in 1944. Looking back, Stegner had vivid memories of some of the literary greats of the twentieth century when they were just beginners coping with the hothouse environment of the writers' conference:

> Eudora Welty sitting worshipfully at the feet of Katherine Anne Porter after a reading, Truman Capote holding himself conspicuously aloof from Louis Untermeyer after Untermeyer had lectured on contemporary poetry and called T. S. Eliot a writer of society verse, Carson McCullers in her starched white boy's shirt deep in talk with W. H. Auden—and deep in my last bottle of bourbon which I had been saving for Sunday, when the liquor store in Brandon would be closed.[13]

Capote, who had taken a vacation to attend Bread Loaf, unintentionally repaid Frost for his discourtesies to MacLeish. Using the name of *The New Yorker*, the young man, who resembled an overgrown boy, gained entrance to the faculty lounge, where Stegner observed him talking with Frost. "I never liked Robert Frost's poetry," Capote told an interviewer years later, "and during the course of a conversation he got the idea that I felt rather indifferent toward him." He waited until Frost had launched into a lecture and then noisily brushed past the others in his row to make a theatrical exit.

The young man knew how to turn nonfiction into fiction. He later spread inflated, competing versions of why it appeared he was sleeping during a Frost reading. Capote claimed that he appeared to have fallen asleep when he leaned over to scratch a mosquito bite on his ankle. A sore neck from the flu kept his head lowered, according to an alternative account. Frost, in response, threw a book at Capote and missed him. "If that's the way *The New Yorker* feels about my poetry," Frost said, according to Capote's version of the incident, "I won't go on reading." Frost then "stomped" out of the room. These stories greatly increased Capote's cachet.

The truth was somewhat different. Frost and others wrote Harold Ross, the editor of the magazine, and complained about Capote's behavior. In Capote's version, he told Ross he was there on his own time and at his own expense and was not representing *The New Yorker*. Capote said he "left" the magazine for about six months and then returned. In fact, he was fired by Ross.

Carson McCullers had submitted the manuscript for *Reflections in a Golden Eye* to the conference staff in 1940. Morrison and Stegner recognized the brilliant writing but had problems with such macabre incidents as a rejected housewife cutting off her nipples with pruning shears and a live cat being stuffed into a mailbox. McCullers attended some of the sessions of the fiction workshop that Stegner conducted but contributed nothing. Outside the classroom, Wally talked to her about her manuscript, "but probably not to her satisfaction, for its distortions were things I could grant as legitimately grotesque without admiring." It was his first contact with "a confirmed devotee of the grotesque, and I found her very interesting, but not easy to know."[14]

Eudora Welty, another southerner, had problems with McCullers's androgynous style of dress. Welty's story "Powerhouse" was not well received in the short story workshop conducted by Mirrielees and in fact was deemed unsalable. At night in Treman Cottage, Welty played the piano and sang songs from her native Mississippi that were counterpoints to Stegner's rawer western ballads. Bread Loaf's "artsy" atmosphere disappointed Welty, and she returned to the less complicated world of Mississippi.

Stegner's last visit to Bread Loaf was as a speaker in 1953. He was asked to return as a member of the staff but declined. By then it was time to move on from those intense two-week sessions.

FROM THE ATMOSPHERICS of Bread Loaf that first summer, Stegner's journey led back to Wisconsin. When Stegner's appointment was not renewed, he wrote Ted Morrison in the fall of 1938 and was overjoyed when he received a letter in return inviting him to teach at Harvard. Once again Schramm, along with DeVoto this time, had made Stegner's advancement possible by supplying the necessary recommendations.

Before moving to Cambridge, Wilbur helped his former roommate again by inviting him to teach at the first summer session of the Iowa Writers' Workshop, in June of 1939. Stegner was one of "eleven writers of national repute" who would be participating. He had just completed a lecture and was answering students' questions when Schramm walked across the platform, silenced the audience, and told his friend quietly that he had just received a telephone call informing him that Wally's father was dead. Stegner's first thought was "So now I know how that damn book ends." He was referring to *The Big Rock Candy Mountain*.[15]

George Stegner had been on the skids, particularly during the last two years, when he had periodically begged his son to send him money. At sixty-one, he was unemployed and too young for Social Security. His mining venture near Winnemucca, Nevada, would surely pan out, said the ever-hopeful George, and he would then repay his son. "This is the last chance for me," wrote the elder Stegner, "and if I fail in this I will end it all."[16] Wally sent his father what he could afford, which wasn't much, and encouraged him to find a job: "Take a brace Bo, and shake it off. Mother would have stiffened her chin and gone along with you. Maybe we could both learn something from remembering how she could take it when it got rough."[17] Bo was the first name of George's fictional counterpart in the family saga Wally was writing.

His father's death was both sensational and lurid and must have been extremely embarrassing to his son, who didn't have to borrow money or an overcoat from Schramm this time to return to Salt Lake City and bury the last remaining member of his immediate family. The news of the murder-suicide was splashed across the front and inside pages of Salt Lake's three daily newspapers for two days.

Shortly after noon on June 15, 1939, George Stegner had obtained a permit from the police to carry a pearl-handled .38-caliber revolver. He said he needed the gun for protection when he visited his Nevada mine. Asked by a police lieutenant if he had a criminal record, the ex-bootlegger replied, "No, I haven't any criminal record—yet."

He returned to the Heron Hotel on East Second Street South, where he had been renting a room since March 1. Stegner went to his room, had a quick drink with the hotel clerk, returned to the lobby, and sat down. He acted like he was drunk, according to witnesses.

A few minutes later Dorothy LeRoy entered the lobby from a shopping trip. She was staying with her mother in the hotel. The striking thirty-eight-year-old woman was described in press accounts as a divorcée, usually code at that time—especially in Utah—for someone suspected of having loose morals. Stegner was described as a retired mining man, which was code for a failure. George had both a business and a personal relationship with Dorothy.

Stegner leaped up and began shouting at her. The clerk saw the bulge of the gun in his pocket, Stegner took it out, and the clerk tried to wrestle it away. George was stronger. The clerk backed away, fearing he would be shot. LeRoy hit Stegner in the face with her pocketbook and fled down a corridor. She opened and then quickly slammed the door in Stegner's face at the rear of the hotel. She braced her back against the door. Stegner fired twice through the closed door, striking LeRoy in the back. One of the bullets pierced her heart. Stegner then shot himself in the temple.

The Deseret News said that Stegner had no known relatives in Salt Lake. *The Salt Lake Tribune* said the only known survivor was a son, Wallace, "formerly of Salt Lake City and now teaching at the University of Wisconsin." George Henry Stegner was buried two days later in an unmarked grave in the city cemetery.

The writing of Wallace Stegner's family and frontier saga went more smoothly after his father's death. Of his struggles with *Big Rock*, Stegner said, "I had a good part of it done when my father made it imperative, and gave it its fated ending, by shooting himself to death in a flea bag Salt Lake hotel in the summer of 1940."[18] (For whatever reason, whether conscious or subconscious, Stegner always got the date of his father's death wrong: it was 1939.)

In the novel the Wallace Stegner–like character leaves his commencement in Minnesota to travel once more back to Salt Lake: "He was going home again, the next to last time, and there was no doubt where his home was, because part of him was already buried in those two graves and in two days another part—admit it—would be buried in the third."[19] The death, and the novel, provided partial expiation. "I was exorcising my father," said Stegner, who could never bring himself to provide a gravestone to mark the site where his father is buried.[20]

UNDER JAMES CONANT, Harvard was being dragged reluctantly into the mid-twentieth century when Stegner arrived on the campus. "Tradition and self-satisfaction flourished with special luxuriance in the Department of English," according to a recent book on Harvard's prewar regeneration.[21] F. O. Matthiessen, Howard Mumford Jones, and Robert Frost were added to the English faculty to beef up the undergraduate American literature component. Frost, who taught at Harvard until 1943, warned Conant that he couldn't teach under the constraints of a regular schedule but would occasionally visit a class, lecture, and meet informally with students.

The required and dreaded freshman composition course was given new life by Morrison. Real writers, like Stegner, would teach it. Morrison thought that the best teachers of writing were writers who were articulate about their craft. They were to be called Briggs-Copeland instructors, after LeBaron Russell Briggs and Charles Townsend Copeland, "the most justly famous writing teachers Harvard has had," said Morrison. Among the original Briggs-Copeland instructors were Mark Schorer, Delmore Schwartz, John Berryman, and Stegner. Only a few, including Stegner, eventually received term appointments as assistant professors.

Stegner was among Morrison's favorites. One of Morrison's former students interviewed him in 1982 for a profile of the emeritus professor of English that appeared in *Harvard Magazine*. In response to a question about writers he had known, Morrison said: "I think a contemporary example of excellence in prose style is Wally Stegner, who can combine the rhetorical resources of vocabulary and of knowledge; without knowledge of some sort, you can't have knowledge in words. I think that he can combine the free, natural-speaking, colloquial kind of language with elegance and refinement, and that is something that I respect and covet."[22]

Stegner's first Harvard writing class, in the fall of 1939, consisted of forty students. He had one teaching assistant, a graduate student by the name of Walter Rideout, who would become a professor of English at the University of Wisconsin. Rideout remembered Stegner as "a very conscientious and gifted teacher," one who tried to draw out each student's special talents rather than attempting to put the Stegner stamp on him. He emphasized Stegner's consideration not only for the students but also for the teaching assistants, who normally read all the papers. Stegner divided the papers between his TAs and himself. He invited the departmental TAs to his home for an evening with Robert Frost, whose long underwear showed above his high-top shoes. A true New Englander and a true human, thought young Rideout.[23]

Stegner found that graduates of eastern prep schools did better the first semester, then loafed while those who had attended public schools in the hinterlands worked hard, caught up, and surpassed the preppies during the second semester. "Old story," said Wally much later, "jackrabbit and tortoise. I must say I'm on the side of the tortoise, who is never as slow as he looks to the jackrabbit."[24]

The new English instructor had problems mastering the colloquialisms of Harvard. "I have declared an embargo on 'Sirs' to preserve my self respect," Stegner told the Grays. He declared that Harvard students were better than the average he had taught at state universities. The Stegners were adjusting to life in the East. He and Molly—as Mary was known to the Grays—had rented a home in suburban Newtonville for $40 a month. A Scottish maid had been dismissed for drinking on the job, and a young French Canadian woman from Cape Breton, who wore her skirts at mid-thigh, was currently helping them.[25]

His second novel, *On a Darkling Plain*, was published during his first year at Harvard. Norman Foerster wrote from the University of Iowa: "Your first novel showed that you could write with beauty; your second that you can write with strength. Therefore I feel much surer than I did of your great promise for the future."[26] The novel's publisher trumpeted in its newsletter: "Stegner is a young man with a great future."

Never one of his favorite novels because he thought it psychologically naive, *On a Darkling Plain* would be reprinted with Stegner's permission only once. And that occurred because his friend Howard Mumford Jones taught English in a German prisoner-of-war camp in the South during World War II. Back in Germany after the war, one of Jones's best students, G. H. Blanke, was asked by the publisher C. Bertelsmann which American novels were worth publishing in translation, and Blanke recommended *On a Darkling Plain*. Upon giving permission for its publication, Stegner said, "Maybe the combination of sentiment and weltschmerz is proper for the German market."[27] Bertelsmann published the book in 1949 and followed it up with translations of *Remembering Laughter* in 1951 and *The Big Rock Candy Mountain* in 1952. Royalties at the time had to remain in Germany, so the ever-frugal Stegner made a side trip to that country in 1950 to collect what was owed him.[28]

The Stegners' social life at Harvard at first consisted of tennis with the Morrisons and dinners with the DeVotos. Then, primarily through the DeVotos, their orbit widened to include Conrad Aiken, Robert Frost, John Kenneth Galbraith, Howard Mumford Jones, F. O. Matthiessen, Arthur Schlesinger Jr., and other Harvard contemporaries. It was a long way from Eastend, Saskatchewan, to Cambridge, Massachusetts, and dining with the Harvard elite.

Whether conservative or liberal, most Harvard students and faculty did not favor involvement in the growing European conflict. There were antiwar demonstrations in Cambridge and clashes between town and gown over veterans' commemoration of Memorial Day, scenes that Stegner would see repeated on the Stanford campus during the Vietnam War years. In a letter to the Grays he commented on the human waste of war:

> And did you ever walk into the reading room at Warren House and see that collection of pictures of Harvard boys killed

in the last war, framed with a sample page of a theme in which they expressed their opinions on the war—generally isolationist, neutral, and Christ almighty how furiously pitiable? There is the answer to a ghoul's prayer. It's the modern equivalent of a charnel house, so help me. So I shall send my children filing by the moldering bones as a theme assignment, and shudder every paper I read. There, but for the grace of God, go we.[29]

Stegner had attended a few meetings of the Young Communist League in Madison and had been unimpressed. At Harvard he joined the teachers' union, headed by Matthiessen, a committed socialist and a noted professor of history and literature. The union was preoccupied with getting Earl Browder, the head of the Communist Party, out of jail. Stegner came home from the meetings muttering, "God damn, that's not what it's *about*."[30]

When war came, Stegner chose to have no part of it. All he wanted to do was write novels. "If I could believe that this whole war business would have a heart and pass little me right on by," he wrote the Grays in April of 1942, "I might see more years ahead for such things as writing novels. . . . If they made this one I could believe in, I'd fight in it. But I see few signs that they're going to, and fewer yet that us little people can make them."[31]

Wally's Selective Service information in 1941 listed him as six feet tall, 160 pounds, with blue eyes, brown hair, and a sallow complexion, and missing the fourth finger of his left hand. He was variously classified between 1-A and 3-A during the war. He was near the upper age limit of the draft, had "a birth-crippled child and an unwell wife," and was plagued by gastric ulcers, which private doctors assured him would keep him out of the military. Teaching in the Army Specialized Training Program at Harvard provided another temporary shelter from the draft.

Stegner declined two unsolicited relatively high-paying war-related jobs in Washington, D.C., one of them in the Office of War Information with Wilbur Schramm. Of the other offer, a job paying $5,600 a year, Stegner said: "That's not a bad wage for an office boy, which is what I would have been. But I thought of novels, I thought of Art, I thought of Greensboro, I thought of Washington, and I answered them no. I wish all temptation was that easy to resist. I'd be a moral paragon." Stegner didn't believe he had the makings of either a conscientious objector or a warrior. "I haven't got up nerve enough to jump either way," he said.[32]

Mary believed he was working himself into a nervous breakdown. Stegner was worried in part because he was facing the possibility of being drafted. He was also teaching, participating in faculty activities, caring for a sick wife and a young son, writing articles for magazines, attempting to complete *The Big Rock Candy Mountain*, and playing with the idea of writing a biography of John Wesley Powell. And he was working on an episodic history of Utah, *Mormon Country*, for the American Folkways Series, edited by Erskine Caldwell. With all that going on, his ulcers acted up.

Stegner undertook *Mormon Country* because he was homesick for Utah. His peers at Harvard viewed him as an academic cowboy who had survived immersion in an alien culture. "What's it like living out there?" they asked. He went back to Utah in the summer of 1941 so that he would be able to tell them: "I wanted to get back West in flesh and spirit and the book gave me an excuse to . . . [return] in both."[33]

What he discovered in that quick dip into Mormon history, and what he would elaborate on later in his nonfiction masterpiece *Beyond the Hundredth Meridian*, was that "this was a country that could be broken only by the united efforts of all. They worked together or they starved out separately, because the supplies of both land and water were extremely limited."[34] Stegner brought his family's homesteading experience to bear on this prescient theme. Perhaps no other work—and certainly none up to that date—captured the uniqueness of that state and the characteristics of its inhabitants as insightfully and sympathetically as Stegner's book, although more rigid Mormons had difficulty accepting its truths.

Stegner needed to complete *The Big Rock Candy Mountain*, however. He couldn't allow any more interruptions. Wally had been working on the novel for five years. A description of the work in 1942 read like his autobiography. "Within the story of this family," he wrote, "are contained, it seems to me, many of the implications of the social and economic history of the West: the anti-social against the social, the restless against the permanent and settled, the morally weak against the morally indomitable." As seen through the eyes of the one surviving son, the "psychological novel . . . [was] concerned with the intimate effects of character on character and generation on generation."[35]

The book meant a lot to Wally, more than anything he had previously written and perhaps more than any book he would ever write. "It is the only novel I have ever attempted in which I was completely and vitally interested," he wrote in a 1942 application for a Guggenheim fellowship. In the foreword to a special edition in 1976, Wally explained: "I wrote it because it happened to me; the significance I found later. A lot of myself is invested in that book. As I wrote some pages of it, I couldn't see the typewriter for tears."[36]

Stegner was in a quandary. If he quit teaching to write full-time, he would be drafted. He had received a five-year appointment in the spring of 1942. Could he ask Morrison for a short leave so soon after receiving that promotion? Morrison gave him a leave for the fall semester of 1942, and he received a small grant from Harvard, ostensibly to work on the Powell book, but he used the time to write the novel.

The only place where the Stegners could afford to stay was Greensboro. Yet their farm was too remote for them to make frequent trips to town, given the constraints of gas rationing. They had spent the two previous Christmases in the Grays' house, which was much closer to Greensboro and the school that Page would attend. May we split wood, pay the utilities, act as winter caretakers, and use your house? The answer from the Grays was, of course, yes.

But before he could concentrate on his novel in Greensboro, Stegner had to resolve a controversy with a Briggs-Copeland colleague, Mark Schorer, who would go on to a distinguished career as an author, critic, and English professor at Berkeley. The argument, carried on mainly in a series of letters but also by word of mouth on the Harvard campus, was symptomatic of the difference in styles between an academic writer and a professional one.

The source of the dispute was that Stegner had paraphrased arguments made by others and had not named all his sources in a December 1942 Harper's magazine article titled "Is the Novel Done For?" The piece drew on Schorer's work, along with the thoughts of others. Schorer's criticism of Stegner's technique was a preview of the sniping that would be aimed at Beyond the Hundredth Meridian and Angle of Repose, Stegner's two greatest works. To Schorer it was a matter of the purity of sources; to Stegner it was the need to produce readable prose. Stegner was susceptible to this type of criticism from academics because he wrote nonfiction for lay audiences using fictional techniques, and he modified real characters, events, and places to meet the fictional needs of his short stories and novels.

In the midst of a long point-by-point rebuttal to Schorer's objections, Stegner blurted out: "I was writing for a popular magazine, for God's sake, not the PMLA," referring to the academic journal of the Modern Language Association. He added, "If my carelessness seemed unfriendly to you, your instant and overheated reaction seems fully as unfriendly to me, and less pardonable, particularly since in effect you were publicly calling me a thief before you had even made an attempt to see if there was any explanation for what you thought my unpardonable actions."[37]

STEGNER PUT THE spat behind him and concentrated on finishing his novel in Greensboro. The summer faded into fall. He gathered berries and raised vegetables for canning and worked with George Hill, a local farmer. Stegner sent Morrison this account of sawing wood:

> Working one full day on the drag saw with a crew of six farmers was something. Not a word was said all morning except when the engine ran out of gas. Then the sawyer said, "Shit, said McGinty," and reached for the [gas] can. A lever kicked back on the little red headed guy dogging the logs under the saw and hit him a dirty one under the chin. One of the farmers spit and laughed and said, "Bust any teeth?" and the redheaded guy wiped off blood from his chin and spit in the same place the other guy had spit and said, "I God, didn't have 'em in." That was the morning. Then we trooped down to the farm and had dinner, a threshing crew spread worth twenty minutes of silence, and then we trooped back and sawed up seven or eight more cords. In silence, I have never been known as garrulous, but I was scratching the empty till for something to say before the day was up.[38]

Never a man to let a good scene go to waste, Stegner drew on that experience to write the short story "Saw Gang." There is an accident. The sawyer, McGinty, asks, "Lose any teeth, Will?" The kid replies, "'Y God, I didn't have them in!" Later in the day the saw runs out of gas. " 'Nuts,' said McGinty." A number of other changes and additions to the account illustrate how Stegner turned fact into fiction.

The Stegners sent the Grays bits and pieces of information. Winter was closing in fast. The "bonfire hills" of autumnal Vermont had disappeared, and the spruces were more clearly etched against the mountains. The larder was full, the cellar being stocked with homemade cider and with apples, squash, potatoes, hams, carrots, and firewood. A cousin of Phil Gray's had sent them fur-lined caribou-skin parkas. They posed with the parkas for a Christmas-card photo. With gas rationed, a phone was installed in case of an emergency. Who the Stegners were was barely known in the community. *Remembering Laughter* was kept in the librarian's desk "for fear of corrupting the young," Mary reported to the Grays.[39]

They lived frugally, turning on the hot-water heater only twice a week, since Wally had determined that it cost twenty-five cents to take a bath. Stegner's day consisted of writing for three hours in the morning, then lunch, sawing wood, reading, dinner, and bed by 9:30 p.m. He felt exceedingly healthy. Page was thriving. As for Mary, she missed doing something active for the war, like working in the Cambridge office of the Socialist Party. Maybe, she mused, Wally would give up teaching and they could work in the Japanese relocation camps in the West. "However, that is not my decision to make and all I can do is influence him a little," Mary wrote to Peg Gray. "He doesn't really have much of a social conscience, I am afraid. Maybe it's a good thing for his writing that he doesn't. At least if he did he probably wouldn't have any time to write."[40]

The temperature hadn't risen above zero for three weeks, having hovered between five and thirty-five degrees below zero. A warmly dressed Stegner had to get up every few minutes from his typewriter to stoke the fire in the living room. For someone who suffered from cold hands and feet, this experience was enough to dissuade him from year-round residency in Greensboro. It was a difficult winter, but some fifty years later Stegner recalled that it had been "the best winter of our lives."[41]

WITH THE RETURN to Cambridge, where they now had an apartment on Trowbridge Street, and the resumption of teaching in February, the pace quickened again. In 1943, Stegner's first important novel was published. *The Big Rock Candy Mountain* is a sweeping, powerful work. As the first exploration of his dysfunctional family and its wanderings, it has a freshness and directness that his later works on the same themes and using some of the same material and characters lack. Of *Big Rock* and the later Salt Lake City novel, *Recapitulation*, Stegner told an interviewer: "I wrote one book, essentially, out of my own life, or more out of my own life than out of imagination. Then I wrote a trailer to it, but it's essentially one book." He told another interviewer that in *Recapitulation* he was looking at "the old problem that was there in *The Big Rock Candy Mountain*, the dominant father who I think wore on me all of my life. Probably a hell of a lot more than any old love affair because I think what he did to my self-confidence was disastrous for a long time."⁴²

History and autobiography served the purposes of fiction in those two books. In a reversal of the process, autobiography and fiction served the needs of history in *Wolf Willow*. "Sometimes I think that my own novels sound like biography, and my biographies like novels, which will give you an idea of where my inclinations lead me," Stegner explained.⁴³

What was easier to write than the personal parts were the sections dealing with the wider historical context of the frontier as it influenced individual lives. He had learned this history from personal experience, and it had been intellectually confirmed by Frederick Jackson Turner: "I guess I got the feeling there of something meaningful to my work in Turner: the importance of the impact of the frontier upon human character and upon human lives." Speaking of Turner's thesis, he said, "I could braid that in with my own family's experience so that it seemed to have a particular meaning." Stegner also borrowed the literary technique of synecdoche from Frost or DeVoto—he wasn't sure just whom he'd borrowed it from since there was so much back-and-forth among the three of them. Wally later explained what he meant by using the personal and the local to establish a wider context: "The most personal reaction to landscape, to people, to ways of living, is that which is rooted in the local. So long as that local is not so absolutely eccentric, so completely out of the stream that it becomes merely local color, a strange picturesque kind of oddity, then the provincial basis is as good as you can get."⁴⁴

Stegner's Harvard colleague Howard Mumford Jones understood what he was attempting. Writing in the *Saturday Review of Literature*, Jones said that Stegner had produced a major novel in a lean year. The story that lay outside the realm of intellectualism but within the kingdom of fiction "is a revelation of life in the contemporary West." *The New York Times* reviewer praised Stegner for evoking life on a homestead but criticized him for lacking "an esthetically significant point of view."⁴⁵

During his Harvard years, Stegner continued to absorb technique, subject matter, and alcohol from DeVoto, who was particularly adept at writing for the popular magazines. For DeVoto and Stegner, selling what they wrote took precedence over publishing in esoteric academic journals. It was a simple matter of economic survival for them. The demeaning academic term for versatility was *pluralism*. Stegner was once asked what pluralistic principles he had learned from DeVoto.

> He told me I ought to be a pro, and I was in an impressionable time. I was green as grass, and I was ambitious, and I was poor. The salary that Harvard paid me to teach freshman English was not excessive, and I cut that in half by choosing to teach only half time. I needed to write stories; I needed to write things for the magazines. At that point I would have done any piece of writing up cheap and neat. I can remember Benny going through his files with me and saying, "Anybody can learn to write for the slick magazines if he wants to give himself about two years to practice. It isn't what you want to do maybe, but that's what they'll pay you for. If you want to be a virgin, all right, be a virgin. But don't pretend you can be a half virgin. You write what the market wants, or you write what you want. Or you do them separately and at different times. But you don't pretend that one is necessarily the other.[46]

It was spring in New England, the last spring the Stegners would experience in Cambridge. In late April of 1944, they walked to a friend's house where fellow summertime residents of Greensboro were assembled and had some beer and a sing. The Boston Pops concerts had begun, the crocuses were blooming, and Stegner was, as ever, attuned to place:

> A New England spring is a fraud, really. You wait and wait and tentatively go without a coat, and catch cold, and recover, and it snows, and then it rains, and the sun shines a little, hopefully, and the much-postponed baseball season gets in a game or two, and then it blows up an east wind and freezes the statues in Monument Square, and then it rains, and then one day all of a sudden it's hot as hell, with a humidity of ninety-eight and that was spring that you just suffered through.[47]

AN OPPORTUNITY SOON presented itself that would allow Stegner to make money from journalism and explore a subject that he—and, for that matter, few others—had barely touched upon.[48] In the process Stegner could circumvent wartime restrictions and travel widely. The subject was racism in America. With race riots occurring in Los Angeles, Detroit, and elsewhere, the editors of *Look* magazine had decided to investigate the "growing wave of intolerance and prejudice." *Look* was one of the slicks. *Big Rock* had attracted the attention of the editors. The magazine's editors commissioned Stegner to do a series of articles on racism that would then be published as a book.

The eighteen-month "wartime-patriotism" assignment—that being Stegner's description—was a complete switch in subject matter and career direction for the assistant professor. Why, he was asked at Cambridge cocktail parties, would he leave Harvard to work for a *magazine*, of all things? Well, for one thing, the money was pretty good, and the assignment "was the best possible way to reach a mass audience with a message about equality and fraternity." There really wasn't much future for him at Harvard. He saw the opportunity in later years as "a real edge of some kind, a divide" in his career path. It also served as an opportunity to return to the West.[49]

Traveling with *Look* photographers by train across the country near the end of World War II was exciting and draining. Stegner lost twenty pounds from a heart infection that incapacitated him for a while. He holed up with his family and typewriter in Santa Barbara in the fall of 1944. They rented a small house on a large estate with a private golf course on the edge of the Pacific Ocean. Wally played golf, swam, wrote, and made forays to Los Angeles and elsewhere on the West Coast to gather material. His Harvard friends kidded him about the good life he was leading during the war, to which he replied, "I know there is a war on because I am the slayer and the slain, and I know too damned well the paths I keep."[50]

At the end of the assignment the editors were no longer interested in a series of articles on racism. "*Look* got scared," Stegner said. "They got afraid that people—the public that reads *Look*—just wouldn't take it." He described the change of mind as "a great wizening of the nerve."[51] The series was condensed into a long, fairly innocuous article with photographs. Stegner scattered the remaining material among various publications, including *The Atlantic, New Republic, Saturday Review*, and *Glamour*, the latter publishing an article titled "Jews Are the Most Misunderstood Minority." A book, *One Nation*, was published in 1945 by Houghton Mifflin and had more bite than the *Look* article. It sold well, received awards, and was read in schools.

· · ·

FIFTY-ONE YEARS LATER and three years after his death, Stegner would be taken to task for his lack of racial inclusiveness. In a chapter in *Why I Can't Read Wallace Stegner and Other Essays: A Tribal Voice*, Elizabeth Cook-Lynn, a Crow Creek Sioux who was described by her publisher as a Native American feminist intellectual, criticized Stegner for not looking back far enough into prehistory to include the "mythological continuity and primordial historiography" of American Indians. Cook-Lynn found fault with Stegner for his "dismissal of indigenousness."

Citing Stegner's remark in *Wolf Willow* that if he was native to anything, it was to the Canadian prairie, Cook-Lynn said: "Stegner simply claims indigenousness and begins to set down the new myths and stories of those newcomers stepping off boats and, in the process, continues the personalization of history and setting that is so dear to the hearts of the so-called regional American writers." There was a loss, a loss in the flow of oral history into written history, when only one era was given credence. Stegner and his cohorts had "claimed possession of the American West." In the meantime, said Cook-Lynn, "my reading in the works of Wallace Stegner is minimally undertaken and then only to remind myself that literature can and does successfully contribute to the politics of possession and dispossession."[52]

Her argument was aimed not only at Stegner but also at those western writers for whom he was an icon. Stegner was a self-declared native of the white experience in the West, not of the Native American experience. He was aware of what the writers of pulp fiction had done to romanticize the Native Americans and mindful of the contributions of those writers who "were closer to the native inhabitants of the continent," such as N. Scott Momaday, James Welch, Leslie Marmon Silko, and Louise Erdrich. He told an interviewer that racial matters were always "much more complex than they seem to outsiders" and that "in a phrase, I am hopelessly culture-bound."[53]

Two white women came to Stegner's defense. He was not infallible, wrote Beth LaDow, the historian of the Canadian–United States border, who had cited Wally's history of Canadian Indians in *Wolf Willow* in her book. She said that *One Nation* demonstrated "a remarkable pre–Civil Rights era model of cultural and racial acceptance." To LaDow, Cook-Lynn's essay was a "thinly argued screed."[54] In a remembrance of Stegner, Patricia Nelson Limerick, a historian of the American West, pointed out that he had not written an East Coast version of race relations in *One Nation* but, rather, had begun with Filipinos,

Japanese Americans, Chinese Americans, Mexicans, Hispanics, and Native Americans in the West and then proceeded eastward to deal with the more widely recognized problems of African Americans, Catholics, and Jews. "On this matter," said Limerick, "and many others, Stegner was far ahead of his time in 1945. He is, in fact, still ahead of *our* time, in 1993."[55]

WITH THE *LOOK* project winding down, Stegner had begun to think about teaching again. Although his appointment at Harvard was not up until 1947, he did not want to return to Cambridge. He would be no closer to academic tenure and was "too close to forty to feel comfortable" looking for other literary work. Besides, it was a seller's market near the end of the war.

Stegner had ten years of teaching experience behind him and had produced five novels (*Remembering Laughter, The Potter's House, On a Darkling Plain, Fire and Ice*, and *The Big Rock Candy Mountain*), one nonfiction book (*Mormon Country*), and numerous short stories and magazine articles. The publication of *One Nation* gave him additional cachet. Bread Loaf and Harvard were names that piqued the interest of chairmen of English departments and the presidents of colleges and universities. He wrote to Ted Morrison from Santa Barbara, "It appears that every damned university in America is all of a sudden hot to find some writer to teach its creative writing."[56] He got nibbles from Wayne State University, the University of Iowa, the University of Kansas, Stanford University, Ohio State University, Stanford University again, UCLA, and Mills College in Oakland.

Mills College's loss was Stanford's gain, and another lesson—as Augustana College had been—in the perils of academe. The president of Mills, Lynn White Jr., recommended Stegner for an American literature post that was being financed by a private donor, whose wishes were represented by an informal committee of one lawyer and two businessmen who had veto power over the nominee. The two businessmen thought certain passages of *Big Rock* were pornographic and said "they did not want to have seventeen-year-old girls studying with a man who could write such things," according to White, who added, "You have been the subject of a major battle which I have lost."[57]

With his Bread Loaf colleague Edith Mirrielees quietly working behind the scenes at Stanford, from which she had recently retired, and counseling Stegner to be patient, Wally eventually received a much better job offer. "I look at a full professorship in a first-class university and I can't see turning it down," he wrote Morrison, "especially when there is every indication that the department wants to spare me committee work and busy work and leave my hands untied to write, and will pay me to start on the basis of five thousand for full time. Edith has apparently laid down some rules about her successor, and I must say her rules are good rules from my point of view. . . . Goddam. Life, it's wonderful."[58]

When he first visited the Stanford campus in January of 1945, there was snow on the nearby Santa Cruz Mountains. It was a cold, clear day with the north wind blowing. Stegner was used to such weather; the Stanford students and faculty were not. He talked with professors in the Department of English and with the vice president. There was agreement on terms: he would be an acting professor the first year and would teach half-time. A full professorship and tenure would follow. It would be a big career leap.

Stegner returned to Santa Barbara and undertook a crash course in Californiana, reading Bret Harte, John Muir, and books on the local color and regional history. He visited nearby ranches and helped the cowboys inoculate cattle against blackleg. The family of three left Santa Barbara in June for Palo Alto, where they would live in a converted rest home until they could find better housing.

The continuum of support had run from Schramm to Morrison to Mirrielees. Stegner had landed with both feet on the West Coast. In his typical aw, shucks manner, Wally attributed his rapid rise to a full professorship at the age of thirty-six to accidents and "pure inertia." His priorities remained the same. One year later, in response to an inquiry from a midwestern university about his availability, he would write: "But I know that for myself I would rather not teach at all than to take on such a burden of teaching that my own writing had to be put aside."[59]

The Stanford Years

Within the academy, of course, there are limited things that a teacher can do, apart from encouraging the environment of interest and criticism within which writing can take place. How can anyone "teach" writing, when he himself, as a writer, is never sure what he is doing?

Wallace Stegner, *On Teaching and Writing Fiction*

S TANFORD UNIVERSITY WAS, and still is, called "the Farm." Whereas Harvard drew on northern Europe for its architectural style, southern Europe was the inspiration for the architects hired by Leland Stanford—railroad baron, California governor, and U.S. senator. Stanford and his wife, Jane, created an instant campus bathed in brilliant, warm sunshine and shaded by palm trees on what had been not a farm but, rather, a vast estate in the late nineteenth century. The money for the private university came from building and operating the transcontinental railroad.

When the Stegners arrived, there was still a slight excuse for calling the campus the Farm. "They were cutting oats right up to the library that day, quite literally against the building," he recalled. Stegner sketched for his friends in Vermont the surroundings of what would become known as Silicon Valley. The date was July 6, 1945.

California, that is Palo Alto, is not wilderness, coming at three thousand an acre and selling altogether too fast at that price. It is very pleasant country, for all that: golden wild-oat hills dotted with marvelous old liveoaks and bay trees, with a dark pine-covered ridge of the coast range behind, and in front the hills dropping down over orchards and towns to the bay, and beyond the bay the barren gold ridge of the San Jose Mountains with Mount Diablo coning up in the midst of it. There are views to knock your eye out all over these hills.[1]

There were few men on the campus near the end of World War II. It seemed to Wally like a girls' college, "and a very quiet one" at that. Then the student population exploded when classes began in the early fall. The enrollment doubled, tripled, quadrupled, and kept increasing during the next three years, with returning veterans taking advantage of the educational benefits of the GI Bill of Rights.

Fortunately, the humanities, which traditionally had suffered from neglect, had just been strengthened. With the hiring of Stegner and Richard F. Jones in the same year, the latter as chairman of the English Department, creative writing was about to be given a tremendous boost. In fact, it is doubtful Stegner could have achieved what he did without Jones as his enthusiastic backer.

Stanford was unprepared for the deluge of students. It was a madhouse. Stegner taught the same two classes Mirrielees had taught, the history of the short story and creative writing. In addition, he taught an American literature course with an enrollment of 160 students the first year. He had to read all the papers because there were no graduate assistants to help him. He also supervised eleven doctoral candidates.

As Stegner was preparing to face his first class at Stanford, he was also becoming involved in another job, as West Coast editor for Houghton Mifflin. And he quickly had a promising manuscript in his hands: his cousin, Tom Heggen, was sending him batches of a novel in progress based on his navy experiences in the Pacific. That work would become the tremendously successful book, play, and movie *Mister Roberts,* and the novel would be Stegner's greatest coup as an acquiring editor.

"The last batch was swell, and the book grows," Wally wrote Tom in August 1945. "You may go on thinking it crap all you please, only write some more." To another editor at the publishing company, Wally wrote that same day: "The kid can write like the angel Gabriel, and if it becomes necessary for anyone to sell the notion of this book to editorial or sales conferences, call on me." From his ship, which was cruising off the coast of Japan, Tom responded to his cousin's enthusiasm with characteristic self-doubt: "I can't tell, and there's no competent criticism on the ship, but I have reason to suspect that it's getting worse all the time." Heggen was subject to periodic bouts of depression.[2]

Stegner read a portion of the manuscript to his first class. It was a story titled "Night Watch." Eugene (Bud) Burdick was sitting in the back row in his navy uniform. He yelled out, "That's the way it was." Stegner sold the story to *The Atlantic* for his cousin, who dropped by

Palo Alto that fall. Heggen went home to Minneapolis, where he completed the book; it was published in 1946. He then went to work for *Reader's Digest* and traveled to Europe and Cuba, searching in vain for another subject to write about. He was found dead in his New York apartment in 1949. Stegner attended the funeral in Minneapolis, where he consoled his aunt Mina. At the time of Heggen's death, *Mister Roberts* had sold more than 100,000 copies, there had been 522 performances of the play, and a movie starring Henry Fonda was about to be made.[3]

One work he couldn't place at Houghton Mifflin, but for which he found an eventual home at Stanford University Press, was Juanita Brooks's groundbreaking *Mountain Meadows Massacre*, the first book-length treatment of the 1857 massacre of California-bound immigrants in southwestern Utah. One man, a Mormon elder named John D. Lee, was made the scapegoat and executed for the crime that some thought had been ordered by the Mormon leader Brigham Young.

Brooks, who was a Mormon, told Stegner that she had written the book "with the idea of learning the facts and presenting them for the few who might be interested, students of western history, LDS who have never been quite satisfied with the accepted church story, and a few curious who have heard of the incident."[4] After being notified of Stanford's acceptance of the manuscript in 1949, Stegner wrote Brooks: "It's a book that evidently deserves publication and I admire your courage in bringing it out."[5] The descendants of Lee also wanted to see it published, as Brooks's book took the full onus off their ancestor. In a few years Stegner would go to work for one of Lee's great-grandsons, Stewart Lee Udall, who would become a good friend and in the 1960s serve as secretary of the interior.

STEGNER, THE TEACHER, was on a roll. The first student's story he read in class was one of Burdick's. "Rest Camp on Maui" was subsequently published in *Harper's*, won an O. Henry Award, and launched Burdick's successful career as a novelist: he would write *The Ninth Wave* and collaborate on *Fail-Safe* and *The Ugly American*. *The Ninth Wave* was Burdick's master's thesis at Stanford. Boris Ilyin, one of the first fellows in the creative writing program, told the following story: "Wright Morris visited us once and Wally read a chapter Bud had written that later was the first chapter of *The Ninth Wave*, and Wright Morris said, 'Well, obviously one is in the presence of a writer.' "[6] Stegner took Burdick back to Vermont as a Bread Loaf Fellow, and there Burdick met William J. Lederer, with whom he collaborated on *The Ugly American* and other books.

The veterans were older, more mature, and more serious about their studies than the other students. Wally felt that he had to do something special for them. He scrounged around and got some money for writing prizes. That wasn't enough, so he drafted a proposal in 1946 for a creative writing program that would grant a master's degree and took it to Jones. The models for the program read like a Stegner résumé. What he constructed contained elements of Iowa, Bread Loaf, and Harvard. It would be the second graduate writing program in the country, after Iowa's, and while under the direction of Stegner it was arguably the better one.

There was the slight problem of money. Richard Jones took him to lunch with his brother, Edward H. (Ned) Jones, a physician, Greek scholar, and Texas oilman. "Well," said Ned Jones at the end of the meal, "I think we can fund it for the first five years and see how it goes." Stegner was ecstatic. As chairman of the Department of English, Richard Jones had to clear the new program with the administration. Donald Tresidder, the university's president, was out of town, so Jones made an appointment to see the vice president, Alvin C. Eurich. Jones told Eurich that the English Department needed shaking up.

"That's why you're here," replied Eurich.

"We have to do something that doesn't threaten anyone in the department."

"I couldn't agree more," said Eurich. "What do you have in mind?"

"Well, no one is doing anything with creative writing. If we set up a writing division in the English Department, we would not threaten anybody."

"Sounds like a good idea to me. What will it cost?"

"About $75,000."

Eurich said he didn't know where he could get that sum of money, but he would try.

"You don't have to get it."

"What?"

"My brother will give me the money. All I need to do is ask him for it. He discovered some oil in Texas, and he'll give us the money."

Did Jones have anyone in mind to run the program?

Yes, he did, as a matter of fact.

"You have the idea, you have the money, and you have the man," said Eurich. "What's holding you up? Why don't we act?"

Tresidder took the proposal to the board of trustees, who approved it.[7]

Stegner wanted to name the fellowships after Ned Jones. Jones said nothing doing; they would be named after Stegner. The Jones Room was named after Ned, and the Jones lectureships after his brother, the chairman of the English Department. Thus was born the most successful writing program conceived and conducted under one director for a quarter century in this country. Those who passed through the creative writing program at Stanford during Stegner's time published many hundreds of books and garnered every conceivable literary award except the Nobel Prize. The diversity of their ideas enriched millions of readers.

WALLACE STEGNER IS remembered primarily as a writer of novels. Too little attention has been paid to how he helped spread the written words of others around the world. He aided not only the students he taught but also those who were in his creative writing program but did not encounter him in the classroom because of his half-time teaching load. His knowledge, experience, and character shaped the program and thus influenced them. A large number of writers sought his assistance outside the classroom. Then there were the writers who never met or corresponded with him but acknowledged his influence.

Among the fiction writers who passed through the Stanford program while Stegner was in charge were Edward Abbey, Peter S. Beagle, Wendell Berry, Eugene Burdick, Evan S. Connell, Ernest J. Gaines, Hannah Green, George V. Higgins, James D. Houston, Ken Kesey, Thomas McGuane, Larry McMurtry, Tillie Olsen, Robert Stone, Scott Turow, and Al Young. Raymond Carver, Harriet Doerr, Allan Gurganus, William Kittredge, and Tobias Wolff were there shortly after he departed. The poets in the program when Stegner was at Stanford included Thom Gunn, Robert Hass, Donald Justice, Philip Levine, N. Scott Momaday, and Robert Pinsky. The separation between prose and poetry during a subsequent career of writing was not as distinct as it had been at Stanford. For instance, Berry later wrote poetry and Momaday wrote novels. Momaday and McMurtry won Pulitzer Prizes, Robert Stone received a National Book Award, and Hass and Pinsky were poets laureate of the United States. Editors who had been students also contributed to the flow of words. Among them were Don Moser, a longtime editor of *Smithsonian* magazine; William Decker, an editor at McGraw-Hill, Dial, and Viking; and Henry Carlisle at Knopf.

The latter two were also novelists. Journalists, such as the environmentalist Harold Gilliam, were particularly prolific.

After he left Stanford, in 1971, Stegner counseled Barry Lopez, Ivan Doig, Terry Tempest Williams, and others in his generous manner. Gretel Ehrlich felt his influence from afar. There was correspondence with Rick Bass and David Rains Wallace. All of these writers had a definite western bias. Stegner, through his own writing, legitimized the topic of the American West among East Coast editors, and he made it possible for others to follow in his footsteps. Since his death, no such literary benefactor has emerged to take Stegner's place in the West.

There were others. The most humbling experience of all, for anyone who has taught, is to read through the files of the creative writing program collection in the Stanford University library. Yes, there are the letters from the great ones, those students who became household names. But there is far more correspondence from those who published little or not at all and wrote apologetically in later years to say thanks and to explain that they had always meant to write, or write more seriously, but just hadn't gotten around to it.

Most former students still addressed him as Professor or Mr. Stegner, some made it to Wally, and Robert Stone called him Prof. For almost all, there was at least time for a postcard in reply from Wally, if not a letter or the requested recommendation for a grant, fellowship, teaching position, or blurb for a forthcoming book. Those requests were themselves a major writing chore for Stegner. A novelist and former fellow wrote to Page, saying that he had told Wally he was too old to keep asking for recommendations for teaching jobs. Page said in reply that his father kept a file of letters for each applicant so that he might just repeat what he had written before and the task would not be too great a chore. The writer got the job.

The remarkable volume of correspondence of this kind from the years during and after Stegner's time at Stanford is a far greater testimony to the effectiveness of his teaching and his students' regard for him than the typical indications of a successful academic career, those being the number of publications, dissertations, and future teachers produced or overseen by a professor.

The creative writing program evolved over time. It included a creative writing center—that being the Jones Room, on the fourth floor of the main library—as well as fellowships and grants and a subsidy for visiting writers, prizes, and publication of an annual book of short stories. The poetry component was overseen by Yvor Winters for the first twenty years. Stegner, aided by his assistant, Richard Scowcroft, directed the overall program and the fiction component. Although Wally taught half-time, his administrative duties ate into the semesters he supposedly devoted full-time to writing.

Usually there were about a half-dozen fellows: two poets and the remainder fiction writers. The selection process was rigorous. To be a fellow was to stand out among one's peers and to be acknowledged as a potential star, although stardom was not always achieved. The writing classes were open to qualified undergraduates and to graduate students in other disciplines. After a time the prizes, in-house publications, and master's degree in creative writing were dropped. Besides the Stegner Fellows, there eventually were fellowships named for Truman Capote, Scowcroft, and Mirrielees. The Jean and Bill Lane Lecture Series brought well-known writers to the campus.[8]

It was Stegner's program regardless of who was responsible for what part of it, and it was to be virtually autonomous within the English Department. When there were encroachments upon his turf, Stegner vigorously defended the integrity and his concept of the program. Sometimes his temper erupted. He was not above academic politics.

FIRST OFF UPON arrival at Stanford, Stegner needed an assistant to help run the program and teach, since he would be absent half the time. Second, he needed a home. The family had been vagabond renters for the eight years it had been a unit of three.

Stegner was euphoric in the new setting. His letters to the people he loved and liked were full of jokes, puns, rhymes, and offhand literary allusions. For instance, he tossed some light verse into a letter to Dick Scowcroft at Harvard:

> *There once was a blonde from Nahant*
> *Whose panties were silken and scant*
> *Her boy was diminutive*
> *And split his infinitive*
> *You finish the damned thing, I can't.*[9]

To Ted Morrison, also at Harvard, he wrote:

> *Two Vermonters in a game of chess*
> *Both in check, both a mess.*

Tiptoe past, don't think them queer.
Trouble is they're Middleburied half the year.[10]

Stegner did not have to look far to find his assistant. Scowcroft, a native of Utah, was also a Briggs-Copeland instructor. They had gone to the same high school. Stegner's father had sold Scowcroft's brother his liquor. Scowcroft had had a five-minute encounter with Stegner at the University of Utah when the student asked the young instructor if he would judge a writing prize being offered by the campus literary magazine, which both men had edited. Scowcroft graduated in 1937, the year Stegner left Utah. He was a graduate student at Harvard, an aspiring writer, and the recent winner of a literary prize in a creative writing contest when he telephoned Wally and reminded him of their brief encounter in Utah. The two Utahans met in a Cambridge bar. Wally said he would get Scowcroft an appointment with Ted Morrison, who immediately hired him to teach freshman English.

Stegner now told Scowcroft that the students at Stanford were "exceptionally good" and were bound to get better because of the money available for fellowships and prizes. They were almost a separate entity in the English Department rather than its stepchild, as they were at Harvard. There were other advantages: they did not have to teach freshman composition courses; promotion was based on writing, not scholarship.[11]

Scowcroft accepted the position in the spring of 1947. He succeeded Stegner as director of the program in 1969 and served as chairman of the Stanford English Department in the 1970s. Scowcroft would write novels with a Utah setting and, like Stegner, be branded a western realist on campus. The two men became close friends, but there was a difference in their teaching techniques. Nancy Packer was a student of both and later taught with them. "Dick was the first among equals in class," she said. "Wally ran the class. He led the discussion."[12]

At the start the creative writing faculty consisted of Stegner, Scowcroft, and the poet Yvor Winters. Wally's office, which lacked a secretary, was the administrative center of the program. Stegner shared the office first with Scowcroft and later with various instructors. Since Stegner and Winters were the only Americanists in the English Department, they alternated teaching the large contemporary American literature survey course. Stegner's literature courses gradually evolved into "The Rise of Realism in the American Novel" and "The Contemporary Novel."

Besides the permanent faculty, which was expanded sparingly over the years, there were a number of writers and editors who taught for one or two sessions. They included Bernard DeVoto, Walter van Tilburg Clark, Malcolm Cowley, Frank O'Connor, and Katherine Anne Porter. Visitors dropped in for a few days. They included Saul Bellow, Elizabeth Bowen, Robert Frost, Aldous Huxley, Ted Morrison, Philip Roth, William Styron, and Jessamyn West.

Every visitor had special needs. The novelist Katherine Anne Porter, whom Stegner had met at Bread Loaf, was an example. Stegner was away the semester of her visit, so it was Scowcroft's task to look after her. After her whirlwind semester, he concluded: "She was an adventure. A vain, arrogant woman but beautiful and exciting, you know." All Porter had had to do was meet a class once a week and talk. Evan S. Connell, who would go on to write *Mrs. Bridge*, *Mr. Bridge*, and *Son of the Morning Star*, was taking Scowcroft's and Porter's classes at the time. Scowcroft gave her the best story in his class to critique, which happened to be one of Connell's. "She was brutal about it . . . and she missed that this was really a talented guy and she tore him to pieces," said Scowcroft. He said Connell "was sick" about what "she'd done to him in this class." At faculty parties the extravagantly dressed Porter would be alternately witty and vicious. In the middle of the semester she disappeared to receive an honorary degree from another college and returned in time to march in the commencement parade with the chairman of the English Department.[13]

LIFE WAS PLEASANT in California, "perhaps too pleasant," Stegner wrote the poet Witter Bynner; "I am suspicious when my saddle blanket has no burr under it."[14] The family lived in a rented house on the campus. They wanted a home and space to keep horses. They joined a cooperative housing venture, named Ladera, but it failed to get off the ground.

They eventually found seven acres on the rolling, oak-studded terrain of Los Altos Hills, borrowed money from Edith Mirrielees, sold a lot in Salt Lake City that they had been holding in case they wanted to return there, and began building their first and last year-round home in 1948. While Wally worked in the Huntington Library in southern California on his John Wesley Powell biography, Mary supervised construction.

The Stegners got some help from writing students. Three were employed to dig a large hole in which the water tank would be hidden. They could hardly dent the hard, dry clay soil. Stegner paid them anyway. They bought a bottle of champagne with the money, returned, and drank it together with the Stegners. The result was that the water tank remained above ground. The students built bookcases and gave them to the Stegners as a gift. The house was completed in 1949.

There were pig farms and orchards scattered along the narrow country road. Gradually there were changes. A white wooden gate, more New England than western, and a "Private Road" sign discouraged unwanted visitors. The driveway ascended steeply under a graceful archway of trees to what Stegner described as "the buttonhook," a reversal of direction at a large oak that flung the visitor backward onto a serene, flat knoll.

The house was a California statement for its time and a declaration by the Stegners that they had arrived, and meant to remain, in the state. The walkway to the house passed the customary California swimming pool, unheated in this case. The angular one-story structure, with floor-to-ceiling living room windows and a cathedral ceiling, encompassed an expansive view of the gently rounded foothills of the Coast Range within whose folds lay the nearby San Andreas Fault. It was a light and airy place in good weather. When it was buffeted by winter storms, it leaked. The house was hard to keep warm during the winter months, with only a living room fireplace. The electric heating system, for some reason embedded by the architect in the ceiling, never worked properly.

The house was best described as Bay Area modern in the style of a Joseph Eichler or as a William W. Wurster–type home set in splendid isolation rather than among the many Palo Alto look-alikes on the flats below Los Altos Hills. Such a home indicated a taste for good design and embraced the indoor-outdoor style of life that was made possible by a balmy climate and promoted by *Sunset* magazine. It was featured in a two-page photo spread in *House & Garden* in August of 1952 under the heading "An open plan, skillfully handled, gives privacy to every member of the family." The family was identified as "a writer, his musical wife, and their 15-year-old son."

The furnishings gave an indication of who lived there. The occupants of the 1,735-square-foot two-bedroom home were obviously rooted in the West but had intellectual interests and sensibilities that ranged much farther. The oak floors were covered with rugs of Mexican and American Indian design. Ansel Adams's photograph of the eastern escarpment of the Sierra Nevada as seen from Lone Pine dominated one wall. To Wally the photograph of dawn breaking over the Owens Valley signified "renewal, rebirth, reassurance" and enriched him, as did the choral movement from Beethoven's Ninth Symphony. Mary's baby grand piano added a musical dimension. The bookcases were filled with volumes that had been read. The furniture was of Scandinavian design.

A few steps outside the sliding glass door, and accessible from the deck, was Stegner's writing studio. More books lined the shelves. The manual typewriter was placed so that Wally wasn't distracted by the view. Light from a band of clerestory windows flooded in behind the desk. The desk, typewriter stand, and credenza were arranged in a U. Stegner was surrounded by comfortable clutter when he wrote.

A short distance below the main residence was a board-and-batten cabin that Wally had originally built as his study. It was first occupied full-time by Page when he was a graduate student at Stanford and then by Page, his wife, and baby son. Page was followed by others, such as the real-life young couple fictionalized in *All the Little Live Things* and various family members, students, instructors, and house sitters. Separate parking for the cottage and a trail that led below the main house meant privacy for the occupants of both residences and a long haul with groceries to the cottage. Wally usually demanded yard work in return for free or reduced rent; he tended to be a strict landlord.

The structures and grounds required a lot of upkeep. Stegner was constantly constructing something, fixing this and that, planting, chopping, mowing, scything to lessen the fire danger, and exterminating pests. The outdoor activity was therapy. He paid Page a quarter for every gopher he dispatched with his .410-gauge shotgun. Allowances were made for the survival of some forms of nature: a hole in the deck, for example, permitted an oak tree to rise unobstructed from below.

Having a home was exceedingly important to Stegner. The overall feeling of the house and the grounds was one of sanctuary. Stegner bought inexpensive cars, at one time purchasing secondhand fleet vehicles from a relative in Pennsylvania. He preferred putting his money into the house, which satisfied "my own need for security."[15]

Stegner quickly absorbed the subtle shifts between seasons in northern California. The storms of winter arrived with a pounce: "The trees heave and creak." The rain produced the anomaly of green grass juxtaposed with leafless trees in winter. Late spring brought strong winds and a sudden change in the grass from green to gold. A summer day began with fog, progressed to heat, and ended with the cool of evening. Fall was divided into October, Wally's least favorite month, when dusty stasis and the danger of brushfires prevailed, and November, when the early rains brought renewal again.

Stegner's life progressed in cycles too: writing and teaching interspersed with travel. It was a disciplined and controlled existence and thus quite productive over a long period of time. On a typical day, Wally rose early, served Mary breakfast in bed, and was writing by 8 a.m. He composed a few letters to warm up his two index fingers on the typewriter and then proceeded to the project at hand. A cigar also helped him start the day. His grandson remembered hearing the staccato clickety-clack of the steel-mounted letters striking the platen and the smell of cigar smoke in the study.

Stegner would knock off around 11 a.m., shower, shave, dress, have lunch, and be on campus for his one o'clock class. That might be his big lecture course, which would be followed by a writing workshop and office hours. Then he would drive home, have a drink or two, and eat dinner. He sat with Mary in the living room in his favorite Danish modern chair during the evening hours, grading papers and reading manuscripts.

There were occasional breaks. They entertained and were entertained in turn, played badminton with friends, went square dancing, and drove to the symphony in San Francisco. They preferred to save money and enjoy the view by having a picnic dinner overlooking the Golden Gate.

A variation on that schedule, if Stegner was not teaching that day or that semester, would involve gardening and odd jobs in the afternoon. One summer he rid the entire adjoining field of star thistles—no small feat. When he trimmed trees, he cut the branches into six-inch lengths to feed the stove in his study. There just might be time in the late afternoon, even if he was teaching, for a ride with Mary on the Stegners' horses, Babe and Trinket. The foothills were free of subdivisions then, and it was possible to ride over private property all the way to La Honda, on the west slope of the Coast Range.

AT THE SAME time, the Stegners were establishing a summer home on the East Coast. The Grays sold them 1.3 acres closer than their old property had been to Greensboro and their residences on Caspian Lake. The ever-frugal Wally salvaged the beams from the old farmhouse and eventually used them to construct the frame for a "shack" on Baker Hill. The planks were secured with wooden pins instead of nails. Page and a local carpenter built the modest cabin, with its high-ceilinged living room, kitchen, indoor bathroom, tiny bedroom, and sleeping loft, in 1963. Page's nearby log house was subsequently constructed from some of the eight thousand Norway pine trees that his father had planted on the first Greensboro property in 1940. The elm mantel and maple dining room table came from trees in his parents' yard. "We grew a house," said father and son on numerous occasions.

Greensboro was both a place without a personal past and familiar territory for Stegner. He could make out of it what he wanted. He felt safe there. New England values, as he perceived them, were his values and the values of an earlier West. Change was seemingly arrested in Vermont. He could detect the same historical cycles of development and abandonment that he wrote about in the West, but in Vermont those cycles were softened by fewer people drifting through the landscape, more families remaining in one place for generations, and the prolific vegetation. Unlike the western landscape, New England's healed quickly. "It demands to be trees. It wants to be trees," said Stegner, who was constantly cutting back the growth that infringed on his cabin and the view of the lake.[16]

Vermont did not mold Stegner as Saskatchewan and Utah had. It attracted him. It gave him the tranquillity, stability, and friendships that enabled him to write about other places. He was accepted by his seasonal peers: academics, other writers, and people of intellect and means. They also had their tiny cabins, called think houses, in which to work during the long summer mornings before it was time for a swim. For the first time in his life, Stegner was part of the landed gentry, albeit at the lower end of the summer economic scale.

And then he made the mistake of writing about Greensboro and had to absent himself from that retreat while feelings healed. Stegner's first novel set in New England was published in 1947. Although he located the lakeside community in New Hampshire and called it Westwick, the setting was a thinly disguised Greensboro, Vermont. Neither the summer residents nor the locals, who did not mix, liked their portrayals in *Second Growth*. Lewis Hill, who became the community historian, wrote Stegner: "There is no doubt that the 'natives' don't fall all over themselves for the campers' friendship: but the reason is obvious; the campers, at least a part of them, don't encourage or expect this equality idea."[17]

The natives were those who were born in Greensboro and lived there year-round. Then there were outsiders and *outsiders*, as depicted in the novel. The first level were the WASP summer residents who had "camps," meaning cabins or houses, as such seasonal structures are described in New Englandese. The second level was the lone Jewish couple, Ruth Liebowitz and Abe Kaplan in the book. They were a thinly disguised Esther and Louis Kesselman in reality, childless friends of the Stegners' who occasionally babysat for Page.

Esther was the Greensboro village librarian for fifteen years. A member of the library board dropped by one day to compliment her on the fine job she was doing. "I didn't know there were Jews like you," he said.

"How many Jews have you known?" asked Esther. "Jews are just people like anyone else," she said.[18]

That was one of the book's messages that didn't go down well in Greensboro. Stegner, who had recently completed *One Nation*, examined the social strata of a small New England community in the novel, and that made some people uncomfortable.

Wally wondered why he and his family were never completely accepted by the natives despite the fact that they had spent a winter in Greensboro and their son had gone to the local school. One of the older native inhabitants explained: "Well, a cat can crawl into the oven and have kittens, but you wouldn't call them biscuits, would you?"[19]

BACK IN CALIFORNIA, Wally was, as usual, extremely busy. Besides working on the Powell book and serving as West Coast editor for Houghton Mifflin, he was teaching at Stanford, writing magazine articles, collecting short stories for a book that would be published as *The Women on the Wall* by Houghton Mifflin in 1950, trying to sell a collection of his travel pieces to the same publisher, suggesting that Houghton Mifflin acquire the rights to *Big Rock*, which had gone out of print, and having a very difficult time shaping a novel that would eventually emerge as *Joe Hill*. Both Stegner and his publisher thought that the historical novel about the militant labor leader of the Industrial Workers of the World, popularly known as the Wobblies, would recapture the success he'd had with *Big Rock*.

Stegner described his writing life at this time to one of the executives at his publishing house, using the third person as if to distance himself from this strange creature:

This business of the literary life of W. Stegner is a little hard to come at. This Stegner goes to his typewriter regularly, and spends certain hours after breakfast. Until recently, when he began teaching again, he did this regularly seven days a week for many months. What emerged from this protracted effort was two short stories, three or four articles, and a certain number of pages of a novel about Joe Hill. This novel we do not think about too much, because it is giving this Stegner hell.[20]

Travel was also an integral part of the Stegners' lives. Most of the trips were working vacations, from which Wally derived material for travel articles, short stories, or books yet to be written. He also worked on novels in progress while on the road.

Beginning with their arrival in Palo Alto, the Stegners explored California and the Southwest. They spent ten days in the Sierra Nevada and the Santa Lucia Mountains above Big Sur in the summer of 1945. Stegner's mind and imagination were always working. Riding horses to the ridgeline of the coastal mountains, Wally and Mary looked down "on waves that have rolled in from Japan and redwoods that were growing there before the Shoguns."[21] They camped, hiked, ran rivers, and rode horses in the interior West. Researching the Powell book was a major incentive, as were revisiting old haunts and discovering new places.

They also traveled widely in foreign lands, mostly at the expense of others. The Rockefeller Foundation, the Guggenheim Foundation, the Fulbright Program, the Department of State, Stanford's overseas program, and the Arabian American Oil Company, better known as Aramco, financed most of their longer trips during Wally's years at Stanford.

The Stegners circled the globe in one seven-month period. The Rockefeller Foundation's purpose for sponsoring the trip in 1950 and 1951 was to connect an American writer with writers in Asia. Young Page went with them. On most trips in the West he had been the only child among adults. Now he was the only child among adults and foreigners of all ages. It was not a happy trip for him. He caught typhoid in Egypt, his father nursing him back to health from near death; spent numerous boring nights alone in hotel rooms while his parents dined with writers; and was hospitalized for two weeks in Manila after suffering a massive reaction to the drugs he had taken to cure the typhoid.

Not all of Stegner's foreign travels were successful ventures. For some reason his more commercially oriented nonfiction projects never worked out as originally envisioned. That had been the case with the *Look* magazine project and was the case as well with his two-week trip to Saudi Arabia in 1955. Stegner's work for Aramco, a subsidiary of two American oil companies, became a victim of company and international politics. What resulted years later was a bland series of articles in the company magazine and a book, *Discovery! The Search for Arabian Oil,* which never circulated outside the confines of the corporation.

Looking backward from the perspective of a post-9/11 world in 2003, Robert Vitalis, a fellow in New York University's International Center for Advanced Study, found Stegner's work overly praiseful of the oil company's accomplishments while denigrating the existence of the Arabs before the Americans' arrival. "The book complicates the picture that we have of Stegner as a destroyer of American western myths and a forerunner of the social and environmental turn in western history," Vitalis wrote. "In writing about Saudi Arabia, Stegner does all the things, deploys all the tropes that his admirers say he avoids in his work on the American West."[22]

The book, much worked over by Stegner and the many fussy hands at Aramco, certainly does that in its introductory chapters but then settles down to an evenhanded narrative. It was, after all, a job handsomely paid for by the company. The subtle twist, not an uncommon Stegner touch, comes at the end, and somehow he got it past the oil company censors when the book was finally published in 1971. It seems unusually prophetic now. "The American involvement in Middle Eastern economic, cultural and political life," Stegner wrote, "would grow deeper, more complicated, and more sobering. Not inconceivably, the thing they all thought of as 'progress' and 'development' would blow them all up, and their world with it."[23]

Mary and Wally made multiple trips to Great Britain and the continent, and single journeys to Scandinavia, Greece, Lebanon, Syria, Iran, Cyprus, Central and South America, Africa, and the South Pacific. "The boundaries of the world that I was dragged out into from Eastend in 1920 had widened beyond belief," said Stegner.[24]

It was Mary who mainly had the travel bug. As the Vietnam War was heating up in the fall of 1967, Stegner wrote Scowcroft from Vermont: "Mary keeps saying why can't we take a trip. My God. It does not seem to me the proper time to bear the blessing of our civilization and the message of our culture to darkest Africa, and I will not take up the State Department's open offer."[25]

. . .

AS THE AROUND-THE-WORLD trip with his parents indicated, it wasn't easy being the son of Wally and Mary. They were an extremely close couple and didn't have much room for anyone else in their tightly woven, interdependent relationship. Page became what was known as a difficult child. His father described him at the age of eleven as a "somewhat unhappy and maladjusted child."[26] Anger and impatience were inbred character traits in the male Stegners. Wally lost his temper with Page just as his father had exploded at him. One time he chased the back-talking teenager with a scythe. Page believed he was fleeing for his life.

Except for what he had written, Stegner's past was a closed book to his son and grandchildren. He never took Page to visit his roots in Iowa or Saskatchewan. The few times they were in Salt Lake City together, they never drove around to see old haunts. "He was very closed about that," said Page, who had to learn about George Stegner from *The Big Rock Candy Mountain*.[27] Wally and Page's son—also named Page, after his grandmother's maiden name—played a game. They addressed each other as George. "Hey, George," one would call to the other, and in that way the grandson learned the name of his paternal great-grandfather. Wally started the game. The grandson's "ready, fire, aim" attitude had reminded him of his father. Toward his grandchildren, Stegner was more patient and less demanding than he had been toward his son. He lectured them about behavior and values. Mary tended to be a fussy, doting, worrying grandmother. The grandchildren don't remember any touching among family members, but they were aware of the presence of love.[28]

Wally and Mary applied high standards to their son, Page. There were few pats on the back. Chores had to be done on time regardless of reasons or excuses. The boy retreated into silence, intransigence, and rebellion during his teenage years. "The real bad times are always adolescence," said Wally "Automobiles, beer, and haircuts and things like that."[29] Perhaps he was recalling his own youth in Salt Lake.

Beginning with Exeter, Page was thrown out of one private boarding school after another. Two weeks before he was supposed to graduate from Palo Alto High School, he was expelled for the same reason: drinking liquor (it was the pre-drug era). He never did graduate from high school. Page enrolled at the University of Colorado and rode freight trains to Boulder. Two years and some good grades later, he was accepted at Stanford, primarily because of his last name, he believes. Page majored in history, and his grades and relationship with his father improved. He was never close to his mother.

It was the 1960s. Page spent time on the fringes of the Ken Kesey crowd in La Honda and played guitar in a bluegrass band. He had capable hands, perhaps the hands of a carpenter or a farmer. However, he chose a career path that led to writing and teaching at the university level. Page obtained a master's degree in journalism at Stanford and entered the doctoral program in the Department of English. His first wife, Marion, worked full-time and helped put him through graduate school. They lived with their baby son in the cabin below the main house, which had been Wally's first study.

Page took his father's course in the contemporary American novel, receiving a B plus. "Room for improvement" was the familiar parental message. Stegner's teaching assistants objected, pointing out that his son's grade average merited an A, and Page got an A as his final grade. His father wrote a friend at the time: "Page maintained himself as a graduate student with an A and B last quarter. Now he mumbles German paradigms and lines from *Tintern Abbey*. This is the strangest thing of all to me, but I keep my peace and do not vent my wonder aloud. How long it lasts is anybody's guess."[30]

Page's career and the places in which he chose to live assumed a familiar pattern. Despite his father's skepticism, his literary interests lasted long enough for him to obtain his degree, begin teaching at Ohio State University, write novels, journalism, and nonfiction, and head the creative writing program at the University of California at Santa Cruz, from which he eventually retired. Page maintains a summer home in Greensboro close to what had been his parents' residence. He bought a house in Salt Lake City but never lived there. During the winter he lives in Santa Fe, where his father died.

THE FIRST TWENTY years at Stanford were Wally's best stretch of teaching. Stegner honed his skills, which were considerable, and his program attracted talented students. An assessment of university-wide courses by the Associated Students of Stanford University had this to say about Stegner's contemporary American fiction class in 1963: "Stegner has a talent for delivering lectures in an easy conversational tone, making four of them a week such an enjoyable experience that a number of students suggested increasing the number to five. . . . The course is highly recommended for anyone who wants to study the modern novel from the point of view of a novelist who communicates both enthusiasm and extensive knowledge."[31]

As for his creative writing course, this was how one student, Ed McClanahan, approached it: "And so when I arrived at Stanford that September, I was still pretty full of myself . . . until the subsequent Wednesday afternoon, which found me cowering in what I realized, too late, was perhaps the most high-powered creative-writing class in all of academe, the Stanford English Department's CW 501, a fabled graduate workshop in which four places were permanently reserved for holders of the coveted Wallace E. Stegner Fellowships in Creative Writing."[32]

When Stegner looked back, it was the initial years at Stanford that he was most nostalgic about. There were barbecues with beer and wine and singing, particularly by Wally, whose western ballads were imprinted for life on the memory of his students. "In the end," he said, "we hobnobbed more with the students than we did with the faculty." In September of each year when Stegner was present, there was a reception for new writing students at his home. They were awed. The light, airy structure on top of the hill seemed like the type of place a writer should inhabit. The students were shown the study, the holy of holies. They absorbed the layout, seeking physical clues for writerly success. "I had never been admitted into a working writer's house," said James Houston. "To be admitted into his study, to see where he sat was a great validation of a place I wanted to get to. Someone has to give you permission to put words on a page in your house," said the novelist, who now works in his home in nearby Santa Cruz.[33]

The teacher learned from his students. "I certainly got a lot more sophisticated about technique than I was before." On the twentieth anniversary of the creative writing program, he said, "Looking back over it, as it was and as it now is, I cannot think of any serious changes that I would make."[34]

Stegner and others adapted the Socratic method to the teaching of creative writing, he refined it, and then his many students spread it further, to the point where it is the dominant technique of teaching writing today. What this method meant in practice was giving students the impression that they were pulling their own teeth or filling their own cavities—under a heavy dose of novocaine, meaning a protective environment—while the teacher gently guided the operation from a distance. Guidance, said Stegner, was the key. "Instead of a lecture, what goes on is a discussion which with luck may lead to some sort of illumination or consensus." It was more an attitude than a technique. The best teaching was done "by members of the class upon one another." A rapport had to be established immediately "because if the students did not feel in the company of friends, there would be no exchange of ideas."[35]

Stegner read most of the manuscripts aloud in class so that students supposedly would not know the author (although invariably the writer was known through various clues), and therefore the ensuing discussion would not be personal. His cultivated, almost clipped voice, with its distinct diction, careful modulation, and lack of any hint of western-ness, took on the full range of material he was required to read. He did not impose himself on the material but simply "put the story in the air," ready for discussion, as one student commented. The exchange of ideas ranged from subdued to spirited, with Stegner serving as a referee and commentator when needed.

Wendell Berry left this description of Stegner as teacher:

> He was not a "colorful" teacher. He was not a dogmatist or a guru, nor did he attempt to be a pal to his students. There was nothing eccentric, odd, or extreme that he tried to pass along. He had, as you would expect, a fairly settled idea of what good writing was, and a fairly settled idea about what it took to be a good writer. He was simply doing his best, always, to help his students become better writers. He did it mainly by paying close attention to what they had written and making practical and often detailed or technical comments about what they had done. Typically, he would come into the class, sit down, receive the attention that he never had to require from his students, read a manuscript, and lead a discussion about it. As a performance, it was utterly undramatic and unegotistical, and it was anything but authoritarian. And yet no teacher that I ever had made me so acutely aware of my obligation to be at work and to work well. I think this was simply because one sensed in him the same sense of obligation.[36]

The creative writing program at Stanford, Stegner explained, fell between the artistic and the critical approaches to teaching writing. The artistic meant freer expression, and the critical was defined by a more traditional, more dogmatic approach. Attitudes toward writing styles had to be flexible, although some thought Wally was fairly rigid in what he tolerated. He certainly had no love of the experimentalism that was the trend of the late 1960s. Invariably, Stegner the writer influenced Stegner the teacher and his students. Stegner was a realist, meaning, as he defined it, that "any good writing is created out of reality," as had been the case with his very first published short story. The creative writer, said Stegner, "does not deal in concepts, in formulated patterns of thought, but in *iconic* ways. . . . He is concerned with people, places, actions, feelings, sensations." The writers Stegner most admired were Mark Twain, Joseph Conrad, Anton Chekhov, Willa Cather, and Robert Frost. They wrote out of the experience of their lives, as did Stegner.[37]

Why was the Stanford Creative Writing Program so successful under Stegner? There was, of course, the writer and teacher himself. There were few such programs in the country at the time; thus there was great demand for the small number of openings and minimal stipend. The selection process conducted by Stegner, Scowcroft, and Winters was extremely rigorous. Last, there was the lure of California—not only the mountains, deserts, rugged coast, and pleasurable cities, but also the salubrious climate and the Mediterranean palaces of the Farm.

Beyond the program and the department was the role of the university in the cold war years. Stegner took on the computer pioneer and Stanford graduate David Packard, who gave a speech to the local chapter of the American Association of University Professors. To Stegner, Packard seemed to advocate "an institution dedicated to the production of technicians, scientists, experts, leaders . . . with half their electrons and with half their nuclei knocked whobberjawed." What was needed, Stegner said in a letter to Packard, and what should be the core of the university was not applied knowledge but "pure" knowledge to be studied for its own sake and "specialists who can generalize and generalists with a specialty."[38]

More broadly, Wally outlined what he believed at the time in a short essay for Edward R. Murrow's book *This I Believe*. Stegner clearly fit the era, which was the dawn of the Eisenhower years. He emphasized moderation and the old-fashioned virtues of generosity, steadfastness, courage, self-control, self-respect, responsibility, and conscience dictated not by organized religion but, rather, by what is absorbed from "the tradition and the society which has bred us." Stegner feared the "immoderate zeal" that was fast bearing down like a rogue asteroid on his generation and would land with a jarring impact during the next decade.[39]

HIS STUDENTS RANGED from the shy and the respectful to the bumptious.

Ed Abbey, who arrived as a Stegner Fellow in 1957, was quiet and meek compared with the voice of the raving dam hater he later assumed on paper. Stegner remembered him as shy, aloof, and, like his son Page, "not as curmudgeonly as they sound." He lived on the coast, in Half Moon Bay.

Abbey and Stegner had what Wally called "a little tiff." Abbey was working on *Desert Solitaire* and wanted to leave Stanford, work on the book, and still collect his fellowship money. Stegner recalled saying, "God, no, we can't give you a fellowship when you aren't here." Wally thought that Abbey was upset over that decision. He later concluded that he should have granted Abbey's request.[40]

Don Moser was a classmate of Abbey's. Before going on to edit *Smithsonian*, Moser was an editor at *Life* magazine, for which Abbey occasionally wrote. Abbey insisted on calling him Mr. Moser. Probably, the editor thought, that was because "you can never trust a guy who wears a necktie." Moser never forgot the lead of a story on mountain lions that Abbey wrote for *Life*: "The mountain lion eats sheep. Any animal that eats sheep can't be all bad."[41]

Abbey took Stegner to task for an "excess of moderation" in a review of a collection of Wally's essays on the West titled *The Sound of Mountain Water*. In *The New York Times Book Review*, Abbey, who had perfected outrageousness as a literary device, found Stegner's "extremity of forbearance" taxing in the face of "that monstrous tragicomedy . . . that we call the United States of North America" in 1969.[42]

Eight years later and six years after publication of *Angle of Repose*, Abbey wrote Stegner rather wistfully: "Dear Stegner—After all these years I finally got around to reading 'Angle of Repose.' A splendid novel—you had me in tears for nearly 400 pages. (I wish I could settle down and write some solid fiction like that. Oh well, what the hell.) Now I'll have to read your other later novels." The note was written on a postcard, the front of which bore a quotation by Stegner about wilderness.[43]

When Abbey died, in 1989, Stegner, who could not attend the memorial service in the desert near Moab, Utah, sent a letter to be read at the gathering by Wendell Berry. "He was a red hot moment in the conscience of the country," Stegner wrote, "and I suspect that the half-life of his intransigence will turn out to be comparable to that of uranium. We will miss him."[44] Berry described the event to Stegner:

> The memorial service for Edward Abbey was held on a big slab of white rock slanting out toward a whole world of mountains and deserts. Many people were there, struggling in singly and in little bunches, on foot, for an hour or an hour and a half. There were some speeches, poems, instrumental music, singing, reminiscences. I read your letter, for which I know that many people were grateful, and then a little statement of my own and a couple of poems. It didn't last long. There was no disturbance of the place. As the people left, you could feel the big stillness returning.[45]

KEN KESEY, WENDELL BERRY, and Larry McMurtry arrived in a clump shortly before 1960. Robert Stone came just afterward. Other writers made their mark during the golden age of the program. Malcolm Cowley, a New York editor and critic and guest lecturer, recalled that six novels being written in his creative writing class at the time were later published, including Kesey's *One Flew over the Cuckoo's Nest*.

Kesey had applied for a creative writing fellowship, was turned down, and entered the program on a Woodrow Wilson fellowship in the fall of 1958. "Neither Wally nor I thought he had a particularly important talent," Scowcroft recalled. "Wally said to me once he was sort of a fairly talented illiterate." Stegner taught Kesey in classes on writing and the development of the short story. At the time, Kesey was working on a novel that was never published. Stegner liked his writing most of the time. What "kind of teed me off," he said, were "his extracurricular activities."[46]

Stegner thought he had been bamboozled when Kesey hiked all the way to his house to ask if he might continue to attend classes after completing the program. Wally said yes, thinking he intended to pay, but that was not the case. Kesey then told Scowcroft that Stegner had said he could attend classes for free. In fact, creative writing fellows were permitted to audit classes after their fellowship expired, but Kesey had been a different type of fellow in many ways. He was one of the first and one of the most publicized free spirits of the 1960s.

Stegner departed for Europe in the summer of 1959 and was gone for one year. He recruited Cowley to teach one quarter. The Irish writer Frank O'Connor taught another quarter. O'Connor told Stegner that he wanted to come to Stanford because his doctor had forbidden him to drink Irish whiskey and put him on a wine diet. Teaching at Stanford would be an opportunity to sample California wines, which he had heard were quite good.

Kesey liked the writing team Stegner had assembled, with one exception. He did not get along with O'Connor, who tended toward a fixed writing formula. "I always compared Stegner to Vince Lombardi," said Kesey; "he put together not only a good team but a good team of supporting coaches. Dick Scowcroft was so sweet and gentle that he complemented Malcolm Cowley, who was a gruff man."[47]

Whatever Kesey said about Stegner afterward, he recognized at the time that Stegner was correct in emphasizing point of view. Point of view—in this case the telling of the story in *Cuckoo's Nest* by Chief Bromden—was "perhaps the most significant . . . [decision] he made in writing the novel," wrote Kesey's biographer, Stephen Tanner. "Most critics agree that his treatment of point of view is a masterstroke," Tanner added. Kesey wrote to his friend Ken Babbs, who had also been a creative writing student at Stanford, "Wally may have been much more correct than us avanting guards wanted to give him credit for—maybe the largest problem in fiction *is* PV."[48]

Cowley remembered Kesey as looking "stolid and self-assured." He had the build of a football halfback and "a neck like the stump of a Douglas fir." He read chapters of *Cuckoo's Nest* to the all-star class that assembled around the oval table in the Jones Room in the fall of 1960. The fifteen students included Kesey, Tillie Olsen, Larry McMurtry, and Peter Beagle (Viking published Beagle's *A Fine and Private Place* that same year). Cowley "was excited by having found something original" in Kesey's work in progress. He described the unfolding of the novel:

His first drafts must have been written at top speed; they were full of typing errors, as if words had come piling out of a Greyhound bus too fast to have their clothes brushed. Later Kesey would redo the manuscript and correct most of the misspellings. He had his visions, but he didn't have the fatal notion of some Beat writers, that the first hasty account of a vision was a sacred text not to be tampered with. He revised, he made deletions and additions; he was working with readers in mind.[49]

Cowley's description of Kesey's careful technique is at odds with Kesey's own description of writing the novel in a drug-induced hallucinatory haze.

Out of curiosity and the need for the $20 a week he was paid for participating, and in keeping with his devil-may-care jock attitude, Kesey volunteered to take a number of hallucinatory drugs as part of the Central Intelligence Agency's supersecret MK-ULTRA project at the veterans hospital in nearby Menlo Park. The drugs included magic mushroom capsules, mescaline, amphetamines, and Kesey's favorite, LSD. He was observed on Tuesdays for eight hours and then released. A job as an orderly in the mental ward of the same hospital allowed him to liberate drugs for home use and gave him the raw material for his novel in progress.

What Kesey and others discovered at the time was a temporary condition that gave them the illusion of increased perception, an illusion that did not necessarily make rational sense on paper. His sudden and only success in writing, Kesey said, came from being "dimensional." That meant, in his words, "I saw that everything that you see from this position, if you're also able to see it from over here, you've got two views of it."[50] Of course, this was gibberish to Stegner.

Cowley informed Stegner in August 1961 that Viking would publish Kesey's novel and that the manuscript had been given to the youngest of its editors. "Much enthusiasm among the younger Viking editors," Cowley wrote. "It's interesting how the judgments on that book divide along age lines—Kesey speaks for the younger generation and, liking his work too, I've been an exception among the gaffers."[51]

The break between teacher and student came in a 1963 published interview with Gordon Lish. At Stanford, Kesey said, he had learned a lot from Cowley, and from Stegner he had learned

> just never to teach in college. You go back and read his early stuff, *On a Darkling Plain* maybe. Fine work. Then you try his later stuff and you find he's not writing to people any longer, not to people he knows and loves, anyway. He's writing to a classroom and his colleagues.
>
> [LISH] And that's the fault of teaching?
>
> Big time teaching, yes. A man becomes accustomed to having two hundred people gather every day at one o'clock giving him all their attention—because he's clever, good looking, famous, and has a beautiful voice. That can't happen without affecting a

man's writing—the wrong way. And when that happens the academic life has come to the end of its usefulness for the writer.[52]

Kesey knew he had made a mistake. He went to Stegner's office immediately after the interview was published to tell him that he hadn't
meant what he said, but he was too late. Stegner's anger was implacable.
His secretary would not allow Kesey to see him. From that point on,
Kesey sought to make amends through public utterances. There was no
public response from Stegner.

There were private letters from Stegner, however, that indicated his
intense dislike of Kesey and what he represented, that being anarchy.
Many, including Stegner's editor at Viking, thought Kesey was his
model for the hippie Jim Peck in *All the Little Live Things*. No, that was
not the case, said Stegner. Peck "is mainly a faddist and fool." He considered Kesey dangerous because he was "a person of more force than
mind. I think Kesey is crazy as a coot, and dangerous, and rather special in his charismatic qualities, and with what was once a fairly big raw
talent."[53]

Wendell Berry sent Wally a copy of *The Country of Marriage* in
1973. It was a lovely collection of poems, said Stegner.

> Then I got to your poem to Ken Kesey and Ken Babbs, and I
> said, in the idiom of my time, Shit, what can Wendell be thinking
> of, commemorating that garbage? He's too good to be raking
> around among that old two-holer privy. Then I thought, maybe
> he's composting it. On that comfort I rest. But you stopped me
> reading, and I haven't got past that page. Prejudice, no doubt.
> But if it's really being composted, I forgive you.

The poem, "Kentucky River Junction," celebrates being apart and yet
together: "Free-hearted men / have the world for words," Berry wrote
of his friends.[54]

Wally refused to meet with Kesey when he came to speak at the university years later. Kesey spoke glowingly of his Stanford experience in
his campus speeches. When he talked with Wally's close friend T. H.
(Tom) Watkins in 1991, Watkins told Stegner, "Kesey allowed as how
you had at one time or another declared him to be 'uneducable.' "
Watkins said, "He seemed to accept the truth of the matter with
equanimity."[55]

When walking with Kesey on a street in New York City, the writer

Barry Lopez asked him about the antipathy between himself and Stegner. Kesey said, "I think he just really misunderstood a callow boy from Oregon." When Lopez telephoned him in 1993 to say that Stegner was in serious condition in a Santa Fe hospital, Kesey replied, "I'm so sorry." Later that year, Kesey minimized their differences, saying they were a matter of contrasting generations: "And whether you liked him or not, and I liked him, and I actually think that he liked me; it's just that we were on different sides of the fence. As I took LSD, and he drank Jack Daniel's, we drew the line between us right there."[56]

MITCHELL J. (MITCH) STRUCINSKI was in the creative writing class with Kesey. As a Stegner Fellow, he was a cut or two above the Woodrow Wilson scholar. The thirty-three-year-old Strucinski hung out with the former frat boy and wrestler from the University of Oregon, but he came from a different background.

Strucinski had quit high school in Chicago and served in the merchant marine during World War II, where a bookish officer encouraged him to write. But he drifted into a life of crime: burglary, larceny, carrying a concealed weapon, mail theft, and forgery, which earned him time in the federal prison on McNeil Island in Washington. The warden there and Edward Weeks, the editor of *The Atlantic*, which had published two of Strucinski's stories, urged Stegner to admit him to the creative writing program. Strucinski took up pipe smoking, married an English major, successfully completed the program, and became a father. He spent much of his time in the special collections section of the library at Stanford, where valuable books and original documents are stored.

In October of 1960, Elmer Robinson, a bibliophile and former mayor of San Francisco, was paging through the catalog of a Manhattan bookstore when he noticed a 1916 letter from Woodrow Wilson on sale—a letter that he had donated, as part of a collection of historical documents, to the Stanford library. Library officials confirmed that the documents were missing, along with a collection of presidential autographs, dating from George Washington's to Stanford's own Herbert Hoover.

Suspicion fell on Strucinski. He denied the thefts and then left town. What kind of person was he? asked a reporter from *Time* magazine. "He was a talented boy," said Stegner. "He earned his fellowship honestly." Stegner wrote his former student, begging him to give himself up for the sake of his wife, who was charged with receiving stolen goods, and his infant son. "You can still salvage something," he said, although conceding that the evidence looked "extremely bad." Strucinski replied that he was concerned about his wife and child and would do nothing to harm them. He added, "You have been a kind and good friend to me, and I thank you . . . once more for everything."[57]

Strucinski surrendered and wrote to Stegner from prison, first apologizing, then expressing regret, and finally stating, "I blew it, all by myself." He added, "I only hope that your experience with me has not chilled your capacity for compassion" because it would then "be a tragedy of a higher order." Strucinski wondered if his teacher had any idea what the quotation in *Time*, about Strucinski's having earned his fellowship honestly, meant to him. "I'd like to thank you for the remark," he wrote, "even though it does have something of the ring of an epitaph."[58]

THE ACTION SHIFTED from the classroom to the small cottages adjacent to the campus, which had been built for the military during the war. Stegner referred to the area as "the ragged little bohemia."[59] That was where Kesey lived with his wife and small child. And that was where the Pied Piper of the creative writing program led those of his fellow classmates who had become disenchanted with O'Connor. The fiery O'Connor was too dogmatic for Kesey and his crowd. Others remained in class to relish the interchanges with someone who talked about "Jimmy Joyce" and "Willie Yeats" and had not only acted in the Abbey Theatre but had also directed productions during the Irish literary revival.

Stegner defined O'Connor's problems with his students and at the same time revealed the essence of the workshop method. He thought O'Connor was too much the actor. "In the writing seminar the actor had no place and the teacher was only another writer," Stegner wrote in an appreciation of O'Connor. "The class was not an audience and the response was not applause, but argument, discussion, debate, dissension, assertion and denial, each one defending his territory and trying to drive off intruders and aggressors who threatened his theory, his art or his ego."[60]

From the first day of class, Peter Beagle recalled, O'Connor listed writers, styles, and genres he couldn't stand, fantasy being one of the latter—and Beagle's forte. That was a challenge to the twenty-one-year-old writer, described by Cowley as having plump cheeks and a solemn, boyish smile. Earlier that year, Stegner had written to Scowcroft about the manuscript Beagle had submitted with his application for a fellowship: "I have been reading Beagle's book, and I don't wonder you gave him a fellowship. He's red hot—terrific. You should have hired him as head of the writing program. Or second assistant, anyway."[61] That manuscript became *A Fine and Private Place*.

After he arrived in Stanford, Beagle—Jewish and from New York City—discovered that he felt more at home in the urban environment of Berkeley. He holed up there for a day and a half and wrote "Come Lady Death," published as a short story in *The Atlantic*, made into an opera, and often anthologized. O'Connor read it to the workshop class in his booming and well-modulated Abbey Theatre voice and then announced grandly: "This is a beautifully written story. I don't like it, and that's that."[62]

In contrast to Beagle's more boisterous classmates, <u>Larry McMurtry</u> was a quiet presence. Shy, thin with a lean face dominated by thick, dark-rimmed glasses, the Texan was working on his second novel, *Leaving Cheyenne*, when he was accepted as a fellow. Shortly before he arrived at Sanford in the early fall of 1960, Harper & Brothers offered him a $250 advance for *Horseman, Pass By*, which would become the movie *Hud*. He first had to produce an "acceptable" manuscript, however. McMurtry worked on *Horseman* in the seminar conducted by Malcolm Cowley.

James Houston, who was in that class, was greatly impressed by the way McMurtry honored his own words. They were impeccably typed on twenty-four-pound bond paper. As McMurtry read, he carefully lifted each page—"like scripture," Houston said—out of a box and set it aside.[63]

Between the workshop readings and an extensive correspondence with his editor at Harper, McMurtry eventually produced a publishable manuscript while at Stanford. But he had felt pressured by his editor and was less than satisfied with the book. He wrote Stegner after *Horseman* was published: "I ran it through one too many drafts. I think if I had quit it about the time I got to Stanford, instead of about December, it would have been all to the good."[64] Cowley described the young McMurtry:

He was a slight, sallow, bespectacled cowboy who wore Texas boots and spoke in a pinched variety of the West Texas drawl.

Gradually I learned that he had read almost everything in English literature, besides a great deal in French, and that he had written a dissertation on the scabrous poetry of John Wilmot, Earl of Rochester. Larry supplemented his Stanford fellowship by finding rare books on the ten-cent tables of Salvation Army outlets and reselling them to dealers; *Book Prices Current* was his bible.[65]

McMurtry was Beagle's first friend on the West Coast. The Texan and his wife lived in San Francisco and were extremely poor. The New Yorker made fun of country music. McMurtry replied gently that where he grew up, people lived by the words and emotions in those songs. From that moment on, Beagle gained an appreciation for such music. Beagle also recalled McMurtry's habit of telling tall tales with a straight face. He got most of his reading done, he said, while driving on the straight country roads of Texas.[66]

Although McMurtry was in Stegner's home for social occasions, he never studied with him because Wally was on leave the year McMurtry was a fellow. They corresponded, and Stegner read his books. He thought those that dealt with the past, like *Horseman* and *Lonesome Dove*, for which McMurtry received the Pulitzer Prize, were good, "intelligible" books. "I think when he gets into the present he's less persuasive," said Stegner, "like so many other western writers."[67]

THE SCENE AT the Kesey house on Perry Lane was one of sex, drugs, and folk songs shading into rock and roll. These were the extracurricular activities that Stegner abhorred. In the words of the denizens of "the dawning of the age of Aquarius," "the times they . . . [were] a-changin'," and Bob Stone was reveling in them. Stone had all the experience in living that a young writer of his time could ever desire and that Stegner could appreciate. He was a self-made man whose life read like an overwrought novel.

Stegner asked Stone in 1967 to furnish him with notes on his life history that he could incorporate into a *Saturday Review* article he was preparing on *A Hall of Mirrors*, Stone's first published novel and the manuscript he had been working on at Stanford. Stone began: "I was born in Brooklyn, grew up in Manhattan. My mother was a school teacher who lost her job in the school system so we lived in a marginal state of near poverty, lapsing on occasion into the Welfare class." His mother was his only known relative. As a young child he lived at a

Catholic boarding school, an experience that resonated with Stegner's time in a Catholic orphanage.

Grades and discipline were issues in school. Stone began writing fiction in high school but dropped out in 1955, at the age of seventeen, to join the navy. His far-right political leanings—he had belonged to a sort of junior John Birch Society and was an admirer of Mussolini ("off the record, for Christ's sake")—began drifting leftward as he cruised the Mediterranean and Antarctic waters. There was a brief stint at New York University. He worked as a copy boy at the New York *Daily News* and was immersed in the New York Beat scene. Marriage followed. The couple moved to New Orleans. Stone got a job with the Census Bureau, joined the seamen's union, and shipped out a couple of times. He also did telephone sales. He and his wife lived in the French Quarter "with all kinds of wild stuff happening around us."[68] New Orleans was the setting for *A Hall of Mirrors*. Then they moved back to New York City.

Stone sent the first chapters of the novel in progress to Stegner and was given a fellowship. Traveling from New York to California in the late summer of 1962 "was like going from black and white to Technicolor." Northern California was "a bloody paradise," said Stone. "It was the most easy-going, pleasant, civilized, laid-back place you can imagine." Of his first class, he wrote, "I found myself sitting across the table from this guy wearing blue suede shoes and a two-toned country-and-western jacket and wrap-around shades and a pompadour and I thought, 'Christ, what kind of yo-yo is this?' "[69] It was Ed McClanahan, a Kentuckian.

McClanahan introduced Stone to the Perry Lane scene. Kesey did not trust Stone at first, thinking he was a Communist. McClanahan smoothed the way for him. McMurtry, who had completed his fellowship and was still living in San Francisco, joined the group. Stone was experienced in psychedelics from his New York coffeehouse days, but dope, which was illegal, had not come out of the closet—where it was smoked on Perry Lane.

It was a tribal scene that had literary and artistic precedents. Perry Lane set the tone for what came later in the decade. "We saw it partly as fun and partly as a spiritual adventure," said Stone. They were pleased with themselves. "We were young and thought that we were just incredibly sophisticated and bohemian to be doing all this far out stuff."[70]

There were trips to San Francisco to hear John Coltrane play mellow jazz and the comedian Lenny Bruce denigrate the establishment.

At the "demise party," held just before the Perry Lane residents were evicted so that the old housing could be demolished, Gurney Norman, who would become the director of the creative writing program at the University of Kentucky, organized the bodies of his fellow partygoers into a huge cat's cradle and then commanded: "All the thumbs raise their hands."[71] Many in that group, including Stone, would be on Kesey's Merry Prankster cross-country bus trip, which was celebrated by Tom Wolfe in *The Electric Kool-Aid Acid Test*. It would be Stanford University's inadvertent contribution to the birth of the counterculture. Stone thought Kesey gave up writing novels to participate in the social revolution that he had anticipated and provoked.

Stegner watched this madness from a distance. He felt protective of Bob Stone's fragile health and talent. "Quiet, nervous, given to black depressions and psychosomatic ailments," Stegner wrote in 1967, "Stone is a completely genuine, however tormented, article." He told an interviewer years later: "All during those years he drank too much and he took all kinds of things and it didn't somehow drown out his really driving impulse to write." Mary Stegner said after her husband died, "Wally certainly thought very highly of Stone's writing." She recalled the time when Stone thought he was losing his mind and Wally rescued him from financial disaster.[72]

After Stone completed his fellowship year, he remained near Stanford to work on his novel. His wife worked. They rented a small house and had very little money. Bob was "tormented and paranoid," said his close friend McClanahan. Besides the drugs, he drank heavily. He began to have splitting headaches and problems with his peripheral vision, seeing "things" to either side of him. Stone went to the Stanford Medical Center and was diagnosed with an inoperable brain tumor. Further tests, including one that involved drilling two holes into his skull, revealed that there was no tumor. But there was a huge medical bill and no money with which to pay it.

McClanahan said that Stone didn't want charity and didn't want anyone, including Stegner, to know about his situation. But somehow Wally found out and arranged for the university to pay all of Stone's medical expenses and to award him $1,250 as a half-year fellowship. "It was just a magnificent, generous thing for him to do," said McClanahan.[73] Stegner had a slightly different version of the incident:

Bob, who had a hypochondriac streak, came in one day with sweat popping out like buckshot on his forehead, and said to me, hoarsely, "I think I'm going blind!" It was right at the end of the term, and the end of Bob's fellowship, as I remember. He was afraid he had a brain tumor. The only thing I could do was to lengthen his fellowship by one quarter, so that he would still be eligible for free medical care as a student. He went over to Student Health and, as he reported it later, they shaved his head and cut a hole in his skull and blew him out with a compressed air hose. As it turned out, he did not have a brain tumor, thank the Lord, and did not go blind.[74]

Stegner could relate to Stone's poverty, wanderings, and realistic approach to writing fiction. It was as if Stegner were speaking of himself when he wrote in the *Saturday Review* article "Hard Experience Talking," which accompanied publication of *A Hall of Mirrors:* "A life of mean streets is not comprehended in a year's residence, and the unsentimental, unself-pitying understanding of skewed lives does not come easily or soon. Bob Stone was preparing for this novel from childhood." Stone's life before Stanford, Stegner said, was "common in the Depression Thirties."[75] Stone had been there, said Stegner, meaning he had experienced firsthand what he wrote about.

A few years after he left Stanford, Stone was working on *Dog Soldiers* and needed time at a writer's retreat. Stegner wrote a strong letter of recommendation to Yaddo. Stone thanked Stegner in a series of "dear prof" letters. "Your response and enthusiasm was tremendously important to me—it made the whole lonely business of finishing much easier and without it I don't know whether I could have gotten over the top," said Stone. "I couldn't have had more breaks, and I owe most of them to you and Stanford."[76] *Dog Soldiers* was given a National Book Award.

THERE IS LITTLE doubt that Wendell Berry was by far Stegner's favorite of the many students who passed through the writing program over the years. Their admiration for each other's work and principles was sustained for thirty-five years.

Before leaving Kentucky for California in the summer of 1958, Berry read Stegner's first novel and his collection of short stories. He thought *Remembering Laughter* was "a perfect little novel, clean and swift and assured." It was the first time he had read a collection of short stories by a single writer. "And so Wallace Stegner became my teacher before I ever laid eyes on him," Berry said, "and he was already teaching me in a way that I have come to see as characteristic of him—by bestowing a kindness that implied an expectation, and by setting an example."[77]

Berry, his wife, and their daughter settled in Mill Valley, then a small village among the redwoods just north of the Golden Gate Bridge and within commuting distance of Stanford. Berry carried the first 111 pages of the manuscript of what would be his first novel, *Nathan Coulter*, to class with him. Also in that class were Ernest Gaines, Ken Kesey, Nancy Packer, and Mitch Strucinski. Berry's deep roots in Henry County, Kentucky, dated back to the county's earliest settlement. Both sides of his family had been slaveholders. In contrast, Gaines was a black man from Louisiana, one of a half-dozen African Americans on the Stanford campus that year.

At the start of the class the two southerners were extremely cautious about criticizing each other's work, constructive criticism being at the heart of the process. Something had to be done. They were at a party, Gaines recalled. "He just called me into the backyard like some cowboy shootout saying, 'Okay, now we have to talk this over. We have to get this out of our way.' And I thought it was just the greatest thing that probably could have happened because after talking we realized that we probably had more in common with each other than we had with many of the other students in the class."

Gaines, who would go on to write a number of novels, including *The Autobiography of Miss Jane Pitman*, and teach writing, said Stegner was a great teacher, "the kind of guy that gives you a lot of leeway, and at the same time he's aware of things." Stegner helped Gaines with point of view and voice, the latter being an important element in the success of the character of the old woman in *Miss Jane Pitman*.[78]

It was during this class that Stegner demonstrated his aplomb in a moment of northern California fright. Objects had begun shaking and rattling in the room. "Don't worry, Mrs. Packer," Wally assured his student, who was pregnant, "you're not having the baby. It's just an earthquake." The class continued uninterrupted.[79]

Berry described the class: "Nancy, I think, was the oldest of us. She had read a great deal, talked well, and was useful to us all. But as a group we had a good deal to say, and Mr. Stegner would let us say it. He would read a piece of somebody's work and then sit back, sometimes with a cigar, listening attentively while we had our say." Unlike O'Connor or Winters, Stegner was not authoritarian. What Berry first thought was Stegner's reticence—meaning that he understated his role as a teacher and did not pontificate, indoctrinate, or evangelize—actually was courtesy: it was "courtesy toward both past and future; courtesy toward the art of writing, which needs to be carefully learned and generously passed on, and courtesy toward us, who as young writers needed all the help we could get, but needed also to be left to our ways."[80]

One important insight Berry gained from Stegner was that a writer could be intelligent and provincial at the same time. (Berry, like Stegner, would be stuck with the label "regional writer.") What was unique about Stegner was that he lived in the West, wrote about the region, and also did his best to protect it "from its would-be exploiters and destroyers." Stegner combined writing with activism to protect his place. "As far as I know," Berry said, "no American storyteller had been that kind of writer before."[81]

After completing his fellowship, Berry was given an appointment as an Edward H. Jones lecturer in creative writing, the same position his fellow Kentuckian McClanahan would hold for seven years. Gurney Norman followed Berry one year later as a Stegner Fellow, and thus, with the inclusion of James Baker Hall, what came to be referred to as the Kentucky mafia passed through Stanford. For Berry a year in Europe on a Guggenheim fellowship was followed by a brief stint teaching at New York University. Stegner had written glowing letters of recommendation for both the fellowship and the teaching job. Berry then returned to his native state; he wasn't bred for New York, he said. Stegner continued to influence him. Berry read *Wolf Willow* and admired it. "I hope to do as well sometime with the facts of my own little neck of the woods," he told Stegner, and he set out to do just that.[82]

Wally and Mary visited Wendell and Tanya Berry in Kentucky. Stegner tried to persuade his former student to teach at Stanford permanently. No, thank you, said Berry, who did lecture on a temporary basis in 1968 and 1969. Berry wrote Stegner in 1970 that he was comforted by the fact that "you are coming to understand my reasons for staying here. . . . I felt that my obligation and opportunity were here together, and that I simply had no choice."[83]

Stegner was asked to nominate candidates for the John D. and Catherine T. MacArthur Foundation fellowships, commonly known as the genius grants, in 1981, the program's inaugural year. He nominated one person for the extremely generous unrestricted, five-year grant.

The Fellowship is such a stupendous opportunity for anyone selected that only people of the highest and most special qualifications should be named. Searching my mind for people of that caliber, especially people still young enough to have their major contributions ahead of them, I come up with only one name, that of Wendell Berry. . . . There is no man I know from whom I ultimately expect more productive and socially useful thought. There is no man I know who, in the five years of freedom permitted by a MacArthur Fellowship, is more likely to justify the confidence placed in him.[84]

There was one problem, the vice president of the foundation wrote Stegner one month later after checking with the potential recipient. Berry did not want to be considered for the fellowship. He said he did not have a "valid need."[85]

Stegner fully understood Berry's rootedness in place during the last few years of his life in California, when he felt the lack of it. He wrote Berry in 1990 that "I was myself guilty of trying to persuade you against your decision, for sometime in the 1960s I alighted at your Kentucky River Farm and tried to talk you into coming to Stanford on some permanent basis. Fortunately, I got nowhere." He added, alluding to the MacArthur fellowship matter, "You and I both know of a more dramatic instance when you refused an opportunity that many writers would sell their souls for. You refused it because you felt that it might obligate you or impede your freedom of mind."[86]

Stegner then inadvertently gave Berry the ultimate compliment, which was a mirror image of who he was:

> From the time when you first appeared as a Fellow in the writing program at Stanford in 1958, I recognized you as one who knew where he was from and who he was. Your career since has given not only me but a large public the spectacle of an entirely principled literary life, a life not merely observant and thoughtful and eloquent but highly responsible, a life in which aesthetics and ethics do not have to be kept apart to prevent their quarreling, but live together in harmony.[87]

Stegner's praise of Berry was lavish by his standards. It was difficult for him to laud people for who they were. It was much easier for Wally to praise their accomplishments, such as their books. Berry was an exception. "It embarrasses my post-Protestant sensibilities to tell a man to his face that I admire him," he wrote in another letter that same year.

It wasn't Berry's "verbal felicity" that he was responding to but, rather, his "qualities of thoughtfulness, character, integrity, and responsibility" that shone through the prose. Berry reciprocated. He credited the "astounding good fortune" that had accompanied him all his life, "a good fortune in which you, your work, and example have figured prominently."[88]

THERE WAS A second category of Stegner students: those who did not make it big or may not have written a single creative word after leaving Stanford. But they, too, are important to any account of Stegner's teaching, because they never forgot their experience, regardless of what they became, and some passed on what they had learned to others, thus greatly increasing Stegner's legacy. They were the majority of students, and they kept in touch with their former professor, primarily through letters, until his death. Their hopes—really pleas in some cases—that he would remember them date back to his Harvard years.

The letters in thick files at the Stanford library begin "I don't know if you remember me" or "It has been some years since we last communicated." Usually Wally replied, and then a correspondence that he could not easily halt ensued. The correspondents asked how he had been and told about their lives. They ranged in the world of education from the wife of the president of the University of Iowa to a Florida schoolteacher to professors in state universities and small colleges. They had read his books, were employing his teaching techniques, and were spreading his writing advice widely. Would he come to speak at their campus, judge a literary contest, accept an award? There were letters from academics and nonacademics alike telling of rejections by agents, editors, and foundations to whom Stegner had written recommendations. At times, Stegner felt as if he were buried under these communications.

A Harvard alumnus wrote that Stegner's freshman writing course in 1940 was "the one, bright guiding light of all my years of school and college." He had spent thirty years on and off Madison Avenue producing advertising copy, writing two nonfiction books, and doing voice-overs for commercials; he was the voice of *The New Yorker* magazine on cable television. Another man, a Stanford graduate, said that although he hadn't written fiction in the thirty-nine years since getting his doctorate under Stegner in 1953, "I have enjoyed a very good life, and I owe much of my happiness to you." He could never have earned his degree "without your support, mentoring, and encouragement"—and he had gone on to become the director of the Writing Center at Harvard University.[89]

A New Yorker sent Stegner the galleys of her second novel and requested that he write a blurb. The former Stegner Fellow said that Wally had once done her the great favor of advising her to rewrite her first book: "For a month I thought my world had disintegrated, and then I started over." What she learned about the necessity for revision had aided her during the last ten years.[90]

Another fellow, who had been a single mother at Stanford in the 1950s, thanked Wally for granting her a fellowship. She'd had problems with the criticisms of male classmates in the workshops and had decided that the writing life was not for her, partly because she had a child to support. She had taken a job as an editor at the Stanford Research Institute and for the last thirty-five years had been looking forward to the time when she no longer had to explain to some offended PhD that *decedent* is not the opposite of *precedent*. That she had done nothing with what she had learned as a fellow except produce a few science fiction stories bothered her. "Maybe they're right," she said, "and educating women is just a waste."[91]

One former student wrote shortly before Stegner's death that he had been haunted for the last forty-three years by a remark Stegner had made in class: that "the sickness of our times is not a political sickness but a soul sickness."[92]

A THIRD CATEGORY of pupil had no formal affiliation with the professor. Even more than his students, those who sought Stegner out beyond the confines of the university had the West and nature in common with him. They learned by reading Stegner's works, occasional meetings with him, and an exchange of letters.

The first time Barry Lopez and Wally met, they sat on the deck of the Los Altos Hills home. Lopez, a young man who had yet to emerge as one of the nation's leading nature writers, was struck by how "humility and wisdom came together" in Stegner. He later visited Wendell Berry in his Kentucky home. They sat at the kitchen table and talked about Stegner. Lopez and Berry agreed that he was the only man they knew who could compliment them about their work in a way that urged them to do better. Stegner made time for writers, encouraged them, and assisted them in a manner that was contrary to what some of them perceived as the fundamental hostility of the West. "I don't think anyone will ever be able to take the measure of how profoundly you've affected American letters," Lopez told Stegner.[93]

The correspondence between Lopez and Stegner is particularly enlightening. A story Stegner told Lopez had haunted him: A student had asked Stegner why he had bothered to write *Wolf Willow*. "Who cares what happened so many years ago?" she asked. "The ignorance of this woman," Lopez said, "has never ceased to frighten rather than amaze me." He observed that history for many people was a nuisance, and he bemoaned the loss of historical perspective. "It requires deliberation and reflection," Lopez wrote Stegner, "neither of which is in vogue in this country. And that attitude is the seedbed of totalitarianism." Lopez wanted to incorporate this theme into his work: "We should practice the conservation of history as we practice the conservation of water." Stegner's contribution to younger writers was considerable, Lopez continued. "You have pointed the way very well for those of us a generation behind in more ways than you know. I am in your debt. And there is a sense of pleasure in this continuity in the anticipation of being able to give to those following me as you have given to my generation."[94]

Stegner replied to Lopez's letter eight days later. He had just finished reading *Arctic Dreams*, for which Lopez would receive a National Book Award: "It is, as I don't have to tell you, a book packed with learning and experience and rich with the sense of history that we both find missing in much of American life."[95]

They shared landscapes. There were finely etched descriptions of fall in Vermont and spring in California in Stegner's letters to Lopez.

Our stay in Vermont is about over. Three or four hard freezes, and our water line has frozen twice in spite of our leaving the water running all night. The geese have been going over for several weeks, and the grosbeaks and other late travelers are around us now. Leaves all gone—lasted quick and were never very bright this year. I begin to have Arctic Dreams—but mine are all of a warmer climate where my hands don't hurt when I type. Never get old—it's a bummer.

[Spring] is over a month early, the second year in a row of drought will put a strain on a lot of things, from the white oaks in the pasture to the ring-necked snakes under the dead leaves. But

there is a pair of wrens nesting in the wisteria and a pair of mock-
ingbirds nesting in the pyracantha and about forty towhees nesting in the bushes roundabout, and a lot of least bushtits nesting
God knows where. This is a season of jubilation, to be followed
shortly by drought, grass fires, water rationing, and cats in the
birds' nests, to be followed at summer's end by hordes of jay-
birds, who survive when all else succumbs.[96]

They were in sync, Lopez and Stegner, as this 1991 exchange indicates:

LOPEZ: I sometimes think that bringing the concerns of literature to the writing of nonfiction is one of the few ways we have to
redress the failure of journalists to live up to their responsibilities
as reporters, not entertainers; and at the same time to take back
from television and advertising some of the power to create
striking images in the public imagination, a power once almost
solely literature's.
STEGNER: You're right about the journalists not living up to
their responsibilities. . . . Now the novelists have to take over
the function of reporters, especially on environmental matters, which seem like the clammy kiss of death to city editors,
apparently.[97]

Ivan Doig recalled that he first crossed paths with Wally shortly
after *The New York Times Magazine* lumped a bunch of western writers,
including Doig, together as "Writers of the Purple Sage" and put
William [*sic*] Stegner at the head of the posse. Linking writers such as
Stegner and Doig with Zane Grey, the author of *Riders of the Purple
Sage* and other western potboilers, was a headline writer's inadvertent
insult. Grey wrote about the myths of the West whereas Stegner was
preoccupied with the realities. The true West, Doig said, citing Stegner
as having set the example for defining it, was "destinies, outlined
against the basic earth. That is the story we all write in the American
West, whether in memory or on the white canyons of paper." Stegner
felt similarly about Doig's work. In response to a request for a blurb for
one of Doig's books, Wally wrote his editor, "Doig does what I have
been wanting western writers to do for a long time: he is finding the
western present in the real, not the mythic, western past."[98]
    Doig had the last word in this exchange, in his 1992 review of Steg-

ner's collection of essays *Where the Bluebird Sings to the Lemonade Springs* in the *Los Angeles Times Sunday Book Review*. After citing the valuable lessons in the craft of writing contained in the essays, Doig added: "More vitally, though, he sweeps us at once into his exploration of the great theme of the West, the clash of its ecologies and its cultures." Three of the essays, he said, represented "the brilliant crystallization of his lifetime of thinking about the American West."[99]

William Kittredge was a Stegner Fellow ("Stegners" they proudly called themselves to mark their difference from the growing number of fellows named for Mirrielees, Jones, Scowcroft, and others) shortly after Wally had departed from Stanford. He was raised on a ranch in southeastern Oregon and later came to appreciate Stegner's description of a soaking rain impacting the dry earth. To Kittredge, "the language seems to call up images from a life which was mine once." He thanked Stegner: "Since I started [writing] you have been a prime model of excellence, not only in the books but in the humanizing, informal influence you have had on life in the West."[100]

Harriet Doerr was a Stegner Fellow in 1980, four years before publishing her first novel at the age of seventy-four. In reply to Stegner's congratulatory letter for winning the National Book Award in 1984 for *Stones for Ibarra*, Doerr wrote: "Your letter made my day, and the day after, and the day after that. Thank you. . . . I'm extremely grateful to the Stanford writing program for taking me in and to you for causing it to exist."[101]

Terry Tempest Williams and Stegner had Salt Lake City and Utah in common. It was where they had both grown up and where Wally and Terry's grandfather had played tennis together in the 1920s. Williams wrote *Refuge: An Unnatural History of Family and Place*, a book about the death of a wildlife refuge and the illness and deaths in her family from cancer caused by radioactive fallout from the Nevada Test Site during the years of nuclear weapons testing. Before the book was published, she wrote Stegner, "You have given me courage to speak as a Mormon woman in the American West." After it was published, Williams was summoned to the church offices and told that it was a woman's duty to have children, not to write about endangered species. When she related her experience to Stegner, he offered to be her patriarch and her Mormon elder. Wally wrote her editor and her agent, "I feel her book from several directions, as I am sure she meant me to."[102]

Gretel Ehrlich and Rick Bass never met Stegner, but he profoundly influenced them. Ehrlich had a small lending library on her northern

Wyoming ranch, where Stegner's books were always in demand and circulated among the neighboring ranches and the sheep, cow, and geology camps. Ehrlich had done something with a book that she had never done before: she had torn out the page that contained Stegner's Wilderness Letter so that she might carry it with her to distant places. Bass sought a refuge in Montana's Yaak Valley only to be surrounded by logging clear-cuts. The story of Yaak Valley "is the dark story of America," wrote Bass, who then paraphrased Stegner's words about the need for wilderness. "He was exemplary in the truest sense of the word," wrote Bass.[103]

IT WASN'T ALL about teaching; there was also academic infighting. To create a program, to mold it to your persona, to find and sustain the funding, and then to hold on to it in a large university entailed watching your back and defending your turf, rather demeaning but necessary occupations that raised Stegner's ire a notch or two from time to time.

He had good relations with Richard Jones, the chairman of the English Department. When Jones's brother died and his death was followed quickly by that of his widow, without the promised provision for continuing the writing program, Jones collected $400,000 from the heirs of the estate. When the chairman suffered a slight heart attack in 1959, Stegner said, "In fifteen years I have got to feeling very filial about that old boy." When he died, six years later, it was like "a sudden silence in a great confusion and yelling" that "puts gooseflesh on my arms."[104]

Within the writing program itself he clashed periodically with Yvor Winters, who ran the poetry section. Winters had been a brilliant faculty member, albeit a loose cannon within the English Department since he began teaching at the university in 1928. He had been denied promotion for years. Then the younger Stegner arrived as a full professor, assumed the directorship of the writing program, and became Winters's boss the next year. Winters took potshots at Stegner behind his back. He insulted Robert Frost when Frost visited the campus, cultivated a clique of graduate students, and insisted, against Stegner's strenuous objections, on giving the two annual poetry fellowships that bore Stegner's name to his graduate students rather than to outside poets. Stegner suspected Winters, somewhat correctly, of wanting to take over the program. Both were strong willed and highly principled.

The poets at Stanford—an unusually talented group in the 1960s—

were divided in their opinion of Winters. Five of them were subsequently collected in *Five American Poets:* Robert Hass, John Matthias, James McMichael, John Peck, and Robert Pinsky. Two of them wrote poems about Winters that were included in the anthology. All were influenced by Winters and knew one another at Stanford.

Donald Justice, a Stanford alumnus who later won a Pulitzer Prize for poetry, cited Winters's "defiantly idiosyncratic but always honorable and hard-headed approach to literature and teaching." Hass was awed by Winters's "single-minded ferocity and passion about poetry" but put off by his "impatience or show of impatience that amounted to contempt" for his students. Hass's classmate, close friend, and fellow United States poet laureate Robert Pinsky thought Winters was both a tyrant and a great teacher.[105]

Hass and Scott Momaday, also a poetry fellow, sought Stegner's company, the former as a fellow westerner lost among a horde of eastern graduate students and the latter for advice on how to write fiction. To Edward Loomis, one of the few graduate students who took classes with both Stegner and Winters, each professor was "a very significant institution," each had his own constituencies that did not mix with each other, and each had his "dominions and borders that were taken very seriously in these little intellectual baronies. There was a certain amount of mutual distrust—or perhaps dislike would be a more accurate characterization."[106]

It got so that Stegner could barely tolerate Winters. "I didn't mind the cantankerousness if he could have laughed," said Wally, "but he had no capacity at all to even like or seem to like anybody with whom he disagreed. He had no capacity to discuss, he could only assert." Mary thought Wally's growing reserve and bitterness dated from the departmental disagreements with Winters. He was no longer the same outgoing man who used to sing western ballads at parties, she said.[107]

After Winters retired, in 1966, there were other problems to deal with. As a way of getting around the realists who dominated the writing program and bringing some experimentalists onto the campus, the English Department hired the son of a distinguished faculty member, who bore the same name as his father, Albert Guérard. At first, Stegner cordially welcomed Guérard. They had taught writing at Harvard at the same time, and along with Mark Schorer and Delmore Schwartz they had been referred to as the bright young stars in that particular firmament. Guérard had recently included one of Stegner's stories in an anthology.

It wasn't long before Stegner began to perceive Guérard as the principal menace to his hold on creative writing. Guérard was very well connected. Besides the interchangeability of father and son (the son succeeded Winters in the literature chair named after his father), there was Guérard's standing in the Department of English: the chairman of the department, who had brought Guérard back to Stanford, had been his protégé at Harvard. Referring to Guérard, Wally wrote to a former student: "The closest friend of the chairman would like to have . . . [the program] in his own fist, to be blunt, and so our appointment and salary needs have been getting late and inadequate attention while the chairman's pal builds up a sort of rival writing establishment in the Freshman English program. It all sounds petty and messy, and is."[108]

Guérard started chipping away at Stegner's sphere of influence. "He wanted to run the program, not be part of it," said Scowcroft.[109] With the graduate-level creative writing program firmly in Wally's hands, Guérard launched his probes at the more vulnerable freshman level, where the teaching of English composition, as it was called, was desultory at best. He initiated the university's first freshman English literature seminar program, codirected the entire freshman English program, and found the federal funding for the Institute of Literary Studies, whose main innovation was commonly known as the Voice Project. Guérard brought another protégé, the postmodern novelist John Hawkes, to Stanford to teach in the new program.

The Voice Project had partial roots in Harvard's Briggs-Copeland fellowships, of which Stegner had been a beneficiary. It brought working novelists to Stanford to teach writing to groups of twenty freshmen. The emphasis was not on technique but, rather, on developing the student's inner voice. "Every genuine writer has a voice of his own," said Guérard, "an inward voice that stems from his temperament as well as from experience. The experienced teacher listens to that voice, helps bring it out."[110]

Stegner shot back: "They may find their voice, but what they don't have is syntax." Voice was certainly something Stegner possessed. Indeed, some might say that he had it in abundance. But it wasn't something he thought could be taught. It was earned—or rather discovered—by hard work. What Guérard's (or Hawkes's) experimental writing produced, in terms of the short story, Stegner said, was "something authentically short, but not authentically story: an open-ended sketch, a whirling gust of images, an impression, a howl, a freehand map of the author's mind."[111]

The young poets, like Hass and Pinsky, and others who were look-ing for an alternative to the drudgery of traditional writing courses and freedom from the constraints of realism rejoiced. "Albert Guérard was a wonderful supporter of literary and progressive graduate students," said Robert Pinsky.[112]

Guérard had his supporters in the English Department; Stegner had his in his creative writing center and in high positions in the university. One of the more balanced observers was David Levin, a member of the English Department faculty. Levin credited Guérard with partial suc-cess in modernizing the department's curriculum. Then Guérard went after the writing program. To Stegner, Levin said, it must have seemed like an invasion. "With equally vigorous ingenuity, Guérard challenged convictions about writing," said Levin. "Neither Stegner nor Winters, whose prescriptive principles Guérard had renounced, welcomed his eagerness to encourage the avant garde."[113]

That was an understatement. Stegner saw Guérard and the depart-ment as a threat to the autonomy of the writing program and Guérard as his possible successor as the program's director. Wally wanted Scow-croft to follow him. Guérard would say years later that he had been offered the job by the chairman of the department but had declined it, partly because he knew Scowcroft was in line for it and partly because he was busy establishing a new graduate English program.

Stegner was angry, said Nancy Packer. He was more than angry, said Scowcroft. "He likes people. He hates a few. And he's capable of real hatred." One of the people he really disliked was Guérard.[114]

THE ACADEMIC INFIGHTING was the prelude to what Stegner ab-horred even more and found extremely difficult to deal with, and that was change. Change in the late 1960s was occurring on a massive scale, and it seemed to come all at once. It consisted of not only literary styles and tastes but also the whole panoply of the youth rebellion of that time. "Throbbing" was the key word Wally used to describe the brief period of upheaval. Add to the mayhem on the Stanford campus the destruction of the California environment that Stegner was trying to help save as a practicing conservationist, and the totality of change resulted in the permanent darkening of the Stegnerian persona.

Stegner went public with his darker vision of the future in an edito-rial that was more a jeremiad in the *Saturday Review*'s California issue of September 1967: California was America in extremis in its environment and culture.[115] It was becoming an "intolerable" place to live. "Having welcomed unlimited growth, the state has the most acute growth problems anywhere." He added a thought that was heretical at the time to all but a few: "Some Californians have begun to look on growth not as a good but as an active evil, ruinous for people and land." He continued, "Like the rest of America, California is unformed, innovative, ahistorical, hedonistic, acquisitive, and energetic—only more so."[116]

California was the last stop on the nation's journey from Europe to Asia. The state rejected—in fact, the youths hated—the Puritanism of the East Coast and embraced the Zen philosophies of the West Coast; witness the work of the poets Allen Ginsberg and Gary Snyder. California was a "hotbed," as it always had been, for extremists, and clearly Stegner didn't like "the hippie aberration" and "California's extreme permissiveness." It was a repudiation of who he was, what he stood for, and where he had come from.

He first located the extremes generally; then he personalized them. The more extreme the Left became, he said, the more the Right "backs up in its rut." Gary Snyder was his symbol for the Left; Governor Ronald Reagan was his stand-in for the Right. It would be tragic if the Right prevailed. "It could be equally unfortunate if the Gary Snyders succeed in their aim of leaving not one value of the old order standing." Clearly describing himself, Stegner wrote, "The man in the middle may be tempted to cry a curse on both their houses, for both extremes hinder the growth of a tradition that might stabilize the society and foster a sense of community in its swollen cities and its creeping slurbs."[117]

The private dialogue between Stegner and Snyder that followed could very well have been the most intelligent discussion at the time—at least in California—of the differences between generations. Snyder took immediate exception to Stegner's characterization of him as the bogeyman of the Left. "I realize you have the Gary Snyders leaving nothing of the old order standing mostly as a rhetorical flourish to provide the second term for a neat pair of opposites, but it's irresponsible," Snyder wrote Stegner from Kyōto, Japan, with a copy of the letter going to the *Saturday Review*. What was unique in Western culture, Snyder said, and what was missing from Asian cultures "is its capacity for self-evaluation and renewal." Some, including Snyder, were attempting to find "the new threads" in the waning old order that still had value. "In the process—and here's where California's young sometimes appear bizarre—a lot has to be put to the test to find if it works or not." The greatest failure of Western civilization was the lack of a proper reverence for nature. Snyder invoked the Mother who was missing from the Trinity, Native Americans, and the Buddha as sources for the new thinking. After all, asked Snyder with his own rhetorical flourish, "Does Jesus save Redwoods?" Some of the solutions lay outside the boundaries of Western culture. "The Gary Snyders and their ilk are, I do most deeply believe, not destroyers but preservers."[118]

Stegner hadn't been teaching and was out of the country when Snyder addressed the creative writing class at Stanford. The report he had received from the students, Stegner said, was that Snyder had said that nothing of the old order should be left standing. It was on that basis that he had made the comments about Snyder in the *Saturday Review* article. He would not accept the charge of irresponsibility, nor would he return it. Stegner believed that values should be codified: "I would say that values aren't values at all until some social order, some social agreement or consensus or acknowledgment, makes them so. Until then, they're only human possibilities, alternatives in the genes and the meat and the mind." He doubted if Snyder's mystical search would yield any tangible results. No, Jesus doesn't save redwoods, he said. "Christians, or pseudo-Christians, cut down all that have been cut." They also save redwoods. It was at this point, he believed, that "we can join hands as preservers." He and Snyder had some interests in common: "wilderness, redwoods, Indians, poetry (I like some of yours), perhaps even intellectual curiosity."[119]

Snyder replied almost immediately: "Blast it I'm sure I'd think twice about characterizing a man as wishing to destroy the good along with the bad—in a national magazine—on the basis of what *I* heard two undergraduates say *they* heard." In the heat of the moment, Snyder had misread Stegner's letter. Wally had broken down what the "writing group" had reported to two students who agreed with Snyder and one who was "appalled" at what he had heard. He had talked with the whole class and the instructor, Stegner replied, and they were consistent in what they had heard Snyder say. He assured Snyder that he was not playing detective. "I guess I simply can't believe in the results of meditation as you do." Redwoods needed to be preserved by action, Stegner wrote Snyder on George Washington's birthday. He would like to talk with Snyder, who jotted "no use in answering" on the envelope.[120]

Stegner took the ideas and some of the wording of a 1969 Snyder broadside and made them part of a more extreme Berkeley hippie manifesto in *Angle of Repose*. He attached Snyder's name to it. The message contained in the manifesto was that the traditional culture would have to be first destroyed and then reconstructed by meditation. When an interviewer told Stegner that he had found the use of Snyder's broadside "ironic and comic" in the novel, Wally smiled and said, "I'm not sure Gary would agree with you."[121] He didn't, nor did he recognize the passage in the novel as his words. "His use of my real name and the rather scurrilous attribution of a text I never wrote was a surprise to me," Snyder said.[122]

Wally wrote to Wendell Berry, who was also a friend of Snyder's, that the California poet had "crossed some boundary, he's like a windigo, he lives outside the safe limits of my tribal territory, we step around each other cautiously when we meet."[123] The two had met and shared a couple of drinks at a conference. Given the opportunity, which never arose, Snyder felt they could have become friends because they were both concerned about the failure of values.

More years passed. In 1992 Snyder asked Stegner to participate in a series of readings, titled "Places on Earth," at the University of California at Davis, stating, "Of all people who might be involved in this series you are the most eminently qualified." Stegner declined, citing health reasons one year ahead of the proffered date. Mary Stegner invited Snyder to attend the dedication of the Wallace Stegner Environmental Center at the new San Francisco Public Library in 1995. Snyder declined, stating that he was finishing a book.[124]

CHANGE WAS OVERTAKING the sybaritic campus of Stanford. If it was true that nobody over the age of thirty could be trusted, then Stegner, who was double that age and could easily have been a grandfather to most Stanford students, certainly fell in the category of the untrustworthy. To some, the older writer and teacher was an anachronism. The graduate students from New York City made fun of him behind his back, concocting stories about violence on the New York City subways that mimicked the violence of Stegner's western heritage. To others he remained the icon of what a writer should be.[125]

Wally, to whom teaching had always been a means, began contemplating his resignation from Stanford. The times were not easy for him, nor for many scholars and administrators on campuses across the country. Stegner could see that his life was passing. There were more books he wanted to write, and he wouldn't get them written if he continued teaching. He needed to devote all his time and energy to his first priority.

Stegner's preference for the writing life was stated most forcefully in 1963, when William Styron turned down his offer to teach at Stanford in order to work on *The Confessions of Nat Turner*, for which he would win the Pulitzer Prize. "Also, I would be the first to think that what you're writing is a hell of a lot more important than what you might be saying to Stanford students," wrote Stegner. "I have daily opportunities for measuring this kind of thing, and it always comes out that I submit to the tyranny of the students and damn them to hell."[126]

He fought back against the changing times in the only way he knew, on paper. His novel *All the Little Live Things* contains all the antihippie venom he could muster. Writing it presented him with problems, and he took the unprecedented step of admitting to his class that he was stumped. Stegner told the students in his fall 1966 workshop that he knew it was someone else's turn to read and then asked if they could postpone that reading for one class. "Please forgive me, but I am at a standstill. I realized this morning that I had lost my way. Forget about my previous books, that I am the director of this program. I just need some help. So don't pull any punches."

The students were stunned. They looked at one another. The unspoken question was, How did Stegner, of all people, lose his way? "It was one of the great lessons of my life," said James Houston. "If you can be that age and wonder what the book is about and be at the edge of your capacity of understanding and deal with that, then you can last as a writer." Stegner recovered his usual equanimity after the reading and the comments. A student asked what would he do if he won the Pulitzer for that book. "I'd drink a better brand of bourbon," he said.[127]

The decision to leave Stanford was made in stages. First, he surrendered the directorship of the program to Scowcroft in 1969. "I am pretty confident that I am a sort of trustee of this job and can pass it on to any qualified person without its becoming a departmental matter," he told his successor.[128] Two years later he resigned—*quit* was his word. He did not retire, he insisted. He hadn't, in fact, reached the age of retirement.

So, what had happened to being a sticker? Can one remain in a place too long? Consider where Wallace Stegner had come from, what he had achieved, and as a result, who he was. Then consider what was occurring at Stanford University at that time. The scenes unfolded relentlessly, one after the other.

The first sit-in was in the spring of 1966. Football players removed the protesters from the president's office. In April of the next year there was a march to the Stanford Research Institute (SRI), which held a number of defense contracts. Eventually the university would sever its ties to that organization. A protest over CIA recruitment on campus was led by H. Bruce Franklin, an English professor turned radical Maoist who had once been Wally's student and would eventually be dismissed from his tenured position. Of Franklin, Stegner said: "The Stanford campus lives on edge, under the constant threat of terrorism, arson, disruption, and retaliation. There are rifts in the academic community, rifts directly traceable to Franklin, that in my opinion will never be healed. He has come a lot closer than many people think to bringing down a great university, and the university has had no option but to defend itself." Stegner admitted he was speaking out of anger when he said of Franklin, "there are some people I would just as soon not call colleague."[129]

There were fights between Arabs and Jews. Soon after Martin Luther King Jr. was assassinated, there was an incident in which black high school students thought they had been unjustly accused of shoplifting in the campus store. The Black Student Union made shouted demands. Buildings were invaded and occupied. Records were perused, destroyed, or—in the case of faculty salaries—publicized. Fires were ignited; the president's office was gutted, and his books destroyed. He departed. It took time for the conservative trustees to hand over the president's job to a liberal replacement. The library was ransacked. The home of the university's personnel director was bombed, and the residences of eight faculty members who had been threatened were guarded around the clock. Sheriff's deputies and local police were called to the campus thirteen times in two months in the spring of 1970. Windows were smashed across the campus. The university decided not to replace them; plywood was nailed over gaping holes. The campus resembled the South Bronx, said the new president. It was a plywood university, said Stegner.

Inside the classrooms it was almost impossible at times to teach. There was disrespect for traditions, for manners, for proper dress, and for learning. "A lot of them came from privilege," said Stegner of the students, "and they expected privilege." Meaning, in his mind, the privilege to destroy. Wendell Berry, who had returned briefly to teach at this time, said of Stegner, "He had grown up deprived of everything these people were taking for granted. And they were very ostentatiously despising it all, and he had a most exquisite sense of the worth of it."[130]

Students came with answers instead of questions; there was questioning of authority and authorities, and the worst part, for Stegner, was that the students who wanted to study were constantly being diverted. The fun was quickly draining out of teaching. "There was a real sense of letdown," Wally said, "a sense that I had wasted a lot of years of my life. I was really disgusted with the teaching business at that point."[131] He vented his anger in the biting introduction to *Twenty Years of Stanford Short Stories:*

> Traditions, including traditional forms in art, go down; the youth who trusts no one over thirty is no devotee of the Great Books. His aim—call it rather a drive—seems to be not to keep his head, but to lose it; he wants not clarity but ecstasy, not understanding but hallucination. According to the apocalypts, orgasm cures wounds, and pot should be sold for balsams, and the academic corollary of this is the "free" university, sans administration, sans buildings, sans fees, sans faculty, sans grades, sans books, sans everything, an assemblage of free souls throbbing together.[132]

Stegner attempted to bridge the difference in generations. He invited Hass into his office, and they talked fairly frequently. "I was his specimen hippie," said Hass. "He really didn't like or get what was going on." Stegner shared his office with Ed McClanahan, a former student in the writing program and a lecturer who styled himself as "Captain Kentucky," in a knee-length red cape, long hair, granny glasses, and Peter Pan boots. They were a study in sartorial opposites. Wally was somewhat bemused by his office mate and treated him with "kindness and unstinting generosity," said McClanahan, who in later years wondered what he had been doing in that costume. To McClanahan, Stegner "was, at all odds, the handsomest, most urbane, most instantly certifiable *gentleman* I'd ever encountered—like one of those 'Men of Distinction' gents in the old Calvert Reserve whiskey ads. I was awestruck."[133]

What disturbed Stegner the most was the rampant sex among the "happily-biological young," and for that activity he reserved the ultimate in obscenities and distasteful images. Nancy Packer thought he saw something of the irresponsibility of his father in the carefree hippies. One of the first writing fellows, Boris Ilyin, spent time with Stegner in the late 1960s. He said, "That was the first time I saw real bitterness in him."[134]

Stegner poured all his loathing into the hippie character of Jim Peck ("Peck's Bad Boy") in *All the Little Live Things*, a novel set in the Los Altos Hills of the 1960s. Peck, described as "a visitation" and as Caliban, becomes Satan incarnate and hijacks the book from the goddess figure of Marian Catlin. He is a rank, bearded, long-haired, lecherous, motorcycle-driving threat to the values of Joe Allston, the Stegner-like narrator whose wisecracking exterior was drawn from Carl Brandt, Stegner's New York literary agent after Baumgarten left the firm.[135]

Peck is a composite character: part a motorcycle-driving physicist whom Page Stegner had given permission to camp on the property when his parents were in Europe, part a tenant in the cottage who planted a patch of marijuana, and part imagination. Referring to another tenant of that period, Stegner sat down at his typewriter and pecked out a four-paragraph rumination titled "Confessions of a Cultural Conservative: A Sort of Dialogue with John McChesney After Three or Four Years—Five Years Maybe." It could be a generational or parental dialogue from any trying period.

> His position—Maoist, Franklinite, confrontationist, freeing Bobby [Seale] and backing the [Black] Panthers, [Eldridge] Cleaver, Angela Davis, hating the cops, fighting the university and participating, probably, in the trashings; resisting Vietnam War, wanting the students to run the institution, assuming the devil theory of the Administration and the liberation theory of all the youth, sub-culture, ethnic, and civil rights agitations of the time.
>
> My position: troubled: agreeing with him on war, civil rights and need of reform in the university and all sorts of areas; opposed to his direct action methods—opposed, that is, to his revolutionary intransigence and hoping to win him to evolutionary reform—not to revolutionary overturn or stoppage, but to evolutionary change—meliorism,* not crashing halt.
>
> His feelings about the black students who trashed the bookstore, then the library; who took over the microphone from the university's president at a meeting and turned the meeting into a shouting of obscenities and denunciations. John's reaction: Hurray. My reaction! I disagreed with their tactics and deplored their manners. "Manners!" he said. I astonished him, I really did. It was as if I had seriously brought the name of Jacqueline Susann into a literary discussion. *Manners!* He had thought better of me.

*BELIEF THAT THE WORLD CAN BECOME BETTER & THAT HUMANS CAN HELP IN ITS BETTERMENT.

We parted somewhat later, and he went off to Antioch to participate in more confrontations, and the last I heard of him he had been forced, by the intransigence of Antioch students, into a position defensive of the faculty and administration. But that is not what I mention him for. I have been conducting a dialogue with him ever since he first came to live in our cottage, because I couldn't understand him, and wanted to. He couldn't understand me, either, though I don't know whether he wanted to or not.

Stegner's credentials as a moderate and a liberal were impeccable. He had been a member of the Kennedy administration, a Democratic Party fund-raiser, a member of the board of the Sierra Club and the American Civil Liberties Union, and a quiet marcher in antiwar parades. At lunch in Palo Alto just after the invasion of Cambodia, he pounded the table and declaimed: "Richard Nixon is an evil man! Richard Nixon is an evil man!" But he couldn't see how the breaking of windows at Stanford helped very much.[136]

By March of 1968 he had had enough of teaching. Stegner wrote his friend Malcolm Cowley, then an editor at Viking: "I've just about decided to retire early and spend my declining years writing books instead of reading bad manuscripts."[137] Thirty-six years after teaching his first classes at Augustana College, Stegner wrote his friend Howard Mumford Jones at Harvard on December 30, 1970: "At this moment, only four dread days away, I face the prospect of resuming pedagogy, alas. I can hardly wait for March 21, when it will end."[138]

Scott Turow was in Stegner's last creative writing class. He thought Wally was guarded with his students, having gone through a few rough years. "His criticisms were adroit, never venomous, although I think he'd gotten past the point where he tried to pull punches."[139] There were four lessons that Turow took from Stegner and applied to his writing career: write every day, be accurate with details, treat writing as a business as well as an art form, and follow the Chekhovian lesson in foreshadowing. "If you say in the first chapter that there is a rifle hanging on a wall, in the second or third chapter it absolutely must go off." Royalties from Turow's best seller *Presumed Innocent* went toward endowing a Stegner fellowship at Stanford. Turow's work has been cited for being "grounded in faithfully depicted realism."[140]

Stegner never regretted his decision to leave teaching. Four years later he wrote his old friend Phil Gray, with whom he had taught at the

University of Wisconsin: "I am never going to miss teaching, as I am sure you do. I never gave it more than half my heart, the ventricle, say." While others around him changed—some radically—Wallace Stegner remained who he was and who he had been. "I never saw Wally insecure during this time," said a teaching colleague.[141]

Reluctant
Conservationist

Of National Parks
and Arid Lands

Instead of the gentle roll of the great valley there were high plains, great mountain ranges, alkali valleys, dead lake bottoms, alluvial benchlands. Instead of trees or oak openings there were grasslands, badlands, timbered mountains, rain forests and rain-shadow deserts, climates that ran the scale from Vermont to the Sahara. And more important than all the variety which was hostile to a too-rigid-traditional pattern was one overmastering unity, the unity of drouth. With local and minor exceptions, the lands beyond the 100th meridian received less than twenty inches of annual rainfall, and twenty inches was the minimum for unaided agriculture. That one simple fact was to be, and is still to be, more fecund of social and economic and institutional change in the West than all the acts of all the Presidents and Congresses from the Louisiana Purchase to the present.

> Wallace Stegner, *Beyond the Hundredth Meridian*

WALLACE STEGNER'S ENVIRONMENTAL commitments peaked during the 1960s. He had participated in the conservationist movement in the previous decade and would remain a committed environmentalist, albeit a thinking and writing one. But during that tumultuous decade, Stegner sacrificed precious time that he would otherwise have devoted to teaching and his beloved writing to attend long meetings, sometimes a continent distant. It was not an entirely happy fit.

In the 1980s, Stegner wrote T. H. Watkins, editor of the Wilderness Society's magazine: "I have not been an effective or even eager activist. . . . Actually I would like, and would always have liked, nothing better than to stay home and write novels and histories. When the compulsions of some book get too strong for me, I have a history of backing away from environmental activism." Watkins, the biographer of Harold Ickes, the activist secretary of the interior under President Franklin D. Roosevelt, thought otherwise. To him and others Stegner was "one of the central figures in the modern conservation movement."[1]

In the nearly forty years Stegner lived after the publication of *Beyond the Hundredth Meridian*—during which time he wrote many essays and articles urging that the destruction of the West be averted and served on various boards, commissions, and committees—he not only influenced and actively shaped legislation at the local, regional, and national levels but also was the conscience, the prodder, and the bard of the conservation movement west of the one hundredth meridian of longitude.

Only David Brower of the Sierra Club, a collaborator with whom Stegner eventually clashed, was as influential with words, primarily those published by the organization itself. However, it was Stegner who had the foresight to warn Brower—who did not heed his advice—against giving away Glen Canyon on the Colorado River in return for no dams on the Green River. The result was a dam named after the canyon and a reservoir named after John Wesley Powell, whom Stegner had raised from obscurity to historical prominence. Brower's decision was one of the great conservation blunders of the century.

Conservation in the 1950s and 1960s meant national parks, national monuments, dams, and wilderness areas. The growing differences between conservationists and environmentalists during the late 1960s and early 1970s seemed to be between those willing to compromise—largely the older generation—and those newer converts whose concerns were wider and whose attitude was increasingly intransigent. Stegner felt more at home in the first category, where he achieved the greatest results, but was able to adapt to the second one, absent the extremes of the environmental movement.

Always susceptible to books and places, Wally applied what he had consciously learned as an academic to what he had unconsciously absorbed as a youth under the vast skies of the northern prairie, the Great Basin, the Rocky Mountains, and the canyonlands of the Plateau Province. He added his acute personal awareness of the scarcity of water to the mix. He demonstrated to a wide audience through his words that the West was an arid land that needed to be considered and treated differently from humid lands.

From the joining of book learning to instinctive feeling for place came Stegner's awareness of John Wesley Powell's importance in western history, which dated to his sophomore year in college. His conservationist stance was a direct outgrowth of Powell's thoughts on the limitations of western land and water and the success of the promotion-minded forces that eventually defeated Powell. What Powell in the nineteenth century and Stegner to a greater extent in the twentieth century achieved as the popularizer of Powell's ideas and as the writer-activist who greatly expanded Powell's basic message was an awakening of the general public and the policy makers in government to the essential issues of the American West. Those issues were—and remain to this day—the aridity that breeds sparseness and the denial of that condition, which leads to overdevelopment.

Along with his illumination of the human condition through the art of fiction and the many accomplished writers that his nearly four decades of teaching produced—some of whom carried the Stegnerian conservation torch even farther—Wally's focus on the limits of the land, the lack of water that kept much of it from blooming, the debunking of the myth of the individual, the need for a collective approach, the fact that most western lands are public, not private, the burgeoning slurbs, and the need for wilderness to cleanse the soul and provide relief from the congestion of the populated areas was one of his most enduring accomplishments.

To achieve his conservationist goals, Stegner temporarily became an organization man, which was near anathema for him. For a brief time in 1961 he worked as a bureaucrat within the paneled precincts of the executive offices of the Department of the Interior in Washington, D.C. He returned to serve for a number of years on an important advisory panel that reported to Secretary of the Interior Stewart L. Udall. In addition to serving on the boards of the Sierra Club, the Wilderness Society, and a local open-space committee, he lent his name to many conservationist and environmental causes.

There was a further dimension to his reluctant activism. The environmentally oriented words that he generated in his journalism, magazine essays, books, interviews, lectures, and radio and television appearances circulated in the ether that infects minds with ideas and pushes them toward action. His words and *active presence*—and this is what really separates him from other nature writers, such as Henry David Thoreau—had a discernible and immediate impact on government policy, regulations, and legislation.

Stegner kept—or, rather, attempted to keep, because he was not entirely successful—his art and advocacy separate. "I don't think that my fiction, or nonfiction for that matter, is very effective advocacy," he told an interviewer. "Partly because I don't want it to be. I keep steering away from advocacy. I try not to make literature into propaganda. On the other hand, the propaganda business is completely necessary. Somebody has to do it, and generally I have to get sort of mad before I do, but I constantly do it. . . . I'm always conscious that I am being a journalist when I'm doing that."[2]

His conversion to the cause was incremental. His conservation learning curve progressed from Saskatchewan to Salt Lake City to his family's cabin on Fish Lake in the Plateau Province of southern Utah to the minor accident that sparked his awareness of Powell and led, eventually, to *Hundredth Meridian*. His awareness of environmental problems was "a very gradual process," Stegner said. "But . . . [I] began to be acutely changed when I began to study John Wesley Powell, who taught me a great deal about what was possible in the West, where I had grown up."[3]

Prodding also came from both coasts. From Cambridge came the urgings of his friend and mentor Benny DeVoto to become more involved in the fight against the western hillbillies, and from San Francisco came David Brower's realization that he could put Stegner's words to work for the goals of the Sierra Club.

John Wesley Powell Rising

> To grow up with the West, or to grow with and through it into national prominence, you had to have the West bred into your bones, you needed it facing you like a dare. You needed a Western education, with all the forming and shaping and the dynamics of special challenge and particular response that such an education implied.
>
> Wallace Stegner, *Beyond the Hundredth Meridian*

> In the Powell biography there is no reminiscence, but some echoes of personal experience. . . . I wouldn't have felt comfortable writing that book if I hadn't gone down the Colorado River in two or three different installments, and if I hadn't spent a half dozen years when I was an adolescent in the southern Utah plateaus.
>
> Wallace Stegner, in *Conversations with Wallace Stegner*

STEGNER WAS HURRYING to a geology exam during his sophomore year at the University of Utah when his thumb got slammed in a car door. He had to go to the hospital, and he missed the test. As a makeup assignment, the professor instructed him to read Clarence E. Dutton's *Tertiary History of the Grand Cañon District* and *Report on the Geology of the High Plateaus of Utah*. Wally was immediately fascinated by the quality of the writing and the illustrations in the two reports. He was also familiar with the terrain. His family's summer cabin was on one of those high plateaus not far from the Grand Canyon.

Dutton was an anomaly. He was a government scientist who could paint landscapes with words and chose his illustrators for their accuracy and powers of evocation. "He was the first literary tourist in a country where tourist travel has become the number one business," wrote Stegner.[1] Dutton's boss in the U.S. Geological Survey was Powell, who looked upon the younger man as his geologic heir. Stegner focused on the more literary Dutton, which made sense for an English major, but he was very aware of the more "sensational" Powell hovering in the background.

Just as he did with his fiction, Stegner became adept at recycling his nonfiction. Dutton was the subject of his doctoral thesis, written in 1935 for the Department of English at the University of Iowa, perhaps the first time a geologist was subjected to a doctoral dissertation's literary assessment at that or any other institution of higher learning. The impoverished graduate student writing in the midst of the Depression could not afford a working copy of *Tertiary History*, so he typed a copy of the entire book. Stegner was not particularly proud of his thesis. He wrote another writer in 1952: "As for my own thesis on Dutton, I don't have a copy and I'd be ashamed to let anyone see it anyway. I did it at a time when Iowa was deemphasizing the doctoral dissertation to the status of a scholarly article."[2]

At the University of Utah, Stegner was facing the publish or perish syndrome. Thus a condensation of the thesis in the form of a booklet was published in 1935 by the University of Utah Press, making it Wally's first published nonfiction work.[3] A further distillation of the Dutton thesis appeared in the July 1937 issue of *The Scientific Monthly*.

Dutton's prose was an object lesson in how to write with clarity and flair, two qualities that were not (and are not) generally esteemed by the scientific and academic communities. Wally took to Dutton, who was as much an exception among scientists as Stegner would be among English professors. He told the campus newspaper shortly after his thesis had been published that Dutton's work was "the finest thing from the standpoint of literary merit in the whole history of American geology." Forty years later Stegner offered another tribute to Dutton: "The prose is evocative and literary and belongs properly with that of Thoreau, Burroughs, Muir, and other 'naturalists' of the time, rather than with works written in the specialized jargon of science."[4]

There were lessons to be learned from Dutton for a lifetime of writing, and Stegner absorbed them. Description did not stand alone. It was not "inert and lifeless" but rather made a point or points and moved the reader along within the overarching narrative. For instance, the horses in Dutton's party plod southward toward the Grand Canyon through desert, plateau, and canyon country with wolves howling at night and geologic observations being made during the day until the goal is reached and, in Dutton's words in *Tertiary History*, "the earth suddenly sinks at our feet to illuminate depths. In an instant, in the twinkling of an eye, the awful scene is before us." In a similar manner, Stegner would lead readers down the Colorado River and into the science and politics of Powell's later years in Washington. Stegner, like Dutton, employed long series of words or phrases linked by commas. For both men serial phrases were a descriptive tic. There are also differences in their styles. Stegner's prose is spare, like the country he describes. He did not mimic Dutton's florid nineteenth-century style.

Stegner wrote the foreword for a new edition of Dutton's work on the Grand Canyon in 1977. He could just as well have been writing about himself when he said: "Dutton was the farthest thing from a narrow specialist. In all his work a habit of metaphor, a quality of imagination and enthusiasm, supplement the sobriety of scientific observation." Dutton's literary qualities, Stegner noted, shone "especially when he is dealing with spectacular country."[5] The foreword appeared as a magazine article the following year; its conception dated backward a half century to Stegner's smashed thumb.

Powell would emerge from behind Dutton as the primary character in *Hundredth Meridian* in 1954. "Dutton was great—he simply opened my eyes in all kinds of ways—and Powell was Dutton's boss," Stegner said, "so that it led naturally from one thing to another."[6]

HARDWORKING, DEDICATED, AMBITIOUS, and with a family to support and tenuous teaching positions to hold on to, Stegner devoted himself to multiple writing projects during the early years of his career. The spectacular canyonlands of the Southwest were secondary to his fiction through the late 1930s and 1940s. The notion of the Powell book took shape sporadically, like rapids on the Colorado River.

By 1942 the core idea for the book had come into focus. It was not so much the rousing adventure story of the first white men to run the canyons of the Green and Colorado Rivers as "the uncovering of Powell's germinal ideas and his enormous labor in laying the foundations for everything under the sun, and the later fruition of those ideas and the completing of the foundations into practical institutions of great importance that intrigues me," said Stegner. In a letter to Edwin Corle, who had also written books about the Southwest, Stegner added, "He has always seemed to me one of the big men on the West, and curiously buried and forgotten."[7]

Stegner received a grant from Harvard that year to work on the Powell book for a semester. But his fiction came first. He spent most of the time finishing *The Big Rock Candy Mountain* in the freezing cold of a Vermont winter. The next year he contacted Juanita Brooks, the Utah historian, asking for information on Powell. She recalled visiting with "Old Brother Spilsbury" before he died. Brother Spilsbury had carried a forty-gallon barrel of wine all night in his buckboard to the celebration of the Powell party's arrival at the end of its journey at the Grand Wash Cliffs, where Lake Mead has now covered the Colorado River. The wine "kicked like a mule in every cup," Spilsbury had told Brooks.[8]

There was "a blow," as Stegner described it, in 1947: Wally discovered that another writer was also working on a Powell biography. That author had contacted Houghton Mifflin, Stegner's publisher at the time. What to do? Conflicts of interest were rife. He wrote DeVoto, "Since he's almost done, there's nothing I can do except to hope he does a bad job and then to come along behind him several years hence, sweeping up his remains."[9] Stegner thought there would be room for two works on Powell. Besides, he was taking a wider view of the subject. DeVoto read the manuscript submitted by William Culp Darrah, who taught at Harvard. He thought it wouldn't hurt his friend's book and might even help him with some of the research. The more conventional biography, by the paleobotanist, was published by Princeton University Press in 1951.[10]

Darrah had been working on his book for ten years. His research was prodigious. He was concerned with "the man" and not, like Stegner, with the story of the West, conservation, and science and government. Darrah made that clear in the preface to his book in order to differentiate it from what he knew would follow. The more literary and historically inclined Stegner was interested in the arc of career set against the context of place.

It was a more civilized time, and both men were gentlemen. They did what would be unthinkable today: Darrah helped Stegner with research, and Stegner tried to find a publisher for Darrah. Stegner wrote his competitor: "I am glad that you feel as I do that we can both work on Powell without getting in each other's hair. They tell me that anyone worth one biography is worth two and that one hand washes the other."[11] Darrah and Stegner credited each other in their respective works on Powell.

Vague similarities and stylistic differences can be found scattered through the two books. The more conventional Darrah wrote, "In 1887 'Big Bill' Stewart of Nevada, after an absence of twelve years, returned to the Senate to fight for two causes—free silver and irrigation." Three years later the following passage appeared in Stegner's book: "When Big Bill Stewart of Nevada was returned to the Senate in 1887 on a platform of free silver and irrigation, he fitted the plot like a St. John the Baptist, saying, 'Prepare ye the way of the Lord.' "[12]

BEING THERE—"there" meaning the setting for a book—was a necessity for Stegner. It lifted his prose from the ordinary and contributed to his conservation activities. To experience the canyon country from the river and to follow partially in Powell's wake, in June of 1947 Wally floated down the San Juan River to where it joins the Colorado and passes through Glen Canyon on its way to Lees Ferry, Arizona. Mary accompanied him.

The Stegners joined a mixed group that included a seventy-two-year-old woman, a ten-year-old girl, and "a fattish and balding guy with marcelled curls around his edges" who was the voice of the Lone Ranger on the radio.[13] Walt Disney was going to make a nature film about the Colorado River Basin, and a photographer lugged a sixteen-millimeter camera along on the trip. Wally obligingly shook the aspen trees on the Kaibab Plateau to simulate a storm for the camera.

The trip was organized and led by Norman Nevills, a pioneer Colorado River boatman. Stegner had come across Nevills and learned of his river trips the year before, when he stopped at his ranch to borrow some baling wire to repair a broken trailer hitch. He didn't have the money or the time to duplicate all of Powell's journey, so the shorter trip would have to do. Stegner planned to do a story for *The Atlantic* ("Backroads River") while getting a feel for the place that could be incorporated into the book.

They floated downstream from Mexican Hat, Utah, in four wooden boats, arriving at Glen Canyon on the third day. Where water is backed up now by Glen Canyon Dam there was at that time a wide, deep, quiet fast-flowing river bending toward the west. Above the salmon-pink canyon walls, high buttes rose on each side. The Navajo sandstone was eroded "in knobs and domes." It was a magic land. There were no people, not even Navajo Indians, just scattered evidence of a more ancient people, the Anasazi. There were no sounds except for the dry rustle of the desert breeze in the tamarisk trees and the sibilant flow of water.

History was present in Glen Canyon in the form of the Crossing of the Fathers, where Fray Silvestre Vélez de Escalante had swum his mules across the river on his way back to Santa Fe in 1776; the trail the Mormons had blasted through Hole-in-the-Rock; and the sites where Powell and prospectors and various entrepreneurs with get-rich schemes and the lesser known and the unknown had lived and camped and raised food and families in years and centuries gone by.

There were no rapids through Glen Canyon. Stegner thought it was "the most serenely beautiful of all the canyons on the Colorado River." The stained and cracked sandstone cliffs were the most gorgeous in the Southwest. "The pockets and alcoves and glens and caves which irregular erosion has worn in the walls are lined with incredible greenery, redbud and tamarisk and willow and the hanging delicacy of maidenhair around springs and seeps."

They explored narrow side canyons where "the walls wave and overhang and cut off the sky," and they waded through waist-deep placid pools. Stegner rhapsodized about Hidden Passage Canyon, concealed behind a wall that masked its presence; waterfalls at the ends of other canyons; the huge domed chamber of Music Temple, where Powell had camped; caves large enough to enclose the Hollywood Bowl; and the tight squeeze into Labyrinth Canyon. Near the end of the trip, Stegner fantasized about avoiding the return to the world beyond the canyon walls. He wished to hide "and watch the river whirl by and write a book."[14]

Paradise was not perfect, however. Snags and logs and driftwood and four stiff legs raised upward from the bloated carcass of a dead deer or sheep floated past on the rising waters that were checked at that time by no large upstream dams.

STEGNER WORKED ON the long-delayed Powell biography in the summer of 1948. He took notes in the private Berkeley library of Francis P. Farquhar, an accountant and writer who had an extensive Powell collection. Farquhar and another Sierra Club member, Dick Leonard, sponsored Stegner for membership in the club, the only means whereby new members were admitted into the organization at that time. "I expect to have a lot of fun out of that organization," said Stegner, who didn't realize that his membership would be a mixed blessing.[15]

The family rented a cabin at the Three Rivers Ranch, forty miles north of Jackson Hole, that summer. The ranch was owned by

Struthers Burt, a well-connected novelist whose book Stegner had panned in a review. Stegner made amends and was told there was a place for him to write at the ranch. Burt recalled sitting on the porch of a New England hotel as a child and hearing Powell relate his adventures. He was also acquainted with the DeVotos and the Alfred Knopfs.

In a letter to his friend Phil Gray, Wally left one of his lyrical sketches of place and people that never saw print—this one dealing with the Teton Range in Wyoming:

> A month, or rather five weeks, in this place has incapacitated us for habitation elsewhere. Apart from the quiet, which is profound, and the thinking which goes on, which is profounder, there are the Tetons, in sight from our windows and very beautiful indeed, and the horse trails which we ride six days a week up through the Grand Teton Monument and the back lakes like Two Ocean and Emma Matilda. There are so many literary influences around the place it feels like Yaddo or the MacDowell colony. Both Struthers Burt and his wife are novelists, his son is a poet and musician, the hasher is writing a dude book, two of the daughters of Maxwell Perkins live in the cottage next to us, and the Filipino cook composes love songs for the guitar, with words like "No girl can love me, No girl can boss me," and "General MacArthur said he would-a come back."[16]

When the New York publisher Alfred Knopf and his wife, Blanche, visited the ranch, he found maps of the West tacked up on the wall of the Stegners' cabin. It was that summer visit to the West that turned the urbane publisher on to the region. He afterward wrote Stegner, "The West has gotten in my blood something awful; I have just got to go out there again to make sure it's real."[17] Knopf's interest led to a search for western authors, the acquisition of books about the West, chairmanship of the federal advisory board on national parks, and such western conservation battles as those fought over dams in Dinosaur National Monument. Stegner and Knopf would combine their talents to produce a book on Dinosaur.

Through most of 1949, Stegner was preoccupied with the troublesome Joe Hill novel. He completed it later that year. Paul Brooks, the editor in chief of Houghton Mifflin, telegraphed Stegner on November 17: "Congratulations on superb job." That same month, Stegner reported that he had completed one hundred pages of the Powell book.

After publication of *The Preacher and the Slave*, later retitled *Joe Hill*, in 1950, Stegner wondered why it had been so poorly received by both reviewers and readers. "This shakes my own belief that I know what a good book is," he wrote his editor, "or know when I've done halfway well. I am not writing any more books until I worry out some answer to this one, so I hope you will give me your wisdom."[18] Perhaps the book was a victim of bad timing came the reply. A far-left labor leader did not have much appeal during the McCarthy era.

There had been no book club deals, no best sellers, and only one "real" critical success in fifteen years of writing fiction, Stegner lamented. He wondered if he was in the right business and took out his frustrations by scything the meadow adjacent to his home. The crisis of confidence in his fiction lasted ten years, which was a good thing, because Stegner's nonfiction, which includes *Beyond the Hundredth Meridian*, blossomed during the 1950s.

One reason for his fiction slump was that his agents at Brandt & Brandt did not represent his book deals during this period. Wally had thought he could adequately represent his own interests and avoid paying the 10 percent agent commission. Bernice Baumgarten still arranged magazine sales and was available as a listening and leaning post. She was there for him in 1953 when, deep in the doldrums, Stegner said that he saw himself as "a professional half-caste, part writer and part teacher."[19]

Being both an editor and a writer for the same publisher had certain advantages and disadvantages. He had entrée to the executive offices. Although he could adequately represent Houghton Mifflin's position to other writers and occasionally did the Boston editors' hatchet work for them, Stegner did not represent his own writing interests very well. The relationship was too tangled.

During this period of struggle, Wally depended on Benny DeVoto for advice on the manuscript of *Beyond the Hundredth Meridian*. Stegner said he wanted to show how fantasy had been overtaken by knowledge of the West in the second half of the nineteenth century. He asked DeVoto: "Who contributed most to the gradually forming shape of the continent and its internal arrangements, and who contributed most to darkness and obfuscation?" Then there were the doubts. He didn't know whom he was writing the book for. "I really am scared to death to let anybody see this, for some reason. Maybe I know the thing stinks."

Back came the encouragement and practical advice. "I don't know that I ever saw a worse attack of literary megrims," wrote DeVoto. LOW SPIRITS

"Why, you God-damned idiot, this is a distinguished book, a fascinating book, and a much needed book." Write for the reader, not the bookstore buyer, he advised. "Never be afraid of length, only superfluity." Trust your first instincts. "Write things the natural and logical way." When you create a climax, make it a real climax, for there is "no point in putting a silencer on the gun when you shoot a sheriff." The book had tremendous scope, added DeVoto. "Look, son, you are writing the book about the culture of the West and the basis of life and society in the West." For that very reason, there will be critics:

> You must, of course, expect the customary dismay from the academics. It has not occurred to any of them that the stuff you work in is history, that history is so multiple or is to be found in such diverse and unfamiliar places, that these things existed, that light was to be had on anything by finding out about them, or that there was any area of history not covered by their lecture notes. You may not enjoy it; I do, but I will also enjoy seeing them on your neck.[20]

Stegner promised his publisher he would rewrite what he had already completed and compose a draft of eight more chapters by June of 1952. "From there on I can tell where the goddamn book is going." He didn't know whether he would get "the Pulitzer Prize or the Booby Prize in Wasted Effort." Houghton Mifflin kept pushing for delivery of the manuscript, which occurred in April 1953. It had been checked by Otis (Doc) Marston, an expert on river runners; representatives of the Bureau of Ethnology and the U.S. Geological Survey; and a triumvirate of historians who had written about the West: DeVoto, Dale Morgan, and Henry Nash Smith.[21]

Stegner now faced a decision that confronts every writer: when to follow gut instincts and when to follow the advice of an editor. Craig Wylie, an editor at Houghton Mifflin, wrote Stegner with the typical sugarcoated good news–bad news response to a manuscript. All that was missing was the vague reference to an anonymous editorial "we." Instead, the editor hid behind the names of other readers.

"I think Benny and Paul [Brooks] have given you the general idea that we all think you have written a potentially very important book with a great deal of spirit and a good broad brush," said Wylie. "There are certain things, however, that seem wrong to Paul and me—and some of them to Benny too—and it is in an attempt to become very specific about these things that I am now reading . . . [the manuscript a second time]." The editor had misrepresented DeVoto, who had written Stegner that his own suggestions were "microscopic." Wylie proceeded to nitpick the manuscript to pieces.

He added, in an attempt to end in an upbeat manner, that they really liked the "tripod" structural device of John Wesley Powell, the self-taught, science-oriented bureaucrat; Henry Adams, the privileged, Harvard-educated easterner; and the Yale-educated geologist Clarence King, the friend of Adams and others in high places. Designed as simplistic foils arrayed against this triad of education, Science (Stegner capitalized the word), and seekers after facts and logic was another triad: the irrational "tribe of Gilpin," represented by Colorado governor William Gilpin, the typical western boomer; an even more ridiculous follower, Captain Samuel Adams; and "Big Bill" Stewart, the development-minded senator from the silver-mining, waterless state of Nevada.

Wylie followed up that note with a long letter containing more than fifty specific comments.[22] Stegner replied in the margins "OK" and "maybe" to a few and "nuts" to most. While Wylie's intent was to clarify almost every detail, the cumulative result would have been to destroy the flow of the narrative. It is the type of editor-author struggle that can shape or destroy a book.

Stegner's reply to Brooks, Wylie's boss, was blistering. Yes, some suggested changes had merit, but others were absurd. "These are literally piddling; they shed no light on Powell and would have no effect on the book except to bog it down in pedestrian declarative sentences about things that don't matter." Such details "don't belong in this book. I worked very hard to keep them out. And I also worked hard to keep chronology from stifling me, especially in the earlier chapters." What Stegner had brought to the nonfiction book that Wylie failed to recognize were the sensibilities of a novelist.

The writer asked, What did Brooks think? "If you don't feel that the book is essentially sound as it is, and that HM can publish it with enthusiasm, then I truly don't believe HM should publish it at all. . . . I don't expect to do much more with it." Stegner had drawn the line. Brooks handed the letter to Wylie, who backtracked without backtracking. No wholesale revision was needed, just clarifying "scattered phrases, sentences, or at worst paragraphs," he said.[23]

But wait, Stegner said after publication of the book had already been ordered by Houghton Mifflin in the fall of 1953. Haven't we forgotten something? Yes, indeed we have, admitted his embarrassed publisher. No contract existed for the work, an important omission that would have been spotted and immediately corrected, in Stegner's favor, by an agent. The $1,500 advance against royalties in the standard Houghton Mifflin contract that Stegner subsequently signed was half what he received for the unsuccessful Joe Hill book, and the royalty rate was lower.

Last, there was the problem of finding the right title. Stegner suggested *Key to the Western Door; The Career of Major John Wesley Powell; Dirty Devil, Bright Angel* (a reference to a river and a creek that emptied into the Colorado that were, respectively, metaphors for the bad guys and the good guys in the book); and *John Wesley Powell and the Opening of the West*. Brooks countered with *John Wesley Powell and the American West* for purposes of the contract. Stegner replied: "I donno. I am about to admit defeat; I am about to suggest things like *The Last of the Explorers* or *The Grandfather Bureaucrat*. If there is respite and nepenthe in the office, I'm grasping for it. Maybe we ought to concentrate on geography and call it simply *Beyond the Hundredth Meridian*."[24] Bingo, they had a title, and a good one at that.

Hundredth Meridian is a hybrid—part history and part biography with a novelist's enlivening touch. The seamless narrative that Stegner fought for was published to general critical acclaim. *The New York Times* said that Stegner had told the life of Powell with "notable gusto and authority" and that the book is more than a life of Powell: "It is an evaluation of the arid West and its meaning in American Life." An exception, as DeVoto had predicted, was the academic response, represented by the *American Historical Review*, whose critic wrote that Stegner failed to "make the grade" as a historian: "Without a standard of selection or discrimination his chapters become a miscellany, or even worse trivial and unoriginal."[25]

To this day, academics have problems with the book. They see it as too novelistic. They also believe it is an extremely important book. "There is an important difference between good history and good novel writing," said Donald Worster, an environmental historian who teaches at the University of Kansas and recently wrote a biography of Powell. When Stegner made Powell the conservationist prophet of the arid West, wrote Worster, "it obscured the fact that he was, above all, an intensely nationalistic American," meaning that he was an advocate of Manifest Destiny. In 1994, as a warm-up for his full-scale biography, which would be published seven years later, Worster asserted that Stegner's work was "one of the most important books ever written about the region."[26]

To Richard White of Stanford University, "Stegner was a skilled writer, but he was not much of an historian." His Powell was too clear-cut, whereas the Powell in the biography by Worster was "more nuanced," said White, who nevertheless referred to Stegner's book as an "environmental classic" in a review of Worster's book for *The New Republic*. Karl Jacoby of Brown University echoed White's opinion in a comparison of the Stegner and Worster biographies in *The Journal of American History*. He thought Worster had been more circumspect in his book, whereas "Stegner's book now ranks as one of the most influential books ever written about the West, and more than any other work its publication explains Powell's resurrection to sainthood after World War II."[27]

Two months after publication of *Hundredth Meridian*, in September of 1954, more than six thousand copies had been sold, and revenues exceeded the small advance. Stegner received a royalty check for $1,253.34. There was talk of a Pulitzer Prize. But the history prize in 1954 went instead to *A Stillness at Appomattox* by Bruce Catton, and *The Spirit of St. Louis* by Charles A. Lindbergh won the biography/autobiography award. *Hundredth Meridian* was too difficult to classify.

Stegner's book remains in print more than fifty years after its publication. It was second on the *San Francisco Chronicle*'s 1999 readers' poll of the best nonfiction books written about or by an author from the West in the twentieth century, the first being Mary Austin's *Land of Little Rain*. Interestingly, the authors of the next four books on the list had close ties to Stegner: Edward Abbey and Evan Connell were his students at Stanford University, Ivan Doig sought his advice and his friendship, and Bernard DeVoto was his mentor.

Both Austin's and Stegner's books are about aridity, and both use synecdoche as a literary device, Austin employing California's Owens Valley as her point of departure and Stegner using Powell to frame his wider-ranging sermon that is disguised as a story. Wally brought the man and place to life, and he gave aridity real meaning for the first time on a region-wide basis. That was a gift the West desperately needed as the postwar dam-building era got under way.

WHO WAS THIS man through whom Stegner narrated the history of the American West in the second half of the nineteenth century and who briefly became, or so Stegner believed, more powerful over this vast domain than any president? By stating up front that he was interested in Powell's career but not his personal life, Stegner was not only declaring his intention for the book but also his model for biographies in general.

As the story of the "small, maimed, whiskery" explorer, scientist, and bureaucrat unfolded, Powell gained form and substance, as did his biographer. There were striking similarities between Powell and his amanuensis. Place shaped the main character, as it had the writer. Powell was "made by wandering," hardship, and deprivation, the frontier of the Middle West, "an outdoor life in small towns and on farms," country schools, and a homemade education "of a special kind," wrote Stegner. Powell did not know enough to be discouraged and was "as single-minded as a buzz saw." The result was "the culmination of an American type." The parallels were carried further. An East versus West theme emerged when Powell was compared with Henry Adams and Clarence King. Powell "started low and West," whereas Adams "started high and East." Clarence King "failed for lack of character, persistence, wholeness," qualities that distinguished Powell and that Stegner admired.[28] Government science was headquartered in Washington but practiced in the West.

The book is part rousing adventure story and part political morality play. Four boats and ten men departed from Green River, Wyoming, on May 24, 1869. Two boats holding six men emerged from the canyons on August 30. Four men had left the foundering expedition; three of them were killed by Indians or Mormons or their own foolishness in the Utah desert. The remainder survived near drownings, fire, loss of supplies and clothing, crippling heat, and always the fear of the unknown. Stegner drew on his firsthand experience to write of the journey:

> Through most of its course the canyoned Green and Colorado, though impressive beyond description, awesome and colorful and bizarre, is scenically disturbing, a trouble to the mind. It works on the nerves, there is no repose in it, nothing that is soft. The water-roar emphasizes what the walls begin: a restlessness and excitement and irritability. But Glen Canyon into which they now floated and which they first called Monument Canyon from the domes and "baldheads" crowning its low walls, is completely different. As beautiful as any of the canyons, it is almost absolutely serene, an interlude for a pastoral flute.[29]

There was a second expedition, and more science was practiced. What Powell derived most from his days of exploring was a close look at the arid lands and their native inhabitants and the public notice that propelled him into a job in Washington. "He was intellectually a plunger," wrote an admiring Stegner, "not a retreater."[30]

Between 1867 and 1877, during which time Powell made numerous fact-finding excursions to the interior West, the story begins to shift from the alternating placid calms and roiling turbulence of the river and the West to the ups and downs of political life in the nation's capital. In doing so, it becomes a fascinating real-life lesson in political science practiced at its most opaque levels—the points where policies bubble up from the bureaucracy to meet the imperatives of the legislative and executive branches of government.

Powell refined the ideas he had acquired while exploring the West by boat, foot, and horseback, first in his 1878 *Report on the Lands of the Arid Region of the United States* and later in his published writings, speeches, reports, and congressional testimony. Both Powell and Stegner, through their familiarity with the Mormons, saw that the winning, and continued viability, of the West depended not upon rugged individuals, as portrayed in dime novels and countless western movies, but rather upon groups and communities working together.

The most natural grouping in the West was watersheds. The rectangular surveys and rigid state and county lines did not fit the irregularities of western watersheds. Landscape should determine jurisdictions, not politically expedient artificial lines. The 160-acre limitation on homesteads was another senseless humid-lands law. It did not reflect the lack or presence of water but assumed a nonexistent constant. "Behind Powell's general plan was something absolutely basic," Stegner wrote, "the willingness to look at what was, rather than at what fantasy, hope, or private interest said should be."[31]

Donald Worster yoked Stegner to Powell in his biography of the latter. He wrote: "The West, according to Wallace Stegner, has not been so much settled as raided—first for its furs, then for its minerals, then for its grass, then in some places for its scenery, and with every raid the raiders have ignored consequences. Powell warned about those consequences, ecological and political, that persistence in old land policies must bring, and the raiders and boosters fought him as they fought reality."[32]

The first position that Powell assumed in Washington was as director of the Bureau of Ethnology, where he became the one person in the country most knowledgeable about Native Americans. He then became the director of the U.S. Geological Survey. Those two positions, along with his professional and social contacts, put him at the head of government science in the 1880s. "There was perhaps not a scientist in the world," wrote Stegner, "who enjoyed as much real power or as many opportunities." In the process of acquiring power, Powell also made enemies.[33]

Stegner explained Powell's downfall: "It was the West itself that beat him . . . the myth-bound West which insisted on running into the future like a streetcar on a gravel road."[34] Myth, which was supported by western politicians, said there was water for everyone and every use. Science, represented by Powell, said, Wait a minute. Let's determine how much water there really is and what it can support. What Powell advocated was an all-wise federal entity that would impose scientifically determined policies. That was a threat to Congress and the mythmakers. In the end, Science was defeated by Myth.

Although not exactly what Powell envisioned, the Bureau of Reclamation soon emerged to do the water interests' bidding by building large dams, reservoirs, and aqueducts. Whereas Stegner saw Powell as a conservationist, Worster thought he was an instrument of development. Both the conservationists and the dam builders would claim Powell as their own. But it was Stegner who constructed the historical foundation and framed the debate over water in the West that continues to this day.

When *Beyond the Hundredth Meridian* was published, Stegner was on the verge of joining the fight against the dams the bureau planned in Dinosaur National Monument. He had acquired the necessary background; now it was time to put his knowledge to practical use and take action.

From Words to Deeds

We are the most dangerous species of life on the planet, and every other species, even the earth itself, has cause to fear our power to exterminate. But we are also the only species which, when it chooses to do so, will go to great effort to save what it might destroy.

Wallace Stegner, in *This Is Dinosaur*

IT WAS HIS memory of what Glen Canyon had been, his knowledge of arid lands, and his contact with David Brower, who had just become the first executive director of the Sierra Club, that propelled Stegner into the fight over two dams in Dinosaur National Monument. Many of the tools, techniques, and attitudes of present-day environmentalists emerged from what has been termed the central event in the narrative of modern conservation.

The battle over dams in Dinosaur was a defining test of the sanctity of national parks, the primary concern of conservationists at the time. The trail led backward to the futile attempt to save Hetch Hetchy Valley in Yosemite National Park in the early years of the century and forward to the next great conservation battle, a legislative solution to the issue of designating wilderness areas on public lands in the 1960s. Like many such clashes of radically opposing concepts, the battle resulted in no clear winners or losers.

Working on the Powell book had prepared Stegner for the fray. DeVoto, who was looking for company in his crusade, launched Stegner. "Benny DeVoto has commanded me to write an article on what is likely to happen to the conservation program in the West under the Republicans," he wrote Baumgarten at Brandt & Brandt. Stegner said he would query the editor of *The Reporter* magazine. "My last chapter on Powell leads me into the conservation business anyway, so I might as well try to gratify Benny and turn a penny all at the same time."[1]

The resulting article about the public lands in the May 1953 issue of *The Reporter* brought him to the attention of the conservationists. Stegner's explanation of public lands and their use, the legacy of Powell, and the "dangerous" policies of the Republican presidents Taft, Hoover, and Eisenhower echoed in a quieter manner the noisier tirades of DeVoto's in *Harper's*.[2]

Leaders of conservation organizations recognized that the sagebrush crown had been passed from the older to the younger man. Olaus J. Murie of the Wilderness Society wrote the editor of *The Reporter* that he had "done the nation a service" in publishing the article. Brower thanked the magazine's public relations director for sending him a copy of the story: "Congratulations to whomever brought Professor Wallace Stegner into the field of conservation writing, congratulations to professor Stegner on a first rate article, and congratulations to *The Reporter* for landing and publishing it," Brower added.[3]

Never one to hesitate and always one to seize an opportunity—especially one involving an important convert to the cause—Brower sent Stegner a copy of his letter and a treatment for a documentary film on Dinosaur. He asked for suggestions and added that he had meant to draw Stegner into the dams in Dinosaur issue earlier. He was about to run the river and hoped to hear from him.

A close working relationship between the two men developed from this initial correspondence. Brower was dedicated, innovative, combative, and driven by the white heat of righteousness or an oversize ego—take your pick, because his contemporaries in the Sierra Club saw it both ways. There was a good fit for a time. Stegner knew the interior West; Brower and other club members didn't. It was a strange land to them. The club had a narrow regional focus, California being its main concern. Dinosaur and the canyonlands of the West were "a long step afield," both physically and in terms of club policy. Few members had heard of the place, and fewer knew where it was. But the integrity of the national park system was at stake. So onward marched the conservationists, like Christian soldiers going off to war.

Stegner warned Brower about the dangers of swimming through the rapids of Split Mountain in Dinosaur National Monument, as Stegner had done as a youth. Brower assured him that the only rapids his party had swum were on the Yampa River, and besides, the water level had been quite low that year.

Brower was interested in learning more about the Four Corners area, that point where the stacked box shapes of Utah, Colorado, New

Mexico, and Arizona converge on the Navajo Indian Reservation. There had just been a story, a map, and color photos in the *National Geographic* suggesting that it was prime country for inclusion in the national park system. He and some members of the Sierra Club board were concerned about "our lack of information on this country. How many more Dinosaur National Monuments are we allowing, through ignorance, to remain essentially unknown and unprotected?" A good question, as it would come to pass. What do you think, Professor Stegner? Can we meet "and talk this problem over with maps and photographs in hand?" And by the way, he added, could you perhaps contribute something to *The Sierra Club Bulletin*?[4]

The film script on Dinosaur, Stegner thought, was "admirable," but there were some errors and omissions. As for Four Corners, he knew it only from one car trip, when he'd had to crawl under a one-wheel trailer and repair the hitch that had been broken on the rough Dinnehotso Road. Four Corners had seemed "extremely barren, and for most people's tastes forbidding" from the road. Since it is part of the Navajo Indian Reservation, "much of it is already preserved after a fashion." The real threat, Stegner said, was in southern Utah, from dams and mineral development, the latter meaning uranium mines and oil and gas wells and all the secondary things, like airports, that accompanied such energy booms. He added, referring to Dinosaur and Four Corners:

> More immediately threatened than either of these regions is the Glen Canyon, which ought properly to be added to the Rainbow Bridge National Monument, but which is already, I guess, doomed by the dam-makers. You probably know Glen Canyon; for my money it is better than the Yampa-Green section, and it has the Navajo Mountain–Rainbow Bridge as well as the Natural Bridges monument on its fringes. Really sound planning could reserve the natural bridges, Glen Canyon, and the Rainbow Bridge as a single national park—and you could throw in the Four Corners without straining probability too much.[5]

No, he did not know Glen Canyon, Brower replied, and he would regret at the time that he didn't.

The warning about Glen Canyon, so clear and prescient in hindsight, went unheeded. Years later, when Stegner was asked by an interviewer whether Brower was pleased to find someone who knew the interior West, he answered: "Well, yes, and he's always said that if he'd listened to me then Glen Canyon Dam might not have gone in, because I kept telling him Glen Canyon was a whole lot more worth saving than Dinosaur. But, you know, at the moment Dinosaur was threatened; Glen Canyon wasn't."[6]

Sure, he would write something for the Bulletin, Stegner told Brower in September of 1953. Perhaps some text could be lifted from his upcoming biography of Powell. He was in Iowa and would soon return to California. Let's have a drink, lunch, a talk. "I'd be pleased," he said, "to know more specifically what the Sierra Club is doing and plans to do, and happy to do what I can to help."

Brower scribbled on the letter, which was passed on to a colleague: "We should try sometime to have a long talk with Stegner. He has the makings of a Western DeVoto and any national magazine such as the *Atlantic, Harper's, New Yorker* would be happy to have his fiction."[7] The two eventually met at a Berkeley cocktail party marking the publication of the Powell book.

THE SHORT DINOSAUR film, made for $500, was just the beginning of Brower's innovative plan of attack, which included a book on Dinosaur that would be the forerunner of the large-format photography books that addressed conservation issues, made publishing history, and nearly drove the club to insolvency in the next decade. He'd had DeVoto in mind as the book's editor, but the author of "The Easy Chair" columns was ailing. He died in late 1955.

Brower then approached Stegner, who knew Dinosaur as he knew Glen Canyon: he had been there. Stegner agreed to edit and contribute the first chapter to the book, whose cost of publication would be paid by the publisher Alfred Knopf, who was chairman of the National Parks Advisory Board.[8] The book, in Knopf's mind, was not entirely a matter of unconditional love for national parks. An organization or group, such as the Sierra Club, needed to buy a certain number of copies in order to at least cover costs and, it was hoped, make a profit. "We simply cannot ourselves afford the loss that publication would undoubtedly involve," Knopf told Stegner and Brower at the outset. He was later bitter that "when it came to putting cash on the barrel head, . . . [the Sierra Club] left us carrying the whole bag."[9]

The plans went forward without any financial commitment from the Sierra Club. The publisher would write the concluding chapter.

Others with a conservation bent and knowledge of the national monument would be enlisted to write chapters. The photos would come from Philip Hyde, a student of Ansel Adams's; Martin Litton, a magazine editor and river runner; and others. It was a rush job. "I had the pleasant, sort of fiendishly pleasant, job of editing Alfred Knopf's prose," said Stegner, "which Alfred didn't like very much. We remained friends. He's a wonderful man, but he was used to being on the other end."[10]

The publisher of Kafka, Camus, Mencken, Cather, and other giants of the written word, who would garner for the firm by the time of his death sixteen Nobel and twenty-seven Pulitzer Prizes, at first gave Stegner carte blanche to edit his essay, stating: "If there is anything I don't fancy myself as, it is as a writer, and if there is anything I don't enjoy doing, it's writing." Knopf urged Stegner to edit rigorously "and throw it out if it is of no use." When confronted with the results of Stegner's editing, Knopf changed his mind. It didn't sound like him. His wife agreed, and two Knopf employees, whose opinions were solicited in a blind reading test of the edited and unedited manuscripts, split on the one they favored. Knopf bolstered his position with the concurring opinion of his production manager.

Stegner had deleted, altered, or rewritten Knopf's angrier passages and personal attacks. One phrase Knopf hated to lose was a comparison of the dam builder—the federal Bureau of Reclamation—to a dog with fleas. "We are trying to sound objective, good-tempered, and without personal rancor (though we burn with it inside)," explained Stegner.[11] Eventually, Knopf agreed with most of the changes.

There was another glitch. At the end of one letter dealing with design matters, Knopf added the caveat "that is assuming there is going to be a book in the end." Stegner immediately shot back: "If I hadn't thought that was settled for sure I wouldn't have started working on it, because although my enthusiasm for Dinosaur is great, my need to earn a living is also great, and I can't waste time on good works that turn out not to be works but idle speculation." Knopf backed down, stating that he was "hooked" on the book.[12]

While in design and production, it became known as the Knopf, not the Dinosaur, book. With galley proofs due in February 1955, Stegner was hoping his job was done. "He has already contributed a tremendous amount of time," noted Brower.[13] The text read well, despite the hurry, but the reproduction of the photos was mediocre, and the layout was uninspired. It was a learning experience for the Sierra Club.

The purpose of the book, said Stegner in the foreword, was "to show—so far as words and pictures can show a region so varied and colorful—what the people would be giving up, what beautiful and instructive and satisfying things their children and their grandchildren and all other Americans from then on would never see." The strategy, in other words, was to demonstrate the relatively unspoiled nature of Dinosaur.

The chapter Stegner wrote was a preliminary exercise for his famous Wilderness Letter, to come six years later. He defined Dinosaur through the historical progression of human usage: "A place is nothing in itself. It has no meaning, it can hardly be said to exist, except in terms of human perception, use, and responses." There was a vast difference between types of uses. "Some uses use things up and some last forever. Recreation, properly controlled, is a perpetual use, and a vital one."[14] In other words, Dinosaur would remain accessible and could still remain a wilderness. "Use, but do no harm" defined wilderness, conservation, and national parks and monuments for Stegner, who chose balance over environmental extremism and, at this time in his life, hope over hopelessness.

At the end of the book, Knopf outlined the purpose of national parks and monuments. Destroy Dinosaur, he said, and you destroy the idea of the national parks. Under "A Note on Contributors," Knopf is identified as "a consistent, tenacious, and informed fighter for conservation policies." The description, which was written by Knopf, or certainly approved by him, went on to state, somewhat tongue in cheek: "He annually practices what he preaches, and takes his refreshment and restoration in the parks which he has done much to protect and support."[15] Knopf was known for the gourmet picnics and fine wines he took on advisory board field trips. He had spent two days on the Green River in 1954.

Five thousand copies were printed, but *This Is Dinosaur* did not sell well. It did, however, serve its primary purpose, as a lobbying tool. Copies were given to every member of Congress, important members of the executive branch, and influential newspaper editors. A brochure titled *What Is Your Stake in Dinosaur?* was published by Brower, inserted into each copy of the book, and circulated separately. It drew parallels between flooding Hetch Hetchy Valley and building the proposed Echo Park and Split Mountain dams in Dinosaur National Monument. The film, an ad in *The Denver Post*, and the printed matter all broke new ground. Undoubtedly they helped, but there was also an incentive for both sides to end the impasse.

A compromise between conservationists and western water interests provided for scrapping the dam projects in Dinosaur (actually down to one dam, in Echo Park, near the end of the fight) in return for a dam in Glen Canyon. Language was inserted into the Colorado River Storage Project Act of 1956 stating that "no dam or reservoir constructed under the authorization of this act shall be within any national park or monument." For the water interests a huge tank in Glen Canyon would serve just as well as, if not better than—except for the leaky sandstone and massive amount of evaporation—a smaller storage facility in Dinosaur. Six months later President Dwight D. Eisenhower detonated by remote control the blast in the Navajo sandstone that signaled the start of construction on Glen Canyon Dam.

One year earlier Brower had confided privately that he did not want to see a dam built in Glen Canyon. "I still want to see Glen Canyon and hope I can make it. From all I have heard it is a beautiful place."[16] In the summer of 1962, Brower floated the Colorado River through Glen Canyon as work progressed on the dam. He wrote Stegner, who by this time was on the publications committee of the Sierra Club:

> A Glen Canyon book might never begin to do so well . . . [as a prior book on wilderness]. All I know is that we've got to get out the best, most beautiful damned book we ever saw.
>
> If Glen goes, the monstrousness of the loss and its perpetrators must never be lost sight of. At long last, you see, I've had a chance to see the place—three chances, 21 days in all, two miles of film—this summer.
>
> There could be no more unconscionable crime against a scenic wonder of the world than Glen Canyon Dam. You said it long ago, and now I know it—Dinosaur doesn't compare.[17]

The main reason why he "sat on his duff instead of acting," Brower said in his autobiography, was that he had not been there. "I had not yet gone through Glen Canyon the several times I was to go with family and friends." If he had, it would have been a different story, he said.[18]

The compromises continued, this time in the Grand Canyon. Brower went back to Washington on a vain mission to plead with Secretary of the Interior Udall not to close the gates on the Glen Canyon diversion dam. He waited in vain outside Udall's office for a brief discussion. Brower finally caught sight of the secretary from the back of the room at a press conference later that January day in 1963. Udall announced a huge Southwest water plan that included two dams in the Grand Canyon. They were not located in the national park proper, but in areas that were later to become part of the park. The reservoir waters would invade the new boundaries of the park.

The Sierra Club would go after those dams in the Grand Canyon with a ferocity and techniques honed by the Dinosaur fight. *The Place No One Knew* (about Glen Canyon) and *Time and the River Flowing* (about the Grand Canyon) followed *This Is Dinosaur.* Bigger and more sophisticated ads were run in newspapers around the country. The result was that there would be no dams between Lake Powell and Lake Mead—but there would be something else.

Brower and the other conservationists who joined the fight against the Grand Canyon dams lacked the foresight to recognize what another compromise would entail. This time they favored nuclear and coal-burning power plants as a substitute for dams. A half-dozen coal plants were built from Four Corners to the southern tip of Nevada. The quality of the traditional style of life, the water resources of the Navajo and Hopi Indians, and the air quality of the national parks in the Southwest deteriorated.

Stegner revisited Glen Canyon as Lake Powell was beginning to fill. It was a bit like looking at a photograph of Miss America from the waist up, he said. "Though they have diminished it," Stegner wrote in an article for *Holiday*, a travel magazine, "they haven't utterly ruined it." There was a different type of beauty. The deep, blue water lapping against the reddish sandstone was "bizarre and somehow exciting." Enough of the canyons remained—meaning their tops—that there was a sense of discovery around each bend: "new colors, new forms, new vistas."[19] From the elevated water level, Navajo Mountain was more visible. Most of all, Stegner missed the places he had once experienced that were now irretrievably lost.

Interestingly, his field notes for the article, written in a small brown notebook embossed with the logo of California Tomorrow, a Bay Area planning and conservation group, were not as sanguine: "The best part of the trip for everybody was the walk [to Rainbow Bridge], which will be gone at higher water. Canyon will be messed up with slime & silt once water rises & recedes." As the lake continued to rise, there would be further changes. "Altogether what will be lost is sense of sanctuary & snugness, except in side canyons, many of which will go under entirely."[20]

Floyd Dominy, the aggressive dam-building commissioner of the

Bureau of Reclamation, read the magazine article and liked it. There was no question that the environment had been radically altered, Dominy wrote Stegner, but what was created was "a lake of extraordinary beauty and attractiveness, as your article points out." Stegner thanked Dominy for beginning a dialogue and reminded him that "we do have some apparently unresolvable differences of opinion about Colorado River dams."[21]

In his book on Dinosaur, *A Symbol of Wilderness*, Mark W. T. Harvey said of the Brower-Stegner-Knopf book: "Behind the pictures and eloquent words of the book came forth the philosophy of wilderness activists in the postwar years." The Wilderness Act of 1964 was an outgrowth of the dams-in-Dinosaur fight. Thirty years after the publication of *This Is Dinosaur*, a more jaded Wallace Stegner told Harvey that it had been a classic western squabble, which he defined as "the endlessly repetitive exploitation v. preservation points of view."[22]

The Next Lone Ranger

It used to be that when so-called "resource-development" interests undertook one of their raids against the public lands, Bernard DeVoto would appear like the Lone Ranger, trail the villains, and end by yanking out their shirt-tails and setting fire to them. If he were alive now, as God knows I wish he were, he would be warming up his blowtorch, not because what he used to call Two-Gun Desmond is shooting up the town again but because conservationists are moving to make at least part of the public domain permanently safe from raids. There comes a time in every horse opera, as Mr. DeVoto knew, when the Better Element set out to clean up the Territory.

> Wallace Stegner, "The War Between the Rough Riders
> and the Bird Watchers"

Altogether, this letter, the labor of an afternoon, has gone farther around the world than any other writings on which I have spent years. . . . Returning to the letter after 20 years, I find that my opinions have not changed. They have actually been sharpened by an increased urgency.

> Wallace Stegner, "The Geography of Hope"

THE EMBOLDENED CONSERVATIONISTS took on wilderness as their next great issue following Dinosaur. The public lands, located primarily in the West and Alaska, amounted to one third of the nation's landmass. They were vulnerable to a host of destructive uses, so a legislative solution similar to what had been obtained for Dinosaur was sought for the wilder lands. The goal was to establish a national system of wilderness areas on federal lands that no executive fiat could overturn.

Wilderness legislation was introduced in Congress in 1957. What was different for the conservationists was the fact that this legislation was an effort to create, not negate. As such, and because of the stakes involved for the opposition, it took a longer time and a greater effort to succeed. Seven years, nine congressional hearings, six thousand pages of testimony, and sixty-six modifications of language and submissions of amended bills later there was wilderness legislation.

From the sidelines, Stegner supplied the *Geist* for the greatest legislative effort in conservation history, which culminated in the passage of the 1964 Wilderness Act. The letter that Stegner produced in one afternoon of two-finger typing on his Remington manual typewriter was "one of the best" postfrontier statements of the philosophy of wilderness, according to the wilderness historian Roderick Nash. To Dan Flores, who specializes in the environmental history of the American West, the Wilderness Letter was "a world-wide classic of environmental history, a galvanizing document . . . [that] with good reason has been endlessly quoted as perhaps the single best statement on behalf of wilderness preservation."[1]

THE LETTER AND how it eventually reached a wide audience evolved in the following manner. Stegner took Brower up on his offer to write for *The Sierra Club Bulletin* and in May of 1959 produced an article titled "The War Between the Rough Riders and the Bird Watchers." Invoking Powell's name and concepts, Stegner sketched the history of public lands and, as he saw them, the heavily weighted pro arguments versus the lightly and ironically sketched con arguments on the subject of wilderness.

His rhetoric was loaded with a somewhat labored historical twist. The interior West, said Stegner, was similar to the South. It evinces "a persistent acrimonious lust after states' rights, which in the West are inextricable from natural resources and the public lands." Both the Mountain West and the South possessed regional guilt. "If the South had black slavery," Stegner wrote, "the West has had its crimes against the land." Aware that the last sentence can be the most powerful, Stegner ended the article: "It has never been man's gift to make wilderness. But he can make deserts, and has."

The antiwilderness forces stalled for time and hoped to defeat the bill by recommending that Congress wait for publication of the National Outdoor Recreation Resources Commission's report, which was not due until 1962. Who knows, the thinking went, the report requested by Congress just might determine that there was no need for wilderness.

The idea for the Wilderness Letter came from a young forester with a penchant for conservation activism who would later defeat a powerful utility company's plans for a nuclear power plant north of San Francisco. David E. Pesonen had just come on board as a research assistant for the Wildlands Research Center at the University of California at Berkeley. The center, a grant-generating unit buried within the School of Forestry, had a one-year contract with the outdoor recreation commission to produce "factual information on the nature, extent, and use of wilderness resources." Pesonen had read *Beyond the Hundredth Meridian*. He knew Stegner could write, and he was having difficulty articulating the idea of what wilderness meant to people.

There were telephone calls between Brower, Pesonen, and Stegner. Pesonen wrote to "Dr. Stegner" on June 15, 1960. The only recipient of a carbon copy noted at the end of the letter was Pesonen's boss, James P. Gilligan, wilderness project director for the center. Brower also received a copy, however, and sent copies of the letter, marked "Not for Publication," to the Sierra Club board and the executive director of the Wilderness Society.

In many ways the request framed the response. The center's personnel felt constrained by the officially mandated parameters of their task, Pesonen explained. They had to consider the place of wilderness in outdoor recreation, which meant quantifying play. Their allotted role was "loaded against wilderness preservation." Instead, said Pesonen, "we shall consider the place of wilderness in the national consciousness, culture, psyche, whatever it is that constitutes a feeling about wilderness, of which science and recreation are only a part."

What Pesonen needed to include in the report was "the Wilderness Idea, abstracted from wilderness use." This was a new concept for Stegner, who had previously linked wilderness to such tangibles as history and current uses. It needed to be demonstrated, Pesonen said, that wilderness was democratic, meaning that it served a large proportion of the population, and that it was a popular, political issue. In this way a wilderness bill could be passed. Stegner, said Pesonen in his admitted "pitch," was the only person qualified to articulate these ideas. He needed a six-page letter within the next four months—six pages because that was all the space they had, and he wouldn't presume to edit it.[2]

Nearly six months later Stegner complied. He wrote not only about wilderness as an idea but also about wilderness as a specific place and the effect of this particular type of place on him. He got mad, said his friend Tom Watkins, and what emerged were a manifesto, a central document, and a coda. The letter reads as though the writer had hit a flow, with Pesonen's specific requests serving to channel him, and followed a pitch-perfect line through the rapids on a swift, intuitive ride.

The wilderness idea, said Stegner, helped form our character and shape our nation's history. The wilderness was a challenge that unrolled and was rolled back as we proceeded westward. If we lose it, we lose our history and our identity in relationship to the surrounding natural environment. We become nothing, in other words, and are committed "to a headlong dive into our technological termite life." As we age, the benefits of wilderness change. "It is good for us when we are young, because of the incomparable sanity it can bring briefly, as vacation and rest, into our insane lives," said the middle-aged writer. "It is important to us when we are old simply because it is there—important, that is, simply as idea." For Stegner, wilderness was a deeply personal issue:

> For myself, I grew up on the empty plains of Saskatchewan and Montana and in the mountains of Utah, and I put a very high valuation on what those places gave me. And if I had not been able periodically to renew myself in the mountains and deserts of western America I would be very nearly bughouse. Even when I can't get to the back country, the thought of the colored deserts of southern Utah, or the reassurance that there are still stretches of prairie where the world can be instantaneously perceived as disk and bowl, and where the little but intensely important human being is exposed to the five directions and the thirty-six winds, is a positive consolation.

The traditional wilderness landscapes, alpine and forested lands, the former coming to be known as "wilderness on the rocks," were fine, but so were the prairie and the desert. The chief values of wilderness were that there were few people and "such a timeless and uncontrolled part of the earth is still there."

Then Stegner brought his argument to a conclusion and gave it the resonance that would propel the last four words into the nature hall of fame: "We simply need that wild country available to us, even if we never do more than drive to its edge and look in. For it can be a means of reassuring ourselves of our sanity as creatures, a part of the geography of hope."[3]

Stegner's letter was contained in the center's report that was sent to the outdoor recreation commission. But it was omitted from the commission's final report, sent to President John F. Kennedy by its chairman, Laurence S. Rockefeller, in January of 1962. Lurking on two inside pages of the final report was the residue of Stegner's concepts. Wilderness areas, the commission determined, "satisfy a deep-seated human need occasionally to get far away from the works of man." There was a "widespread feeling" that in order to preserve them, Congress should take "prompt and effective action."[4]

THE LETTER BEGAN to find a life of its own through informal channels. Shortly after Udall had been named secretary of the interior, Stegner sent him a copy of *Beyond the Hundredth Meridian.* "I thought there might be something in it that he could make use of," said Stegner.[5] Udall invited Stegner to drop by his office when he was in Washington, and Wally and Mary did so in January of 1961. The two men, both westerners, immediately liked each other. Stegner gave Udall a copy of the letter as he walked out the door.

The secretary had been invited to speak at the Sierra Club's Seventh Biennial Wilderness Conference in San Francisco in April. "It was so powerful and so eloquent and so poetic a statement concerning wilderness," said Udall, "that I thought, when I attempted later to write a text of my own, that it would be foolish not to read it."[6] Udall telephoned Stegner at Williamsburg, Virginia, where the author was making a stop on a speaking tour, and asked permission to read the letter at the conference. Stegner gave his consent.

Udall toured by helicopter on April 7 what would become Point Reyes National Seashore (which now contains officially declared wilderness). He spoke that night in the Gold Room of the Sheraton Palace Hotel, where he was introduced by Supreme Court Justice William O. Douglas, a great wilderness lover. Besides Justice Douglas, such big names in the wilderness movement as Howard Zahniser of the Wilderness Society, Joseph W. Penfold and Sigurd Olson of the Izaak Walton League, the urban planner Catherine Bauer Wurster, the photographer Ansel Adams, the writer Joseph Wood Krutch, Sierra Club president Edgar Wayburn, and of course David Brower were participants in the conference. Stegner was not present.

The letter was the highlight of the very successful wilderness conference. The Friday-night banquet was attended by seven hundred people, and the proceedings were broadcast over the radio. Two sixteen-millimeter cameras recorded the event. The Sierra Club was besieged for copies of "that wonderful Stegner letter." Later that year, Brower published the conference's proceedings, which contained the first printed version of the letter.

Its popularity spread. Stegner saw the letter posted in a game park in Kenya, and references to it appeared on posters in Rhodesia, South Africa, Australia, Canada, and Israel. The phrase "geography of hope" is contained in the title of at least seven books. Either the entire text or the key phrase has appeared in countless newspapers, magazines, and books. A search of the Internet reveals thousands of references.

With the publication of the entire letter in *The Washington Post*, it was viewed by far more decision makers than was the outdoor recreation commission's report. The momentum that would climax in the passage of the Wilderness Act three years later had begun to build.

Closer to Home

Some of the things that go on outside our windows are less reassuring, incomparably swifter, immeasurably more destructive,
and a thousand times more visible than natural forces produce.
Industrial society in an area of expansive growth does not move
with the dignity of geological change. The roads, cuts, and
buildings of subdivisions, even much landscaping, have no
slow inevitability about them. They are imposed on the hills by
force, they obey no natural laws, they do not conform themselves to the terrain but conform the terrain to themselves. . . .
Most of what people have done to the hills they have done
ruthlessly, against the grain, without foresight or concern for
consequences.

Wallace Stegner, "The Peninsula," in *20-20 Vision:
In Celebration of the Peninsula Hills*

WILDERNESS IS MACRO, a vast expanse of fairly pristine
land removed from cities and their appendages. Open
space is micro, a lot, a marsh, a hillside, or rolling hills in
an urban or suburban setting. Stegner was concerned with both not
long after he bought the oak-dotted property in Los Altos Hills.

For a man who had passed through many places in his lifetime,
rented more than his share of residences, and finally owned a home on
seven paradisiacal acres in one of the most pleasant climatic zones in
the country, there should have been a sense of finality, of rootedness, of
settling in and coming to rest in one place. The Stegners, after all,
spent more than half their lives in this one house. But California and
the West bred transience, with Stegner one of its better-known off-
spring. Movement was inherent in the landscape. California was never
home to Stegner, at least not in the way he chose to define it. California
personified change, and he despaired over it.

Unfortunately, as it turned out, Stegner chose the wrong place to live. He found himself residing in the midst of massive change. From the mid-1940s through the 1960s what was known as the pastoral Valley of the Heart's Desire was transformed into the valley of desire for instant riches and what would become known as Silicon Valley. "The coming of the electronic city," as the geographer Richard A. Walker referred to it, caused massive dislocations.

The new Stanford Industrial Park, with its high-tech tenants, symbolized the industrial landscape of the future in America. Around it huddled huge housing tracts. The population exploded in the Santa Clara Valley from just under three hundred thousand to just over one million during the first quarter century after World War II. Planning and zoning were in the hands of the developers. "Towns set aside vast tracts of empty space for industry and approved every housing subdivision that came forward," wrote Walker. "Elite suburbs like Los Altos Hills and Saratoga established large lot sizes to enforce their social character and keep out the subdividers. No one looked to the collective effects."[1]

In the 1950s, Stegner saw what was coming. Citing growth figures thought to be rampant in those days but minuscule in comparison to what was to come, he said in the year that Glen Canyon was lost: "The enormously swollen future haunts my dreams." Speaking at an open-space conference sponsored by the local chapter of the Sierra Club in 1956, Stegner said that conservation began with very small things, like a single lot. He had seen a sign in India a few years before that asked, "Who Planted the Trees?" then answered, "A Friend of God." We should all be such a friend was his message. We need open space, the urban equivalent of wilderness. How would we get it? This was his advice: "Organize, talk it up, and get into groups."[2]

The peninsula south of San Francisco was no ordinary place in the second half of the twentieth century. The city of Palo Alto was the privileged appendage of Stanford University, and the encircling communities that lived off the university's largesse constituted an enclave within the affluent white suburbs of the peninsula. Brains and horses, relatively large lots, and high incomes predominated within the small circle. African Americans were grouped in East Palo Alto.

In a Voice of America broadcast and a magazine article, Stegner publicly took notice of the divisions and inequities on the peninsula that were precisely demarcated by the Bayshore Freeway. West of Highway 101 the democratic process worked well in Los Altos Hills, where "without snobbery and class divisions" the citizens sought to preserve "the charms of climate and landscape." In the "authentic ghetto" of East Palo Alto, on the other side of the freeway, open space was not an overriding concern. There were other, more pressing problems, Stegner said. The residents were confronted with de facto school segregation and the lack of basic social and economic necessities. His idealistic solution was for the whites to supply money and political muscle.[3]

For those people, like the Stegners, who had arrived from elsewhere during the postwar years, the peninsula was nirvana. Who needed snow and ice and humid heat? When it got too hot, nature herself turned on the air conditioner, and a cooling fog enveloped the ridgeline and spread over the foothills and bay-side flats. "Waterfall fog, one of the most beautiful sights in nature, visible in only a few places on earth, commonplace here. And salutary," wrote Stegner.[4]

For a change of season or terrain the new arrival had only to drive a few miles. A short distance to the west was the vast expanse of the Pacific Ocean. In the opposite direction was the San Joaquin Valley, with its striking agricultural fecundity. Beyond were the rugged fourteen-thousand-foot-high peaks of the Sierra Nevada and the abyss of Death Valley. The abundance and the variety of landscapes were staggering, and they seemed to stun the fictional characters whom Stegner located in this place.

The couple in *All the Little Live Things*, who could very well have been the Stegners, took a walk on their Los Altos Hills property:

> Somewhere along there we always stopped to admire the view, with our backs to the orchard and our faces toward the pasture and woodland rolling steeply down and then more steeply up, ravine and ridge, to the dark forested mountainside and the crest. Across the mountain the pale air swept in from remote places—Hawaii, Midway, illimitable Japans. I have never anywhere else had so strong a feeling of the vast continuity of air in which we live. On a walk, we flew up into that gusty envelope like climbing kites.[5]

Stegner was attuned to the duality of the California landscape, seemingly gentle but harboring the potential for great violence. Of the San Andreas Fault, that seamed dividing line between two great tectonic plates not far from his home, he wrote: "In a cross-eyed sort of way I have been comforted by the thought of that crack under the smiling hills: the devil's in his diocese, all's right with the world. . . . Where you find the greatest Good, there you will also find the greatest Evil, for Evil likes Paradise every bit as much as Good does."[6]

Natural disasters in northern California, as Stegner well knew, took different forms. He told fellow inhabitants of the peninsula's foothills that they faced the same problems as those who lived in arid lands: the ground cover was minimal, slopes were steep, and runoff from violent rainstorms produced "migrating tract homes." As he put it with his customary pithy, literary flair: "I will lift up mine eyes unto the hills, whence cometh my floods, whence cometh my mudslides, whence cometh my neighbor's house."[7]

California was a land of extremes: extreme mountains and deserts, extreme conservationists, and extreme developers. Stegner had already addressed the wilder lands of the interior West in the Powell book. In *All the Little Live Things* he sketched the historic land-use pattern of the California rural-suburban interface in the postwar years.

The white newcomers, whether Hispanic or Anglo, claimed the land in the name of a deity, king, or president. They displaced the natives with guns and liquor. The white men burned the woods and drained the swamps. There were skirmishes between the whites and the remaining red men. The Indians were pauperized. The whites took the land and became farmers and ranchers. Some, whose families had lived there long enough to believe they had "rights," attempted to profit by dividing their large parcels into small lots. The Stegners and other postwar immigrants were the newest of the newcomers; they would be followed by others.

A SMALL, "TIGHT group," as Stegner described it, opposed Stanford University's plans to build "factories" in the foothills. The university wanted to develop an industrial park on 254 acres. Stegner and others opposed it. A referendum was held in 1959, and the advocates of open space lost.

Faced with such threats as new freeways, denser developments, and high-voltage electric lines, twenty-five of Stegner's friends, neighbors, and fellow conservationists formed the Committee for Green Foothills in May of 1962. The name had the positive Stegner touch—it was "for" something. Stegner was one of the founders and served as the committee's first president. As such, he represented the committee in front of boards and commissions "because he had not only the name recognition but the force of Stanford behind him and then he would just give it to them. He did it so graciously," said a committee member. Another recalled that Stegner "became our environmental guru, our leader, our spiritual guide, and really the inspiration for what we felt."[8]

The region was the nation's center of environmental consciousness and activity at the time. Many similar committees had formed in the Bay Area in the 1960s to deal with local issues, while the Sierra Club had cast its net over increasingly vaster sections of the West. There were a few victories and many defeats. "You win some and you lose some, and you win far fewer than you lose," said Stegner.[9]

Effectively employing the gunslinger myth of the Old West, Stegner told a 1964 hearing that a proposed freeway from east to west across the peninsula was "a loaded and cocked gun, aimed straight at the heart of the last splendid open space on the Peninsula."[10] The freeway was defeated for many reasons, not the least of which was that it would have crossed some highly landslide-prone terrain.

The committee was less successful in Los Altos Hills because it was "a developer's paradise." Stegner described the destiny of the foothill community: "It got taken over as the Peninsula filled in. Newcomers came in who hadn't any particular feel for the country, and a lot of those newcomers turned out to be development-minded, with their eye on a profit, getting some cheap land and splitting it up later."[11] They were aided and abetted by city officials. It was a cozy relationship, not unknown elsewhere in California.

In turn, Stegner and his fellow committee members were accused of NIMBYism (NIMBY standing for "Not In My BackYard"). He replied:

> There is a cynical assumption in some quarters that those who fight for a degree of naturalness in the foothills are fighting to preserve for their own selfish benefit a place in which they arrived luckily early. I don't acknowledge that for myself and I don't believe it of any Green Foothills member I know. Many who work hard to protect the hills don't live in them, and those who do live in them fight just as hard to protect Alaska wilderness or Montana grassland that they will never see. They want the hills protected for the simple reason that they love and respect the earth, know its value for other purposes than profit, and want to leave to their children and grandchildren a heritage that has not been dug up and paved over and—it is an ironic word—humanized.[12]

The disappearance of the orchards in the valley and the foothills haunted Stegner through the 1960s and beyond. He recalled their orderliness, the spring blossoms, the apricot picking. "The drama of change," he wrote, "in this brief Eden could approximately end with the final stage directions in Chekhov's *The Cherry Orchard*." The directions read: "A distant sound is heard, coming as if out of the sky, like the sound of a strong snapping, slowly and sadly dying away. Silence ensues, broken only by the sound of an ax striking a tree in the orchard far away."[13]

A National Agenda

We spent all morning trying to get across to the Escalante rim by jeep; lunch on the slick rock halfway across; got lost from one another, scouting, for an hour or more. . . . We can look up Stevens Canyon on the other side, and up the Escalante—a vast broken country of piers and domes and cliffs. . . . Just below us on the rim is a long talus of blown sand almost up to the rim of a dead bend. Down this (a ten-foot jump off or so) rustlers used to mill and chase cattle, picking up the survivors and driving them into the Escalante Canyon, down that to the Colorado, and across the Colorado into Arizona. This jump-off would make a superb trail-head into the wilderness.

Wallace Stegner, notes from a southern Utah field trip

It *is* time for development of a cultural policy by the Federal Government; and though I do not have too much faith in arts policies which are developed simply as instruments in the cold war, I do think that a sympathetic and helpful attitude toward all the arts on the part of the Government cannot help having useful international results. But I think the Government should support and encourage the arts because they are the arts, the expression of much of the best in this civilization, and not because by supporting them we will win friends abroad.

Wallace Stegner, memorandum to Secretary of the Interior Stewart L. Udall

THE YEAR 1961 was the dawn of the New Frontier, a time of hope infused with youthful energy following the administration of an aging president. For conservationists there was a chance to acquire new national parks and monuments, something that had not previously occurred other than by carving out segments of the public domain or receiving gifts from such philanthropists as the Rockefeller family.

Without missing a beat, Stegner went from the classrooms of Stanford and the meeting rooms of local planning commissions, city councils, and boards of supervisors to a high position in the executive branch of the federal government in Washington.

Stegner's gift to Udall of a copy of *Beyond the Hundredth Meridian* and the Wilderness Letter had an unintended result. After their meeting in Udall's office, the Stegners had proceeded to Williamsburg. Udall first wrote, then, realizing Stegner was nearby, telephoned. Along with the request to read the Wilderness Letter, there was a general discussion. The new secretary of the interior wrote Stegner in May that he had been trying "to get up my nerve" to ask Stegner to take a leave of absence for a semester or two and join his personal staff.[1] He wanted to do a better job of communicating with the public, and a New York publisher had asked if he would write a book on "the quiet crisis" in conservation. He would need help with the book because he was "too busy to do a first-rate job" by himself.

Stegner's other duties in Udall's office would enable him to affect public policy directly. "It would be my intention to give you a prime policy-making function in terms of conservation," Udall said, "and I would want you to participate in all policy-making decisions and to assist in coordination in this department of the general conservation plan which I am now proposing to the president." Udall then asked: "How'd you like to come to Washington and work with us while we work out a program of conservation, parks acquisition, and so on for eight years of the Kennedy Administration?"[2] Stegner declined, stating he was scheduled to teach in the fall.

A Phi Beta Kappa speaking tour took Wally to Pullman, Washington, home of Washington State University. Udall met with him there and tried to persuade him to go to Washington as his special assistant. It was tempting, and the offer prompted memories of his family's drive through Yellowstone National Park in the 1920s. A few years later he got his first look at the national parks that stretched across southern Utah and northern Arizona. Now there would be a chance to create more of them.

Yes, he would come on board, he finally wrote Udall in June. The salary of $16,000 a year matched what he was making at Stanford. He would need to return home by Christmas in order to prepare to teach the next year. He commented on Udall's ideas for the book. Udall wrote back, thanking Stegner for his "penetrating memorandum" and said he agreed with nearly all his suggestions.[3]

In September, Stegner traveled to the Olympic Peninsula, in the Northwest, where the National Parks Advisory Board was meeting. He attended the meeting as the representative of the secretary of the interior. By this time, Knopf was no longer on the board, although he maintained an active interest in its proceedings. The board functioned only to advise the director of the National Park Service and the secretary of the interior. Its members during Stegner's association with it, as special assistant and as a board member, tended to be older white men (with one exception) and prominent. They included John B. Oakes of *The New York Times*, Robert G. Sproul of the University of California, and Melville B. Grosvenor of the National Geographic Society.

The discussions during the five-day meeting in Olympic National Park dealt with issues Stegner was familiar with. The board endorsed a compromise size for the proposed Canyonlands National Park in southern Utah, noting that there was political pressure both for and against it. Grazing and mining could continue in the new park, it was determined, since that concession would hasten congressional approval. There was talk of designating Dinosaur National Monument a national park. The current proposal for dams at either end of Grand Canyon National Park was discussed.

The Stegners traveled to Washington, D.C., later in September. Between the former Arizona congressman of Mormon ancestry turned cabinet member and the former Utah resident turned university professor and author there was a close working relationship and a friendship that would last after Wally's tenure in Washington. "We sort of think alike," Stegner said twenty years later, "and we come out of the same kind of background."[4]

In follow-up memos on the advisory board meeting, Stegner suggested that a documentary be made about the national parks that would impart "a broader, warmer, friendlier, and more humane view of America." He thought the advisory board was "actually more concerned with corroborating and supporting than with advising." His memos tended to be enthusiastic and overly long for a busy secretary of the interior to absorb. He soon learned to shorten them.[5]

The early-October days in Washington were "exciting and strenuous," and held the possibility that tangible results could be achieved. For Mary the bleak "three story barn" they had rented sight unseen was "a little lonesome and tedious." During long hours at the Department of the Interior, Stegner said, "I am trying to promote conservation thinking and conservation acting in as many ways as I can."[6] He wrote a correspondent:

You speak of the writer's involvement in his society. I think too many writers are far too little involved. They sit in the middle of their own skulls, or their endocrines, and snipe at the saints, politicians, working people, housewives, and bureaucrats who have to keep their world running. This doesn't mean I am anti-literary. The highest thing I can think of doing is literary. But literature does not exist in a vacuum, or even in a partial vacuum. We are neither detached nor semi-detached, but are linked to our world by a million interdependencies. To deny the interdependencies, while living on the comforts and services that they make possible, is adolescent when it isn't downright dishonest. And I would as soon say it to Henry Miller as to the book reviewer on the *Des Moines Register*.[7]

Work on the Udall book took most of Stegner's time in Washington. Stegner and Udall developed a draft outline. "I did a little research in the Library of Congress for him," Stegner said, "and we tried it out on a panel of people, including [presidential speechwriter] Ted Sorensen and some others to see if they thought that was the way it should go, and everybody seemed to approve of that." After Stegner left Washington, work on the text proceeded according to Stegner's outline. He continued to advise Udall and his staff from California. A series of hastily scribbled, handwritten notes went back and forth between the two. "Writing history is murder," said Udall in one of the notes.

Two of Stegner's Stanford writing students, Don Moser and Harold Gilliam, went to work for Udall as special assistants and helped him complete the book. Other staff members pitched in with the research. Stegner had written four draft chapters. With the deadline looming— the manuscript was to be completed by June 1, 1962—Moser reported to his former professor: "All the troops are getting a little scratchy around the eyes every morning."[8]

The Quiet Crisis was published in 1963 with an introduction by President Kennedy. Stegner thought it was "a splendid job." The best seller became one of the conservation canons of the 1960s—it was to land use what Rachel Carson's *Silent Spring* was to toxic chemicals. Many people thought Stegner had written the book. No, he said, he had contributed only the outline. Udall had his own style. "Even when he would get a draft chapter from some helper," Stegner said, "he tore it all apart and made it over again in his own way, so it's his book, I think."[9]

. . .

DURING HIS TIME in Washington, Stegner participated in discussions that led to some of the most significant conservation and cultural bills that would be passed by Congress in the next few years. He had unrestricted access to Udall's office and was present when summoned or when he chose to take part. He wrote a California friend this description of the excitement in the early days of the Kennedy administration:

> My chores are concerned mainly with policy and planning in several areas of conservation, and . . . [implementation] by whatever means offers itself. It's a little like a three-headed boy trying to scratch his head with both hands full of pencils. But it's exciting, and there's an opportunity to do something, right now, that if it isn't done now can never be done again. So on occasion we even get urgent.[10]

He worked on early drafts of the wilderness bill and on the act that created the Land and Water Conservation Fund, which provides money for the acquisition and enlargement of national parks and other types of nature refuges. He was present for the start of discussions about the possibility of building dams in the Grand Canyon. He defended Udall on this controversial issue in later years: "Stewart was against them and wanted to find some way, but he didn't think he could just nix them out. In fact, he couldn't as secretary. This was a congressional matter, but he had to exert his influence as he could."[11]

While assuming the mantle of a conservationist by way of his aggressive additions to the national park system and the publication of his book, Udall both publicly and privately advocated the construction of dams that would provide the money, through the sale of hydroelectricity, to build the aqueducts that would transport water from the Colorado River to the interior of his home state of Arizona. What "we all agreed" to in the end, said Stegner—in reference to conservationists, dam builders, Congress, and the Kennedy and Johnson administrations—were the coal-burning power plants that brought air pollution to the parklands of the Southwest. "There was no good alternative," he said.[12]

Others disagreed with his enthusiastic endorsement of the Kennedy administration's conservation policies during his first month in Washington. His close friend and Sierra Club board member Ansel Adams sent him a letter that was cautionary. Yes, Udall seemed to be doing "a perfectly wonderful job," but could he control the Bureau of Reclamation? "I for one," Adams said, "do not trust the administration of the Park Service," whose emphasis was on physical structures, not values. What about a Golden Gate national monument? He was going to fight for it personally because he didn't think the Park Service had "the taste or the imagination" to realize "what a wonderful thing this project could be."[13] Years later Tom Watkins said that Les Line, the editor of *Audubon* magazine, had asked him to do a profile of Udall. He begged off. "His record on the Grand Canyon dams and the enforcement of reclamation law makes me nervous," Watkins said.[14]

Where Udall would eventually make his mark, with the help of Stegner at the start, was with the expansion of the national park system through annexation of public lands and the purchase of private property. Creating Canyonlands National Park was one of his first priorities. Udall sent his special assistant on a fact-finding trip in October 1961 to the Plateau Province, which he had written about so eloquently in the Powell book.

What a glorious, uncomplicated journey it was back to the earlier years of his life in southern Utah and away from bureaucratic Washington. Stegner toured the area with park superintendents from the region for one week via jeep, horseback, and foot. The group set out by car from Moab to Capitol Reef National Monument, then down the length of the Kaiparowits Plateau to Hole-in-the-Rock. By horseback they descended to the Colorado River and were among the last to see Cathedral in the Desert before it was inundated by the waters of Lake Powell.

The party paused at one of the greatest overlooks in the West after an early-season snowstorm on October 10. The view southward from Boulder Mountain was a wilderness of rocks. The language Stegner employed in his notes to describe the scene on the Aquarius Plateau surpassed Dutton's more florid description of the same area:

> Aspens all around us on the overlook are shedding ice with a scolding sort of clatter; they sound like fussy women sweeping their porches clean of litter after a storm. Where they have not shed, they glitter in sheaths of white ice. The air pure, without haze; the sun warming up, the snow soft, the trail thawing in the ruts and against north banks. A mule deer buck with a rack like an elk takes off into the aspens just before the Forest Service lookout. Further west, a beaver dam and a lot of felled aspens lying crisscrossed in the woods.[15]

Along with recommending that Capitol Reef be expanded, Stegner thought that the Bureau of Land Management, a grazing- and mining-oriented agency within the Department of the Interior, should designate the spectacular canyonlands in the Escalante River Basin as official wilderness. By combining Capitol Reef with the Escalante basin, Stegner said, a huge wilderness could be formed. Public access "should be peripheral, permitting views. . . . Within the canyons themselves access should be only by foot, horse, or restricted non-motorized forms of boating. Held back thus from heavy visitation, the two adjacent areas would form a magnificent wilderness with a rim road offering great views: it could thus serve both the casual tourist and the wilderness camper."[16] Thirty-five years later much of this area was designated the Grand Staircase–Escalante National Monument by President Bill Clinton.

Six days after his return to Washington, Stegner discussed his trip with Udall. Later that day he wrote the secretary a memorandum titled "Building a Conservation Backfire in Utah." It was his most naked assessment of land use and leadership in the state.

Stegner first outlined how public opinion of new or expanded national parks in Utah and elsewhere in the West was molded: "Where it is formed at all, it is likely to be formed by resource interests such as uranium, oil, and grazing, and by the politicians subservient to these." The hierarchy of the Mormon Church was "in the same camp, drawn there by its considerable wealth and by its general conservatism. This frame of mind, the Resource-Republican variety of States Rightism," he continued, "is common enough throughout the West. It is probably least diluted in Wyoming, where the stockmen dominate the State, and in Utah, where the existence of the Mormon Church creates a special condition and a special difficulty."

Stegner described the cohesiveness that made Utah different from any other state. The church and the state's two U.S. senators were in agreement. Referring to the former, he said: "It controls the media of communication, and since it absolutely controls Brigham Young University, largely controls Utah State, and considerably dominates the University of Utah, the organization of any opposition will be difficult and slow." The solution was the following formula, which has subsequently been adopted by local environmental groups: "The first step must be the organization of the scattered supporters of the park-and-wilderness philosophy into some body which can, with both the force and the anonymity of a group, create a conservation movement in Utah and make it clear that [Governor George] Clyde and [Senator Wallace]

Bennett speak not for the people of Utah but for special interests, and not for the welfare of the State but for the fast buck benefiting the few."

Stegner offered to "communicate discreetly with a certain few people in Utah of whose opinions and energy we are sure." He would help them organize. In many ways, he told Udall, he was the ideal person for such a task. He offered this appraisal of his standing in Utah:

> In all of this I stand in a rather odd position. I am known to be a liberal and a Democrat, and I was active in the Dinosaur fight, and for these I am looked on with suspicion. On the other hand, I am in many eyes a Local Boy Who Made Good, and besides that I have written a good many things about Utah, and Utah is fantastically sensitive to praise and publicity "outside." I think that anything on Utah's park possibilities that I wrote would be more persuasive to university people, especially, than someone else's writings on the same subject. I am supposed to Know, in a hometown way, and to be sympathetic with Utah at large. For that matter, I am.[17]

As Stegner found out, policy making at the higher levels of government meant running from brushfire to brushfire and then back again to the original blaze. In addition to working on Udall's book and trying to expand national parks and wilderness areas, Stegner participated in the Kennedy administration's first discussions about a national cultural policy.

For the short time that he was in Washington, Stegner was Udall's point man on the issue. He wrote the secretary memos in favor of federal support of the arts: "We have a long national history of indifference to the arts, or even hostility, to live down." Government support was important, Stegner thought, because "about the greatest encouragement one can give the arts is to buy a talented man's time and let him work, and to honor or reward distinguished performance." He would also like to see something done about stimulating the different audiences for the arts, but he realized that was a longer-term issue "achieved only by massive changes in our national attitudes, educational system, and entertainment patterns."[18]

Stegner lunched with his former Harvard colleague Arthur Schlesinger Jr., who headed the White House effort to develop an arts policy. Stegner told Udall that he "couldn't agree more" with a draft policy drawn up by the Department of State, which was later described as being "suggestive of the mood of the early sixties, when notions of Camelot captured the national attention."[19] Noting the success of a glittering evening featuring a performance by the cellist Pablo Casals at the White House, President Kennedy adopted the arts as one of the symbols of his administration. Two years after Kennedy died, President Lyndon Johnson signed the act creating the National Endowment for the Arts and the National Endowment for the Humanities.

Stegner was not an indiscriminate supporter of government; rather, he believed in federal support of the arts and the freedom of artists to create. He declined the National Medal of Arts, which was to be presented to him by President George H. W. Bush in 1992, on the grounds that the government was attempting to censor, not support, the arts. For his refusal to accept the medal he was given the Freedom to Write Award by PEN USA.

THE ARTS WERE a diversion from Stegner's main chores at Interior. Shortly after he returned home in time for Christmas, he sent Udall the final outline for *The Quiet Crisis* and offered some helpful advice: "As one who has written too many books, and got trapped in too many of the customary pitfalls, let me urge you not to think of this outline as anything holy." The four chapters he had written were only rough drafts. "Insert, delete and revise several times before letting go of them," he warned. On letting go of a manuscript, Stegner wrote:

> And always, always, there is the possibility of more learning, more knowledge. No book is ever finished, in the sense that its author knows the whole subject and has said it just as he wants to. Every book is eventually relinquished, with bugs still in it, and weak spots, and places where the author would like to do some more reading and thinking. In a quick book like this one, the discomforts of early relinquishment may be greater than usual.[20]

Canyonlands National Park was created not long after Stegner departed from Washington. Capitol Reef was expanded and, along with Arches National Monument—where Ed Abbey had worked as a seasonal ranger and gathered the material for *Desert Solitaire*—was upgraded from national monument to national park status. From inside

and, later, outside government, Stegner played a role in these conservation successes. It was a rare opportunity and "an exhilarating experience," Stegner later recalled. He had been able to mold public policy
from the knowledge gained from his personal experience and writing
articles and books. But he wasn't done yet.

IT WASN'T LONG before Stegner was back in Washington on national
parks business. Udall appointed him to a six-year term on the National
Parks Advisory Board in June 1962. He attended his first meeting at
Hawaii Volcanoes National Park during October of that year. The
spring meetings were held in the Washington area. During his time on
the board, Stegner served on a subcommittee that reviewed the Park
Service's recommendations for the Redwood National Park in California, on the history and natural resource committees, and as the board's
vice chairman and chairman. The perks were seeing some beautiful
country, being kept informed about national parks matters, and having
an impact on policy. Board members received no payment for their service, other than reimbursements of transportation costs and $16 per
diem.[21]

Stegner was more familiar with the issues, Udall's thinking, and
Department of the Interior personnel than the other board members.
He told his colleagues that it was the secretary's opinion that national
parks and monuments did not have to be absolutely pristine. There
needed, however, to be a "core of pureness" around which such pre-
serves could be created. There was an urgent need, he said, to move
quickly before acquisition costs rose too high. New policies advocated
by the board during Stegner's tenure resulted in the creation of national
seashores on the Atlantic, Gulf, and Pacific coasts and national recreation areas near major cities.

He also possessed what other board members lacked, and that was
direct, informal access to Udall. There wasn't much to say about the
Hawaii meeting, he reported, other than that "we all had the hell of a
good time, saw Hawaii going to the devil even faster than California,
ate indigenous and drank exotic, and came home with the flu."[22]

Although he missed the two 1963 meetings, Stegner was active
behind the scenes promoting the Sierra Club's position on the proposed Redwood National Park and criticizing lumber companies,
including the one in which he held stock, for their clear-cutting practices. He toured the redwood country in northwestern California by

auto and light plane. He told the two less active members on his national parks subcommittee, Grosvenor and Sproul, that the Park Service's recommendations for a national park were not enough. The entire watershed of Redwood Creek, not just part of it, needed to be protected. Depending upon a cooperative agreement with the logging companies was "whistling in a windstorm." He added, "But I doubt that we lose anything by going for what would really be a safe and protected park of a size commensurate with the dignity and value of the trees themselves and suitable to the overcrowded future."²³ These were his personal views, Stegner said, and he had communicated them to Udall. Unfortunately, that concept was not shared by Congress. Logging companies, environmentalists, local communities, and state and federal agencies struggled with the uncertainties of half a park through the next decade.

Stegner was present at the spring 1964 meeting in Washington at which a study of national parks and monument sites with agricultural significance was presented to the advisory board. The sites were mostly in the East. Stegner added Pipe Spring National Monument in northern Arizona to the list; the desert spring had been a Native American and Mormon agricultural outpost.

By the fall 1964 meeting, in Great Smoky Mountains National Park, Stegner had become vice chairman of the board. There were reports on passage of the Land and Water Conservation Fund Act and the wilderness bill, both of which he had worked on while in Washington. Not all the members were happy with the wilderness bill. Grosvenor opposed designating any wilderness areas in Yellowstone National Park. The park, he said, had been formed "to preserve the natural wonders as pleasuring grounds." Only one person in one thousand wanted wilderness, claimed the head of the National Geographic Society.²⁴

Word had trickled down to Udall, and then to the advisory board, that President Johnson wanted his Texas birthplace designated a national historic site. This demand offended Stegner, who could recognize the difference between an egotistic whim of the moment and a proposal of true historical significance. Knowing at the April 1965 meeting what the board would be facing in the near future, Stegner, now its chairman, urged adoption of a policy stating that birthplaces and burial grounds not be considered as national historic sites "except in cases of historical figures of transcendent importance." Historic sites associated with the career of such individuals, he said, were more important than the place where they were born or buried. Living persons, regardless of their importance, should not be so honored. He later wrote Udall: "One or two of the recommendations and resolutions you probably won't much like. Alas, they are what we felt."[25]

The advisory board, with Udall and various Interior Department and Park Service officials in attendance, traveled to Alaska in early August of 1965 to inspect existing and proposed national park sites. Udall departed, and the board was left in the hands of lesser department officials. They took the train from Fairbanks to Mount McKinley (now Denali) National Park. The board held a meeting on August 4 in the club car of the train, which was operated by the Park Service. Stegner led the discussion in which he opposed designating Johnson's birthplace a national historic site. With two members opposed, the board voted to reaffirm the policy Stegner had proposed. It attempted to soften the blow by stating that an "appropriate site" for a sitting president could be "identified and considered" for classification as a national landmark (a status less prestigious than that of a national historic site).

Word came back immediately from Udall, according to Stegner, that "we damn well had to" designate Johnson's birthplace a national historic site, "so swallow and hold your nose and do it." The board held firm. "The board itself was absolutely right," said its chairman. "The political situation was such that Stewart just couldn't go home without having that done." A face- and job-saving compromise for Udall was devised: the board's decision was put in the form of a confidential memorandum to the interior secretary. A formal resolution would have had to have been made public. Udall could live with that. "After all," said Stegner, "a vain man in the White House whose vanity would be flattered by that and whose vanity would be very much irritated by what we proposed, could just throw him out of office."[26]

From Mount McKinley they traveled on to Anchorage, where their reception was mixed. "Everybody was out there with red carpets or flags or shotguns at the railroad stations as we came by," Stegner recalled. At a dinner hosted by the Anchorage Chamber of Commerce, Wally and his fellow board members were berated for meddling in Alaskan affairs by proposing additional national parks in the state.

Near the end of the three-week tour, the group flew out to Katmai National Monument, where Alaska's lone congressman joined the party to discuss the future of national parks in Alaska. The board's minutes noted: "Chairman Stegner said that it was the right time for development of the Alaskan parks."[27] Actually, it wasn't, since Native Alaskans' claims had to be resolved first. Additional parks were created in the 1970s after the claims issue was settled.

Photos taken on the trip show a burr-headed Udall looking at plans, uniformed Park Service officials standing in the background in their wide-brimmed hats, and white-haired board members wearing neckties or western bolos. A more youthful, lanky Stegner posed in gunslinger fashion, a cigar in his hand, squinting into the sun. He is wearing an open-collar sport shirt. Mary stands next to him in a Windbreaker.

Stegner did not complete his six-year term, leaving the board shortly after the Alaska trip to travel to Italy and work on a book. As he had done while a member of the National Parks Advisory Board—and as he would continue to do while serving on the Sierra Club board— Stegner defended Udall, mostly in a series of *Saturday Review* articles and editorials on environmental issues. Referring to the Grand Canyon dam controversy, and conveniently forgetting about the legacy of Harold Ickes, Stegner wrote: "Caught in the middle is Secretary of the Interior Stewart Udall, the strongest conservationist who ever held this post." If Udall had opposed both dams, Stegner argued, he would have lost control of the Bureau of Reclamation, which had strong supporters in Congress. Udall thanked Stegner for defending him against "the whips and scorns of Sierra Club zealots."[28]

Looking back on Udall's long tenure in office, Stegner said: "Udall as secretary was completely on the side of the environment, a good steward. It is true he was often hampered by the power of certain bureaus, especially Reclamation, and that on occasion environmental groups sued him to enforce or ventilate an issue. But he welcomed even the intransigent environmental people because, as he said, somebody had to take that view in order to balance equally intransigent views from the exploitative side."[29] Of Udall's failure to persuade Johnson to make wholesale additions to the national park system shortly before leaving office, Stegner believed that Johnson "wasn't that bold, or that convinced." Wally wrote Stu: "It's been a tremendous eight years. You're in the history books."[30]

The Sierra Club Years

I hear lamentable things about the Sierra Club. Almost I hate to ask anybody what's happening, for fear I'll find out. So don't consider yourself asked unless you feel the need of a listening and probably sympathetic ear.

Wallace Stegner, letter to Ansel Adams

H IS FRIEND ANSEL Adams convinced Stegner to run for election to the Sierra Club board, on which Adams served. Stegner won a place and took his seat at the May 1964 meeting. His time, he wrote the Sierra Club president that summer, was "very pinched," and he didn't think he could remain on the publication committee. He also doubted that he would be a good board member: "My willingness is not in question, only my capacity, together with the certainty that I shall be often away."[1] In fact, the next week he was heading to Vermont, and from there he would go on to a National Parks Advisory Board meeting in the South.

Establishing the Redwood National Park and keeping dams out of the Grand Canyon were the most visible of the Sierra Club's issues, but a Walt Disney ski resort in Mineral King Valley, in the southern Sierra Nevada, and a nuclear power plant in Diablo Canyon, on the California coast, took up most of the board's time. Both California issues involved a switch in the club's previous positions, and Stegner wasn't particularly knowledgeable about either one. Although he didn't like the projects, Stegner thought a deal was a deal. It was a bit like accepting coal-burning power plants as an alternative to dams in the Grand Canyon. "You accept one thing," he said, "and you take another with it."[2]

Stegner missed a number of meetings and took no leadership role, preferring to follow the lead, and second the motions, of the veteran director Edgar Wayburn. He stayed out of the Mineral King debate and missed the vote but seconded motions that Wayburn made on establishing a scenic-area classification for the Ruby Mountains in Nevada and a stronger California Forest Practices Act.

There were those within and outside the club who believed it was an elitist organization during and after Stegner's tenure on the board. Damn right, Stegner said. "I don't apologize for being an elitist. God knows, my background is about as democratic and lumpenproletariat as you could get. But it does seem to me that the world progresses only through its special people, and that instead of resenting them, it's time we acknowledge them. An Ansel Adams is worth ten thousand of us. We ought to admit that."[3]

Two years after joining the Sierra Club board, he submitted his resignation, stating that he had accepted a temporary position at an overseas branch of Stanford University. "Again, I went abroad," Stegner recalled years later. "So I was never an effective or a good member. I found it interesting but difficult. I just couldn't get loose to get to meetings." He later assessed his role as an environmental activist in a letter to Tom Watkins, who was preparing an article on his conservationist activities for *Audubon* magazine: "I am a paper tiger, Watkins, typewritten on both sides. Get that in somewhere." He did.[4]

STEGNER STAYED OUT of internal Sierra Club politics until the Brower controversy erupted in 1968 and 1969. Depending on which side was talking, Brower was the savior of the earth or an egomaniac who was financially ruining the Sierra Club. Stegner sided with those directors, including Adams, who thought Brower should be fired. In the process, he made one of the few noticeable mistakes in his life—he lost his famous cool in public.

He was hesitant to ask Adams for details of what was happening internally in the Sierra Club in late 1968, but he would listen if his friend needed a sympathetic ear. The ebullient photographer immediately poured his thoughts out on paper: "The Sierra Club is in a truly lamentable situation. I do not like to be a Jeremiah, but we are confronted with possible financial disaster. The obdurate, recalcitrant, myth-weaving, unilateral character of our Executive Director hath brought the startling possibility of catastrophe. I hope and pray for some SIGN from above—some miracle."[5] Adams was most bothered by the specter of the club's bankruptcy, for which individual directors could be held personally liable. One estimate of the losses of the publications program over the previous five years was $230,000. Brower had set up a London office without the board's approval, incurring a further cost.

In later years, when he could look back on the internecine struggle for power within the organization with some perspective, Stegner thought that Brower was "sucked into the spirit of the times, which was the sixties." He would have preferred Brower's taking a "somewhat milder, not necessarily less resolute" approach, which "might have been more effective."[6]

In 1969, however, he lacked that perspective and lashed out publicly at Brower, who had brought him into the fold of the Sierra Club, of which he was now an honorary life member. Stegner's "Bitten by Worm of Power" letter, as it was prominently headlined on the op-ed page, appeared in the *Palo Alto Times*, the daily newspaper that served the greater Stanford area. The letter was in response to what Stegner considered a number of misrepresentations, among which was the implication that Stegner was aligned with the senile traditionalists who opposed Brower and that Brower represented the new wave of environmentalists. "I write because Brower has ceased to be what he was. He had been bitten by some worm of power," declared Stegner. He had been one of Brower's supporters—Brower was "a kind of genius"—but "in his grab for absolute power he will wreck the Sierra Club."[7] Brower and his family were deeply wounded by this public attack.

The letter was reprinted widely. Shortly after its initial publication the board suggested that Brower take a leave of absence and appointed an acting executive director. A pro-Brower slate of directors lost in the ensuing election; Brower was fired and then alternatively given a chance to resign in early May, which he took.

Stegner didn't regret Brower's departure; it was, he thought, in the best interests of the Sierra Club. He did come to regret his intemperate outburst, however. "I didn't express myself very well in that editorial," he said, "and later I regretted in many ways having written it, because I liked Dave and I like him yet." When Brower sent him a copy of his autobiography in 1990, Stegner replied: "Though we have not always agreed on tactics, particularly in that one bruising instance, I never doubted that you were and are the most effective fighter for the environment in the whole round world. . . . I hope you live forever, and in a sense you will."[8]

By the end of the 1960s, at the age of sixty, Stegner was soured on conservation politics, California's growth, teaching, hippie lifestyles, and the war in Vietnam. He was ready to pull up the drawbridge and focus on his fiction. A few years later he invited Stewart Udall and his wife, Lee, to visit this "very quiet backwater" for a night or two. "I am getting old, I find. I eschew social contacts. I love my chain saw, and especially my Swedish pulp saw, more than my fellowman, and my woodpile above my social life."[9]

Prominent Author

Angle of Unrest

My grandparents had to live their way out of one world and into another, or into several others, making new out of old the way corals live their reef upward. I am on my grandparents' side. I believe in Time, as they did, and in the life chronological rather than in the life existential. We live in time and through it, we build our huts in its ruins, or used to, and we cannot afford all these abandonings.

Wallace Stegner, narration of Lyman Ward in *Angle of Repose*

I began to read Stegner in 1978 when I moved to California from points east (Chicago and New York), and I found him, as I think most Eastern critics have, impressive and yet strangely unimpressive. . . . The frontier spirit that, in its twilight, shaped Wallace Stegner was a rough spirit. Stegner first fled it, then seized it and turned . . . [it] into his art. The California of 1993, more than a century after the official closing of the frontier in 1890, may seem to suffer more from artificially and, if you will, from a surfeit of smoothness than from any such roughness. But what a Czech visitor recently described to me as "your incredible California helpfulness" grows in us from a Stegnerian habit of saving what we can from the Western wreckage. The literary equivalent of "California helpfulness," faintly offputting as it is to Easterners, is what, 15 years ago, made Wallace Stegner seem strange to me. He was calmly putting things together when I believed, instinctively, that what strong writers did was tear things apart. The same quality in him, I recognize with a small jolt, is what now makes him seem familiar. In the interim, I have become a Californian, and a Westerner, myself.

Jack Miles, *Los Angeles Times Sunday Book Review*

STEGNER CUT HIS formal ties to Stanford University in 1971. He was completing the novel *Angle of Repose*, which would be to fiction what *Beyond the Hundredth Meridian* was to nonfiction—one of the outstanding books in its genre ever written about the American West. *Angle* is a multigenerational and geographic saga of operatic dimensions. It won a Pulitzer Prize and was voted by readers of the *San Francisco Chronicle* the best novel "written in or about—or by an author from—" the American West in the twentieth century. They rated it over books by John Steinbeck, Jack London, and Stegner's student Ken Kesey.[1]

Stegner's greatest literary triumphs—the Pulitzer and a National Book Award for *The Spectator Bird*—occurred in the 1970s. At last he had received national recognition. But his greatest achievements were deflated by the barbs of critics. On the surface he was very successful; underneath he was disappointed and hurt. It was a bittersweet time. The fault or faults, if any can or need be assigned, lay in the nature of Stegner's fiction, which drew heavily on his own and others' experiences, the attitudes of *The New York Times Book Review*, and Stegner's anger and tendency to hold a grudge. The story itself is worthy of a realistic novel.

From the very beginning of his writing career, Stegner got into trouble for not sufficiently disguising factual material. For obvious reasons, he never faced such criticism for his more autobiographical works. The characters and plot that drew on the stories of others in *Angle of Repose* brought allegations of slander and plagiarism. Stegner was vulnerable to such accusations. He found his material in life, and then used his imaginative powers to shape the accounts into the fictions that fit his needs. "I begin with the real world, obviously. I hope I don't end there," he said.[2]

In his first novel, *Remembering Laughter*, Wally retained enough of the facts to embarrass people in Iowa. Mary Stegner's two aunts, on whom he had based the book, were Mary and Janet Armour. He was ashamed of that episode. "It never occurred to me that it would be published," he later told an interviewer.[3]

In 1940 and again in 1950 (during which interval he published six novels) he wrote articles in national magazines on bending, or "warping," truth in fiction. At both ends of that productive decade, Stegner emphasized that the details embedded in reality could be faked or altered. By faked details, which he dealt with in the first article, he meant that unimportant details need not be researched. Imagined details of weather and place, for instance, could be substituted for unknown particulars. Of altering, he said in the second article, which expanded his concept: "It is often necessary for a writer to distort the particulars of experience in order to see them better."[4]

Two of his books written during this decade serve as examples of how Stegner altered factual realities to fit fictional needs. Wally's editor, on the advice of a lawyer, suggested that Stegner change some names and switch the location of the village in *Second Growth* from Vermont to New Hampshire. But Westwick, New Hampshire, still resembled Greensboro too closely. "If what I did in the book was wrong," Stegner explained, "then all fiction is an instrument of the devil, as Cotton Mather said it was, because all fiction is made that way, if it has any relevance and meaning at all." He explained his fictional technique to his fellow Greensboro summer resident Phil Gray, who complained that Wally had depicted the village as a sinister place: "Actually, if you can clear your mind of G[reensboro] and look at it as a novel, you'll see that three quarters of it at least is pure fiction, and that the other quarter is pretty much improvised from a few incidents. Actually, too, I took situations from the town, the situations that seemed to me symbolic and characteristic, and bent them to fit what I was doing."[5]

The novel *Joe Hill* is the story of a union organizer for the Wobblies who is convicted of killing a father and his son in a Salt Lake City butcher shop. "It is not history," he emphasized, "though it deals here and there with historical episodes and sometimes incorporates historical documents; and it is not biography, though it deals with a life. It is fiction, with fiction's prerogatives and none of history's limiting obligations. I hope and believe it is after a kind of truth, but a different kind from that which historians follow."[6] His deflation of the Joe Hill myth, popularized in romantic ballads that depict Hill as a martyr, did not endear him to union members, who picketed the offices of *The New Republic* in 1948 after that magazine published a nonfiction account by Stegner stating that Hill "probably" was guilty of the killings. The novel, published two years later, attracted very little attention.

Stegner used a family's diaries for background material for *A Shooting Star*, one of his less successful novels, which was published in 1961. The diaries were written by the mother of Mrs. Gardiner Hammond, the Stegners' Santa Barbara landlady. The material provided the family background for the novel's protagonist, Sabrina Castro. He used the location of the diaries (in a trunk), "some hints" from the diaries, "as well as a few details of Mrs. Hammond's personality and household, modified to fit the purposes of my book." He had Mrs. Hammond's written permission to use the diaries.[7]

In *Angle of Repose*, Stegner took the basic outline of the lives of Arthur and Mary Hallock Foote and bent it to fit his fictional needs. Why did he do it? "As for using historical people for a partly fictional purpose, so did Hawthorne, and for the same reason: the search for a usable past."[8] He also altered Gary Snyder's words in the same novel to the point where the poet could not recognize them.

STEGNER'S BRAND OF realism, described as humanistic and palpable, was on a collision course with the more inventive experimentalism of the late 1960s and the 1970s. For a time it would be eclipsed. Robert Canzoneri, an English professor at Ohio State University, was sympathetic to Stegner's plight. He wrote tongue in cheek in 1973: "Since in Stegner's work neither style, method, nor form is exotic, doctrinaire, distorted, violent, or romantic, and since none of his fiction depends upon myth, symbol, current psychology, or neotheology, what is there to write about, teach about, or talk about?" In other words, Canzoneri continued, Stegner's novels fell into "that unfashionable, anachronistic category called realism."[9]

Stegner was perfectly comfortable being associated with a passé category of fiction: "I'm a realist, I guess, and what I'm interested in is showing the West as it is and as it has been, not as it might have been and not as imagination has re-created it. *Angle of Repose* is built on quite a lot of historical research," he told an interviewer.[10]

The spectacular was not for Stegner. What he had absorbed from the Russian short story writer and playwright Anton Chekhov, he said, was the rheostat effect: "the kind of story in which nothing changes but everything gradually gets clearer and brighter and the situation is exactly the same at the end as it was at the beginning."[11]

What Stegner would accomplish with his fictional masterpiece, which contains no violence or any of the trite romanticism found in such sagas, is a portrait of the real West, which was dependent upon water for crops and the extraction of minerals for wealth. At its center is a married couple whose life is narrated by their grandson, Lyman Ward. Using this mechanism, Stegner moved back and forth in time and across landscapes that stretched from California to New York to

Mexico to Colorado to Idaho and back to California, where the book ends.

His primary purpose was to bind the past to the present and thus create a discernible history for the American West, just as he had done for the Canadian prairie provinces in *Wolf Willow:*

> For years I have wondered why no western writer had been able to make a continuity between the past and the present, why so many are sunk in the mythic twilight of horse opera, why the various Wests seem to have produced no culture or literature comparable to those of New England, the South, and the Midwest, why no westerner had managed to do for his territory what Faulkner did for Yoknapatawpha County. Well, here was my chance to give it a try.[12]

He needed a particular story to illustrate the general concept and found it in the life and letters of Mary Hallock Foote. "I had the life," Stegner explained, "and wrote it up as fact and imagination suggested it had to go, and let any general ideas about past and present, East and West, art and making a living, [and] career and marriage evolve from it naturally."[13]

The story also appealed to Wally on a personal level. As with his family and the characters in *The Big Rock Candy Mountain*, there was "the boomer husband and the nesting wife," albeit at a higher social level. Of this central concern in his fiction he later said, in reference to *Big Rock* and *Angle:* "It's perfectly clear that if every writer is born to write one story, that's my story. I wrote it at least two ways, but I certainly wasn't aware of it."[14]

The three main characters in *Angle* form a triangle, with Lyman Ward at the apex. Ward is an aging historian who is crippled emotionally and physically. He looks backward in time to his grandparents, Susan Burling Ward and Oliver Ward, for answers to questions posed by the present, that being the late 1960s. Lyman's physical disability was borrowed from Stegner's old University of Iowa professor Norman Foerster, whom he discovered living near Palo Alto with one leg and a frozen spine. The disability allows Lyman Ward to fixate on the past or, in Stegner's words, to view it with "tunnel vision."[15]

The problem, as it would develop, was that the characters of Susan and Oliver Ward were derived from real people who were recognizable. Some aspects of their lives were changed, and not always in flattering ways. Mary Hallock Foote was a prominent writer and illustrator in the late nineteenth and early twentieth centuries. She was married to Arthur D. Foote, a mining engineer. Stegner both borrowed from and added to their story. Minimal credit was given to the sources because the Footes' relatives desired anonymity for their grandparents. The granddaughters didn't like the results, and critics were divided on whether the borrowing was a valid fiction technique or outright plagiarism. Stegner's novel and the feminist movement that coalesced in the 1970s were the primary reasons for a Foote boomlet that has continued into the present.

The controversy has circulated at a relatively low level among scholars, feminists, and Stegner aficionados for years, only occasionally erupting into print in obscure academic journals and books. The full story—told here for the first time—deserves a wider audience because the novel was awarded a Pulitzer Prize, continues to sell briskly, is Stegner's best-known and most treasured work, and because recently the issue of plagiarism has received increasing public attention. Ironically, the more reflexive elements of the media have come down hard on borrowers, while the more reflective elements have excused the borrowers on the basis of creative imitation, meaning that all art is derivative to some extent and what follows should add value to the original.[16]

ANGLE OF REPOSE began to emerge in fits and starts. Then the book gathered steam like a locomotive crossing the very continent its words encompassed. It was an evolving process.

While researching a chapter for *Literary History of the United States*, an anthology published in 1948, Stegner came across Foote's writings, which he judged quite good. "I suppose she appealed to me because she was western and not southern or Midwestern," he said. In his chapter in the anthology, "Western Record and Romance," Stegner placed Foote among the local colorists who "avoided the commonplace, concerned themselves chiefly with the unusual, were incurably romantic, obsessed with the picturesque, and accurate only to the superficial aspects of their chosen materials."[17] Foote was, in his assessment, among the best of this group, but Stegner predicted that by midcentury her reputation was likely to dwindle further. He placed one of her novels on the reading list for his "Rise of Realism" course.

Stegner mentioned in a 1954 class that "a biography of Mrs. Foote was greatly needed."[18] This remark attracted the attention of one of his

students, George H. McMurry, who was looking for a dissertation subject. McMurry volunteered to obtain Foote's letters from her granddaughter Janet Micoleau, who lived in the Sierra Nevada foothill
community of Grass Valley. With the help of a letter of support from
Stegner to Micoleau, McMurry began the process whereby the Foote
letters were acquired by the Stanford University library in July of 1955,
thus beating out the Bancroft Library at the University of California at
Berkeley, which was also interested in obtaining the documents. Stegner wrote Micoleau: "It has long been my opinion that Mrs. Foote was
one of the very best of the Western local color writers and her emi-
nence as an illustrator gives her an additional distinction."[19] He hoped
that Stanford could acquire all her materials. McMurry began tran-
scribing the letters with the idea of writing his doctoral thesis under
Stegner.

Wally was working on a story about the gold rush for *Holiday* magazine and needed to do some research in Grass Valley. He met Janet and
her husband, Tyler Micoleau, for the first time in late March of 1957 at
the home of Ruth and Alfred Heller in nearby Nevada City. Ruth had
been Stegner's part-time secretary at Stanford, and Alfred had been a
creative writing student at the university. Stegner and Micoleau talked
about the letters. He took home some short stories of Foote's, had them
copied, and returned them. He told Micoleau that he was urging
McMurry to write a critical biography of Foote for his dissertation and
then have it published by Stanford University Press.

The following month, Stegner asked Micoleau for permission to
include the Foote short story "How the Pump Stopped at the Morning
Watch" in *Selected American Prose, 1841–1900,* an anthology that was to
be published in 1958. The year 1900 was selected by the publisher,
Rinehart & Company, because no permissions fees had to be paid for
stories published prior to that date, according to the copyright laws of
the time. Not knowing when or if it had been previously published,
Stegner asked McMurry to research the copyright. McMurry said that
it had never been published. He was wrong. It had appeared in the July
1899 issue of *Century* magazine.

The story combines two incidents that occurred at the North Star
Mine in Grass Valley while Arthur Foote was its manager. The second
event did not occur in the way Foote depicted it. Stegner wrote that her
work thus demonstrated "how fiction, even realistic fiction, may legitimately warp history and fact to arrive at a human truth larger than the
factual truth."[20]

By the mid-1960s, Stegner was looking around for a topic for a historical novel with a wide scope that would link the past to the present. He contacted Micoleau in August 1967. By that time it was obvious that McMurry was going nowhere with the subject.[21] Wally had "a vague query" for Micoleau, vague because he had not yet thought it through to a solid book proposal:

> Out of the so-typical and so-comprehensive western life of Arthur and Mary Foote I might work out the outlines of a big western novel of a kind I have not yet seen written. I am very serious about this, and thinking hard about it. Of course it would not be a biography, and it would have to depart, when necessary—which might be often—from both facts of their careers and the facts of their characters. It would probably not be recognizable as based on MHF & AF, but it *would* be. They were so many places, he had the big ideas early—always too early—and their life was close to the big national movements and to big national figures in a way no ordinary pioneer lives were. Our usual pioneers were dirt-diggers; these were cultivated people transplanting a civilization. It is a theme Willa Cather would have liked, and so do I. Since it would involve no recognizable characterizations and no quotations direct from the letters, I assume this sort of book is more or less open to me. If it isn't, for any reason, I wish you would let me know. It's a long project, two or three years at the least I should guess, and I don't want to get deep into it without giving you a chance to object, if you feel that way.[22]

Micoleau replied three weeks later. The war in Vietnam and the strife throughout the country had preoccupied her. Too much time had slipped by since his last letter. She said, "We'd be delighted to have the MHF materials used as background for a novel." She would make "anything that you can use" available to him. "We gave George McMurry a copy of the *Reminiscences,* and I think he has some other material as well. He took a box-load of stuff once, so long ago that I can't remember what it was. Perhaps he could pass on to you anything that you can use and return the rest to me." The "Reminiscences," or "Rems" as Foote referred to her unpublished memoir, was in manuscript form. Micoleau hadn't known what to do with all the Foote material. "I am very grateful to you for your continued interest in MHF and for rescuing me from my dilemma!"[23]

Wally replied immediately: "I'm grateful for your blanket approval, and though I don't myself know yet exactly the best way to make use of the letters and other MHF papers, I'm sure they are too rich to lie around in the archives unused."[24]

What "background" meant and who the "we" in Micoleau's letter actually referred to, from what Stegner derived "blanket approval," and exactly how he was going to use the Foote material and attribute its source were not specified before publication. Within this zone of vagueness that encompassed both Stegner and the Foote family lay the difficulties that rankle some scholars and certain members of the Foote family to this day.

Stegner assumed that Micoleau spoke for the entire family.[25] The copyright, meaning the right to grant permission to quote from the letters, was held by Foote's heirs. Janet Micoleau granted Stegner that right on the condition that he get the permission of Rosamond Gilder in New York. The letters were owned by Gilder; she had inherited them from her mother, Helena de Kay Gilder, Mary Foote's close friend and confidante (Augusta in Stegner's novel). The correspondence was between Mary and Helena.[26]

Hold everything, said Gilder; she had never received the transcribed copies of the letters that the Stanford library had promised to send her in return for her giving the library the letters. Gilder was also planning a book on Foote based on the letters to her mother. The librarians at Stanford finally sent her the transcribed letters, which had been promised twelve years earlier, thus clearing the way for Stegner to use them.

In October 1967 Stegner was still not sure what he was going to write. He told Gilder, "I think either a biography, in which case I may come hat in hand to ask your help, or a novel, in which case I can move much more freely within the materials." By the next year he was leaning toward a novel. He thought Foote was a better illustrator than a writer. "She just wasn't a big enough figure for a biography to be a big book," he said.[27]

Stegner was an astute judge of the realities of the New York literary marketplace. His later critics, mostly feminists and some members of the Foote family who viewed her as a major literary figure, thought he had demeaned Foote by not believing she was worthy of a biography. He had meant "big" in terms of public renown, thematic scope, and the potential sales that would attract a major publisher and an adequate advance. He had just given up the steady income derived from teaching and was seeking to replace it. He was right, as later sales figures proved.

Mary Hallock Foote: Author-Illustrator of the American West by Darlis A. Miller was published by the University of Oklahoma Press in 2002. Four years later less than one thousand hardcover copies had been sold, and the book had not made it into a softcover edition. By way of contrast, sales of the hardcover and paperback editions of *Angle of Repose* between 1971 and 2007 numbered 570,000 copies.[28]

After reading Foote's unpublished memoir, which Micoleau had sent him, Stegner settled on a novel in early 1968. "Quite a book, really, and quite a life," he told her, referring to the "Reminiscences," which provided him with the basic plot and specific scenes from the Footes' lives. He wrote Micoleau that he'd like "to test your response to the mixture of history and fiction that I may want to stir up." Referring to the fact-mixed-with-fiction technique of *In Cold Blood*, Stegner said: "If Truman Capote can do it about a murder, I ought to be able to do it about a good constructive pair of lives. Don't you think so?"[29]

BEHIND MOST RENOWNED writers there are capable agents, because producing and publishing a book is a minefield of hidden obstacles, any one of which can explode in the author's face. It is the agent's job, which is no small task, to be an effective mine detector and clear the path for the author.

Except for a few years after World War II, when he was West Coast editor for Houghton Mifflin and mistakenly thought he could adequately represent his own interests, Wally was a client of Brandt & Brandt Literary Agents from 1937 until his death in 1993. He said he had returned to the agency "convinced that publishers were not to be trusted and that I did indeed need a keeper."[30]

While Stegner remained with one agency, he changed publishers fairly frequently, mostly when he thought they weren't paying enough attention to him in terms of marketing or advances. More conventional wisdom, he said, was to stick with one publisher, and that firm would push a writer's backlist along with the most recent book. The progression of publishers was Little, Brown; Harcourt, Brace; Duell, Sloan and Pearce; Houghton Mifflin; McGraw-Hill; Viking Press; Doubleday; E. P. Dutton; and Random House.

His agents at Brandt & Brandt arranged the changes in publishers. He worked successively with Bernice Baumgarten; Carl Brandt; his wife, Carol Brandt; and their son Carl D. Brandt.[31] The literary agency, now known as Brandt & Hochman, is perhaps the oldest in New York.

It was formed shortly before World War I by Mary Kirkpatrick, who hired Carl Brandt to sweep the floors. Brandt took over after the war. Up to the mid-1950s most of the income earned by writers and agents came from sales to the many popular magazines, but television eviscerated that market. As Carl's health began to fail in 1956, Carol joined Brandt & Brandt. She had previously stolen some of her husband's clients and run a boutique literary agency. Carol and Bernice did not get along, and Baumgarten departed in 1957, shortly after Carl's death.

Stegner had a close and productive relationship with Carol. They were more than agent and client. She said that Stegner was "not only a valued client but a very close friend." When he won the Pulitzer Prize for *Angle of Repose*, Wally thanked Carol for her "affectionate support."[32] Carol was Wally's financial, legal, literary, and, for Mary's health problems, medical adviser. The correspondence with her was his most extensive and personal in an era when letters were the principal form of communication for people living and working on opposite coasts. They cared for and trusted each other. Whenever Wally didn't mention Mary's health problems, which was infrequently, Carol assumed that Mary was okay. When he did mention them, it was sometimes in the form of an unburdening about lesser or greater woes. Carol replied with a woman's and a friend's perspective.

She was a cheerleader when Stegner needed bucking up, and she kept him focused on the task at hand when diversions threatened in the form of other book and film projects. Brandt was responsible for the multibook contract that allowed Stegner to quit teaching, gave him insightful advice when he had second thoughts about cutting the cord with Stanford (for which he called her Mother Cassandra), and was at least partially responsible for his successes in the 1970s. When Stegner was depressed about the critical reception and sales of *Angle*, she wrote, referring to his editor and publisher: "Sandy, Doubleday, and I all love you dearly. So does Mary. Get back to your typewriter."

The book she worked hardest on was one of his less successful projects, *American Places*, published in 1981. Six parties were involved in that book, whose text, a collection of essays, was a collaborative effort by Page and Wallace Stegner. There were father and son and their two agents, the photographer Eliot Porter, and Jack Macrae, the editor and the president of E. P. Dutton. Carol's accomplishment was to keep them all talking through their many differences, the major one being the Stegners' and Macrae's views of what the text should cover and the latter's lack of communication with the authors. "Still no response from

Macrae to the manuscript," Wally fumed. "Either he despises it, or he is the most dilatory man alive, or both." Calm down was Carol's message. The result of the project, which stretched over six years, was a book Stegner was only "moderately pleased" with.[33]

Stegner was not a passive client. He took an active interest in the business affairs of writing, not only in the advances and royalties but also the fine print in contracts. He was concerned about making too little or too much money in a given year, meaning that he might ask Carol for a short-term loan at the end of a year to cover Christmas expenses or request that a publisher's payment be spread over two years in order to escape the tax consequences of a single payment. Ultimately, if there was a difference of opinion between writer and agent, he deferred to Carol's judgment.

At a time when men dominated the book industry, the agency had a history of employing powerful women. Carol mixed toughness with grace. She dressed well, wore expensive jewelry, and stayed in the best hotels on her European trips. Her apartments in New York had Park Avenue and Central Park South addresses. If she wasn't lunching with a client or an editor, she might order a sandwich from Chock full o'Nuts and drink a scotch and water at her desk. Mary Stegner found Carol "very stagy, sort of an elegant lady, and very, very kind. She was very nice to Wally." Late in his writing career Stegner said that beginning with Bernice and ending with the Brandts' son, he couldn't have been in better hands. "I've been through them all," he said, "and worn them all out."[34]

BY EARLY 1968, Carol and Wally were exasperated by the lack of advertising for Stegner's most recent novel, *All the Little Live Things*, published the previous year by Viking. Sensing his dissatisfaction, two editors from Doubleday, Luther Nichols and Ken McCormick, visited Stegner at Stanford, as did E. L. Doctorow, then an editor with Dial Press. Stegner concluded: "One, I am leaving Viking, no matter what. And two, I am very interested in some sort of package deal that will let me retire from teaching four or five years early, and write books." He preferred Doubleday because of its paperback lines and book clubs. If Doubleday offered him a contract that would ensure his being treated "as one of their race horses," he would sign it.[35]

Carol went to work on the company's offer of $70,000. "Ma'am, you are a potent negotiator," declared Stegner, "Up fifty thousand in the first round must be some sort of record." His friend Malcolm Cowley at Viking heard what was transpiring and was distressed. Stegner told him, "I was not getting at Viking what I left Houghton Mifflin hoping to get and what I thought was assured me. And I haven't got a hell of a lot more time. So I will have to go hunting."[36] At fifty-nine, Stegner felt that time was getting short.

Carol and Wally finalized the contract with Doubleday in May. He liked his editors, Ken McCormick and Stewart (Sandy) Richardson. McCormick said, "I think we are going to have a great time together."[37] The six-book contract, for $127,500, came close to matching the $150,000 in lost salary from Stanford that would be incurred by retiring early. The six books were *The Sound of Mountain Water*, a collection of essays; paperback reprints of *The Big Rock Candy Mountain* and *The Preacher and the Slave*, retitled *Joe Hill*; *Angle of Repose*; *The Uneasy Chair: A Biography of Bernard DeVoto*; and *The Letters of Bernard DeVoto*. Three books were added later: the novels *The Spectator Bird* and *Recapitulation*, and *One Way to Spell Man*, another collection of essays. Those nine books, spread over fourteen years, represented Stegner's longest association with one publisher.

WITH THE FINANCIAL arrangements out of the way, Stegner began working on *Angle* in May 1968. He was making daily progress "of a kind" and promised delivery of the manuscript in one year. To keep himself motivated, he would promise an early completion date, which he would later have to revise.

Writing was hard work seven mornings a week. Every book was a struggle for Stegner, with some more difficult than others. "I'll type a single page so many times to get it right before I go onto the next one that there never is a proper first draft. But certainly one of the things that happens before going on from page one to page twenty of that preliminary draft is trying to get the feel and the emotion right." The creative process was a series of small jerks forward and backward with, it was hoped, a net gain at the end of each day.

His "progress of a kind" consisted of making three attempts at a start. The conventional wisdom is that if a writer gets the beginning right, the remainder of the book will fall into place. Melville's first sentence in *Moby-Dick* ("Call me Ishmael") is the classic example. These are Stegner's first three tries. The story is viewed retrospectively by Lyman Ward, grandson of the Wards and a crippled historian; Rodman is his son.

I begin by jotting down the place and time: Zodiac Cottage, Grass Valley, California, April 12, 1968, and while I thus establish the present, the present has moved on. Before I can finish saying I am, I was. But am or was, I am cumulative. I am everything I ever had been, and much of what my family has been—inherited stature, coloring, bone (that part unfortunate); transmitted scruple, pride, and prejudice. My antecedents are rooted in me like weeds in a field, and time is a moving shadow across them and me.

Rodman's visit today clinches it. They will not interfere, at least until the rainy season reactivates their worry mechanisms, and that gives me seven months, every day of it pure gain over what they had in mind for me. Sufficient unto the day. I will not fret myself making plans for how to combat them until they show signs of renewing their campaign against my freedom. So I can sit here now and jot down the place and time of this beginning: Zodiac Cottage, Grass Valley, California, April 12, 1968.

It's all right, I feel certain they will not bother me, at least until the rainy season reactivates their worry mechanisms. Rodman came to snoop out signs of my incompetence but he went home without any of what he would call data. So now I can sit here, where I like to be, and by myself as I like to be, and jot down the time and place of this beginning: *Zodiac Cottage, Grass Valley, California, April 12, 1968.*[38]

And the published version:

Now I believe they will leave me alone. Obviously Rodman came up hoping to find evidence of my incompetence—though how an incompetent could have got this place renovated, moved his library up, and got himself transported to it without arousing the suspicion of his watchful children, ought to be a hard one for Rodman to answer. I take some pride in the way I managed all that. And he went away this afternoon without a scrap of what he would call data.

So tonight I can sit here with the tape recorder whirring no more noisily than electrified time, and say into the microphone the place and date of a sort of beginning and a sort of return: Zodiac Cottage, Grass Valley, California, April 12, 1970.[39]

It took this rearranging and honing of words to transfer Stegner's intent more perfectly from his mind to the page in a manner that would instantly engage the reader and resonate throughout the book. The hardest part was throwing away what was good but didn't quite fit, like the evocative sentence "My antecedents are rooted in me like weeds in a field, and time is a moving shadow across them and me."

From lecturing, Stegner had shifted into the storytelling mode. Thesis gave way to action. "Call me Ishmael" became "Call me Lyman Ward," the narrator. The scrappy character, the authorial voice stripped of such flourishes as "Sufficient unto the day" and "fret myself," the passage of time, the generational conflict, the preferred machinery of historical inquiry (oral history captured on a tape recorder versus the computer data that his son favors), and place, where the novel conceivably begins and ends within a longer stretch of time (thus the "sort of") are all established in 127 words—no small achievement.

Stegner's creation of the character Lyman Ward and his use of Mary Hallock Foote's writings allowed him to contrast the present of the late 1960s with the Victorian past. It gave him a way of avoiding a single point of view and telling two related stories that were separated by time and different cultural mores. Of his use of Foote's letters, he said: "A few of them are almost unchanged, some are half changed, and some are totally changed. Sometimes I'm utilizing documents, and sometimes I'm writing pretend-documentary. All of which, it seems to me, is making maximum use of the tools that are there. It gives you maximum freedom."[40]

Random thoughts were captured by Stegner in green ink on scraps of paper to be used or discarded later. He plumbed his mind thus:

> Why writing this book? (Is it a book? I'm just trying to settle some things in my mind.) Maybe how two very different people, with profoundly different aims and faiths, manage to make a solid marriage.
>
> They do it by giving up things. Is it good to give up things? You only got one life.
>
> Depends on whether you want to depart with character or with an exhaustion of sensation.[41]

Was it Hilda or George Stegner, Mary or Arthur Foote, Mary or Wallace Stegner who preferred not to give up anything—or an amalgam of all three couples plus friends and acquaintances? Or was it the universal condition of two people living together that formed the deep well from which Stegner drew the water to irrigate his study of past and present time and a marriage?

The differences between the East (from where both Footes and Wards had emigrated) and the West (where they lived most of their married lives) are interwoven throughout the book. Another scrap of paper illustrates Stegner's thoughts about Susan Ward's geographic and cultural transformation: "In the end, too, she will be a Westerner—she will have abdicated what she thought her most precious heritage, she will be less sure what is a lady, she will have less faith in magnificent moral gestures and renunciations learned from Henry James, she will be humble, tried, durable, and old."[42]

FROM GREENSBORO IN August of 1968, Wally wrote Carol Brandt: "I'm back in my gloomy little shack at work again on the novel. I wish I had some bright posters of Faulkner accepting the Nobel Prize and Truman Capote vacationing in Marrakech. Then I'd maybe *believe* in the literary life." Three months later he had thrown away the first five chapters "and improved it like mad. Oh pray for us."[43]

One year later Stegner reported, "The novel bumps and grinds on." There might be a completed manuscript by the end of 1969. Then the admission: "This is palaver—I may be slower than expected." By January 1970 he was seventy-five pages short of a draft, but "after that there'll be a good deal of yanking and combing and carding before it's a manuscript."[44]

In the spring of 1970 there was an important exchange of letters between Stegner and Janet Micoleau. "Probably you thought I was dead, paralyzed, struck dumb or otherwise incapacitated," he wrote. "I am none of those. I am only slow as a sinful conscience." He had completed more than five hundred manuscript pages and had the entire last section to write. "Some parts of it I like a good deal. But as I warned you, the process of making a novel from real people has led me to bend them where I had to, and you may not recognize your ancestors when I get through with them. On the other hand, I have availed myself of your invitation to use the letters and 'Reminiscences' as I pleased, and so there are passages from both in my novel, stolen outright. Not long passages: a paragraph at a time at most."[45] Actually, they would be considerably longer.

The previous week, Stegner wrote Micoleau, he had had a telephone call from Rodman W. Paul, a history professor at the California

Institute of Technology. Paul said he was beginning work on the editing of Foote's memoir. Stegner and Paul began a correspondence. For a local colorist, Foote was rather distant from her subjects, Paul thought: she was "an educated outsider who had little contact with the people and communities that were her successive western homes." He added: "One thinks of parallel cases of upper-class, educated eastern ladies who were protected by their husbands and their own tastes from intimate contact with an intriguing but crude new society: Martha Summerhayes, Dame Shirley." He looked forward to meeting and discussing Mary Hallock Foote with Stegner later in the spring.[46]

Stegner told Micoleau that publication of the "Rems" was "a splendid idea" and "long past due." He had agreed to read Paul's introduction. There was one problem, however, and that was how to preserve the anonymity of the Footes, as Micoleau had requested. That would have been difficult enough with anyone familiar with her work; it would be harder after publication of the memoir. "But sometime before Paul gets the *Reminiscences* ready for publication, which won't be soon, I'd like your word on what I should do about my threads of actual fact." He couldn't change the history of their lives, but he could modify "the actual language" and names if he really had to. "Will you let me know?"[47]

He'd also like to send Micoleau a draft of the manuscript. "Would you read it? It'll take you a week. And it won't of course be final. Neither will it be true to all the details of the Footes' lives. For reasons of drama, if nothing else, I'm having to foreshorten, and I'm having to throw in a domestic tragedy of an entirely fictional nature. But I think I'm not too far from their real characters."[48] The tragedy was the scene in which Susan Ward's daughter drowns while she is involved in an intense emotional exchange that hints at adultery with a young engineer. The invention of this scene, which suggests both adultery and filicide, was what most disturbed Foote's family and critics of Stegner's use of the material.

Five weeks after Stegner wrote, Janet Micoleau replied. She apologized. She had once again gotten her priorities "reversed." There were committee meetings to attend, mailings to get out, a county zoning ordinance to consider, and a campaign for state superintendent of public instruction to back.

> I'm glad you haven't abandoned the idea of the book—
> I thought you might possibly have become discouraged with it—
> and I appreciate your thoughtfulness in consulting us again now

that the "Rems" are to be published. I see no need for you to change or modify anything. Perhaps in an introduction you could explain your interweaving of truth & fiction for the benefit of those who have read the "Rems" and might recognize the threads of truth amidst the fiction. But that's up to you—I'm sure all concerned are content to trust your judgment. We all wish you well with the undertaking, & have no desire to censor or interfere with it in any way.[49]

As for reading the manuscript, Micoleau said: "Thank you for offering to send the 600 page manuscript for me to read but that's a lot of trouble. I'd just as soon wait until it's in print and easier to mail."[50]

THERE WERE INTERRUPTIONS and temptations for Stegner to deal with, like a film for the National Film Board of Canada and offers from *Reader's Digest* to write a historical novel about John James Audubon and from Time-Life to write the text for a book of photographs on the canyonlands of the Southwest. The money was tempting, but with Carol's subtle prodding Stegner said no to both writing projects. Brandt pointed out that the "editorial meddling" at Time-Life Books "would remind one of a Vassar senior."[51]

Then, too, it was a very difficult time in America for Stegner, who wrote his agent:

Too much disruption and emotional exhaustion and other symptoms from the campus and the White House. It's hard to believe in Mary Hallock Foote when I listen to the radio and television or pick my way to the office through the barricades and broken glass and the smell of tear gas. . . . It ain't the easiest time to write a genteel novel. Bless your stars you have no connection with any college campus. And curse your fate at having Him [Richard Nixon] in the White House.[52]

Stegner knew he was out of step with what was occurring around him. To Howard Mumford Jones, the critic and professor of English at Harvard who had won a Pulitzer Prize for the first in a series of books on American culture, Wally wrote that he was writing a "long, sexless, violence-less novel about a genteel female." He added: "I rather like the Genteel Tradition. I can think of a lot of people and some civilizations that a touch of gentility would not harm."[53]

Wallace, Hilda, and Cecil Stegner, Christmas 1913

Wally emerging from a swim in the Frenchman River behind the Stegners' Eastend home

Left: A young Wallace Stegner

Right: A young Mary Page

A friend and Stegner at Fish Lake in 1928

George and Wallace
Stegner and an
unidentified man on
the right

The photo of Hilda Stegner that Wally
kept on his desk

Wally and Mary shortly after being
married in 1934

Above: Mary and Wally, first and third from the left, with their close friends Peg and Phil Gray and an unidentified woman on the far right preparing for the pack trip in 1938 that was described in *Crossing to Safety*

The family Christmas card for 1942, when they wintered in Greensboro

The Briggs-Copeland writing instructor at Harvard University in 1943.

Below: Wally and Page at their Stanford University rented house in 1947

Opposite top: Wally, the shortest figure in the back row, with Mary just below him in Glen Canyon during the float trip down the San Juan River in 1947

Opposite bottom: The Los Altos Hills home under construction in 1949 and the empty landscape surrounding it at the time

Wally, Mary, and Page in their home with Smokey the dog and Baghdad the cat in 1953

Right: Teaching the creative writing workshop in the Jones Room in the Stanford Library

A 1960 class at the Stegner home with Ed McClanahan on the far left and Larry McMurtry to Stegner's right

Wally and Mary on the Alaska field trip of the National Park Service advisory committee in 1965

Wallace Stegner in his writing studio in 1982 *(Leo Holub photo)*

Opposite: Signing copies of *Collected Stories* in 1990

Mary Stegner in their Vermont home the second summer after Wally's death. The photo was taken by their close friend Tom Watkins.

Opposite bottom: Eastend, Saskatchewan: the two-story structure toward the right next to the tree is the former Pastime Theater

The reservoir on the homestead site, the only remaining evidence of the family's summers of toil on the prairie

The Stegners' Eastend home, now an artists' and writers' residence

Page, Lynn, and Alison Stegner at the Davis Gulch campsite on the Lake Powell trip

Opposite bottom: The porch at Treman Cottage, where the faculty socialized during the Bread Loaf Writers' Conference

Right: In the foreground are the gravestones for Cecil and Hilda Stegner in the Salt Lake City Cemetery

Where Wallace Stegner's ashes were scattered outside his Greensboro, Vermont, summer home

Canyonlands, the heart of Stegner country *(Alex Fradkin photo)*

Stegner sent Brandt the first two thirds of the manuscript in May 1970. She wrote him: "I love the 400 pages, and they will go to Ken today." To McCormick she wrote: "I like it very much. I so hope you and Sandy will." They did.[54]

He fled the turmoil of Stanford and in June was in tranquil Greensboro, working on both the novel and the biography of Bernard DeVoto and enjoying an early summer in New England. One of Stegner's most evocative descriptive passages was sandwiched between what was otherwise a dull but necessary business letter to Carol:

> The walks are across sphagnum moss four inches thick, with wild strawberries poking their red heads out. The mornings are full of choirs of thrushes and white-throats. I work two hours a day with some brutal machine such as a chain saw, and in the evenings we sit and listen to Schubert quintets by one candle, with ten million fireflies winking around the grove outside. We not only live with the earth, we live in the dirt, and love it.[55]

An Airedale puppy lying before the stove completed the scene far from the madding crowd.

Sandy Richardson visited Stegner in June to go over the manuscript that Wally had just completed the previous night, when, feeling he lacked an effective ending, he had written the concluding dream sequence in one intense sitting. Wally reported to Carol: "Sandy after three drinks talks Book of the Month and Pulitzer Prize. I keep my intake down to *two* drinks and keep my sanity."[56]

Brandt and Richardson had problems with one small section of the manuscript, however. Reviewers would focus on it, and the negative attention would affect sales. "Nobody can be sure of this," said Carol, "but you know how strongly he and I feel about this passage."[57] Stegner said he would take a look at it.

Oliver and Susan are in Boise. His plans to build an irrigation canal and ditches have failed. Stegner needed a short transition chapter to move the story quickly forward to the next scene. He hauled out Uncle Remus and had him narrate the passage in a vaudevillian Negro dialect that went on for five double-spaced pages. Richardson slashed a line across each page with the notation to the typesetter "Do Not Set."

The solution that Stegner quickly supplied was to have Lyman narrate the transition chapter. Of Oliver's failed attempts, Stegner had written: "He sho nuff tried, honey, Brer Ward did. Tried en tried, sho's you born." The passage now reads in Lyman's words: "About this time

I need some Mister Bones to say to me, 'Doesn't this story have any-thing in it but hard luck and waiting? Isn't the man ever going to get that ditch dug?' Then I can reply in summary fashion, and get by this dead time." Good agents and editors earn their commissions and salaries, which were not inconsiderable in Stegner's opinion, on the basis of these seemingly small but potentially fateful corrections.

There was the remaining problem of how to credit the sources for the material on which much of the novel was based while not identify-ing the family. Stegner's solution was a one-paragraph statement in the front of the book.

> My thanks to J.M. and her sister for the loan of their ances-tors. Though I have used many details of their lives and charac-ters, I have not hesitated to warp both personalities and events to fictional needs. This is a novel which utilizes selected facts from their real lives. It is in no sense a family history.

Given the publication of Foote's memoir, the remote possibility that Gilder might produce a book, and the fact that Foote was a published writer and illustrator famous in her time, some people—especially in Grass Valley—would inevitably associate Foote with Ward. Even if they read the caveat, they would have no way to separate fact from fic-tion and would tend to read the book as family history. They would gossip, and the granddaughters would hear and react to what was being said in the small community. In such an ordinary manner a literary con-troversy would arise.

ENTHUSIASM FOR THE novel began mounting within Doubleday during the fall of 1970. "The excitement that is building up around the house about the novel is really wonderful," McCormick told Wally. Forty thousand dollars was budgeted for the advertising campaign. "We will know about mid-January whether we make the 40,000 advance sale," said Richardson. "I would be happy with around 30,000 because I am confident the book will sell—both men and women are crazy about it. This is a good sign."[58]

The predicted Book-of-the-Month Club selection failed to materi-alize because Richardson opted for a guaranteed $50,000 Literary Guild selection instead of waiting a few days for the $125,000 BOMC offer. "I was, of course, sick," said Richardson, who added, "Suffice it to say that the whole matter was painful to everyone here, and doubly so to you."[59]

One of the first reactions to the book from outside publishing circles came from Janet Micoleau in March. Stegner had sent prepublication copies to Janet and her husband, Tyler, and to Janet's sister Marian Foote Conway, who lived near Janet. He was not aware that there was a third sister, Evelyn Foote Gardiner, who resided in southern California. Janet wrote Wally:

> Although I have only dipped into *Angle of Repose* and listened to and discussed parts read to me by Tyler, I'm already delighted and fascinated with it, and am looking forward to reading it properly from beginning to end. Then I shall write you a proper letter about it. You needn't fear that any of us will be offended—and I am sure I can speak for all the family—by your blending of fiction with fact. I've read enough of it to know that this enhances the fascination of the book for me—discovering the threads of fact in the intricate pattern, while admiring the design and the skill of the craftsman. Since none of us has read the letters, we may not always detect which were altered and which invented.[60]

A less favorable reaction came from his son, Page, to whom the novel was dedicated. Wally's testy answer to the criticisms contained insightful comments about the book. His novelist–writing teacher son was bothered about Susan Ward's gentility and the ending. As for Ward, Stegner answered:

> I find your faulty judgments about art and posterity and such easy to condone, and I agree with you about Susan Ward. If you didn't dislike her gentility you weren't reading me. . . . I may have been trying to do something impossible in showing, through two long lives and several shorter ones, that in any social context individuals will be colored by their times, for good and ill, and that in the end one social context is about as good as another, so long as it is subscribed to fully and is binding on the people born to it. I suppose I also wanted to throw in the notion that one time, despite its assumed freedom and emancipation from history and human cussedness, can be about as foolish as another.

The ending had been a problem. "How would *you* get out of that book?" Wally asked Page. He had tried writing a realistic ending, with Ward's wife returning to take care of him. It was too long and wrong. "The dream bit was a kind of cheap way out, but the only one I could think of." Somebody, probably his wife, would rescue Ward, and his independence would be bent "by vile necessity."[61] Although Malcolm Cowley also had problems with the ending, Stegner believed it worked. It connected the past to the present.

TWO WEEKS AFTER publication, in April 1971, 30,000 copies had been sold. Sales then hovered around that figure. The book was briefly on the best-seller lists of *Publishers Weekly*, *Time* magazine, and *The New York Times Book Review*. At a time when there were many more book-review sections and pages devoted to books in the print media, *Angle* was widely and favorably reviewed throughout the country. The critics praised Stegner for what he had imagined and what he had taken from Foote's letters, published stories, and unpublished memoir. None cited Foote as the source. William Abrahams in *The Atlantic Monthly* thought the letters were "a triumph of verisimilitude, perfectly matched to Mr. Stegner's carefully rendered locales and social discriminations."[62]

No review, however, had yet appeared in the Sunday *New York Times Book Review*, the only daily newspaper review section with national pretensions. The book review was edited by John Leonard, who, in his own words, had been hired by the *Times* in 1971 "out of the anti-war movement." (The book had been assigned for review, Leonard later recalled, but the review was "a disaster." It was *Times* policy not to reassign a review so that the newspaper could not be accused of dictating judgment.)[63] However, *Angle* was mentioned in a Saturday "Books of the Times" column, written by Thomas Lask. "It's a long, relaxed and relaxing piece of work, not terribly demanding," wrote Lask. Stegner had a tactile feeling for the West and "the authentic ring of history." The old-fashioned virtues promoted in the book were more likely to appeal to members of the local garden club than to the younger generation, Lask said. Stegner wrote to Carol Brandt: "Lask in the daily *Times* was the usual condescending New Yorker (why do you live in that town?)."[64]

Wally was depressed. The book did not remain on the *Times* best-seller list very long, "for which I owe the *Times* and I suppose Leonard an undying grudge—and I am a good grudge holder." He saw *Angle* as "probably my last chance to make it with a novel. After sixty the spirit doesn't rally so fast from these knockdowns. But I suppose the old habits will still work one time more, and so I am wiping this one out and thinking about the next one, which will of course (don't tell Doubleday) sell six thousand copies at the top. So, having failed to get the bullion box, let's gather up the watches and small change and vamanos," he said.[65]

Malcolm Cowley, who in addition to being an author and editor was an influential book critic, consoled Wally:

> I think of how you've run into bad luck with critics on account of the operation of almost physical laws of literary force. For a long time it was your being a Western writer at a time when the ruling establishment was first Eastern, then Southern, then New York Jewish. Right now it is the disorderly advance of a new generation bent on annihilating everything old. Nothing like that has happened since the 1920s—for almost half a century the new people came on rather tamely, or at least they chose certain of their elders to exalt at the expense of others, but now they want to abolish all of them.[66]

The next knockdown—the knockout punch would come soon—appeared two months later. Leonard ran a column by William DuBois in the Sunday *Times Book Review* titled "The Last Word: The Well-Made Novel." *Angle* was described as "a jumbo that illumines one man's Western heritage, a dynastic chronicle that contrasts the American past and present with dazzling expertise." DuBois said he liked it. "Why, then, did I close this big but never boring novel with a sense of circular motion in a maze?" It was well made. "Unfortunately," said DuBois, "it's too well made. The paradox is defensible." He could not deal with the back-and-forth in time rather than a straightforward chronological narrative, nor could he lose himself in the characters. He gave Stegner, the former professor, an A minus.[67]

To Cowley, who wrote Stegner the day the column appeared, DuBois's comments didn't make sense unless one considered that the essay was Leonard's one-page apology for not reviewing *Angle*: "It's the *Times* eating crow and pretending that it's duck, hence the mental confusion." As far as Cowley could determine, Stegner had been censured "for writing a big novel that is easy to read and at the same time soundly constructed."[68]

The book sold slowly, Doubleday recovered its costs, and there was some talk about movie rights. Stegner reported to his editor that he was making good progress on his DeVoto biography. The DuBois article made him gag. He repeated Cowley's duck versus crow line, making it Peking duck, and added: "The hell with the whole goddamn ingrown outfit."[69]

Sandy Richardson's prophecy, made two years previously, came true on May 1, 1972. Over "too many" drinks at 2 a.m., Doubleday publisher Sam Vaughan was tipped off by a juror that *Angle of Repose* had been awarded, by a unanimous vote, the Pulitzer Prize for fiction. The next morning he passed his "hunch" on to the sales manager, checked to make sure there was sufficient inventory (there was), shipped more books, and planned an ad campaign. Wally missed Carol's excited phone call and was given the news by a United Press International reporter one hour later. The much bigger news that day was that *The New York Times* had won a Pulitzer for publishing the Pentagon Papers.

Stegner's grudge against the *Times* dominated his guarded response to Carol Brandt. He regretted missing her phone call. Learning about the prize from a wire-service reporter was "an indignity I find it easy to bear, especially after what the reviewers of your town did to the book." He had two wishes: "That the prize turns out in most people's opinion to be deserved as these things usually are and that the *Times* book review has to admit it, if only in the privacy of its own withered heart."[70] Neither wish would be granted.

Stegner was flooded with congratulations from family, friends, former students, faculty members, acquaintances, and complete strangers. From Port Royal, Kentucky, came a letter from Wendell Berry:

> It has moved me as few books ever have. From the beginning it accepts all its challenges and grows steadily broader and deeper. I read it with the sense of something large and fine being added both to my mind and to the country, and with the warmest gratitude to you. It is preeminently an American book—the most *continental* of the American books that I know—and yet it is, as a novel, more Russian than American; it made me think of Tolstoy and Pasternak.[71]

It was difficult for Wally to show his feelings. That was not part of the frontier code. He could, however, confide his more personal thoughts to a select few, like his old friend Phil Gray.

One of the nicest things about this Pulitzer Prize is all sorts of people call up, and wire, and write. It's bettern Christmas cards. And it touches us, it really does, to see how many people seem genuinely to wish us well. When a TV man asked how I felt, I said I felt humble, and Mary briskly kicked my shins. But I wasn't talking about the damn prize. Hell, I've deserved that since my first book (How's that, Molly?). But I felt humble about that telephone ringing from all over, and really jubilant voices, as pleased for us as if it had happened to them. God bless people, wot I say. Except some I'd like to strangle, but that's another week and another mood.[72]

The brief moment of celebration was quickly eradicated by a renewed attack on the book and Stegner by the editor of the *Times Book Review*. A new layer was added to the shell that Stegner lugged through life. It was just as well the carapace was in place because he needed all the armor he could muster.

In "The Last Word" column of May 14, titled "The Pulitzer Prizes: Fail-Safe Again," John Leonard wrote that Stegner did not deserve the prize. The column transcended professional criticism for those in the know, like Stegner, in that it contained personal references designed to hurt. Leonard set up his target by citing the DuBois column and another published a year previously in the book review by Walter Clemons.

Mr. Clemons enunciated four rules of thumb which govern the awarding of Pulitzer Prizes for fiction: (1) middlebrows get it early—Louis Bromfield, Edna Ferber, Herman Wouk, James Michener and Allen Drury; (2) better writers get it late, for inferior books—William Faulkner and Willa Cather; (3) moral uplift helps; and (4) imitating your betters helps even more.

He followed that paragraph with the sentence "This year the jurors danced themselves dizzy around the Maypole and bumped into Wallace Stegner, an estimable man." Leonard then unleashed his broadside:

But for those of us who care about what is happening to fiction in this country, the selection of "Angle of Repose" is another in a long, apparently endless, line of Pulitzer disappointments: Forthright, yes; and morally uplifting; and middlebrow. As safe as N. Scott Momaday's "House Made of Dawn" (1969), a kind of Pontiac in the age of Apollo, an Ed Muskie in the fiction sweepstakes ("Trust Me"). Remember: the Pulitzer people are saying, in effect, that Mr. Stegner's novel is the only "distinguished work of fiction by an American author" *in the last two years*. Eat your heart out, John Hawkes.[73]

Very few except Stegner, some Stanford graduate students, and members of the university's Department of English would have known that Momaday had been a Stegner Fellow and that John Hawkes, the postmodern author of *The Lime Twig* and *Second Skin*, had been the experimental novelist hired by Albert Guérard for the Voice Project, which Stegner had viewed as a threat to his creative writing program.[74]

Leonard had more to say, and he said it vehemently and in a particularly nasty manner. He attacked "reviewers who treat experiments in form and technique as a personal insult" and Pulitzer jurors who settle "for whatever is comfortable, tame, toothless and affectionate—a pet instead of a work of art." The column concluded: "We have obviously settled for pacifiers, and one hopes we choke on them."

Stegner wouldn't read the column, believing that Leonard had not read his book. "The *Times* did not treat the novel," he said; "it attempted to destroy it."[75] He soldiered on, only to be again attacked by the newspaper's critics a few years later.

His editor, however, was furious. By May 1972, Sandy Richardson had been promoted from senior editor to editor in chief of Doubleday. An editor who has many books under consideration for review by the *Times* does not lightly attack someone like Leonard. The editor of the *Times Book Review* has the single most powerful voice in the industry. Richardson wrote Stegner:

> I got so furious over John Leonard's THE LAST WORD (because it was dastardly and because I was *convinced* he hadn't read your book) that I rang him up and gave him hell. . . . I told him that the essay, if it could be so dignified, was shallow and in extremely bad taste, and, in view of his knowledge of the book, inexcusable.
>
> Then I felt better. But not about that son of a bitch.[76]

(John Leonard, however, recalls no such phone call and said he would have had it occurred. "My 'Last Word' on Pulitzers is what it is, intemperate I think now, but no great shakes in the snark department of litcrit today," said Leonard in 2007. He was originally from the West Coast, Leonard said, and "one of the many biases I brought to the *TBR* was western, which is why we published as much Joan Didion as we could get our hands on.")[77]

Stegner urged his publishers to put their advertising dollars for *Angle* into California publications, in order to focus on his greatest audience: "I think a writer like me has his most natural reading public in the area where geographically and psychologically he's at home." He suggested the Sunday *San Francisco Chronicle-Examiner*, which, he said, had a mediocre book-review section and critic, that being William Hogan. The *Los Angeles Times*, he said, had a low advertising rate, high circulation, and "a very good" critic in Robert Kirsch. How about an advertising boycott of *The New York Times Book Review*? "The point is, I think the TBR has lost its moxie, it's a sinking ship, and us rats ought to get off it and demonstrate the feasibility of sailing on other craft."[78] Such a radical departure from custom was not a realistic course of action, mainly because there were no other review media that gave books such national exposure and editors and publishers such market exposure and cachet on their home ground.[79]

In a notebook titled "Biography and Fiction" that Stegner kept at this time, he jotted down his private thoughts on the role of regionalism and the review media.

> In literary terms, regionalism . . . can be healthy if there is an overall supervision or vision or criticism. That is performed by critical and review journals. But when these are captured by cliques or coteries or groups, and when there is no super-journal of great prestige to top their narrower judgments, then chaos ensues.
>
> It is John Leonard's distinction that in less than a year he made the only possible super-journal, *The New York Times Book Review*, into a coterie sheet of shrill partisanship and no authority, intense advocacy and most imperfect coverage. The further in that direction it goes, the further literary and cultural Balkanization has succeeded.

This most influential and acclaimed writer living in the American West elaborated on his opinions of eastern publishers and the review media in the *Palo Alto Weekly*, which published an impressive quarterly book-review section in the 1970s. Regional review outlets were important, Stegner said, because from the time a New York publisher accepts or rejects a manuscript to the time *The New York Times Book Review* and, to a lesser extent, *The New Yorker* and *The New York Review of Books* approve or disapprove of it, "book readers and book writers the country over are helplessly in the hands of those who make and express New York opinion."

A publisher who can sell books to the eastern market does not have to depend upon the remainder of the country for financial success. This results, said Stegner, in a sameness of product and book fashions that writers attempt to copy. "Without a local body of opinion to back up their own notions about themselves, they are subject to the temptation to imitate what seems to be attractive in New York; or they get picked up by New York as quaint Auslanders. Either way, integrity and confidence suffer." New York City, to Stegner, was "the Cave of the Winds from which literary opinion issues."[80]

Leonard left his job as editor of the book review in 1975 and went on to write and to review books, movies, and television for *The Nation*, *The New York Review of Books*, *Harper's*, *New York* magazine, *Sunday Morning* on CBS, and the *Times*. A few years after Leonard's departure, an interviewer asked Stegner why he thought *Angle of Repose* had had such a negative reception at the *Times*. Stegner replied:

> John Leonard was the editor at that point. I don't know him, but evidently my stuff infuriates him, bores him to death, or something. I know he got a lot of angry letters from people, denouncing him for not reviewing it, because many sent me copies. A national book review journal has the obligation of reporting books to the whole reading public. You can't be idiosyncratically selective; you can't leave out books you happen to have a personal antipathy to. It's notable that Leonard didn't last as editor. So I suspect we got our revenge.[81]

Revenge was an integral part of Stegner's persona. "Revenge," he once said, "I have dreamed of a lot."[82]

STEGNER WAS UNEASY about how the Foote family would respond to the entire novel once they had read it. Shortly after it was published, he again told Janet that he had been unable to stick to all the facts of her grandparents' lives, and he described the reason why: fiction had increasingly displaced fact.

> I had to warp it—it warped itself as the novel progressed, and she got farther and farther from Mary Hallock Foote, while still retaining at least loosely the structure of her life. Until near the end. Then fiction takes over entirely. And this makes a funny combination, since I quote fairly freely from her letters (though I rewrite those, too, when I have to, and sometimes invent entire letters that have to be in my book but aren't in Mrs. Foote's file) and in effect make your grandmother bolster with her authentic letters the false portrait I am painting of her. The ways of fiction are devious indeed. I couldn't have written this book without the strong help I got from the letters and reminiscences; and yet I couldn't have written it without bending those authentic and often wonderful materials to a purpose that your grandmother would have thought pretty ungenteel.

He urged her to think of the woman in the novel not as Mary Foote but as Susan Ward, hoped she liked the book, thanked her for the loan of her ancestors, and said he felt like "a character in literary history," which he would become.[83]

The Foote family had second thoughts about the novel after reading the book in its entirety and being confronted by the gossip that circulated through the small community. The main problem stemmed from the "domestic tragedy" Stegner had created. There are tensions in the fictional depiction of the Wards' marriage. An attraction develops between Susan Ward and Frank Sargent, a composite of all the young mining engineers who circulated in orbits around Mary Hallock Foote, seeking culture and a home atmosphere in the "skinned land" of western mining camps. Frank falls in love with the fictional Susan. Lyman, looking backward into the past with the help of his grandmother's letters and writings, guesses that their first intimate encounter was "no sooner ignited by touch than it was put out by conscience."[84]

The second, more enigmatic encounter occurs when Susan takes her young daughter (named Agnes, as was the Footes' daughter) with her to say good-bye to Frank on the banks of an Idaho irrigation canal. Agnes wandered away while the "two adults held their tense, nearly silent interview." The child falls into the canal and drowns. (The real

Agnes died in Grass Valley of appendicitis when she was a teenager.) A few days later Frank commits suicide.

In reconstructing what happened, Lyman emphasizes his lack of exact knowledge. It was Stegner's intention that the precise act between the two adults that leads to the drowning of the child be ambiguous. Did Stegner achieve his purpose in this controversial scene? There are differing opinions. James Houston, the novelist, former Stegner Fellow, and teacher of creative writing, believes "the scene on July 4 between Susan and Frank is rendered in ambiguous language that leaves open the possibility that something physical could have happened between them." Another interpretation is offered by the feminist scholar Linda K. Karrell: "It is important to note that Susan does not necessarily have an affair with Frank Sargent. Even Lyman says, 'I gravely doubt they "had sex." ' "[85]

Stegner wanted to push this very proper Victorian woman toward the edge, to "put her through all kinds of wringers that she never went through in real life," and to "suggest the full lives of people who lived in an essentially different culture" from the present, meaning the late 1960s. Obviously, Foote's life, or at least how she portrayed it in "Reminiscences," was not complete enough for his fictional purposes. Wally went on to explain the metamorphosis of the scene:

> Often, I don't suppose I deliberately build toward certain climaxes because very often I don't know where the book is going. I change things to build toward a climax without being aware I'm doing it. But before you're through, it's an accident you see coming. You can see it coming on the page. In *Angle of Repose* I wasn't even thinking, I'm sure, about the building toward that one act of infidelity. And when it came, if you notice, I blurred that infidelity very, very deliberately. It's ambiguous whether anything happened or not. Probably it didn't. In Victorian terms it didn't make any difference. Infidelity is of many kinds. It's of the mind and spirit as well as of the body.[86]

Susan and Oliver eventually arrive at a "happily-unhappily" relationship lasting for "year after irrelevant year" in Grass Valley. Oliver never forgives Susan for what led to the death of their daughter. Facing the break with his wife, who has left him for another man, and the vague possibility of an eventual reconciliation, Lyman Ward describes his grandparents as "vertical people, they lived by pride." Ward/Steg-

ner indicates that a better alternative is the angle of repose, a geologic phrase Stegner borrowed from professional geologists and Foote.
He defined it as "the angle at which two lines prop each other up, the
leaning-together from the vertical which produces the false arch. For
lack of a keystone, the false arch may be as much as one can expect in
this life. Only the very lucky discover the keystone."[87]

THE FIRST OPPORTUNITY to compare the novel with the life of Mary
Hallock Foote arose with publication of *The Reminiscences* in 1972.
Rodman Paul evaluated *Angle of Repose* in a bibliographic note as "a
book that has a high value as a novel but should not be regarded as a
factual explanation of Mary Hallock Foote and her career," especially
the Idaho years. In the first assessment of Stegner's fact-into-fiction
technique, as employed in *Angle of Repose*, Paul wrote: "Although the
basic settings and the cast of characters have been re-created out of
Mary Hallock Foote's own descriptions, with few changes and only the
thin disguise of a slight alternation of names, nevertheless the personalities and their individual destinies have been developed through a
blending of fact, perceptive interpretation, and sheer invention—at
times, unrestrained intervention."[88]

Four relatively quiet years passed. During this period, when there
was a surge in feminist activities, interest in Foote as a woman who
wrote about the West increased. Stegner's use of the Foote materials
received additional attention when the novel was transformed into an
opera by the San Francisco Opera in celebration of the bicentennial
year 1976.

The three-act opera with music by the modernist composer Andrew
Imbrie of the University of California at Berkeley and libretto by the
California novelist Oakley Hall had its world premiere on November 6. Stegner explained to operagoers in the program notes: "The
story of Susan Ward, which I adapted (with some drastic changes) from
the life of a real literary-artistic Victorian lady whose papers are in the
Stanford University Library, derives its technique from the literal
process of historical research. Its pretense is that it is reconstructed
from actual documents, pieced out with the memories of Lyman Ward,
some speculation, and some frank guessing." In the same publication,
Oakley Hall said that he respected the novel, which he found "rich and
complex."[89]

In preparation for the opening, *San Francisco Chronicle* reporter

Blake Green wrote a story headlined "The Genteel Western Lady Behind This Season's New Opera." She interviewed Stegner in person and telephoned Janet Micoleau, who gave the first public indication that the family was distancing itself from the book. Micoleau, having now read the whole book, objected that Stegner "didn't fictionalize it enough," meaning that he hadn't lessened the resemblance to her grandmother. Apologizing for having "done you wrong" in the Green article, Micoleau wrote Stegner three days after the newspaper story appeared: "She did me wrong as a result, I suppose, of my stupidity." Micoleau added: "I gave her the general family reaction that much of the novel followed MHF's life so closely in almost every detail that the departures from fact seemed incongruous and out of character. I immediately regretted having said this, and told her that I did not want to be quoted, that this was the personal reaction of people who remembered MHF, and not an objective criticism of the novel."

She was sorry, she told Wally, that Green emphasized "the family's emotional over-reaction to what would seem 'no big thing' to an outsider" and blamed herself for pointing the reporter in the direction of "this crime, as Green sarcastically calls it." The reporter had written that Stegner's "greatest crime" was in not finding Foote's life interesting enough to write a biography.[90]

Micoleau had referred Green to her sister, Marian Conway, admitting to Stegner that this "was stupidity #2 because I know Marian is really bitter about *Angle of Repose* and I should have known that she would probably sound off." She continued: "I have told Marian that if she feels cheated it is largely my fault, because without consulting her I waived the opportunity you gave us of reading the manuscript; and when, having heard that the 'Rems' were to be published, you offered to make changes in your story. I decided it was not necessary, again without consulting her."[91]

Marian Conway was quoted in Green's article as stating that after publication of the book, people recognized her grandparents, who had lived in Grass Valley. They "asked us about things that never happened and we've resented it." Conway elaborated on the local reaction: "People who had barely known M. H. Foote would stop me on the street and say, in essence, 'I never knew your grandmother did *that*!' Even though some of them listened politely to denials of all these evil doings, it was only a matter of time until a man in our local book store said to my brother-in-law, 'Don't worry—there's one in every family.' "[92]

Green heard from a television reporter that Stegner felt she had stabbed him in the back. The story was accurate, Green told Stegner, so she assumed "your objection is to my having opened doors that you felt were best left closed." The information she uncovered gave the story "a rather different angle" from what she had indicated when interviewing him.[93]

Stegner replied that Green had disregarded his and Janet's request not to exploit their differences and had offended both of them. "Do I have to tell you that the freedom of the press implies responsibilities of the press," Stegner lectured the reporter. He ended the letter by charging Green with sensationalizing what would otherwise have been a dull story.[94]

TWO FACULTY MEMBERS at Idaho State University in Pocatello were having lunch in late 1978. Mary Ellen Williams Walsh of the English Department and Richard W. Etulain, a historian, were discussing Stegner. Walsh, who specialized in western women writers, was newly arrived in Idaho and immersing herself in Stegner's books. Etulain had approached Stegner with the idea of conducting a series of taped interviews, the result of which would be published as *Conversations with Wallace Stegner* in 1983. Etulain was also president of the Western Literature Association. He suggested that Walsh present a paper at the association's 1979 conference on the sources of *Angle of Repose*. Walsh read "Succubi and Other Monsters: The Women in *Angle of Repose*" at the conference. It was not complimentary to Stegner. She described the reaction:

> There were about 20–25 people at the session, probably two-thirds were men. The negative reactions were on the order of accusations that I didn't understand Stegner, that I didn't know what I was talking about, that I hadn't done the necessary research—in other words, how dare you suggest anything negative about Stegner? The positive reactions were that Tony Arthur asked me to do the expanded version for the essay collection and that several people told me privately that they were pleased that I had indeed dared to say what I had.[95]

Anthony Arthur taught American literature at California State University at Northridge and was compiling a collection of essays on Stegner for publication.

Shortly after giving the paper, Walsh got in touch with Marian Conway, who welcomed the professor's defense of Mary Hallock Foote and the opportunity to set the record straight. Conway sent Walsh Stegner's letters to Janet Micoleau. Walsh's immediate comment upon reading them was "What an astonishing record Stegner's letters present. And how easily he forgave himself for his 'selected theft.' . . . He manages very skillfully never to suggest he's done anything other than what he should have done."[96]

Conway also sent Walsh a copy of an unpublished Foote story, "The Miniature." When Walsh read it, she was shocked. She thought there were striking similarities to the Lyman Ward character and his situation in *Angle of Repose*. "To discover that Mary Hallock Foote helped him even with that is astonishing, to say the least. . . . I think that from a literary scholar's point of view, that story may be one of the most important pieces of information that you have uncovered," Walsh wrote Conway. In her essay for Arthur, Walsh termed the unpublished story "the most significant discovery I have made in my research into the sources of the novel." She concluded that it provided "the idea and the basic outline" for the character of Lyman Ward, who previously had been thought of as Stegner's most fictional creation.[97]

The similarities seem, from further remove, to be superficial and forced. The story is set in Grass Valley. A nurse easily lifts a crippled man from a wheelchair. The man had been paralyzed after diving into a swimming pool. He is haunted by the spirit of a drowned woman who committed suicide by jumping into the Pacific Ocean from an ocean liner. Foote's short story explores the psychic and dream worlds with stock characters. Stegner was familiar with Grass Valley from having visited it and from having read about it in "Reminiscences" and stories of Foote's, such as the one he had published in 1958. The helper in *Angle* struggles mightily to lift Lyman into the bathtub. Although Lyman is also confined to a wheelchair, Stegner had borrowed Lyman's very different physical condition from Norman Foerster. The disabled character in "The Miniature" is described by Foote as "a perfectly modern boy," whereas Ward is a crusty old historian. When asked about Walsh's "discovery," Stegner said he had never read the story.[98]

Walsh posed a series of questions concerning Stegner's behavior to herself and to Conway:

And finally, I keep asking myself, why did he do it? He is a person with an established reputation. Why did he need, so late in his career, to steal from somebody else? And where did he get his confidence that he could simply get away with it? Perhaps he felt that he was covered by the "permissions" from Mrs. Micoleau and Miss Gilder. Will we ever be able to find out exactly what those permissions were?[99]

It was a key question left unanswered until the present.

During the spring of 1980, Walsh had difficulties with her editor on the expanded essay. She said that Arthur wanted a more positive assessment of Stegner and added in a letter to Conway: "But I am slugging through all this heaviness so that no one with any shred of integrity can dispute the conclusions that I reached about how Stegner, in fact, stole everything. The revised version of the paper also does not contain the rather heavily emotive language that I used in the first paper, again at the insistence of the editor. But what I am doing here is letting the evidence itself hang Stegner."[100] Arthur later explained, "What she originally sent me was much longer than the published essay, and much more inflammatory, if not libelous."[101]

In late May, Walsh sent a final version of her essay to Conway, asking for permission to quote briefly from "The Miniature" and certain letters. She also asked for and received permission to summarize Stegner's correspondence with Micoleau, stating that it would preempt his argument.[102] "Otherwise," Walsh wrote, "his supporters will gladly believe him when he states, as he will, that he had Mrs. Micoleau's permission to use the papers but that he didn't identify his sources because she asked him not to."[103]

Walsh also asked for and received permission to use the quotation in Conway's letter indicating that townspeople believed her grandmother had done "that," meaning that she'd committed adultery. "My editor objected to my use of the word *slander* in the first version of my paper. The passage from your letter demonstrates very clearly that *slander* is not too strong a word."[104] The word *slander* is used in the published version of the essay.

The manuscript was published under the innocuous title "*Angle of Repose* and the Writings of Mary Hallock Foote: A Source Study" in the 1982 book *Critical Essays on Wallace Stegner*, edited by Arthur. The twenty-five-page essay, with one additional page of endnotes, was the first extensive airing of the issue and has been repeatedly cited by Stegner's critics as a reliable source. But the book did not circulate widely. Beyond a letter from Stegner stating that he was distressed that Arthur had commissioned the essay, the editor received no other response to the one negative appraisal of Stegner in the entire volume.[105]

In the recent words of its author, the essay is "stodgy almost." There were, however, "ethical issues" that she believed needed to be addressed. In her essay, Walsh uses the word *borrow*, not *plagiarize*. She explained her reasoning for not using the *p* word: "I guess that was because I didn't want to be seen as attacking. I think I very clearly showed the plagiarism, and anyone who reads the text of the letters and the memoir and follows the parallels I have cited will see it. I didn't want to attack. I just wanted to show it."[106]

To Arthur it seemed that "the evidence Walsh lays out is strong and her argument that Stegner's practice here is unethical is restrained and responsible." He did not agree with Walsh that Stegner's use of the Foote material was unethical. "I did hope for debate on the general subject of transforming life into art, which I think Stegner accomplished, but my impression afterward was that the dispute was seen as an *ad hominem* feminist attack on a writer of great integrity and dignity."[107]

The Walsh essay and subsequent criticism had two major flaws. Walsh had not attempted to contact Stegner. Nor have other scholars taken the time to search for, read, and cite the Micoleau letters in their published works. Stegner held the exculpatory letters on the permission issue until his death. They were deposited in the University of Utah library two years later, in 1995.

When asked why she never contacted Stegner for his side of the story, Walsh said she had assumed Stegner would not talk to her or let her see Micoleau's letters. "I think it is quite true that Mrs. Micoleau wrote those letters to Stegner," she said, "but I think it is equally true that he arrogantly assumed that he could plagiarize from this basically unknown woman and nobody would notice."[108]

THE BEST WAY to judge Walsh's conclusions, and the contentions of later critics, is to attempt to measure, compare, and examine what both Foote and Stegner wrote, keeping in mind the loose understanding between Stegner and Micoleau. An overall assessment is possible; exactness is impossible because of all the variables. Not the law but literary ethics, which have changed with time and the prevailing fashion, seem to be the deciding factor.

The directly quoted portions of the memoir and letters, set off from the narrative in a smaller typeface and closer line spacing, measure 5 percent of the book's length. Using a different methodology, based on a page count, Jackson Benson, who wrote a previous biography, came up with a 10 percent figure.[109] Perhaps if the condensed sections were expanded to the size of the narrative text, the figure would be close to 10 percent. The quotations vary from a short paragraph to nearly sixteen pages. From Foote's letters, short stories, and unpublished memoir, Stegner invented, made substantial changes, altered her words slightly, or used blocks of text verbatim. The "Reminiscences" provided the overall plot of the book. The stories and letters filled in the details.

One example of Stegner's use of a letter by Foote is the correspondence that Walsh and others believe he introduced to establish a lesbian relationship between the two women.[110] But the letter may very well be an example of how Victorian women expressed feelings of close friendship to other women, and Stegner may only have wanted to give verisimilitude to an era and a particular type of friendship.[111] The version of Foote's September 23, 1873, letter to Gilder that appears in *Angle of Repose* follows, with words in boldface showing Stegner's additions and strikeouts showing his deletions. The bracketed exclamation "*what*, Grandmother?" is Lyman Ward's comment. Not shown are a few minor punctuation changes and Foote's use of the ampersand. Stegner also broke Foote's one long paragraph into two, as shown here:

My dear dear **girl** ~~Girl~~

Your note came this afternoon just after **Bessie** ~~Phil~~ and I had been getting your room ready and making your bed—*our* bed where I thought I should lie tonight with my dear girl's arm under my head. It gave me a queer little sick trembly feeling that I've had only once or twice in my life—and then I thought I **must** ~~must~~ see you, not to "talk things over"—I don't care about **things** ~~things~~, I only want you to love me.

So I hurried after supper and changed my dress and pulled my ruffle down low in front to please my girl [*what,* **Grandmother?**] and rushed into the garden for a bunch of roses—your June roses, blooming late just for you (**we** ~~We~~ have been hoarding them and begging the buds to wait a few days longer for your coming)—**and** then down to the **night** ~~Albany~~ boat. I thought I'd either coax you to land or go with you as far as West Point.[112]

From an overall comparison of the texts and specific passages, Walsh concluded that Stegner had made "few changes" in Foote's life. "The changes he made, however, are substantial ones which, as he remarks in his note, 'warp' Foote's life and personality." She added: "Stegner chose to make Susan Burling Ward an adulteress, to make her responsible for the death of a child, to show her estranged from her son for ten years, and to create a terrible rift between her and her husband because of her adultery and her responsibility for the child's death. None of these negative events occurred in Mary Hallock Foote's life."

As for the permission issue, Walsh wrote in her essay: "By writing 'fiction,' is Stegner absolved from obtaining permission to quote Foote's letters when other scholars must do so?" Stegner should have avoided "slandering Mary Hallock Foote through Susan Burling Ward." By inventing the drowning scene, he had made Foote "an adulteress and a filicide." In a footnote, Walsh accused Stegner of using the letter "to advance the lesbianism theme" in the novel.[113]

Stegner's only public reply to Walsh's criticism was in Etulain's *Conversations.* It was rather abrupt and dismissive. He was, he said, "a little irritated at that particular holier-than-thou attack"; the book was a novel, not a biography that required documentation of sources; he had mixed history and fiction before (and would do so again); and fact could legitimately serve the needs of fiction and vice versa, as it had in *Wolf Willow. Angle of Repose* "has nothing to do with the actual life of Mary Hallock Foote except I borrowed a lot of her experiences. So I don't, I guess, feel very guilty about that. It is a method that I've used, as you've said, to mix history and fiction."[114]

Stegner's immediate impulse was to sue. Then he decided to ignore "the scurrilities of the Walsh woman" because he didn't want to give "her paranoia any further publicity." If she felt Foote had been slandered, well then, he felt that he had been slandered by her. Stegner confided to James Hepworth, who was writing a doctoral dissertation about him: "You're irked by Stegner criticism. So am I, as it happens, by its absence, by its presence, and sometimes by its trend."[115]

THE SUBJECT DID not end with Walsh. The third granddaughter, Evelyn Gardiner, contributed her opinion when she was interviewed by Jackson Benson. By 1993, Marian Conway was dead, and Janet Micoleau was in a rest home. Stegner had permission to write the book "from all of us," Gardiner said. She added: "I don't know whether I wrote my permission, but Janet called me on the telephone and said, 'Would you give your permission for Wallace Stegner to write a biographical novel about Mary Hallock Foote?' And I thought that was very wonderful. I know he's a very good writer, and I liked some of his books a lot."

The problem was that Gardiner thought Stegner would write a different kind of book. "I thought he would write something like Irving Stone's biographical novels. That he would invent conversations and all of that, but that he would pretty much stick to the facts of their . . . [lives]." She continued: "We all felt it was a good book and a readable book. But we just didn't like the whole letters." They also didn't like the scene at the irrigation ditch. "I resent the fact that he got the Pulitzer Prize for his sense of place, when most of the things that establish the sense of place are direct quotes of what my grandmother wrote."

Besides Walsh, with whom she was working on the publication of her grandmother's letters, Gardiner had been in contact with other Stegner critics. Referring to her grandmother, Gardiner said: "She's been taken up by the feminists, and boy, every once in a while I run into some lesbian feminist who wants to make her out as this downtrodden woman who supported this drunken husband."[116]

MOST FEMINISTS, SCHOLARS, and writers discovered Foote through Stegner; a few came upon Stegner through Foote. After additional research they discovered Walsh. Most went no further. It was a sorry exercise in scholarship.

One problem is the lack of a word or phrase that is nonjudgmental and describes the situation precisely and accurately: *borrow, copy, plagiarize, steal, fraud, piracy, slander,* and *libel* don't work in the entirety of their implications. Ethics are certainly involved, but whose and from what time period? Opinions on the issue cover the gamut of emotions and reasoning and make for a fascinating case study of the use of facts for fictional purposes.

David Lavender, a respected author of numerous nonfiction works on western history, has said that one way to deal with historically based fiction is to "cloud" the facts. Writing about the controversy, Lavender said: "This device is legitimate, I think—*up to a point.*" He added: "But when the clouding is used to falsify, that is something else." Lavender's sources for his essay were Stegner's novel, Foote's published memoir, and Etulain's *Conversations*. He apparently was not aware of Walsh's essay.

The historian thought the novel "a beautifully crafted, densely textured story revolving around skillfully realized characters." With their names changed—"clouded" in Lavender's terms—the characters could be seen as "real people" and not "similarities." Stegner then "slanders them cruelly—there simply are no other words for what he does— in order to smite the reader with a powerful but wholly fictitious conclusion."

Lavender then posed the question: Was this legitimate? He avoided an outright answer beyond stating that Stegner's "extensive borrowings" and "calculated distortions" could be called "plagiarisms." But, he asked, hadn't William Shakespeare, in one of his historical plays, made the benign Richard III a diabolical murderer?[117]

To James Hepworth, a writer, publisher, and teacher living in Walsh's home state of Idaho, Walsh's essay "typifies the degenerate state of Stegner criticism as it currently exists." In his dissertation, Hepworth went on to state: "I know of no more chronic case of critical pedantry in Stegner criticism than Mary Ellen Williams Walsh's 'essay.'" A passionate defender of Stegner whose interviews of the writer appeared in *The Paris Review*, *The Bloomsbury Review*, and a book titled *Stealing Glances*, Hepworth added in an essay that appeared four years after Wally's death: "Essentially, Walsh and [Elizabeth] Cook-Lynn use Stegner as their whipping boy to call attention to their own political agendas."[118]

Jackson Benson was also critical of Walsh. He wrote in his Stegner biography:

> She has taken all the family's objections at face value, become their spear carrier, and set out to slay the male dragon in an essay. . . . It is a nasty piece of character assassination. There was no attempt to get Stegner's side of the story, nor to give him at any point the benefit of the doubt, no possibility that there may have been a misunderstanding or that Janet and the other heirs may have contributed to the misunderstanding—he is portrayed as a deliberate fraud, a thorough villain.[119]

There were serious lapses on Benson's part, too. In his extensive interviews with Stegner in the late 1980s and early 1990s, he avoided sensitive issues. Benson was also constrained in what he could use in his

1996 biography by Wally, who said his personal life was off limits, and then more overtly by Mary, who was a staunch defender of her husband's reputation after Stegner's death.[120] He never contacted Walsh to ask for her views. The use of Foote's work, he wrote in an introduction to a new edition of *Angle of Repose* in 2000, had brought "accusations of plagiarism, charges of misuse of source materials, and even angry denunciations by feminists who claimed that a male writer had deliberately set out to destroy the reputation of an accomplished female artist. Some of the charges grew out of misunderstanding and miscommunication; some, out of spite and, no doubt, jealousy."[121] Mary Stegner asked Benson and his editor for a draft copy of the introduction. She requested some minor changes, not all of which were granted, and then said that four books by or about Foote—none of which dealt with the controversy—should be eliminated from the introduction's bibliography. That was done.

From a feminist scholar at the University of New Hampshire who specialized in western studies came a different viewpoint: Stegner was a literary pioneer in the field of feminism. Melody Graulich thought that he enhanced the role of women in the West by rethinking western myths. *Angle* "was especially insightful for a book published in 1971" because of "the presence, indeed the centrality" of Foote/Ward. Graulich wrote: "Stegner argues for the importance of Susan's point of view, the 'woman's point of view,' in our literary history." She believed Stegner's works belonged on the bookshelf along with such authors as George Eliot, Louisa May Alcott, Kate Chopin, and Edith Wharton. Graulich said that "dozens of feminist scholars" followed his lead by rediscovering "minor" women writers and defining "marriage as a crucial theme of late-nineteenth-century women's literature."

To Graulich the Foote/Ward letters tell "a rich, complex, and very new western story," one that ironically had not been published as of 1971. That Stegner borrowed, stole, or plagiarized the letters did not bother her. She mentioned in a footnote that she had read the Walsh critique and then added: "Foote deserves attention as a fine western writer and illustrator, and I find Stegner's realization of her importance and attention to her life and work, in the late 1960s, quite remarkable. I choose to see Stegner as using Foote's life and work to think seriously about the role of gender in western literary traditions."[122]

Graulich became a professor of English and American studies at Utah State University and editor of the journal *Western American Literature* and was editing Foote's letters for publication in their original form, a chore others had attempted for the last half century. She avoided the plagiarism issue in public discussions, she said, because she wrote about both Stegner and Foote. But she felt that Stegner had made "a major mistake" in using Foote's language so extensively without a more detailed acknowledgment. In two classes that Graulich taught at the Utah university, she assigned *Angle of Repose* and some Foote materials.

> Then ensues a spirited discussion in which many students feel "duped" by Stegner because they so loved the novel and especially his ability to "capture" a woman's point of view in the letters, and they now feel betrayed. Others argue that the fact that Foote was "a real woman" adds to the novel's "authenticity," despite the fact that Stegner so dramatically distorts Foote's life by imagining an affair that never occurred. On other occasions, I have asked the students to read the Foote materials before reading the novel, which creates quite a different response where students attend more to how Stegner manipulates the historical details of her life and works to his own ends.[123]

Writing shortly before the nonfiction writers Stephen Ambrose and Doris Kearns Goodwin were criticized for not putting quotation marks around what they had "borrowed" but had credited in footnotes, Linda Karrell, then an associate professor of English at Montana State University, stated: "Certainly our contemporary idea of plagiarism describes well his use of Foote's material in *Angle of Repose*." Karrell added that Stegner had appeared "clumsy and defensive in his anxious efforts to articulate how his relationship to Foote's work is different than the term plagiarism would suggest." She cited Walsh's essay as "the most fully documented and the most adamantly critical of Stegner's use of Foote's papers" and repeated Walsh's accusation of slander, basing her conclusion on Stegner's drawing attention to "a possible lesbian attraction" between the two women and Susan Ward's "inattention and potential infidelity" as the cause of her daughter's death.[124]

Sands Hall, the daughter of Oakley Hall, the California novelist and librettist for the opera of *Angle of Repose*, weighed in with an assessment in the form of a play that was performed at academic conferences and small theaters in the West during the early years of the present century. Hall is a playwright, novelist, and teacher of writing. The play

Fair Use contains the following dialogue between a historian-father and a playwright-daughter:

PLAYWRIGHT: He's using her words, Dad.
HISTORIAN: Who is?
PLAYWRIGHT: Wallace Stegner.
HISTORIAN: Oh, that tired old accusation.
PLAYWRIGHT: That salt and roses bit, for instance. It's in *Angle of Repose*, page 33. But it's from Mary Hallock Foote's *Reminiscences*, page 97.
HISTORIAN: So? (They stare at each other.) Well, I see why he left it in.
PLAYWRIGHT: Dad.
HISTORIAN: It's an apt metaphor! Reveals a lot about the woman and the time.
PLAYWRIGHT: It is. It is. But she came up with it. And everyone who reads his novel thinks Stegner did.
HISTORIAN: He often mixed history—fact—with fiction. He was a novelist. It's what they *do*. All writers do. You used your mother and me in your last "drama." I shudder to remember.
(He tries to go back to his book, but the playwright has located his dictionary and is looking up a word.)
PLAYWRIGHT: I used elements of your relationship. Those characters weren't you.
HISTORIAN: Proves my point: you can't copyright a life. Anyway. All writers borrow.
PLAYWRIGHT: He didn't just "borrow," if that's the right word, the *life* of Mary Hallock Foote. (Finds the word she is looking for.) "*Plagiarize*: Verb. One—"
HISTORIAN: This is so ridiculous. That controversy is ancient history.
PLAYWRIGHT: "To steal and use the ideas or writing of another *as one's own*—"[125]

Linda Karrell, who saw the play performed at the 2002 Western Literature Association conference in Tucson, termed it "a complex feminist look at the ongoing debates regarding originality and plagiarism." To Karrell, the Stegner character in *Fair Use* emerged "more guilty than innocent" of plagiarism, a form of cheating, she said, for which students are expelled from school.[126] The issue, said Hall, who speaks through the character of the playwright, was about proper acknowledgment. She did not think a legal issue was involved.

The most complete journalistic account of the controversy was written in 2003 for the *Los Angeles Times Magazine* by Susan Salter Reynolds, a *Times* staff writer and book reviewer. Titled "Tangle of Repose," Reynolds's article recounts the "murky" history of permission and the arguments of the Walsh essay. Susan Ward, in Reynolds's view, is "potentially a lesbian and adulteress." Reynolds tracked down Micoleau's letters at the University of Utah, but she did not make extensive use of them. The writer broke his promise, she said, to use no direct quotations from the letters. To Reynolds, Foote was "the West's consummate 19th century storyteller and traveler, equal parts Amelia Earhart, Susan Sontag, Edith Wharton, and Isabella Bird." She credited Sands Hall with bringing the issue into the open and had interviewed Page Stegner, who questioned the relevance of the topic and said he was not the keeper of his father's literary legacy. Christine Hill Smith, who taught English at the Colorado School of Mines, told Reynolds that it was a feminist issue on one level and on another "it's just the facts."[127]

The facts, as Smith outlined them in her own publication, were that Walsh's scholarship had held up over time, Stegner had appropriated Foote's words, and the novelist could hardly be faulted for wanting to "liven up" Foote's "two-dimensional" prose for his own purposes. "Certainly any creative writing student in a graduate program would face intense scrutiny about such 'borrowings,'" Smith wrote, "but Stegner as a revered western American author seems to have weathered the criticism."[128]

It seemed to come down to how would Wally have judged the output of one of his writing students if it had been similarly based on someone else's writings and lacked a clear acknowledgment of the source. Would that student have been thrown out of Stanford? Applying the literary ethics of that time—if they could be determined— would be the fairest way to decide the issue. It would avoid the sticky problem of presentism, which nags scholars (and which they conveniently forget when it suits their purposes). *Presentism* is a critical term used mainly by academic historians that refers to judging the past by present-day standards.

There was irony in the fact that some feminists were critical of Stegner. His female characters are generally regarded as being portrayed with sympathy and understanding. His male characters, however, tend to take over his books. They are not always admirable. Stegner wrote from the depths of what he had experienced and who he was. He was not a feminist, at least as the term came to be defined in its politically correct sense. He "did not hold the fundamental feminist conviction that women are oppressed," wrote Krista Comer of Rice University. She added: "He imagined women, in his own novels, not as symbols of entrapment but as complex characters with legitimate motivations and understandable needs." In other words, she said, his women characters mattered.[129]

WHAT ARE PLAGIARISM and libel as they may, or may not, pertain to Stegner's use of the Foote material? A clearly articulated dictionary definition and the most relevant is contained in the 2000 edition of the Random House *Webster's Unabridged Dictionary:* "The unauthorized use or close imitation of the language and thoughts of another author and the representation of them as one's own original work." A broad, working definition of plagiarism, in reference to the Ambrose and Goodwin cases, was offered by Richard A. Posner in *The Atlantic Monthly:* "unacknowledged copying."[130]

A far more detailed and nuanced definition is contained in Posner's erudite handbook *The Little Book of Plagiarism.* Posner is a federal appellate court judge who specializes, on the bench and in the classes he teaches at the University of Chicago Law School, in the law and economics of intellectual property. In calling for "a cool appraisal rather than fervid condemnation" and admitting to "the ambiguity of the concept," he further defined plagiarism as "a species of intellectual fraud."

> It consists of unauthorized copying that the copier claims (whether explicitly or implicitly, and whether deliberately or carelessly) is original with him and the claim causes the copier's audience to behave otherwise than it would if it knew the truth. This change in behavior, as when it takes the form of readers' buying the copier's book under the misapprehension that it is original, can harm both the person who is copied and the competitors of the copier.[131]

The attraction of the Stegner case is its complexity. There simply are no easy answers. Stegner received permission and acknowledged use of the materials, sort of. Awkwardness of acknowledgment, Posner said, can excuse plagiarism. Readers of the novel may or may not feel cheated by the knowledge that much of the book is derivative. Then again, as Posner wrote in general terms that apply to *Angle of Repose* and Mary Hallock Foote, "Creative imitation produces value that should undercut a judgment of plagiarism—indeed an imitator may produce greater value than an originator."

Harm was possibly done, however, to readers who felt that they had been fooled, to Foote's moral reputation, and to her immediate family, although one granddaughter had the opportunity to comment on the offending passages prior to the novel's publication. What is clear from Posner's book is that Stegner's fabrication of the scene hinting at adultery and resulting in Agnes's death is "literary deceit," which "has consequences similar to those of plagiarism."[132]

The legal term that covers the ethical concept of plagiarism is *copyright infringement*. The way to avoid a lawsuit involving copyright infringement is to employ the slippery concept of fair use, meaning that one should use someone else's words very sparingly and attribute them to their source if the material is copyrighted. If it is not copyrighted, it is in the public domain and can be used more freely. What was copyrighted when Foote wrote her letters, her published and unpublished stories, and her unpublished memoir and what laws covered their use at the time and later, when Stegner published his novel, are such tangled issues that it would be impossible to pursue the legality of what Stegner did or did not do in terms of copyright infringement without engaging in protracted and costly litigation. There is no libel issue, because a person can be libeled only if he or she is living.

The popular concept of what constitutes plagiarism has changed in the last forty years. In a recent discussion of the issue as it pertained to a Broadway play, Malcolm Gladwell wrote in *The New Yorker:* "We have somehow decided that copying is *never* acceptable." Of those types of publications that are most critical of borrowers, Gladwell cited the "heavily derivative nature" of journalism, the nonfiction genre that most frequently raises the issue of plagiarism. It was an earlier article of Gladwell's in *The New Yorker* that had been "borrowed" for a play. "Instead of feeling that my words had been taken from me," he wrote, "I felt that they had become part of some grander cause," a reference to creative imitation.[133]

So who is to blame in the *Angle of Repose* case? In hindsight and given a perfect world, it seems that mistakes were made by everyone. Stegner should have told the family how many of the letters and how much of the memoir he planned to use and the length of the passages as the novel evolved during the writing and editing processes. He should have insisted that the manuscript, or at least the potentially offensive passages, be read before publication. His terse explanation at the start of the book citing the borrowing of "selected facts" should have contained the additional information that the letters and the material from the memoir had a definite source, that they had been adapted for fictional purposes, and that a more specific acknowledgment was not included because the relatives of the source did not wish that person to be identified.[134]

Given the need to disguise the source, Stegner still used portions of Foote family names for his fictional characters. They include Agnes, Bessie, Burling, Rodman, Lyman, and Ward. Agnes, as has been pointed out, was the Footes' daughter in real life and is the daughter of their counterparts in the novel; Bessie was Mary Hallock Foote's sister in real life and is her sister in the novel; Burling, the maiden name of Mary Hallock Foote's mother and the middle name of the Footes' son, is Susan Ward's middle name in the novel; Rodman was the first name of the husband of the Footes' daughter Elizabeth and of Helena Gilder's oldest son and is the name of Lyman Ward's son in the novel. Lyman Ward's name in the novel, which is also his grandparents' last name, seems to have been derived from two Foote family names. Lyman Beecher, a famous preacher and the father of Henry Ward Beecher, an even more famous preacher, married Arthur Foote's aunt. Ward was the name of relatives on Arthur Foote's side of the family.

All of these names would have been available to Stegner through Foote's memoir, her letters, and members of the Foote family. An alternative to consciously borrowing the names, which makes little sense since Stegner was sympathetic to the need to hide the family's identity, is cryptomnesia, experiencing a memory as if it were one's own sudden inspiration. The theory, advanced by Carl Jung in *Man and His Symbols*, may also account for the vague similarities between Foote's short story "The Miniature" and the Lyman Ward character.

The Foote family also made mistakes. Since they had the opportunity, at least one member of the family—and ideally all three granddaughters—should have read the manuscript and made her or their feelings known to Stegner before their reactions were influenced by others.

Walsh should have—at the very least—attempted to interview Stegner and been less hasty in her judgment. Benson should have talked to

Walsh and been less protective of Stegner. Hepworth also falls into the overly protective category. Lavender didn't do his homework. Other scholars who followed Walsh's lead should have researched all the primary sources, including Micoleau's letters to Stegner.

Stegner certainly learned from the experience. He asked all six children of Peg and Phil Gray, on whom he based the characters Charity and Sid Lang in *Crossing to Safety*, to approve the manuscript for the novel before it was published. None voiced any objections.

The Coup de Grâce
by the Times

WILLIAM STEGNER: "The West does not need to explore its myths much further," he writes; "it has already relied on them too long."

Caption under photograph of Wallace Stegner,
The New York Times Magazine

JOHN LEONARD WAS not the complete western-realist-hating ogre that Stegner made him out to be. Wally credited "that least of editors" for running Malcolm Cowley's lengthy review of Stegner's biography of Bernard DeVoto on the front page of the *Times Book Review* in February 1974. He had mixed feelings, however, about that review of *The Uneasy Chair.* He regretted that Cowley, along with a few other reviewers, "have seen fit to dredge up what they think was Benny's belligerence and bad manners." But he couldn't argue with the space the reviews had been given, not only in the *Times* but also in other publications.[1]

Throughout the 1970s, Stegner and Fawn Brodie, another biographer with Utah roots, albeit deep within the leadership of the Church of Jesus Christ of Latter-day Saints, engaged in a correspondence on the nature of biography, history, fiction, their mutual friends, and their respective books. Brodie wrote searching biographies of the Mormon leader Joseph Smith, the explorer Richard Burton, and presidents Thomas Jefferson and Richard Nixon.

Stegner began work on the DeVoto biography in 1968, before he had written a word of *Angle of Repose*. He then switched to the novel and wrote Brodie in 1970. Wally said he was sorry that he hadn't gotten to Salt Lake City to hear Brodie talk at a conference on the manipulation of history and then added: "Since I have been manipulating history for the purposes of fiction for three years, I'm interested. Is it O.K. if I twist events and personalities for fictional purposes? Or have I sinned? (I'm fairly sure I have—I've got that feeling)."²

They discussed the extent to which private matters should be revealed in public biographies. He had assured DeVoto's widow: "I can edit around any hot spots, or in a pinch omit whole letters, because there's God's plenty, and on every sort of subject."³ In *The Uneasy Chair,* Stegner danced around DeVoto's extramarital affairs. Brodie, on the other hand, had disclosed Jefferson's sexual relationship with Sally Hemings, one of his slaves. Of her intent, she wrote Stegner: "I am pursuing the inner man and I am trying to justify my pretensions to being a historian by relating his private life to his public life. So it will not be a mere piece of gossip."⁴

After *The Uneasy Chair* was published, Brodie said that she could understand "the selective process that went into it, since you were an old and valued friend" of DeVoto's. She pointed out that as a novelist, Stegner had revealed more about himself and his family than anyone else was knowledgeable about. Brodie added: "But in fiction you have the advantage of conscious distortion."⁵ Wally wrote back:

> On the issue of "censorship," I suppose I have to plead guilty. I had a choice to make, and made it for what I hoped was better but what may have been worse. The fact is, I wasn't, and am not now, particularly interested in Benny's private life insofar as that private life was sexual or conjugal. That's *his* business, so far as I am concerned. And, as you remark, Avis [DeVoto's wife and Stegner's friend] is still alive. So are the two boys. . . . So somewhere in midstream I decided that his private life, his life as husband, lover, and father, was none of my business, and that I would write of his private life only as it plainly affected his career and his solution of his problems by work. So I concentrated on his depressions and his panics and his triumphs over them. Revealing the emotional life of a man like Benny can make him look like an awful fool, perhaps an irretrievable fool. And that was not what my biography wanted to say. What I wanted to say was that he survived his own worst enemy, himself.⁶

Stegner thought that Brodie had a different situation with Jefferson and had handled it in a "splendid" manner. She had "enriched the world by taking a figurehead off his pedestal . . . and humanizing him."

There was a match between the private and the public man, he said, and Brodie had no personal relationship with Jefferson. Would she, Stegner asked, have written the same type of revealing biography of a beloved relative?[7]

In this manner these two practicing writers discussed the problem of depth of revelations in their respective books.

THE PATTERN OF being first ignored and then pummeled in the *Times* continued after Leonard's departure. Stegner, the ever-frugal writer, salvaged material he had collected in Denmark in 1954, thinking at that time to link the history of an older Danish village with a New England town and Eastend. The result would have been a study of how village institutions grow from their beginnings. The concept proved too abstract, *Wolf Willow* resulted from the Canadian research, and the story of the Danish countess with whom the Stegners had lodged in Copenhagen languished and was then incorporated into *The Spectator Bird*, published in 1976 as part of the Doubleday contract.

He began working on that novel in 1974. As usual, there were problems. "Trouble is," he wrote Howard Mumford Jones, "I am trying to combine a story about Denmark in 1954 with one about old age in California in 1974, and somehow there's a sort of organ-rejection going on."[8]

When it was published, *Spectator Bird* was a small book with none of the in-house Doubleday enthusiasm behind it that *Angle* had generated. Stegner summarized the reviews for Carol Brandt: "*Saturday Review* and *New Yorker* snippy, *Atlantic* so-so, and the good old NYTimes BR, living up to itself to the hilt, silent. I wish you could explain that sheet to me sometime." As for the lack of excitement, Stegner concluded, rather presciently as it turned out, "I do think there's a generation gap. In fact, I applaud it. Nobody under fifty is competent to review that magnificent book."[9]

The book went through two printings for a total of 22,500 hardcover copies. There was no immediate paperback edition. It was nevertheless nominated for a National Book Award. "No *Times* review, no paperback sale, and the Book Award would make a nice tripod," Stegner thought.[10]

At the time of the nomination, Stegner's publisher, Ken McCormick, had won "his long battle in the Bay Area." Wally had complained that, five years after publication of *Angle of Repose*, bookstores where he lived and where the opera had been performed were not carrying the novel. McCormick got the novel into nine Bay Area bookstores by giving each one a free copy of the tremendously popular novel *Roots* by Alex Haley, which Doubleday had just published. "The point of this bribery," he told Carol Brandt, "is that there are so many new titles being sold, that by and large on reissues, putting some things back in stock, the managers say an automatic no." He cautioned her not to say anything about the bribery.[11]

It came as a surprise to nearly everyone that *Spectator Bird* won the National Book Award's fiction prize in 1977. Stegner had thought it was a legitimate candidate. He got a break, he said, because he knew two of the three elderly judges who were assessing books with "something like the same standards I was writing them by." Otherwise, he said, *The Spectator Bird* could easily have fallen through the cracks.[12]

The *Times* story on the awards was written by Herbert Mitgang. The mention of the Stegner novel appeared under the notation "Arthritic's Last Years." The fiction award, Mitgang wrote, was particularly controversial that year because none of the nominated books had received much critical attention. The Stegner novel was about "the difficult last years of life of a 69-year-old arthritic man,"[13] hardly a great commendation or an accurate description of the book. Other finalists in the fiction category were Raymond Carver (a former Stegner Fellow at Stanford), Ursula K. Le Guin, and Cynthia Propper Seton.

The next day the *Times* published a follow-up story criticizing the elderly fiction judges. They favored older writers and "were not *au courant* with the latest fiction," Mitgang said. One publisher, whose book did not win, was quoted as stating that it was like Veterans Day at Yankee Stadium, with the judges out there rooting for Joe DiMaggio and Phil Rizzuto. The average age of the judges on the fiction panel was sixty-seven, which was approximately the same age as Stegner, a columnist for the Cleveland *Plain Dealer* pointed out.[14]

Stegner knew the book critic Orville Prescott and the novelist Erskine Caldwell, both of whom were judges. Caldwell, a member of the sponsoring American Academy and Institute of Arts and Letters, was chairman of the fiction panel, which also included the novelist, poet, and critic George Elliott. Caldwell had been the editor of the American Folkways Series, for which Stegner had written *Mormon Country* in the early 1940s. They had corresponded but had never met. Caldwell's wife, Virginia, was a fan of Stegner's, and later said that she had read all the nominated books and she and her husband thought *Spectator Bird* was "an absolutely perfect book."[15]

Orville Prescott, a former in-house book critic for the *Times*, replied to a thank-you note from Stegner:

> I am delighted that you think the *Times* reviewing has declined since I retired. Hardly surprisingly, I think so, too! But I think I left at the right time. I could have stayed for at least five more years, but if I had I would have become an old scold fighting lost battles. There seems to be a huge generation gap between you and me and the writers and critics now in their forties and younger. They admire pretentious and unreadable experimenta-tion in form, self-pitying exposures of emotional turmoil and intellectual confusion, and explorations of degeneracy. You can't imagine the stuff I had to read for the National Book Award. Some women writers described sexual abominations of which I had never even heard.[16]

There was no question that there was a generational void between Stegner and some important opinion makers in the book world of the 1970s. From the publication in 1967 of *All the Little Live Things*, which features a retiree who is entangled in the youth revolution of that decade, through the two elderly couples in 1987's *Crossing to Safety*, Stegner filled a gap in American literature. He wrote books for ma-ture readers on such topics as marriage and friendship that were devoid of explicit sex, violence, and experimental techniques. Therein lay the rub.

The New York Times took an inadvertent parting shot at Stegner at the beginning of the next decade. In a *Times Magazine* article in 1981 on western writers, Wally was identified prominently as "William" in the caption under a photograph of him and, less noticeably, as "Wal-lace" in the text. It was a caption writer's and proofreader's mistake, but fellow western writers took it as symptomatic of the newspaper's and, by extension, the eastern literary establishment's disinterest in what was being written west of the Hudson River.

Stegner's friends rode to the rescue. Citing the story's use of the adjective *western*, as in the phrase "western writer," and the incorrect name, Wendell Berry wrote: "The adjective 'Western,' as all regional writers will understand, would have been dismissive, even if the name had been correctly given. This is the regional-ism of New York, which will use the West, and depend on it, but not care for it." To Ivan Doig, the photograph and caption were presented to the readership of the *Times* in a "big hey-look-who-we've-discovered typeface as: William

Stegner. West of the Hudson River, of course, that first name has always been pronounced 'Wallace.' "[17]

The article and cover photo on the magazine promoted the usual horsey-cowboy stereotypes that Stegner had spent a lifetime attempting to demolish. The novelist and screenwriter Larry McMurtry, who reviewed books on the West for *The New York Review of Books*, would write what a hopeless task that was. "The romance of the West is so powerful, you can't really swim against the current," wrote the former Stegner Fellow. "Whatever truth about the West is printed, the legend is always more potent."[18]

The cute cover of a cowboy pecking away on a manual typewriter precariously perched on a horse's neck was followed inside the magazine by the equally cute title of the article, "Writers of the Purple Sage." The text, written by Russell Martin, identified as a fourth-generation Colorado writer, was generally complimentary. Wally was identified as "the dean of Western American letters."[19] Stegner thought that the coupling of William with the title of dean, which implies great age, was characteristic of the *Times*'s derogatory treatment of him. Grouped around "the dean" in the photos and the text were some of his "grandchildren," meaning writers who had studied at Stanford or had acknowledged his help. They went by the names of Abbey, Doig, Kittredge, McGuane, McMurtry, and Momaday.

Taking Leave

I wonder if I have ever felt more alive, more competent in my mind and more at ease with myself and my world, than I feel for a few minutes on the shoulder of that known hill while I watch the sun climb powerfully and confidently and see below me the unchanged village, the lake like a pool of mercury, the varying greens of hayfields and meadows and sugarbush and black spruce woods, all of it lifting and warming as the stretched shadows shorten.

There it was, there it is, the place where during the best time of our lives friendship had its home and happiness its headquarters.

Wallace Stegner, description of Greensboro, Vermont,
in *Crossing to Safety*

D ESPITE HIS ADVANCING years, it would take time before Stegner's wheels would stop spinning and he could finally come to rest in Vermont. First, he had to take leave of California.

Wally had seen change coming to the Santa Clara Valley as far back as 1962, when he helped organize the Committee for Green Foothills. The committee and Stegner had initially been concerned about aesthetics. The issues, as they tend to do in California, rapidly escalated. Thirty years later he felt inundated, helpless, and displaced, not only in what had become known as Silicon Valley but also in the remainder of the West. Stegner could not deal with the second western constant—the first being aridity and the second rapid change. Change would alienate Stegner from his native place.

As Stegner's life encompassed the radical shifts of the twentieth-century American West, so his residency in California spanned the state's post–World War II transformation from an agrarian to a high-tech economy. From raising fruit to national defense to the computer, the Santa Clara Valley morphed into Silicon Valley. Up, up, and up went the population, to the point where San Jose outnumbered slumbering San Francisco. The suburban tract homes spread to the east and south while the trophy homes of the newly rich were plopped down on all sides of the Stegner hillside.

New industries and businesses based on the silicon wafer flocked to the valley. There was a 133 percent increase in office space, the largest jump in such growth in any urban area in the state during the 1980s. The real estate madness peaked in 1989. The newest boom brought with it high housing costs, traffic jams, air and water pollution, crowded schools, fiscal crises for local governments, and particularly for Wallace Stegner, a bleak reminder of the transient nature of the West he had spent a lifetime trying to avoid.

While San Jose became the largest city in Silicon Valley, Palo Alto, at the north end of the valley, became the financial, legal, and high-end shopping and restaurant center. The sleek hegemony of the groomed, tree-shaded city was the result of its proximity to prosperous Stanford University, the intellectual center of all this activity. Money and brains made nearby Los Altos Hills, once home to pig farms and affordable housing for young professors, a highly desirable semirural neighborhood within easy commuting distance of the action.

By the 1990s, Silicon Valley had become the economic engine that was driving the San Francisco Bay Area. In fact, traditional roles had been reversed. San Francisco had become a suburb of the valley. It was a historic and a nearly instantaneous flip-flop. There were twice as many Fortune 500 firms in the valley as in the city. For many the real city was a more desirable place to live than the faux cities to the south. They commuted from the city in the morning and then returned at night. It was the gold rush all over again, this time in a valley and not in the mountains. Los Altos Hills, in particular, was known for its "monster homes."[1]

Nor was it any different elsewhere in the West. As Stegner looked about, it seemed that individuality had been subsumed by mass culture. San Jose and Silicon Valley were clones of Los Angeles, as were the metropolitan areas of Seattle, Salt Lake City, Denver, Albuquerque, Phoenix, and Las Vegas. Only Eastend, to which he chose not to return, remained the same.

Stegner's locally aimed environmental writings reflected a growing alienation from his chosen place. Nearly thirty years after building the only year-round residence he ever owned, Wally wrote: "I have seen many changes, and the changes have not been by any means all for the good." He wondered why history had "to repeat itself so drearily."² On the twentieth anniversary of the founding of the Committee for Green Foothills, Stegner described what the developers had done to the peninsula:

> What is more, they little by little take the joy out of daily living, they push us toward the desperate termite life of Paterson, New Jersey. They leave no room for the wild species, they obliterate the ecology of grassy hills and wooded ravines and brushy creek banks, they overflow the winter creeks and dry up the summer ones, they unknowingly or uncaringly doom dozens of species of wild things to local extinction. And they starve the eye that craves beauty. They substitute for voluptuous bare hills and green slopes formed and softened by natural forces the crude shelves and benches and cuts of bulldozers.³

Committee members and friends gathered in the tasteful Los Altos Hills garden of one of their own on a spring afternoon in 1987 to honor Stegner. It was the type of gathering of the affluent, the powerful, and the white elite that made one wonder if they were celebrating the maintenance of their natural surroundings, to which they were accustomed, or good works that had benefited a wider swath of society. A large population of Asians and Latinos had recently arrived in Silicon Valley. Donald Kennedy, the president of Stanford, introduced Stegner, who ended his brief remarks thus: "Many of you have been more dedicated and more effective than I have been. But I can tell you I am proud to be, and grateful to be, among friends, and that our purpose is as strong as it ever was. This, finally, is my place. The very first memories I have, from about the age of three, are of an orphanage in Seattle. I would be content if my last ones could be of a gathering like this, among these people, here."⁴

Stegner was denied those last memories. He would die in Santa Fe, and his ashes would be scattered in Vermont. New England had become the symbol of a more stable culture, one that reminded him more of his frontier upbringing in Canada, which he now treasured more than the good life he had experienced for forty-five years in California.

HIS ANGER DID not mellow with age. A row with Stanford in 1982 contributed to the California university's losing his papers to the University of Utah. It began when Albert Guérard, his English Department nemesis, brought the white-haired writer storming down off his hilltop to the campus eleven years after he had resigned his faculty position. Stegner saw the hand of Guérard behind the hiring of Gilbert Sorrentino as a creative writing professor.

The Department of English search committee recommended Sorrentino, who was backed not only by his friend Guérard but also by the postmodern-literature faction in the department. The creative writing program's director at the time, John L'Heureux, was on the search committee. He later had second thoughts and stated that Sorrentino was "not an outstanding writer and as an experimentalist he was interested in experiment as an end in itself."[5] The writing program's faculty, headed by Nancy Packer, opposed Sorrentino's appointment but was overruled.

<u>Stegner, possessed by the temper he had inherited from his father and that, with Mary's help, he could usually control</u>, made the rounds of the dean, provost, and president of Stanford. His fear was that the creative writing program was coming under the control of the English Department. He wrote L'Heureux and told him to take his name off the fellowships. Robert Polhemus, who was the chair of the Department of English at the time, said years later that he liked and admired Stegner, "but he could be a very hard man."[6]

L'Heureux gave various reasons why Wally should reconsider his request. "It is wrong," said L'Heureux. "It is the breaking of an essential bond that connects the very best of the Stanford Writing Program with the very best it can once again become." Do it, said Stegner. Sorrentino is "a coterie writer of minimum distinction" and represents "a danger to the future of the writing program and a complete repudiation of everything I tried to do when I was building it." He asked that his name be taken off the fellowships, catalogs, leaflets, and announcements. "That's all it takes to make us all easier in our minds," said Stegner.[7]

It didn't make everyone feel easier. Nancy Packer replaced L'Heureux as director. She instituted a delaying action. With Mary's calming influence, they got Wally to rescind his demands. "Wally was furious," said Packer, "and it cost this university a lot."[8] It cost Stanford the bulk of Stegner's papers.

The papers had been stored at Stanford since 1976 and added to periodically by Stegner since then. The original agreement was that they would remain at Stanford for ten years, they could be withdrawn at any time, and the public would have access only to the fan mail. David C. Weber, director of the Stanford University Libraries, had written Stegner: "I note with pleasure your comment as to your intentions that the papers will eventually come to Stanford."⁹

Shortly after Sorrentino took his place on the faculty, Stegner wrote a correspondent: "Nobody has my papers, but they will probably go to the University of Utah (don't broadcast this). Utah has been good to me, and consistently supportive, and it's where I came from, and its library [which Stegner had dedicated] could use a little strengthening. Any scholar who has to go to Salt Lake to study Stegner will get a bonus by being lured into good country."¹⁰ Utah library officials had actively courted Stegner. Stanford librarians, who simply assumed they would get the papers, were taken aback by his decision.

Sorrentino taught—"lackadaisically" said one of his colleagues—at Stanford for fifteen years and then returned to New York City. To Sorrentino, who saw himself as a New Yorker's New Yorker, "the entire Bay Area, with the source of infection being, of course, that citadel of provincialism, San Francisco, has the air of an amateur stage production set in sinister natural surroundings."¹¹

PLACE TO A great extent formed Stegner's character and the characters in his novels. He first thought of locating *Crossing to Safety* in California, but that just didn't feel right. Yes, the Grays, on whom the characters Sid and Charity were based, had spent a number of years in southern California, but they were more rooted in Vermont. He explained: "I suppose I do subscribe to the notion that places (which include social habits, memory, attics, relatives, graveyards, and much else) have a lot to do with the formation of character—that at least in well established regions there is a sort of regional character. Maybe I felt that in California there is no such established pattern, and that characters who . . . would look appropriate in New England would only look bizarre in California."¹²

Stegner's last novel is about the reaffirmation of a friendship that takes place in Vermont during the course of one day. Wally thought of the ideal friendship as being *amicitia*, the working title for the book drawn from Cicero's *De amicitia*. The relationship of friend to friend was regarded as being on the same plane as that of brother to brother in the ancient world and had its own philosophical code.

The subject, like that in most of Stegner's novels, is not overly dramatic. Although it deals with two couples who resemble the Stegners and the Grays, it does not involve wife or husband swapping, a fatal accident, murder, or any other mayhem, just the scramble for academic tenure. An indirect reference to the novel in progress was contained in Stegner's letter to Wendell Berry's editor praising his former student's book *A Place on Earth:*

> It has no side, there is nothing flashy about it, it can't be read backwards as readily as forward, it has a beginning middle and end, it closes a stretch of life-history and town-history and it leads through feeling to a profound satisfaction. What a pleasure it is to read a book about decent people who love or like or at least tolerate each other, who know, for themselves at least, what the good and the bad are, and who try, and sometimes succeed, to live by "virtue," by obeying their sense of conduct.[13]

As with his other books, Wally had problems writing *Crossing to Safety*. He wrote Carol Brandt:

> One day I think I have the clue to where all this work is leading, I'm just about to grab it, like the meaning of the universe glimpsed in a dream. Next day the whole thing is a dull family chronicle without point or end or pertinence or meaning or interest or even continuity, and I'm back where I started. I don't know. Maybe it's a lost cause. Maybe, on the other hand, I *will* get that ultimate clue, and the whole thing will stitch together in one triumphant sewing machine operation.[14]

It finally did come together. Before sending the manuscript to his publisher, Stegner wanted it read by the Grays' six children, their parents having died. He told his agent, "There is nothing libelous, or anything like that; but I don't want even hurt feelings." If one of the children had objected, he would not have published the book. One of them, Nancy Gray Keyes, said, "I thought, 'Boy, he doesn't want to get burned a second time,'" referring to the *Angle of Repose* controversy. Speaking for the family, she told Wally, "We feel it is a privilege to have the essence of Greensboro and my family captured so beautifully and sadly by you."[15]

Stegner had followed Sam Vaughan, the publisher of Doubleday, to Random House, where Vaughan was a senior vice president. Vaughan would publish Stegner's last three books. He wrote Wally an eight-page memo detailing his thoughts on the novel. His remarkably detailed and insightful letter began:

I have thought for a long time about friendship, as a form of love. . . . As I wrote in a report to my colleagues here, yours is a novel about the complex forms of love called friendship—about love and marriage and the "marriage" of friendships that is sometimes possible, wherein four people become some kind of unit. It is about the perils and pleasures of friendship; of giving and getting; of bonds as strong—and sometimes as limiting— as family; of selfless generosity of what in some cases turns out to be an inadvertently selfish attempt not just to give but to dominate.

Vaughan suggested some minor changes, one being the title *Amicitia*, which he and Carl D. Brandt thought no one would recognize outside of "Bill Buckley and a few botanists" who were learned in Latin.[16] Stegner chose *Crossing to Safety* from a Robert Frost poem.

Fortunately, *The New York Times Book Review* assigned the review to the novelist Doris Grumbach, who was approaching the age of seventy. She complimented Stegner for avoiding such "currently popular subjects" as kinky sex and violence and concentrating instead on the "quiet re-examination of what, close to the end, seems not only worth living but happy and almost fulfilled."[17]

After the book was published, in a talk to the Intermountain Booksellers Association in Salt Lake City, Stegner linked *Crossing to Safety* to his growing despair about the West:

Without my intending it, *Crossing to Safety* became, during the writing and rewriting and rewriting of it, almost a *complaint* against the West—against a liberty that too easily frays out into chaos, against the mobility that prevents a deep sense of family, community and place, against the brevity of time and the limited or attenuated nature of the group memory, against the thinness and fragility of the social fabric, against the loss of all that is given up in a new country. If going west meant emancipation from past history, past oppression and injustice, past poverty, it also meant deprivation of much that in older societies made life secure and satisfying.

The Morgans (Stegners) see in the Langs (Grays) all of that which they covet. The Langs see in the Morgans the emancipation from the dead hands of the past. I don't try to adjudicate that difference of view, unless to suggest that my westerners, coming from deprivation, may be a little tougher and more flexible in

their wrestle with chaos than their friends are, and more deter-
minedly hungry for what they want than their friends are. It may
be I am talking about differences between people brought up
poor and people brought up rich as much as I am talking about
people brought up west or east. But I think the cultural hunger is
real. I have felt it myself.[18]

THE NEED TO be recognized—to be the "good boy" his mother
wanted him to be—ate at Stegner to the end of his working life. For
Stegner at the age of seventy-eight, *Crossing to Safety* represented his
last chance for success. "I am interested in seeing my reputation climb
out of the hole the NY Times et-all dug for it," he told a correspondent. Stegner wanted "this book to make me rich and famous. Money,
though not the major consideration, is a consideration."[19] Sales were
moderate, however, as was to be expected for an author who defined
fiction as being about "conduct in a place." What did he need to do to
become famous? "I guess I need to knife my wife, or be caught bugger-
ing a statue of Reagan in the park."[20]

Through the late 1970s and early 1980s, Stegner suffered a loss in
popularity, and his book sales dipped precipitously. New York publishers let his books languish or drift out of print. They were acquired and
republished with plain covers by the University of Nebraska Press. The
university press, said Stegner, makes "pleasant-looking books on good
paper, and works hard, at least in the West, at keeping them in bookstores."[21] Although the advances were minuscule, the advantages were
that his books would stay in print and appear as part of a series.

Literary fashions changed, as they frequently do, and New York
book editors again became interested in Stegner. Dan Frank at Viking-
Penguin was one of those editors. He was interested in reprinting the
titles held by Nebraska. Carl Brandt wrote to the university press's
director: "I am sorry. You were faithful to Wally in the days when the
demand was not great, and somehow it isn't fair that such faithfulness
shouldn't be rewarded. But I do believe that it is important for Wally to
be distributed as widely as possible."[22]

Frank was a young editorial assistant at Knopf in the late 1970s
when he first read one of Stegner's books. His fiancée had suggested he
read *Angle of Repose*. On their honeymoon, in Paris, they read *The Spectator Bird*. He became an editor at Viking-Penguin in the next decade
and acquired the paperback rights to most of Stegner's books. "In short,

your books have given my wife and me much pleasure. We are grateful," Dan wrote Wally.[23] Along with Steinbeck titles, Stegner paperbacks now dominate the *S's* in the fiction and literature sections of bookstores in the West and have kept his reputation as a writer alive.

SAM VAUGHAN WAS interested in acquiring Stegner's next books after publishing *Crossing to Safety.* He edited volumes of Stegner's collected short stories and nonfiction essays, respectively titled *Collected Stories of Wallace Stegner* and *Where the Bluebird Sings to the Lemonade Springs. Collected Stories* was nominated for a National Book Critics Circle Award in 1990 but did not win. John Updike won the award that year. Stegner had edged out Updike for the Pulitzer Prize in 1972.[24]

Shortly after publication of *Collected Stories,* Stegner prepared a speech to accompany a reading. He lashed out at his critics and defended his type of fiction:

> And one kind of critics, the deconstructionist magi of Yale and its colonies, have declared themselves superior to fiction, and to literature in general. It is a joke. Both it and its makers are themselves fictions, mosaics of culturally constructed myths, fragments of previous texts and stereotyped values, phatic verbiage, reverberations of old delusions, echoes of echoes. The delight of these critics is to show what shopworn stuff literature is made of and what shoddy tricks it employs. They destroy their own justification for being, and before long, like the snake that took hold of its own tail and swallowed itself, they will vanish like all the other over-subtle and scholastic aberrations of history. Perhaps once we have had them, we will be immune, as we are after having had the measles.

As for the type of fiction he preferred and wrote, Stegner said:

> The point is, our fiction—what we write and what we read— is likely to be as frivolous or as serious as our lives are. If we never examine our lives, we are not likely to get much out of fiction that makes such examination its function. . . . Because I tend to take life seriously, what I like about it and what I don't, I believe in fiction, not only in its do-ability but in its importance. For the writer, whose life is as often as not a mess, it can clean up a murky

and littered mind as snails clean up a fish tank. And at its best it leaves behind a purified residue, an artifact, something shaped and created and capable of communicating whatever wisdom it has arrived at. Even a deconstructionist could benefit from it if he would.

As an example, Stegner gave the background for "Goin' to Town," first published in *The Atlantic* in 1940, next as a chapter in *The Big Rock Candy Mountain*, first collected in *The Women on the Wall*, and again published in his last short story collection. The purpose of the story, he said, was to get even with his father "for what I felt was both an injustice and an unkindness" and to understand why his father hit him "a swift backhand blow that knocked the boy staggering." He continued:

> But I think hoarded resentment was not the only reason my subconscious sent up this story from the cellar. There was regret and guilt as well as resentment involved. As I recreated that bad day on the homestead in 1917 I began to realize that I was not only outraged by my father's act, I was desolated by it, I wanted it not to happen, I wanted to admire him and be loved by him, I wanted not to have offended him with my crybabyishness, I wanted to be the sort of son he could be proud of. Getting even was only one impulse, and a not very attractive one, of what moved me. I also found myself wanting to understand, to make a reconciliation of some kind, to soothe my own anger and unease, to lay his troubled and troubling ghost . . . [to rest].[25]

Stegner's lifelong attempt to heal himself—he termed it "self-therapy"—didn't work. He thought he finally had achieved it in *Recapitulation,* but he hadn't, which doesn't mean that he didn't try mightily. Of that autobiographical novel, Stegner said, "I measure the strength of the intention by the difficulty and exasperation of getting a handle on it."[26] Shortly after *Recapitulation* was published, in 1979, Stegner vowed he would never buy a tombstone for his father's grave.

NEAR THE END of his life there were newspaper and magazine articles to write, awards to accept, books to sign at bookstores, and speeches to give. He summarized his life in a San Francisco lecture: "My first fifteen years were migrant and deprived. My next fifteen were aspiring and academic and literary and deprived. My last fifty have been academic and literary and not quite so deprived. It is progress of a sort. But I am still the person my first fifteen years made me. Without consciously intending to, I have written my life."[27]

As autobiographical works, Stegner cited *The Big Rock Candy Mountain*, *Wolf Willow*, and *Recapitulation* as defining his life in the interior West; *A Shooting Star*, *All the Little Live Things*, *Angle of Repose*, and *Spectator Bird* contained shards of his California experience; and *Crossing to Safety* touched upon the Vermont years. The closest Stegner came to a nonfiction autobiography was writing ten thousand words in 1988 for the Gale Research series on contemporary authors. He offered the manuscript to his agent for a possible magazine sale, with the caveat, "Of course I've written it all before, but that was fiction." Stegner toyed with the idea of expanding it into a full-scale autobiography. "Eighty is a good round year to write your autobiography in," he wrote Carl Brandt, but he never pursued it.[28]

There were down times and up times. A bad back, arthritis, ulcers, and a hip replacement slowed him down. He used a cane. Mary needed constant medical attention. It felt like the end of an era on the hilltop. Acid rain, drought, and pear blight wrecked the trees. The mother of a friend died. "Your relationship with your mother, even with all the difficulties of age and growing infirmity, is something I envy," Stegner wrote the friend shortly before his own death. "I would have liked the chance to live alone with my own mother for a while, to get her out of her imprisonment and share some of the good things of life."[29]

In his last years, Stegner issued from his hilltop "the razor-sharp warnings of a modern day Cassandra" about the environmental health of the West. The West had been "the geography of hope"; but he now qualified the word, stating that "the wrong kinds [of hope], in excessive amounts, go with human failure and environmental damage as boom goes with bust."[30] The emphasis was now on caution and, ultimately, despair about the region's future.

One year before his death, Stegner bemoaned the losses, particularly in his beloved southern Utah, of wilderness and the quality of national park lands: "We have already lost a good deal; the further it goes, the more we lose. Trying to think of ways to prevent further losses of this kind, all I can think of is acceptance, acknowledgment, and restraint—acceptance of the limitations of the country, acknowledgment of the incompatibility of solitude and resort activities, and restraint of our devouring greed."[31]

Stegner wrote in longhand "The Real Line," a short summary of his life, to guide the filmmaker Stephen Fisher, who was making a documentary. Under the heading "What I learned," he wrote in reference to the West:

- respect for the land and its history
- contrition for my part in spoiling it
- some sense of responsibility, as a citizen at last of the whole country, for trying to repair and preserve
- suspicion and dislike for those who in continuing and inexcusable ignorance, or in disregard for land ethics and human ethics, go on raping the West (and also the world at large) in cycles of boom and bust, growing desertification, bad sociology, bad human living[32]

He welcomed a new granddaughter into the family and wondered who would be able to afford Allison's Stanford education.[33] Wally and Mary traveled. He worked with Fisher on the television documentary, which was narrated by Robert Redford, and cooperated with Jackson Benson on his biography. He flew to Bozeman, Montana, to be present at the unveiling of a chair in western American studies established in his name at Montana State University, only to be struck down by flu on the stage and hauled off to a hospital in an ambulance.

If New York City had its coteries, well then, Wally had his clique of western writers. He was more a lodestone at the apex of a pyramid than the dean, as *The New York Times* had christened him. His closest relationship was with T. H. Watkins. A native of the Bay Area, Tom had edited *American West* magazine, whose birth Stegner had overseen, before going to Washington to edit *The Living Wilderness*, the magazine of the Wilderness Society. They had a father-son, master-mentor relationship that was similar to the DeVoto-Stegner bond. Watkins wrote a glowing profile of Stegner for *Audubon* magazine. He also nominated Stegner for the Nobel Prize in Literature.[34] Watkins became the first Wallace Stegner Distinguished Professor of Western American Studies at Montana State University. He died in 2000.[35]

The clique, who met and corresponded with Wally during his last years, paid tribute to him, and Stegner praised their work. It was a mutual admiration society with Stegner the fulcrum. The problem, as Stegner had recognized, was that no overarching publication served the region. So the dialogue remained mostly private.[36] Barry Lopez wrote that he had visited Wendell Berry in Kentucky and they had agreed "how profoundly" Stegner had affected American letters.[37]

Montana was a mecca for writers, many of whom Stegner knew personally. Asked by the Montana writer William Kittredge for a list of his favorite Montana authors, Stegner replied: "I am not so much of a regionalist that I keep icons in the niche, but I have enjoyed everything by William Kittredge, everything by James Welch, everything but the whodunits by Bud Guthrie, everything by Dorothy Johnson, whatever I have read of Richard Hugo, everything by Ivan Doig."[38]

Two authors and professors who taught at the University of Colorado and were well versed in the West sought Stegner out. Charles F. Wilkinson, a law professor, had considered writing a biography of Stegner but bowed out when Watkins said he was interested.[39] Wilkinson wrote a New York editor, "His thinking was the most luminous I have ever known, and it molded my work." To a letter from Wilkinson, Stegner replied, "Nothing would please me better than to have been even 2% responsible for starting you on your career of making the West work."[40]

Patricia Limerick, of the University of Colorado, described her meteoric rise in the ranks of western historians. "Two or three years ago," she wrote Stegner in 1989, "I could not get on the WHA [Western History Association] program to save my life . . . and now I am the authority figure." As chair of the program committee, she was in a position to determine the agenda for the next conference. Limerick had defined and promoted the concept of an inclusive "new" western history in *The Legacy of Conquest*. Now, she wrote, she had been rereading Stegner's books "and was struck by how much *Legacy* seems to have been cribbed from you (through that marginally honorable process of reading, thinking, letting years pass, and then writing)." Cross-pollination was occurring. One year earlier Stegner had written Wilkinson that he had been "reading and stealing" ideas from Limerick's book.[41]

There were fewer letters from the East, where teaching colleagues and fellow writers with whom he had lifted a few drinks had died or contacts had withered with age and distance. He wasn't entirely forgotten, however. David McCullough wrote Stegner in 1990: "Someone asked me recently, 'Who is your favorite living American writer?' I said, 'Wallace Stegner.' "[42]

He returned to Stanford to give the keynote address at the 1991 Founders' Day celebration on the university's centennial. It was a gracious speech. Stegner lauded Stanford for being "one of the handful of the greatest universities in the world" and ignored in his remarks the students outside Memorial Auditorium who were protesting yet another war. They lay as if dead or injured, a woman draped in black wailed, and a sign stated "Parents' Day in Baghdad."[43] It had been twenty years since Stegner had left the university during similar protests.

Mary and Wally were planning to visit Eastend in the summer of 1993. The Stegner home had been restored by a local group as a visiting artists' and writers' residence. His most vivid memory of Saskatchewan during the intervening years, he told the leader of that effort, had hit him unexpectedly when he visited the Serengeti Plain in Tanzania. "I got out of the car and was struck absolutely dumb by a combined memory and vision: it was the same earth and the same sky I had grown up in, only it had some wildebeest and zebras in it instead of horses and Herefords."[44]

Summing up his literary output, Stegner seemed almost reconciled to being defined, by default, as a western writer. He wrote Carol Brandt:

> It's an odd feeling to become a bigger and bigger frog in this western puddle while fading like breath on a windowpane on your coast. To coin a metaphor, I'm just beginning to realize that I've been pretty much forced to be a "western" writer, something I never intended to be and don't think I really am. Between local puffing and far-flung disregard, I turn out to be world famous all over California, and [I may] eventually make up my mind to dance with the guys that brung me.[45]

Stegner maintained with blind insistence to the end of his life that there was only one kind of fiction writing. It came from the writer's own life and experiences. He took a parting shot at Ken Kesey, who continued to be a burr under his saddle. Kesey's advice in a *New York Times Magazine* article to "write what you don't know" struck him "as balderdash. That is the way to produce unknowing and unfeeling books, the way to send with a dead [telegraph] key, the way to convince ourselves and perhaps others that antic motions in a void, a meaningless mugging and hoofing, are what literature is supposed to be."[46]

Stegner emphasized the transient quality of human life in the West, as shaped by its landscape. He returned to the defining theme of aridity, which he had popularized. The West "is arid country and aridity enforces space, which in turn enforces mobility." Life was not as settled in the West as it was in, say, New England. Why? "Space does something to the vision: It makes the country itself, for lack of human coagulation and illusions of human importance, into something formidable and ever-present, and it tends to make humans as migratory as antelope."[47]

"Changing everywhere," Stegner wrote in the fall of 1992, "America changes fastest west of the 100th meridian."[48] He had increasingly been looking eastward. Vermont was now described by Stegner as the ideal place. Wally wrote: "For there is something in Vermont—in its climate, people, history, laws—that wins people to it in love and loyalty, and does not welcome speculation and the unearned increment and the treatment of land and water as commodities. Here, if anywhere in the United States, land is a heritage as well as a resource, and ownership suggests stewardship, not exploitation."[49]

Heritage meant knowing and treasuring history. Silicon Valley, he told an interviewer, has "no sense of history, no regard for history." It was "full of people who, like Henry Ford, think of history as bunk. What you have to pay attention to is what is on the screen of your computer. That's where the competition is; that's where the challenge is." What he was drawn to in Vermont, he said, was "family and tradition and history."[50]

Although he would continue to live in warmer California—the winters in New England being too cold—he had decided he would seek his final resting place, his angle of repose, in Vermont. When Benson interviewed Stegner in June 1989, he was shocked by this disclosure from a writer who had traded so extensively on his nativeness and sense of place in the American West.

SANTA FE HAD always been a pleasant stopping place for the Stegners. In fact, Wally and Mary had once given some thought to living there. They had good friends in the city, including Lee and Stewart Udall.

The Stegners went to Santa Fe in March 1993 in order for Wally to accept an award from the Mountains & Plains Independent Booksellers Association. Wally had been ill the year before and had had to decline the booksellers' "Spirit of the West" Literary Achievement Award. One of the conditions of the award was that the recipient be present. This year David Lavender would get that award, and Stegner would receive one of four regional book awards for *Where the Bluebird Sings*.[51] Before leaving Los Altos Hills, Wally made out a to-do list that contained eight items. An introduction to a book of essays by Page was at the top of the list. There were other introductions and forewords to books and remarks to compose for various events, such as an upcoming Earth Day celebration.

The awards were presented at a banquet on the evening of March 27. The following evening, on a Santa Fe highway, Wally pulled out into the path of an oncoming car bearing down on his left. Stegner was at fault, police said. He was cited for violating the right-of-way.[52] The driver's side of the large rental car was crushed. Stegner's ribs and collarbone were broken on his left side. Mary was not injured.

"How could I have done this to you?" Wally said to his wife of nearly fifty-nine years as he lay in St. Vincent Hospital the next day. Complications, including a heart attack and pneumonia, followed, and Wallace Stegner died in the hospital on April 13.[53] He was eighty-four years old. Death from injuries suffered in an automobile accident far from home and in the stylized city of Santa Fe seemed an inappropriate end for Stegner, the celebrator of wilderness and reality.

At least two acquaintances dreamed of Stegner's death on the night he died, before they knew about it. Both were reasonable people. They lived twelve hundred miles apart and recorded their dreams in separate publications shortly after his death. They were Donald Kennedy, the former president of Stanford University and a biology professor, and Sharon Butala, a prize-winning Canadian author who lived on a ranch near Eastend and had corresponded with Wally.[54]

Kennedy's account of his dream was published in *The Stanford Daily*. He was standing in front a strange map of North America, one that showed all the major river basins. The Colorado River watershed stretched far beyond its true limits and took in the upper Midwest. How strange, Kennedy said to Stegner, that the river seemed to drain one half of the country yet accounted for less than one quarter of its fresh water supply. Kennedy reminded Stegner of his writings about aridity and the oasis civilization of the West. He had no explanation for the dream.[55]

Butala wrote in a Canadian literary magazine: "The night Wallace Stegner died and came to meet me no tea was poured or whiskey drunk. What I sensed in the room was the distilled essence of the man, a clear, questing intelligence; there was little intimacy, little of what I think of as human warmth, affection, or concern—except perhaps there was a touch of the most eloquent and moving sadness, a sense of him still not having found whatever he had spent his life searching for."[56]

The obituaries, including a generous one in *The New York Times*, were long and numerous.[57] Tributes flooded the electronic and print media. There were gatherings at Stanford Memorial Church, Kepler's bookstore in Menlo Park, the Herbst Theatre in San Francisco, the University of Portland, the Wallace Stegner House in Eastend, and the Department of the Interior in Washington.

A Democratic administration reminiscent of John F. Kennedy's had just taken office. Bruce Babbitt, the new secretary of the interior, an Arizonan, had read *Beyond the Hundredth Meridian* shortly after it was published, in 1954. He reread it during his first week on the job in Washington. "Each generation," he told the gathering, "is given another chance to consider that balance" between the exploitation and conservation of natural resources in the West that Stegner had so evocatively portrayed.[58]

Lesser-known individuals also voiced their grief. An admirer wrote Wally an imagined letter a few days after his death: "In some way, all of your books have spoken directly to my soul."[59]

Wallace Stegner had, at last, crossed to safety, and his many legacies would enable others to understand that the geography of the West is varied; it includes despair as well as hope.

Epilogue

Saskatchewan

June 29, 1984: 11:10 a.m. It is 91 degrees F. and the wind must be blowing up to 50 m.p.h. That hot wind and lack of moisture (last July we had a 3-day rain and virtually nothing since) is ruining the hay and the grain crops. Even my vegetable and flower gardens won't grow. The sky is a pale, dusty blue at the horizon and higher up where the dust doesn't reach it, it is the usual bright blue of summer. Anxiety Butte is faded by the haze of dust in the air. The hay crop is short and thin and burning at the bottom and the crested wheat grass in the yard has whitish tips and is pale dun below. The road is crumbling to dust. Everything looks white, even the air, even the grass and trees that have been watered and are green, and the earth between the back door and the carangana hedge is blown bare and is white and cracking. People who are overextended are worried sick.

Sharon Butala, *Perfection of the Morning:*
A Woman's Awakening in Nature

I T'S DIFFICULT FOR me and others who have attempted to arrange the West in meaningful ways not to feel at least partly in Wallace Stegner's shadow when traveling through, thinking about, or writing on the region. His teaching, conservation, and writing legacies are scattered like cottonwood fluff across the landscapes of the American West.

After I completed research on the historical components of this book, I embarked on a series of contemporary journeys. I went searching for traces of Stegner's spoor, his places and some of mine that we had shared at different times and links between the past and present and between him and me and others. I traveled the Stegner Trail to those landscapes in Saskatchewan, Utah, California, and Vermont that had been most important to him. I was testing his premise: if the past keeps feeding into the present, as Stegner maintained, then there should be sightings of him more than a dozen years after his death.

I think he would have appreciated this additional effort to make his life and work meaningful. And I think he would have learned from it, too, because I went to places that he had dared not revisit, the first being the site of the Stegner homestead on the Saskatchewan prairie. Stegner had written that he was afraid to return to the blistering prairie: "I don't want to find, as I know I will if I go down there, that we have vanished without a trace like a boat sunk in mid-ocean."[1]

He thought the only remnants of his family's fleeting existence would be a few willow trees and the "rezavoy." There were no willow trees, let alone trees or signs of habitation of any description. I did find the reservoir, enlarged since 1920 to accommodate cattle grazing on the Prairie Farm Rehabilitation Administration's Battle Creek Community Pasture. There were still a few native plants mixed with the invasive crested wheatgrass, which dominates the mixed-grass prairie. Sagebrush and cacti were familiar to me from excursions to the south. Burnouts where topsoil is lacking and hardpan predominates reduce the productivity of the pastureland.

Neither the land nor its transient occupants have prospered since 1920. The grazing capacity is four cows per 160 acres. Two hundred thirty head of beef cattle were spread across the community pasture— the same type of government land and the same type of land use that Stegner had written about in articles about the public domain in the United States. Privatizing public lands, a periodic movement in the American West, is not as big an issue in Canada, but access is more controlled. I needed a right-of-entry license for "miscellaneous activities" to visit the Stegner homestead.

By means of research in the provincial archives, a global positioning system receiver, and local knowledge supplied by Sharon and Peter Butala, who took me in their four-wheel-drive pickup to the steel peg that marks the northwest side of the Stegners' quarter section, we arrived at this formative place in Wally's life on a hot August day. Along the empty graded dirt roads, dirt tracks marked by two sets of wheels, and through numerous barbed-wire gates, which needed continual opening and closing, we saw coyotes, deer, and pronghorn antelope. No gophers showed their heads. Perhaps the Stegner brothers had exterminated them, but I doubted it.

A few minutes after we arrived, as if cued by our presence, a light plane passed from west to east a few hundred feet above the sixty-foot swath that marks the United States–Canadian border. Big Brother, in the form of the U.S. Department of Homeland Security, was watching in this age of terrorism. The fences, including the one along the border, were for cattle; the plane was for sighting two-legged creatures. Because of its remote and desolate nature, nothing much happens along this stretch of the border that lies between the Cypress Hills to the north and the Bear Paw Mountains to the south.

True ghost towns, not the make-believe ones in the American West, which glorify minerals, dot both sides of the border. The weathered-gray clapboard structures are wind-battered creaking testimonials to the decline of agriculture on relatively small parcels of land like the Stegners' occupied.

PETER BUTALA'S FAMILY arrived in 1913, one year before the Stegners. They were stickers. Peter has watched while droughts and economics have reduced the number of ranches. His wife, Sharon, came from the city and led the effort to save the Stegner House. She had corresponded with Wally and talked with him on the telephone. They never met, although they were attempting to arrange his visit for the summer of 1993 when he died.

Wally had commiserated with Sharon about their isolation from the mainstream of book publishing in their respective countries. "I understand your frustration about being 'way out in the boondocks.' I have been out in the boondocks most of my life, and it always makes me mad how hard it is to get anybody's ear." Stegner greatly appreciated her efforts to restore the family home in Eastend. "That was the only house my mother ever owned, and she owned it about three years. The rest of her life she lived in tents, rentals, and tenements. Having the house restored might anchor her poor ghost."[2]

We needed to keep watch for bulls that might be grazing in the pasture. I warily followed Peter and Sharon down a faint track, once a wagon road, paralleling a shallow coulee. It gradually deepened and emptied into the dirt-dammed reservoir. Peter told me about the waves of homesteaders and more current ranchers who had failed and departed. Sharon wrote the following about the 1984 drought: "Raised for at least two generations on the myth that we were 'the breadbasket of the world,' we didn't find it easy to look in the eye so basic a belief, the framework on which three generations had built their lives and a whole society, and see that this was no longer true and, in fact, probably never had been."[3] My god, I thought when I read that, Stegner redux.

The cattle were grouped around the reservoir, the water level low.

We looked for pieces of the rusted metal that Peter had found on a prior visit but failed to find any. By myself I cut across the two quarter sections that the Stegners had claimed in order to experience a type of space that was new to me. The Butalas returned to the pickup. We would meet at the border fence.

I felt alone and isolated from the world—much more so than on my customary solitary coastal, mountain, and desert hikes—although I knew that the Butalas were nearby and would not leave without me. The crunch of dry grass was the dominant sound as I walked south. In the distance I could see the deserted ranch where Peter had fallen in the cistern and his father had rescued him. Trees to the south marked the place where the community of Hydro had existed on the other side of the border. I walked carefully so as not to sprain an ankle or break a leg in a gopher hole.

I lay down in front of the tallest nearby object, a wavy-leaved thistle that is native to the region. There were crickets and a few scattered birdcalls. Then silence. I rose. At a height of six feet two inches I was the most exposed object in that vast space and extremely vulnerable to the elements, which on any given day could be benign but might instantly take the form of a number of interesting combinations: fierce winds, biting cold, extreme heat, intense drought, driving rain, thunder, lightning, and tornadoes. The heat rose from the baking prairie in waves. A shimmering lump to the west was a single tree upon the horizon. The land flowed south like a vast bedsheet with occasional folds. The water collected in the Milk River and ended up in the Gulf of Mexico via the Mississippi River system. The Stegners had flowed south across this prairie to Great Falls.

Peter's vision was more attuned to shifts in the prairie landscape than was mine. He could see a subtle difference in the grass where George Stegner had plowed a narrow north-south strip and planted it with wheat nearly ninety years before. The strip was plowed in that direction to minimize the loss of soil to the prevailing westerly winds.

After a steak dinner at the Butala ranch that night, I returned to Eastend and my camping spot alongside the Frenchman River, near where Wally and Mary had stayed in their trailer in 1953. I had a copy of *Wolf Willow*. I lit the propane lamp in my camper and read the passage that described what Wally had derived from that homestead experience:

> One who has lived the dream, the temporary fulfillment, and the disappointment has had the full course. He may lack a thou-

sand things that the rest of the world takes for granted, and because his experience is belated he may feel like an anachronism all his life. But he will know one thing about what it means to be an American, because he has known the raw continent, and not as tourist but as denizen. Some of the beauty, the innocence, and the callousness must stick to him, and some of the regret.[4]

The authenticity of Stegner's words was brought home to me by where I had been and with whom I had spent that day and by knowing the breadth of Stegner's career and something about the history of the West. Few if any of us shadow writers who had followed in his tracks could match that legitimacy.

IN THE SUMMER young Wally learned firsthand about aridity on the prairie. Fall, winter, and spring he was taught the value of community in Eastend. He would later unite these experiences into a lesson for the West that was further distilled from the life of John Wesley Powell. It was communities or like-minded groups, not the mythical gunslingers, who had carved out habitable islands of living space in the basically inhospitable terrain.

Stegner's model, like Powell's, was the small Mormon villages in southern Utah. If any community resembled those original hamlets today (Utahans' having sold their southwestern souls to the tourist trade), it was Eastend, about which Stegner said years later: "I can't escape the perception that Eastend did a lot more for me than I ever did for it. All I ever did was remember it, fondly, probably inaccurately, and forever."[5]

The picturesque town of some six hundred residents is contained on three sides by the sinuous flow of the Frenchman River. As in Mormon farming communities and European villages, development has been kept within reasonable bounds so as not to infringe upon the productive fields. No motels, gas stations, or fast-food chains stretch beyond the town limits, nor are there any of the latter in Eastend. The tallest structures remain the grain elevators.

On its Web site, Eastend boasts of two seemingly paradoxical claims to fame: being in the midst of dinosaur country and being in "the middle of nowhere and miles from the nearest city."[6] Highway 13 is the wide, uncongested main street. Along with the gleaming new T.rex Discovery Centre on a nearby hillside, there have been other attempts to generate a tourist trade that might eventually put Eastend in the position of being somewhere.

The highway has been named Red Coat Drive within the town's limits, after the dress uniform of the country's constabulary force. Outside town it is known as the Red Coat Trail. Ten handcrafted banners on the main street celebrated local craftspeople and artists, cowgirls and cowboys, Sitting Bull and the Royal Canadian Mounted Police, Hudson's Bay Company blankets, and last but not least, Wallace Stegner. Ranchers also sought attention, the most prevalent bumper sticker in town being "Support Our Ranchers, Eat Canadian Beef," which I had done at the Butalas' ranch.

Today Eastend is poised on a fulcrum. The ranching culture is giving way to an artists' and second-home retreat setting. The Stegner House is the main cultural draw. While I was there, an art gallery opened nearby with a show by the artist in residence at the Stegner House. Inexpensive homes and the sheltered orderliness of the tree-shaded town on the banks of the river have lured urban refugees from Canadian cities to the north. I was told that even a California couple had purchased a home in town. There was an excellent bookstore, and espresso was available in an offbeat café. Near the end of his life, Stegner realized Eastend was changing. He wrote Butala: "In *Wolf Willow* I sort of disparaged the dream of the rural Athens, but I think I underestimated Eastend, and I didn't then know about you."[7]

The town, on the other hand, has managed, at least for the time being, to remain a living museum and a model for how a relative lack of change can itself produce a certain vitality. Eastend has a visible history that is demonstrable by functioning structures with connections to the past.

The Stegner Trail through town began for me with breakfast at Jack's Café, the original owner having been known as the Greek when Stegner bought ice cream from him. The café is now run by his grandniece. Visitors from out of town are taken to Jack's for dinner and sit in the dining room. I selected a booth near the counter in order to view the large mural covering three walls. Stegner would have smiled wryly.

The mural is an idealized portrait of southwestern Saskatchewan that resembles New England (or, in this case, the Maritime Provinces of Canada) more closely than the realities of the dry, dusty prairie. It proved to me that Canadians are just as adept at fooling themselves as Americans and brought home Larry McMurtry's remark that the romance of the West was always more potent than the truth. The land is green, the cows fat, the grain ripe, the barns red, the rivers full, the hills conical, and the distant city a pleasant, vertical presence upon a verdant plain.

The historical museum was housed a few doors east on Red Coat Drive in the former Pastime Theatre, where Wally used to watch silent movies to the accompaniment of a local pianist. I stopped to examine a photo on the wall taken on January 8, 1919, when the temperature was 85 degrees above zero. Nine men are relaxing on the porch of the rebuilt Cypress Hotel, which stands across the street from the museum. The hotel had burned in 1916 (along with the Stegners' potato crop, which was stored in the basement) and subsequently had been replaced. There is George Stegner, identified as Fats Stegner in the photo because of his husky build. His legs are crossed at a jaunty angle. George wears suspenders and a necktie. A cigar is clamped in his mouth. Stegner's hat brim is drawn down over his eyes, giving him the appearance of a small-town gambler. I realized it was the same photo that Corky Jones had described to Wally.

North on Elm Street three blocks, left at the river, and there was the Z-X Ranch house, built in 1903. The Stegner brothers had gotten their cowboy education at the ranch. Treeless then, now there was a carefully tended lawn, flowers, and a satellite-television dish. The house was painted a jaunty yellow above what resembled the brown bottom paint of a ship. Should the river rise, there would be a clear waterline, it seemed to me.

There have been three owners, the current one being Bea Tasche, the widow of the former postmaster. She was in her eighties. Her father had known George Stegner, she said. No, she didn't want to talk about George. "That's not very nice history." Bea Tasche's father, who represented Eastend in the Canadian Parliament, had never talked about the flu epidemic.[8] Ethel Wills, who ran the Stegner House, told me that Eastend was an upbeat place. Dating back to the first issues of the *East End Enterprise* and its coverage of the flu epidemic, it appeared that the town preferred its history nice.

Back on Elm and right on Pottery Street for two blocks, and there was the schoolhouse built in 1915 that had served as a hospital during the flu epidemic. It was a senior center now. I had been in Eastend long enough to determine that there was a healthy crop of seniors, as the center's eighty-six-year-old volunteer janitor, who served as my guide, exemplified. There were lively Saturday-night dances, card games, shuffleboard, and pool in the same brick structure where Wally had learned an eastern Canadian version of history and his family had been quarantined with the flu.

Walking farther west, I took a left on Tamarack Avenue and passed the Snooz 'n' crooZ Guest House. The nearby Stegner home was in impeccable condition. No member of the Stegner family has ever visited it. I think they would be pleased at what the people of Eastend have achieved. The town raised the money to restore the house. In the fifteen years since it opened, in 1990, it had welcomed sixty-five artists and writers from Canada, five from the United States, and one from Japan.

The Frenchman River flows in back. It was a short walk to the place where Wally, his brother, and their friends enjoyed late-season "shivery" swims. Wolf willow flowers in May and June. I had missed its pungent phase. I was told that once experienced, the smell is never forgotten. That certainly had been true for Wallace Stegner.

Utah

As an American writer, I have found no subject to be as intellectually challenging as writing about wilderness. How can I convey the scale and power of these big wide-open lands to those who have never seen them, let alone to those who have? How can I learn to write out of my own experience, out of my deep love for wild country, while still maintaining a language that opens minds rather than closes them? How to write again and again from every conceivable angle to stay the hand of development? How to write as clearly as one can from the heart and still be credible?

In the middle of the Utah wilderness campaign in 1996, Mary Page Stegner sent some inspiring words by her late husband, Wallace Stegner, about why paving the Burr Trail outside Capitol Reef National Park was a wrong-headed idea:

> *Why? So people coming up dammed Glen Canyon in power boats can get out of the water and make it more easily from ramp to ramp. And anyone on the fringes of that lovely stone wilderness will hear their motors ten, fifteen, twenty miles away across the garbed stone, reverberating off the Kaiparowits Cliffs, ricocheting off the Waterpocket Fold.*
>
> *As there has been nothing to interrupt the silence in this desert, so there is nothing to break the view of watercourses, of cliff lines and gulch and bare bald heads and domes, so there will be nothing to intercept the view of cut and fill highways.*
>
> *This road as proposed by the Utah highway commission, would be a tragedy, the dimmest of "wilderness breaking." Poverty program, public works? Yes—poverty of intelligence, poverty of imagination, poverty of sensibility. And a greater poverty for Utah's future, once that last wilderness is split, shattered, and brought down to size.*
> *Wallace Stegner*
> *Unpublished journal entry, 1966*

Terry Tempest Williams, *Red: Passion and Patience in the Desert*

URING THE EARLY years of the new century—years of exceptional drought in the Colorado River watershed, a circumstance that confirmed Stegner's descriptions of the future of this arid land—I searched southern Utah for signs of the man. During this dry period, people talked about moving away, shifting water priorities, and using less water, all of which came to naught when the rains and snow returned briefly in mid-decade. But it had been a very close call, and the next sustained drought or the one after that, and so on, might very well force the drastic measures that no one seemed willing to take in order to bring population growth into balance with the available water supply.

Southern Utah is classic Stegner Country for many reasons. It was the southernmost boundary of the happiest years of Stegner's life in Salt Lake City. His friend's father took the two boys on a camping trip through the national parks. He returned with his family to spend summers at Fish Lake. Wally studied the region and Clarence Edward Dutton in his undergraduate years. The place and the man were the subjects of his doctoral dissertation. He explored the river that ran through the canyonlands in order to give zest to the prose in *Beyond the Hundredth Meridian.* Stegner returned to the region on a jeep and horseback field trip during his stint in the Kennedy administration, and he continued the fight for the creation and enlargement of its national parks while on the National Parks Advisory Board and the boards of the Sierra Club and the Wilderness Society. He made overland camping and white-water boating forays into its wilderness recesses with friends in his later years.

The creation of the 1.7-million-acre Grand Staircase–Escalante National Monument by President Clinton's executive order in 1996, over the strenuous objections of many southern Utahans, occurred after Stegner had laid the groundwork, defined the opposition, and sketched the conflicts concerning resources. Perhaps some of his ashes should have been spread in the canyonland hinterlands, where there has been the least amount of change in the entire country because of the remoteness, the aridity, and the conservation efforts of such people as Wallace Stegner.

THE STEGNER TRAIL led inevitably to the Colorado River. My son, Alex, then twelve years old, and I had gone down the river from Lees

Ferry to Lake Mead in 1977 in one of Martin Litton's Grand Canyon dories, the craft that came closest to matching Powell's wooden rowboats. Like Wally's trip on the San Juan, it was a research voyage. I wrote about the twenty-one-day trip in *A River No More*, a book Stegner had favorably reviewed in *The New Republic*.

OARS (Outdoor Adventure River Specialists) had acquired Litton's company during the intervening years. So I contacted the rafting company for this second trip on the Colorado River. Alex would accompany me again. We would spend six days floating nearly one hundred miles, from Moab to the mouth of the Dirty Devil River. The Web site for the rafting company noted: "Lake Powell will be at its lowest level since the completion of Glen Canyon Dam in 1963 and we will be able to connect past with present as the canyon is partially returning to its natural state." How Stegnerian, I thought.

There were thirteen of us: three boatmen, two doctors, two journalists, a software designer, the owner of a picture-framing shop, a retired architect, a civil servant, a photographer (Alex), and me. Our homes spanned the continent, from California to Vermont. The river molded us into a cohesive group. At night we discussed Stegner's message of the need for community and wilderness in the West.

We slipped quietly through Canyonlands National Park, for whose creation Stegner had pushed. There were glimpses of ancient Indian ruins and bighorn sheep. At the confluence of the Green and Colorado Rivers, where years before I had hiked down the route that Powell had ascended, a park ranger had us in sight with his binoculars, checking to see if the stenciled OARS logo corresponded to the necessary permits.

Two days later we stood and surveyed the boiling cauldron of Big Drop Rapids. Inscribed in a rock was the following message, or statement:

Capsized

No. 3

7-15-40

NEVILLS

Was Norman Nevills warning us or boasting to succeeding generations of boatmen that he had survived, or was it a little bit of both? Nevills had played an important role in the evolution of the design of white-water craft and in initiating commercial trips on the Colorado and San Juan Rivers. Such political opposites and canyon lovers as Barry Goldwater and Wallace Stegner had floated through Glen

Canyon with Nevills. The flat-bottomed wooden boats of Nevills's design had been replaced by inflatable rubber rafts, three of which were transporting us down the river.

Once past Cataract Canyon, had the water been at its pre-drought level, we would have been floating on Lake Powell and using an outboard engine to propel us across the flat surface of the reservoir to the marina at Hite. However, we had come at a historic time. The river was flowing again. The submerged Navajo sandstone on the mainstream and in the side canyons had risen like a slimy monster from the depths. Some of the rocks were still covered with silt, but much had been washed away by recent rainstorms. I had always doubted the aesthetic argument for draining the reservoir because it seemed it would remain an encrusted disaster zone forever. That clearly wasn't the case.

New tamarisk shrubs grew in front of the older ranks of this invasive species. Where the silt had been washed away by the river's meandering current, their long roots dangled like so many veins seeking water for life, but falling short of that vital substance. The ceaseless flow of water had undermined the fragile silt banks that calved into the mocha-colored river. In this manner temporary rapids were formed where there had been the still water of an artificial lake.

Lake Powell had destroyed the river. Now the river was reclaiming its right to flow down a natural gradient, eating and cutting its way through layers of Lake Powell sediment. The question was, Would this layer of silt remain long enough to earn a geologic designation? The answer was no in terms of human time, because eventually the lake would rise again and cover it, but perhaps yes in terms of geologic time, providing there was someone present to name it.

We hiked up Dark Canyon through Lake Powell silt. It took forty minutes of navigating the gentle incline through the remnants of the lake bed, which had been shredded by recent flash floods, to reach the highest point of the reservoir's penetration. The pad and claw tracks of some type of wild cat and the indentations from the soles of expensive sandals that had just preceded me marked the way. The creek that drained the surrounding land was the color of dry blood.

Our trip ended that same day, and a small plane whisked us back to Moab. I asked the pilot to bank left and pass over the first delta of the Colorado River, the last and true delta being many miles distant in Mexico. The brown river and the turquoise reservoir met in a still pool. We flew back over the creases and wrinkles and boils of Canyonlands National Park.

. . .

ONE YEAR LATER my descent of the Colorado River through Stegner Country continued not far from where the previous trip had ended. Whereas I had previously been on a high-end (salmon-for-dinner) oar-propelled white-water raft trip, I was now on a budget-conscious flat-water, engine-powered foray on Lake Powell.

We were in "dammed Glen Canyon," as Wally had referred to this portion of the Colorado River, chugging along in a decrepit catamaran. The small group consisted of the Stegners' son, Page; his wife, Lynn; their daughter, Allison; my son, Alex; and Bob Clotworthy and his son Bruce, who was the legal research director for the Glen Canyon Institute, which is dedicated to the impossible task of getting rid of Glen Canyon Dam at the very most and lessening its effects on the magnificent canyonlands that surround Lake Powell at the very least.

The three-day trip had not gotten off to a good start. First, there were the two National Park Service rangers who inspected our safety equipment as we were poised on the launching ramp at Bullfrog Marina. The rangers were courteous; they said we needed to rent another life jacket. That done, we motored across Lake Powell in our ancient pontoon craft to fill our gas cans at Halls Crossing.

An unmanned water cannon mounted on the deck of a Park Service patrol vessel tracked our slow progress across the lake, its arc of water falling just short of our craft. Strange, I thought. Immediately upon docking, we were approached by two rangers who pulled up in the patrol boat. They jumped out smartly and strode toward us, bristling with lethal weapons strapped to their waists.

"We have issues with you," said one. They were not courteous.

In this age of fear of terrorism, the fact that the boat was registered to the Glen Canyon Institute possibly linked us to members of an aging Monkey Wrench Gang. Granted, the nonprofit institute was guilty of some previous minor infractions of regulations, but the rangers' agenda clearly exceeded a paper chase.

They asked us repeatedly where we were from and whether we were paying for the trip. It was an obvious attempt to rattle our cages. The answers were: various places and no. The interrogative technique was more suited to Iraq or Guantánamo Bay than to Lake Powell. I had no doubt the two sets of rangers had radio contact. Once again we were told to haul out the life preservers to be counted. Clearly, we were being harassed. I wanted to shout: "But don't you know what legacy we represent?" They wouldn't have recognized the name of Wallace Stegner. Best to keep quiet. They finally let us go.

Our troubles continued. The engine balked periodically; at times we thought the pontoons were leaking and we were sinking; we were never sure we had enough gas for the projected round-trip. The outing became an adventure. We lurched, much like the *African Queen*, into the heart of the reservoir that had once been a river.

As the boat toiled eastward toward the Escalante River, I told Lynn and Page a story I had recently heard in Salt Lake City. I had located the daughter of Juanita Crawford, to whom Wally was once engaged. Juanita had dropped Wally for his friend Marv Broberg while Stegner was in graduate school in Iowa. Juanita and Marv had had an unhappy marriage, and she had never forgotten Wally.

Juanita's daughter, Anne Riordan, a slim woman in her early seventies, lived in a comfortable section of town near the University of Utah, where she had taught dance. We talked for a few minutes. I asked her some basic questions, and then the following story—told only sparingly before—emerged.

During one of the Brobergs' separations in 1949, there had been a knock on the door. Young Anne opened it. She didn't clearly see the stranger because it was dark. He was hatless, which was unusual for Salt Lake City men at the time. The stranger asked for her mother.

"What are you doing here?" her mother had asked the man, whose name may have been Wally. Anne wasn't sure; she didn't hear the name clearly.

Juanita told Anne to go to bed, but her daughter lingered in the hallway, where there was a clear view of the living room. "I was kind of frozen there," she said.

The couple whispered, and then the man took Juanita in his arms and kissed her on the lips. "It was a very romantic kiss," said Riordan, who had been startled. Nothing like that had ever occurred before. They whispered some more, and then the man left. Juanita sat alone in the living room for a long time.

Anne sensed that the stranger was Wallace Stegner. "It was just something I knew in my bones." It was "a kiss of remembrance," she said. "He looked for her and found her for one moment."

Juanita died in 1974. A few years later Riordan took her father to a lecture Stegner was giving at the university. Afterward they waited in line to talk to him. The two men shook hands warmly. Broberg told Stegner that Juanita had died. "I'm glad you told me," Wally replied. "I knew she did."[1]

How wonderfully chaste and how beautiful, I thought, for this man who controlled his feelings so tightly, except when they imploded in anger or were committed to paper. I was touched by the story, and so were Lynn and Page when I related it to them on the boat.

We sputtered along. When Page took over the helm, he exhibited an almost instinctive ability to steer the clumsy rectangular-shaped craft through the labyrinthine entrances to side canyons of the Escalante River drainage that were flooded by the waters of Lake Powell. First we entered Clear Creek Canyon, our goal being Cathedral in the Desert. The huge grotto had emerged dripping from years of submersion as the water level dropped during the drought years. It had been dry just two months earlier. The lake had risen forty feet in the meantime, and we floated in.

I had given the Stegner family a copy of the handwritten notes Wally had made on a March 1965 Lake Powell trip. Wally was being taken on a tour on a Park Service patrol vessel to see the reservoir, which had been filling for the last two years. At the time he was chairman of the National Parks Advisory Board.

Before the reservoir had replaced the two rivers, it had been a long hike up the Escalante from the Colorado and then one mile up Clear Creek. For Stegner in 1965 it was a three-quarter-mile hike from the rising lake. The banks were lined with willows, reeds, and tall grasses. A rock wall ahead seemed impenetrable, but the stream bent, and suddenly a vast interior space lighted by angled columns of sunshine opened up. "This is another Music Temple," Stegner wrote, "perhaps higher in the walls—a domed grotto in the overhang with a skylight [and a] trickle of a fall into a pool at the head, then level sand."[2] In photographs of the empty chamber, people are mere dots within a huge curved space dedicated to the worship of nature.

We had come too late to judge the beauty of the cathedral for ourselves. Forty years after Wally's brief visit and two months after the reservoir had begun to rise again, there was no sacred space. There was just a motorboat-clogged cave. The top of the waterfall and further exploration of the canyon beyond it were accessible from the deck of a boat, but a sleek cigar-shaped vessel blocked our way. The owner said he would put towels down so that our feet would not dirty his deck and we could then cross it, but we decided to move on and camp elsewhere.

We proceeded up the Escalante. All the camping spots were taken. Page steered left into Davis Gulch. The winding arm of the reservoir had drowned the lower reaches of the slickrock canyon. We passed the sepulchral arms of dead cottonwood trees. The passage narrowed. The walls towered over the boat. The stagnant water was capped by a thin layer of scum, which consisted of plant life flushed down the canyon by flash floods and detritus from boaters. We found a camping spot near the end of the inlet and laid our sleeping bags under a giant overhang of Navajo sandstone. At last, peace from the noisy boat traffic on the main freeway of the river.

After dinner we arranged our folding chairs in a circle. We passed a copy of *The Sound of Mountain Water* around, and each of us read two pages from Stegner's essay "Glen Canyon Submersus." The article, for *Holiday* magazine, had been written from his 1965 notes. For Stegner there were both advantages and disadvantages in the changes he observed between 1947 and 1965. "In gaining the lovely and the usable," he wrote in the article, "we have given up the incomparable."[3] The words echoed in the narrow canyon and came back to us as if through a filter of time.

The campsite was redolent with environmental issues and history that Stegner would have appreciated. Recent torrential rains had incised the silt deposited on the exposed lake bed, revealing layers of garbage that resembled, in a more compact form, past civilizations at an archaeological dig in the Middle East. Allison bent down and picked up the shells of striped zebra mussels that lay like a thin carpet over the dry lake bed. The mussels, which can clog engine intakes and alter the ecosystems of lakes and rivers, were also a problem in Saskatchewan and New England.

The name Dunn was incised on the wall of the overhang. That was a familiar name, I thought, but I couldn't place it until I returned home and opened a copy of *Beyond the Hundredth Meridian*. William Dunn was a rebellious member of the 1869 Powell expedition that floated down the Colorado River. Three men, including Dunn, had left the expedition shortly before its end and walked overland. They were never seen again. A fourth had departed upriver.

Four decades ago Stegner had observed, while camped nearby: "Why not, we say, sitting in chilly fire-flushed darkness under mica stars, why not throw a boom across the mouth of the Escalante Canyon and hold this one precious arm of Lake Powell for the experiencing of silence?"[4] Such a sanctuary would be a fitting memorial to a river and a man. Why not, with the centennial of Wallace Stegner's birth approaching in 2009, take this first small step toward righting a wrong.

California

Often I thought of one of their phrases, "the angle of repose," which was too good to waste on rockslides or heaps of sand. Each one of us in the Cañon was slipping and crawling and grinding along seeking what to us was that angle, but we were not any of us ready for repose.

Mary Hallock Foote, *A Victorian Gentlewoman in the Far West*

IT WAS DIFFICULT finding a place in California where I could grab hold of Wally. He kept slipping from my grasp in the state where he had lived the longest. It seemed as though he had more substance elsewhere.

He was still a presence, albeit a fading one, in the creative writing program at Stanford. Each year ten new Stegner Fellows were chosen from some fifteen hundred applicants. I spent a day at the house in nearby Los Altos Hills and then returned and spent a night with Page Stegner just before the house was sold. We talked in the living room where the Ansel Adams print *Sierra Nevada, from Lone Pine* still hung on the wall.

I searched the grounds. I could see the various projects he had worked on over the years: the swaybacked brick patio he laid, the golden grasses he repeatedly scythed, and the two eastern birch trees—not western aspen trees, mind you—that he carefully tended at the entrance to the house. I walked down the curving driveway to the white gate and the "Private Road" sign, which sought to seal the property off from the world, and back up through the arched canopy of trees. Then the house was sold, with Stanford University showing no interest in acquiring it.

There was a decided pull in one direction, however, and that was toward Grass Valley and Mary Hallock Foote. Wally had been drawn to her life. Maybe she could tell me something about him, and perhaps I could give her a life beyond her fictional ending.

Mary and Arthur Foote had come to rest in this thriving mining district in 1895 after roaming the West. The fictional historian Lyman Ward takes up residence in the same place in the late 1960s to research the lives of his grandparents, Susan and Oliver Ward. I arrived for a short visit in 2006. The past fed into the present, just as Stegner had said.

The descriptions of Zodiac Cottage in *Angle of Repose* match the North Star House, not the North Star Cottage. The Footes lived for ten years with their three children in the cottage and then moved to the nearby house, which had been designed by Julia Morgan and completed in 1905. The architect believed in using native building materials. The stone façade that covers the first story came from North Star Mine tailings. The cedar shakes on the façade of the second story and the roof and the pine floors were milled from local woods. The eighteen-thousand-square-foot mansion containing twenty-two rooms cost $23,000 to construct.

The Foote house, as it is called by architectural historians, was Morgan's first significant arts-and-crafts-style residential commission outside the Bay Area. In a long career, Morgan would fulfill various architectural commissions for the Hearst family, including William Randolph Hearst's coastal castle known as San Simeon. In the novel, Stegner credited as the designer another Bay Area architect with whom Julia Morgan had worked. "One of the earliest [Bernard] Maybeck houses," Stegner's character Lyman Ward says, "this—a landmark. A pity if they should ever tear it down. It ought to be turned over, and I would see that it was, to the National Trust."

Through neglect, vandalism, the predations of squatters, and a fire department training exercise, only the foundation of the cottage remains. The North Star House was damaged, but it has not been obliterated. The Nevada County Land Trust stabilized the structure and is hoping to raise the millions of dollars needed to restore it. The graffiti on the walls referring to sex, drugs, and various mystical experiences would have repulsed Foote and Stegner, who lived by rigid codes of behavior, and they would have reminded Wally of the loathsome hippie years.

THE PHOTOGRAPHIC PORTRAITS of Mary Hallock Foote are either wistful or demure, the standard poses for gentlewomen in the genteel tradition. They do not indicate any passion or show that she was under five feet tall and a sticker in the Stegnerian sense of the word. Foote marketed her art and writings relentlessly and with a keen sense of their monetary worth. She had to. When her engineer husband was out of work or earning minimal wages, she supported the family. A Quaker, Foote had a "secret dread," and that was her husband's periodic drinking bouts. Her "one great sorrow" was her daughter Agnes's untimely death.

Foote achieved fame as an illustrator and short story and novel writer on western subjects and had a solid marriage. For the first time in the marriage there was financial security, a permanent place to live in Grass Valley, and a place that fit her perceived station in society. Behind the façade, however, there was reality. The Footes didn't own the various residences scattered about the grounds. They had to serve as hosts, with the help of a half-dozen servants, for the visiting mining-company directors, investors, and engineers. Arthur was the superintendent of the North Star Mine. His brother-in-law owned the houses and the mine.

After all that wandering and lack of appreciation for his talents, Arthur found his niche in Grass Valley. His engineering skills were appreciated, he cultivated roses, and he took stunning photographs of California mines. Mary's memoir, written in the 1920s, dealt briefly with Grass Valley, where she lived for thirty-seven years and wrote her finest novels. In Grass Valley she found a refuge but not complete fulfillment. Foote titled the Grass Valley chapter of her memoir "The Safer Life, or Dreams Kept Under."

During the Grass Valley years there were a number of tragic deaths, both within and outside the immediate family circle. Agnes's death from appendicitis struck Foote extremely hard. "This was the house of success," wrote Foote in reference to the North Star House, "but sorrow was built into its walls."[1]

The Footes left Grass Valley in 1932 to live their last years with a daughter in Massachusetts, not far from where Mary Foote had been raised in New York State. When Mary died, at the age of ninety in 1938, she chose not to be buried beside her husband in the Foote family plot in Connecticut but, rather, to have her ashes interred alongside Agnes's remains in Grass Valley. It was a measure of her great sense of loss for her beloved daughter and an indication why her family was so incensed at the manner in which Agnes was dispatched by Wallace Stegner in *Angle of Repose*.

Vermont

During the question-and-answer period following a reading
my father gave in San Francisco, a man in the crowd stood up
and said, "Mr. Stegner, you are America's most prominent western writer. Yet for the past fifty years you have maintained a
residence in New England, where you spend some part of
every year. Can you tell us, sir, what attracts you to such an alien
environment?"

I waited eagerly for the answer as the laughter died away (we
were, after all, a regional audience), but my father said something vague that got muddied by the bad acoustics under the balcony where I was seated, and sidestepped to another questioner.
By the end of his performance, the issue had slipped my mind.

Page Stegner, "Where the Heart Is"

I N A SENSE, it began here and ended here. Stegner got his big
break at Bread Loaf, making the contacts that would elevate him
from an obscure assistant professor in a midwestern university to a
celebrated writer. The road into the Green Mountains above Middlebury, Vermont, is a gentle incline that levels off onto a meadow at an
elevation of fifteen hundred feet. I was confronted in this otherwise syl-
van scene by the jarring view of the four-story ochre-colored Victorian
Bread Loaf Inn, the headquarters of the writing conference. I hadn't
encountered such a startling earth color since leaving the western
desert.

To establish a New England setting, Adirondack chairs were scattered about the campus of this summer extension of Middlebury College. The rain, the smell of mold, the predominance of green, the
cloying humidity, the soft warmth, the screens covering windows and
doors, the low mountains, and the generally subaqueous atmosphere
were vaguely familiar to me from summers spent as a youth in a New
England camp.

I wondered how first impressions had affected the Stegners in 1938. Wally was a thin, awkward stranger armed with little else than intelligence, ambition, and the ability to play tennis and sing cowboy songs. Would there be any trace of him more than sixty-five years later?

Bread Loaf had changed since Stegner's time, his last appearance there having been as a lecturer in 1953. Tuition, room, and board for eleven days were up from over $100 to over $2,000. The heavy drinking had given way to drugs in the 1970s. The opportunities for sexual encounters varied only by degrees over the years, there now being a politically correct harassment policy that verged on the redundant for writers: "If someone believes that another's speech is offensive or wrong or hurtful, he or she is encouraged to express that judgment in the exercise of his or her freedom." For liquor and drug offenses, dismissal without a refund was the punishment.

The intensity, seriousness, and ultimate exhaustion of participants and faculty were the same. Bread Loaf was now the oldest and most prestigious of the hundreds of writing conferences that were spread across the country from Key West, Florida, to Sitka, Alaska. They all operated on the principle that writing can be taught in a week or two.

Was there a Welty, a Capote, or a McCullers here, as there had been during Stegner's time? At the reception on the first night I asked questions of some of the two hundred hopeful writers gathered in the Barn.

A Cincinnati woman in her eighties, who published her novels as e-books, sat on a couch with her husband, a retiree who had been a medical researcher. The younger crowd stood and assumed various cocktail-party poses with their wine and mineral water. A young Salt Lake City woman who had just graduated from Middlebury was interested in family history, not an unusual topic for the Mormon-dominated culture. An African American woman with a medical degree was working on a novel about race and medicine. An editor from Houghton Mifflin stood with her author, whose first book, a historical novel about World War I involving a woman with a venereal disease, had just been acquired. A tall male novelist asked me if Stegner wasn't considered conventional, at least that was what he had heard.

Later that evening at Treman Cottage, where the faculty gathered, I talked to a Stegner Fellow who was on his way to the University of Wisconsin to teach. I told him I hoped he would enjoy his experience there more than Stegner had enjoyed his. Two years later, when I wanted to question him, his Madison e-mail address was no longer operative, and he wasn't listed as a faculty member.

A granddaughter of Ted and Kay Morrison was one of the students. She was staying at the Homer Noble Farm, the Frost summer residence just down the road from Bread Loaf. She was scheduled, according to the conference's daily newsletter, *The Crumb*, to give a reading that evening in the Blue Parlor, a room meant to resemble a Parisian literary salon.

The Morrisons' granddaughter, Jessamyn Smyth, read "Celibacy," a poem from her cross-genre novel. It began, "I am in bed with Kafka." We talked briefly afterward. Yes, she said, the affair between her grandmother and Robert Frost during that tumultuous summer of 1938 was "a skeleton in the family closet." Somehow, she said, they all had been able to manage it discreetly.[1]

ON THE FIRST day of classes I gravitated toward two writers who lived and worked in the West. I had already come across Wally's "Dear Bill" letters to William Kittredge and the latter's eulogy, which read in part: "Both Wallace Stegner and my mother told me, the one in his work, the other in the privacy of the room where she died, that I'd better get down to defining those things I hold sacred and taking what measures I can to preserve them. Which means saying what I mean, as directly and unequivocally as I can manage."[2]

Wally and Bill had become acquainted. There were similarities between the two men. Kittredge wrote of his early years on a ranch where he had "fed off examples like Wallace Stegner, a boy out of the rural West who had gone on to have an important career."[3] He had been raised on a ranch in the Upper Klamath Basin of southeastern Oregon and northeastern California and had worked there until his mid-thirties. His family, like Stegner's, made mistakes in land use in the middle of nowhere. He departed for Missoula, Montana, to teach and write and had hung out and drunk with another Stegner Fellow, Raymond Carver.

Kittredge was a veteran writing teacher. In addition to his year at Stanford, he had attended the writers' workshop at the University of Iowa and had taught writing at many summer conferences and at the University of Montana. He employed the standard workshop technique at Bread Loaf, which dated back to Socrates and forward to Stegner's time at Iowa and to the Stanford creative writing courses of today. He posed questions and made short observations as a way to extract responses from the students, who would then learn from what they had just heard themselves and others say.

In Ron Carlson, also a member of the Bread Loaf faculty that summer, there was another contemporary mirror into Stegner's past. "I was
lit by his use of places in Salt Lake which were familiar to me," Carlson
said. There were other parallels as well. Carlson's parents were the off-
spring of South Dakota farmers. The family moved in 1950 to Salt
Lake City, where his father took a job as a welder. They lived on the
west side, meaning the industrial section of town—the other side of
both the railroad tracks and the Jordan River. Even the outlaw Stegners
had managed to stay on the east side.

Like young Wally, Carlson had a Tom Sawyer–type youth in Salt
Lake. His Poplar Grove neighborhood was a boys' paradise. A large
park, vacant lots, abandoned houses, the dangerous railroad, and "the
river full of mystery and legend" were playgrounds for Carlson and
his friends. Fenderless bikes were their means of transportation.
They slept outside most nights during the summer months. For
Carlson, baseball, not tennis—as it had been for Stegner—was the
means to acquire status. He hit eight home runs in one Little League
season. The family was non-Mormon, but Carlson, like Stegner, did
not feel particularly excluded. "It pinched at times," he said, "but not
generally."

Carlson wrote in high school and at the University of Utah when
there was time during his job as a night watchman at a local technical
college. At the university he took a writing-workshop course from Ed
Abbey. "Abbey was not a good teacher," Carlson said. "He was a good
guy, and we had a few beers, but his workshop was a shambles." Carlson's first published story appeared in the campus literary magazine,
the *Pen* in Stegner's day, which had morphed into the short-lived
Wasatch Front of 1971. After getting a graduate degree from Utah,
where he wrote short stories to meet the requirements, Carlson drove
east with his wife to begin climbing the teaching and writing ladders.[4]
He now taught at Arizona State University, where he was a regents'
professor and the author of eight works of fiction, mostly collections of
short stories. Carlson was mindful of the warning Bernice Baumgarten
had given Stegner that "a short-story writer lives on his principal, giving up beginnings and endings." Carlson would publish a novel in 2007.

GREENSBORO WAS THE last stop on the Stegner Trail.

My wife and I went for a row on Caspian Lake in the late afternoon
of the day we arrived. We were surrounded by a landscape that was soft
and warm and edgeless. There were couples, families, and groups of

families with children on the beach who knew one another, who had been returning to this very spot in the summertime—as had the Stegner family—for generations. We were accustomed to being among strangers in the West. Here being a stranger was being in the minority; there it was the norm.

Children splashing and shouting in the water and the distant buzz of an outboard motor were the dominant human sounds. The haunting call of a loon on the lake contrasted with the joyful, descending trill of a canyon wren in the Southwest. As we rowed across the lake, we talked about how difficult the crossing part of crossing to safety was and whether there was any such thing as safety. For instance, I said, those dark clouds forming in the west could contain a tornado. Tornadoes and Vermont didn't seem to go together, but as a westerner accustomed to extremes in weather, and in many other things for that matter, cyclonic winds were as close as I could come to a fitting analogy.

I rowed close to shore, and we coasted among massive granite boulders that promised stability should the water roil. That night at dinner in the Highland Lodge our waitress recalled serving Mary and Wally. It was very unlikely that a waitperson in the West would have worked that long in the same restaurant. We were surrounded by stability. The same family had run the lodge for three generations.

Stegner told an interviewer during his last summer in Greensboro: "This is a place you feel loyal about. Maybe it's because it's a stable community—the kind of community that I had never lived in. Even the summer people here—the 'campers,' as folks up here call them—are often fourth-generation campers." Wally showed the visitor the ferns and joe-pye weed that would absorb his ashes the next summer, the "think house" where he had written so many books about the West, and the recycled shack, as he called it, which contained the beams from the farmhouse purchased in the summer of 1938.

He was attracted to Vermont, he said, because "it heals. The rest of the country—the West—when you damage it, you get a wasteland. Here we spend half our time cutting trees just to keep a view of the lake open. Then you turn your back, you come back the next year, and it's woods again."

Northeast Vermont was the frontier of his youth—wild and rough with resourceful year-round residents who could fix anything, survived harsh winters, worked hard, had integrity, and were stickers. There was too much money to be had in California, he thought, and that resulted in a certain shoddiness of place and character.

After interviewing him, the contributing editor of *Vermont Magazine* had written in a manner that both served the editorial needs of that publication and reflected Wally's thinking: "Stegner sighs, disgusted and pained. Although he once wrote, memorably, that the West was 'hope's native home,' he now admits that he is 'not really hopeful' about the region's future. 'It'll survive, I suppose. The race has a way of recovering from its mistakes just in time. But not fully recovering. The land that's been turned from a viable kind of dryland ecology into wasteland will stay wasteland for a long time.' "5

The next day, Page Stegner took us to the cemetery where no Stegner was buried and then to Baker Hill where Wally's ashes had been scattered on the lush vegetation. We walked around and through the cottage. The straight lines of the weathered brown-hued planks were offset by one bowed window. Page recalled his father's frugality with the building materials and the furnishings.

I walked to the back of the cottage and up a gentle slope into the edge of the forest where the ten-by-twelve-foot writing shack stood in the cool shade. On the small table facing the single window and a view toward the lake was the laptop computer of the current owner, a friend of the Stegners'. It was here that Wally had written the ending of *Angle of Repose* in one all-night session on a manual typewriter.

What Stegner chose in the end was a return to his beginnings. What he found in Vermont, as he had in Eastend, was a convergence of nature and human history. Why was that so attractive? Because, as he told an audience shortly before he died, "the business of studying the relations between places and people, and the ways in which people's living is conditioned by the place, is one of the best ways I know of finding out about ourselves."6

ACKNOWLEDGMENTS

THE FOLLOWING people read and commented on substantial portions of the text: Wendell Berry, Sharon and Peter Butala, Ann Gardiner, Sands Hall, Elizabeth Haskell, Robert Hass, James Houston, Jonathan Kirsch, Nancy Packer, David Pesonen, Gary Snyder, Robert Stone, and Donald Worster. Carl D. Brandt, Richard W. Etulain, Dianne Fradkin, Michael and Connie Mery, Doris Ober, Jo Ann Rogers, and Page Stegner read and commented on the entire manuscript. I thank them all. Of course, I am responsible for the final product.

Letters and other written materials in their possession were given to me by Wendell Berry, Carl D. Brandt, Sharon Butala, Robert Canzoneri, Ann Gardiner, Sands Hall, James Hepworth, Robert Irvine, Beth LaDow, Barry Lopez, Jo Ann Rogers, Page Stegner, Richard Walker, Mary Ellen Walsh, and Charles Wilkinson. I would especially like to acknowledge Anne Riordan for entrusting me with the story of her mother and Wally. I thank all of the above and others for replying generously to my requests.

Once again I used my traveling office, a Volkswagen van, to good advantage. The problem was it tended to break down in inconvenient places, such as the Utah desert, the Saskatchewan prairie, and just outside Yellowstone National Park. I upgraded the 1989 Vanagon to a newer Eurovan camper model for the last stages of research.

I stayed at the well-run Kampgrounds of America campground in downtown Salt Lake City. At the University of Utah's Marriott Library, Gregory Thompson, Karen Carver, and Kirk Baddley were quite helpful with requests and information concerning the Stegner Papers. In California my daily commute from the state park in Half Moon Bay to Stanford always ended with the able assistance of Margaret Kimball and Polly Armstrong at Stanford's Special Collections and University Archives. The Harvard Libraries contain information on Stegner's Cambridge years. The University of California, Berkeley, Library never failed to produce the volumes that filled a particular need. The Sierra

Club collections at Berkeley's Bancroft Library yielded information on Wally's conservation activities. Gary Snyder's papers are stored in the Department of Special Collections at the library of the University of California, Davis. The Stewart Udall papers at the University of Arizona Library contain information on Stegner's Department of the Interior activities. The Middlebury College Library yielded documents and photographs from the Bread Loaf Writers' Conference. I found helpful secondary materials in the University Libraries at the University of Nevada, Reno. From the University of Iowa Libraries came information on Wally's graduate years. The public libraries in Great Falls, Montana, and Greensboro, Vermont, filled small gaps in the narrative. As usual, the smallest library yielded some of the best results—in this case the Eastend Library, with its back issues of the local newspaper and its local histories covering the years the Stegners lived in Saskatchewan.

In Eastend everyone was friendly, and the Butalas and Ethel Wills were particularly helpful and hospitable. Gerald Davidson and the Butalas helped me locate the Stegner homestead. OARS furnished transportation down the Colorado River. The Glen Canyon Institute took me the rest of the way. Grant Johnson of Escalante Canyon Outfitters was my guide in the canyon country of southern Utah, where I gathered material for this and another book. Sands Hall was my escort in Grass Valley and Nevada City. Two great-granddaughters of the Footes, Elizabeth Haskell and Ann Gardiner, gave me Stegner letters, other correspondence, and information that was not available elsewhere. Gardiner found a copy of "The Miniature" in her files. I had searched in vain elsewhere for the unpublished short story.

Page Stegner and Jo Ann Rogers, who had joint power of attorney over the Stegner estate while I worked on this project, provided unrestricted access to places, photographs, letters, other documents, and other information. Page talked to me at length and answered all my queries. I had the initial idea for the biography, approached Page, and requested his cooperation. Page made very clear from the start that he did not want another hagiography.

I have returned to Knopf and Ashbel Green, the editor of the Colorado River book and one other book of mine. I have also returned to my agent Carl D. Brandt for this book. We are all older, and the arcs of our separate lives and careers have been reunited in this project. I think Wally would have appreciated this linking of the past with the present. Also at Knopf I would like to thank Luba Ostashevsky, Sara Sherbill, Abigail Winograd, Barbara de Wilde, Sarah Robinson, and Pamela Henstell, the West Coast publicist with whom I also began my book career.

WORKS BY AND ABOUT
WALLACE STEGNER

What follows is a list of Stegner's novels, histories, biographies, interviews, and short story and essay collections. Most are in print in quality paperback editions. The dates given with these titles in the notes section do not match these dates: I worked from less expensive paperback editions. The chronological list of first editions in this bibliography gives a good idea of the order, flow, and extent of Stegner's body of work.

This list does not include all the works Stegner edited or contributed to, just the ones that are most significant, in my opinion. The most complete bibliography, lacking only work produced in the last five years of Stegner's life, is Nancy Colberg's *Wallace Stegner: A Descriptive Bibliography* (Lewiston, Idaho: Confluence Press, 1990). In the section dealing with what others have written about Wallace Stegner, I have chosen those books and magazine and newspaper articles that are most helpful and should be available in a larger library.

Works by Wallace Stegner

Clarence Edward Dutton: An Appraisal. Salt Lake City: University of Utah Press, 1935.
Remembering Laughter. Boston: Little, Brown, 1937.
The Potter's House. Muscatine, Iowa: Prairie Press, 1938.
On a Darkling Plain. New York: Harcourt, Brace, 1940.
Fire and Ice. New York: Duell, Sloan and Pearce, 1941.
Mormon Country. New York: Duell, Sloan and Pearce, 1942.
The Big Rock Candy Mountain. New York: Duell, Sloan and Pearce, 1943.
One Nation. Boston: Houghton Mifflin, 1945.
Second Growth. Boston: Houghton Mifflin, 1947.
The Women on the Wall. Boston: Houghton Mifflin, 1950.
Joe Hill. Originally published as *The Preacher and the Slave.* Boston: Houghton Mifflin, 1950.
Beyond the Hundredth Meridian: John Wesley Powell and the Second Opening of the West. Boston: Houghton Mifflin, 1954.
This Is Dinosaur: Echo Park and Its Magic Rivers. Edited with a contribution by Wallace Stegner. New York: Alfred A. Knopf, 1955.
The City of the Living. Boston: Houghton Mifflin, 1956.
A Shooting Star. New York: Viking Press, 1961.
Wolf Willow: A History, a Story, and a Memory of the Last Plains Frontier. New York: Viking Press, 1962.
John Wesley Powell, *Report on the Lands of the Arid Region of the United States, with a More Detailed Account of the Lands of Utah.* Edited with an introduction by Wallace Stegner. Cambridge, Mass.: Belknap Press / Harvard University Press, 1962.
The Gathering of Zion: The Story of the Mormon Trail. New York: McGraw-Hill, 1964.

Twenty Years of Stanford Short Stories. Edited by Wallace Stegner and Richard Scow-
    croft. Palo Alto, Calif.: Stanford University Press, 1966.
All the Little Live Things. New York: Viking Press, 1967.
The Sound of Mountain Water: The Changing American West. Garden City, N.Y.: Dou-
    bleday, 1969.
Discovery! The Search for Arabian Oil. Beirut, Lebanon: Middle East Export Press,
    1971.
Angle of Repose. Garden City, N.Y.: Doubleday, 1971.
The Uneasy Chair: A Biography of Bernard DeVoto. Garden City, N.Y.: Doubleday, 1974.
The Letters of Bernard DeVoto. Edited by Wallace Stegner. Garden City, N.Y.: Double-
    day, 1975.
The Spectator Bird. Garden City, N.Y.: Doubleday, 1976.
Recapitulation. Garden City, N.Y.: Doubleday, 1979.
American Places. By Wallace Stegner and Page Stegner, with photographs by Eliot
    Porter. New York: E. P. Dutton, 1981.
One Way to Spell Man. Garden City, N.Y.: Doubleday, 1982.
Conversations with Wallace Stegner on Western History and Literature. Edited by Wallace
    Stegner and Richard W. Etulain. Salt Lake City: University of Utah Press, 1983.
Crossing to Safety. New York: Random House, 1987.
The American West as Living Space. Ann Arbor: University of Michigan Press, 1987.
"Wallace Stegner." In vol. 9 of *Contemporary Authors Autobiography Series,* edited by
    Mark Zadrozny. Detroit: Gale Research, 1989.
Collected Stories of Wallace Stegner. New York: Random House, 1990.
"Finding the Place." In *Growing Up Western,* edited by Clarus Backes. New York:
    Alfred A. Knopf, 1990.
Where the Bluebird Sings to the Lemonade Springs: Living and Writing in the West. New
    York: Random House, 1992.
Marking the Sparrow's Fall. Edited by Page Stegner. New York: Henry Holt, 1998.
On Teaching and Writing Fiction. Edited by Lynn Stegner. New York: Penguin Books,
    2002.

WORKS RELATING TO WALLACE STEGNER

BOOKS

Arthur, Anthony, ed. *Critical Essays on Wallace Stegner.* Boston: G. K. Hall, 1982. This
    book contains the Mary Ellen Williams Walsh essay "*Angle of Repose* and the Writ-
    ings of Mary Hallock Foote: A Source Study."
Benson, Jackson J. *Wallace Stegner: His Life and Work.* New York: Viking Press, 1996.
————. Introduction to *Angle of Repose* by Wallace Stegner. New York: Penguin Clas-
    sics, 2000.
————. *Down by the Lemonade Springs: Essays on Wallace Stegner.* Reno: University of
    Nevada Press, 2001.
Cook-Lynn, Elizabeth. *Why I Can't Read Wallace Stegner and Other Essays: A Tribal
    Voice.* Madison: University of Wisconsin Press, 1996.
Flora, Joseph M. "Wallace Stegner: An Update and a Retrospect." In *Updating the Lit-
    erary West,* sponsored by the Western Literature Association. Fort Worth: Texas
    Christian University Press, 1997.
Haglund, Elizabeth, ed. *Remembering the University of Utah.* Salt Lake City: University
    of Utah Press, 1981.

Hepworth, James. "Wallace Stegner's *Angle of Repose:* One Reader's Response." Ph.D. thesis, University of Arizona, 1989.

————. *Stealing Glances: Three Interviews with Wallace Stegner.* Albuquerque: University of New Mexico Press, 1998.

Meine, Curt, ed. *Wallace Stegner and the Continental Vision: Essays on Literature, History, and Landscape.* Washington, D.C.: Island Press, 1997.

Paul, Rodman W. *A Victorian Gentlewoman in the Far West: The Reminiscences of Mary Hallock Foote.* San Marino, Calif.: Huntington Library, 1972.

Rankin, Charles E. *Wallace Stegner: Man & Writer.* Albuquerque: University of New Mexico Press, 1996.

Robinson, Forrest G., and Margaret G. Robinson. *Wallace Stegner.* Boston: Twayne, 1977.

Stegner, Page, and Mary Stegner, eds. *The Geography of Hope.* San Francisco: Sierra Club Books, 1996.

Thomas, John L. *A Country in the Mind: Wallace Stegner, Bernard DeVoto, History, and the American Land.* New York: Routledge, 2002.

Topping, Gary. *Utah Historians and the Reconstruction of Western History.* Norman: University of Oklahoma Press, 2003.

MAGAZINE, JOURNAL, AND NEWSPAPER ARTICLES

Bass, Rick. "On Wilderness and Wallace Stegner." *Amicus Journal,* Spring 1997.

Burrows, Russell. "Wallace Stegner's Version of Pastoral." *Western American Literature,* Spring 1990.

Canzoneri, Robert. "Wallace Stegner: Trial by Existence." *Southern Review* 9, no. 3–4 (1973).

Doig, Ivan. "Under the Great Wide Sky." *Los Angeles Times Book Review,* April 12, 1992.

Foley, Jim. "On the Edge of Nowhere." *Stanford Magazine,* September/October 2001.

Houston, James D. "Wallace Stegner—Universal Truths Rooted in a Region." *Los Angeles Times Book Review,* November 23, 1980.

Kirgo, Julie. "The Healing Country." *Vermont Magazine,* January/February 1993.

Martin, Russell. "Writers of the Purple Sage: Voices in Western Literature." *New York Times Magazine,* December 27, 1981.

Miles, Jack. "Frontier Spirits." *Los Angeles Times Sunday Book Review,* March 7, 1993.

Olsen, Brett J. "Wallace Stegner and the Environmental Ethic: Environmentalism as a Rejection of Western Myth." *Western American Literature,* Summer 1994.

Reynolds, Susan Salter. "Tangle of Repose." *Los Angeles Times Magazine,* March 23, 2003.

Robinson, Forrest G. "Wallace Stegner's Family Saga." *Western American Literature,* Summer 1982.

————. "Clio Bereft of Calliope: Literature and the New Western History." *Arizona Quarterly,* Summer 1997.

————. "Fathers and Sons in Stegner's Ordered Dream of Man." *Arizona Quarterly,* Autumn 2003.

Robinson, Forrest G., and Margaret G. Robinson. "An Interview with Wallace Stegner." *American West,* January/February 1978.

Smith, Dinitia. "Puncturing the Myth of the West." *New York Times,* September 8, 1997.

South Dakota Review, Winter 1985. This issue is devoted entirely to Stegner.

Streitfeld, David. "Appreciation: Wallace Stegner and the West Years of His Life. *Washington Post*, April 15, 1993.

Stegner, Wallace. "Wallace Stegner: The Artist as Environmental Advocate." By Anne Lage, Sierra Club Oral History Series. Regional Oral History Office, Bancroft Library, University of California, Berkeley, 1983.

Tyburski, Susan J. "Wallace Stegner's Vision of Wilderness." *Western American Literature*, Summer 1983.

Watkins, T. H. "Typewritten on Both Sides: The Conservation Career of Wallace Stegner." *Audubon*, September 1987.

TELEVISION AND RADIO DOCUMENTARIES

Fisher, Stephen. *Wallace Stegner: A Writer's Life.* Los Angeles: Stephen Fisher Productions and KCET, 1996.

Bonetti, Kay. *Interview with Wallace Stegner.* Columbia, Mo.: American Audio Prose Library, 1987.

NOTES

THE SPECIAL COLLECTIONS DEPARTMENT of the J. Willard Marriott Library at the University of Utah, for reasons made obvious in the text, is the principal source for Stegners' photographs and written materials. Next in importance is the Special Collections and University Archives at the Stanford University Libraries. The main difference between the two collections is that the Salt Lake City library spans the whole of Stegner's life whereas Stanford focuses on his teaching years at that university. Also at Stanford are the invaluable transcripts of the Jackson Benson interviews, mentioned earlier.

Except for his letters to the various agents at Brandt & Brandt, which are now preserved in their entirety at the Utah library, Wally tended not to save copies of his outgoing personal correspondence, or it was discarded after his death by his wife. The Brandt & Brandt correspondence is intact only because it was held by the literary agency and then donated to the Utah library. Finding Stegner's letters meant contacting anyone who knew him to some extent and asking for them. Almost all of those people were cooperative. Page Stegner, who was working on a volume of selected correspondence at the same time, and I traded the letters we received. Page and Jo Ann Rogers also made available family letters and photos that had not yet been forwarded to the Utah archive. Members of the Stegner family and others answered questions in letters, e-mails, interviews conducted on the phone or in person, and informal conversations.

As far as I know, only three substantial sources of information about Wallace Stegner are not in archives. The widow of T. H. Watkins said that Wally's letters to Tom, his close friend in later years, were not available; she gave no explanation. The conditions that the filmmaker Stephen Fisher imposed for viewing outtakes and written materials were too burdensome. The relatives of Mary Hallock Foote have some Foote letters and unpublished stories, the remainder being at Stanford. I have encouraged all three parties to sell or donate their documents to the appropriate archives. At some time in an as yet undetermined library I will deposit all the materials I have collected.

I HAVE CHOSEN to use endnotes to cite the sources of most quotations and explanations that expand upon what is contained in the narrative. Because Stegner's letters are from many different sources and quite a few are in private hands, I have not designated their location. For materials in libraries, a search can be made online in guides that are quite detailed. If a serious researcher is stumped and wants to persist, he or she can contact me by e-mail through my Web site, www.philipfradkin.com.

The initials WS refer, of course, to Wallace Stegner.

Prologue

1. WS to Ronald Rayman, October 12, 1975.
2. WS, *Crossing to Safety* (New York: Penguin Books, 1988), p. 78.

UNFORMED YOUTH

Seattle

1. Stegner was nominated for the Nobel Prize for Literature. His former student Edward Abbey said he was "the only living American worthy of the Nobel."
2. Wendell Berry, "Author's Legacy Extends Beyond Words of the Land to Its Preservation," *San Jose Mercury News*, April 18, 1993.
3. WS to James Hepworth, July 2, 1985.
4. WS, "Greek Trip with the American Academy," brown notebook, n.d.
5. Kenneth Arrow, interview by Jackson Benson, August 9, 1988.
6. WS, interview by Jackson Benson, January 27, 1988.
7. WS, *The Big Rock Candy Mountain* (New York: Penguin Books, 1991), p. 457.
8. Redmond is described on its Web site as "home to everything from one person start-ups to Microsoft."
9. WS, *Where the Bluebird Sings to the Lemonade Springs: Living and Writing in the West* (New York: Modern Library, 2002), p. 30.
10. Mina Paulson Heggen to WS, n.d. Mina Paulson returned to Iowa in 1914 and married Thomas Heggen.
11. WS, interviews by Jackson Benson, May 7, June 2, and June 5, 1987. Reminiscences in the following two paragraphs also come from these interviews.
12. Lynn Stegner, who had similar experiences in a later version of the same Seattle orphanage and school, pointed me in the general direction that enabled me to make the link to Sacred Heart.
13. Blind pigs had attractions such as pool that customers paid to play or view; in turn, they were served a complimentary drink so that blue laws and the restrictions of Prohibition were circumvented.
14. Mina Paulson Heggen to WS, n.d.
15. "Wallace Stegner," in *Contemporary Authors Autobiography Series*, ed. Mark Zadrozny (Detroit: Gale Research, 1989), 9:258–60.
16. WS and Richard W. Etulain, *Conversations with Wallace Stegner on Western History and Literature* (Salt Lake City: University of Utah Press, 1990), p. 43. The most recent edition of this book was published by the University of Nevada Press in 1996.

Eastend

1. WS, "Finding the Place," in *Growing Up Western*, ed. Clarus Backes (New York: HarperPerennial, 1991), p. 162. Stegner made this point again and again. For instance: "I remember it better than any place I ever lived." WS to Mrs. Grant Carlton, January 7, 1957.
2. Forrest G. Robinson and Margaret G. Robinson, *Wallace Stegner* (Boston: Twayne, 1977), p. 21.
3. A democrat wagon had large, narrow wheels and a light frame. WS to Carl Brandt, January 17, 1953.
4. WS to Margaret Kecskemeti, May 29, 1986.
5. Ibid.

6. WS, *Wolf Willow: A History, a Story, and a Memory of the Last Plains Frontier* (New York: Penguin Books, 2000), p. 283.

7. Edward McCourt, *Saskatchewan* (Toronto: Macmillan of Canada, 1968), p. 5.

8. Gerald Friesen, *The Canadian Prairies: A History* (Lincoln: University of Nebraska Press, 1984), p. 7.

9. Ibid., p. 328.

10. Quoted in Clyde A. Milner II, Carol A. O'Connor, and Martha A. Sandweiss, eds., *The Oxford History of the American West* (New York: Oxford University Press, 1996), pp. 3–4.

11. Beth LaDow, *The Medicine Line: Life and Death on a North American Borderland* (New York: Routledge, 2002), p. 8.

12. H. S. Jones to WS, November 16, 1954, September 6, 1955, December 13, 1955.

13. H. S. Jones, "Eastend: 1885–1914."

14. Ibid.; LaDow, *Medicine Line*, p. 121; WS, *Wolf Willow*, pp. 137–38.

15. WS to Beth LaDow, March 13, 1990.

16. WS, *Wolf Willow*, p. 243.

17. Ibid., p. 6.

18. WS, "Finding the Place," p. 165.

19. Ibid., p. 292.

20. WS to Beth LaDow, March 13, 1990.

21. WS to Beth LaDow, December 5, 1990.

22. Ralph Gregg, recollection, in Eastend Historical Society, *Range Riders and "Sodbusters"* (North Battleford, Saskatchewan: Turner-Warwick 1984), p. 445; letter to the editor, *Eastend Enterprise*, March 5, 1964.

23. WS, *Wolf Willow*, p. 112.

24. WS and Etulain, *Conversations*, p. 3.

25. WS, *Wolf Willow*, p. 132.

26. Ibid., p. 16.

27. WS and Etulain, *Conversations*, p. 9; WS, *Where the Bluebird Sings*, p. 25.

28. WS, "Autobiography," handwritten notes on one page, written in about 1989.

29. Richard Scowcroft, interview by Jackson Benson, November 5, 1987; Forrest G. Robinson and Margaret G. Robinson, "An Interview with Wallace Stegner," *American West*, January/February 1978, p. 63.

30. WS, *Wolf Willow*, p. 23; WS, "Finding the Place," p. 179.

31. Mrs. J. E. Adair to WS, January 17, 1954.

32. WS, "The Geography of Hope," *Living Wilderness*, December 1980, p. 17.

33. WS, *Wolf Willow*, p. 275.

34. Ibid., p. 277.

35. WS, *Big Rock Candy Mountain*, pp. 340–41.

36. This account is based on Carl A. Krause, *Two Apples in a Jar* (Saskatoon, Saskatchewan: Pupil Profiles, 1977), the story of the murder written by a grand-nephew of Jacob Krause's, who was puzzled by the gaps in the story, and on Carl A. Krause, personal communication.

37. WS to Beth LaDow, December 5, 1990.

38. *East End Enterprise*, November 14, 1918.

39. WS, *On a Darkling Plain* (New York: Harcourt, Brace, 1940), p. 230.

40. *East End Enterprise*, August 7, 1919.

41. Eileen Huffman Starrett to WS, September 9, 1989; Mrs. J. E. Adair to WS, November 12, 1953.

42. H. S. Jones to WS, July 13, 1953.
43. WS, *Wolf Willow*, pp. 9, 283.
44. WS to Phil and Peg Gray, June 22, 1953.
45. WS to Corky Jones, December 26, 1953.
46. Jones was referring to Canadian Broadcasting Corporation radio programs. Corky Jones to WS, July 13, 1953.
47. WS to Mrs. Grant Carlton, January 7, 1957.
48. Sharon Butala, personal communication.

Great Falls

1. "Wallace Stegner," in *Contemporary Authors*, 9:261.
2. William J. Furdell and Elizabeth Lane Furdell, *Great Falls: A Pictorial History* (Norfolk, Va.: Downing, n.d.), p. 148.
3. WS, *Wolf Willow*, p. 24.
4. WS, "That Great Falls Year," in *Marking the Sparrow's Fall: Wallace Stegner's American West*, ed. Page Stegner (New York: Henry Holt, 1998), p. 20.
5. WS, "Finding the Place," p. 173.
6. WS, "That Great Falls Year," p. 28.
7. Ibid., p. 6.
8. WS, *Big Rock Candy Mountain*, p. 347.

Salt Lake City

1. WS, *The Gathering of Zion: The Story of the Mormon Trail* (Lincoln: University of Nebraska Press, 1992), p. 314.
2. WS, *Mormon Country* (Lincoln: University of Nebraska Press, 1981), p. 62.
3. Ibid., p. 51.
4. Ibid., p. 349.
5. WS, "Finding the Place," p. 177.
6. WS, *The Sound of Mountain Water: The Changing American West* (Lincoln: University of Nebraska Press, 1985), p. 42.
7. WS, notes for *Recapitulation*, scraps of paper, n.d.
8. WS to Phil Gray, November 16, 1944.
9. David L. Freed, September 1992, Everett L. Cooley Oral History Project, Marriott Library, University of Utah.
10. Thomas G. Alexander, *Utah: The Right Place* (Salt Lake City: Gibbs-Smith, 1995), pp. 276–307.
11. Helen Z. Papanikolas, "Bootlegging in Zion," *Utah Historical Quarterly*, Summer 1985, p. 286.
12. Ibid., p. 287.
13. Ibid., p. 289.
14. WS, *Recapitulation* (New York: Penguin Books, 1997), p. 35.
15. WS and Etulain, *Conversations*, p. 51.
16. WS, "The Best Idea We Ever Had," *Wilderness*, Spring 1983, p. 4.
17. WS, *Mormon Country*, pp. 188–89.
18. WS, "Finding the Place," p. 177.
19. David L. Freed, interview by Jackson Benson, May 25, 1989; WS, *Recapitulation*, pp. 85–86.

The University of Utah

1. WS, *Recapitulation*, p. 103.
2. WS to Jack Irvine, nine letters, August–November 1927.

3. WS to Jack Irvine, September 6, 1974; WS to Annie Irvine, December 22, 1987.

4. WS, "It Is the Love of Books I Owe Them," in *Remembering the University of Utah*, ed. Elizabeth Haglund (Salt Lake City: University of Utah Press, 1981), n.p.

5. Ibid.

6. WS and Etulain, *Conversations*, p. 24; WS to Tim Woodward, April 1, 1984.

7. WS, "It Is the Love of Books," n.p.

8. Ibid.

9. "Radical Talks at University," *Deseret News*, February 11, 1927.

10. WS, "The Personality," in *Four Portraits and One Subject: Bernard DeVoto*, by C. D. Bowen, E. R. Mirrielees, A. M. Schlesinger Jr., and WS (Boston: Houghton Mifflin, 1963), p. 82.

11. WS, "It Is the Love of Books," n.p.; WS, *Where the Bluebird Sings*, p. 17.

12. Vardis Fisher, *God or Caesar: The Writing of Fiction for Beginners* (Caldwell, Idaho: Caxton, 1953), p. 147.

13. "Wallace Stegner," in *Contemporary Authors*, 9:262. This was a sentiment Wally repeated often.

14. WS, "How the Smart People Escaped Annihilation," *Pen*, January 1930, p. 17.

15. "Wallace Stegner," in *Contemporary Authors*, 9:262; WS, "Literary by Accident," *Utah Libraries*, Fall 1975, p. 9.

The Iowa Years

1. WS, "Finding the Place," pp. 179–80.

2. WS to Stephen Wilbers, February 26, 1976.

3. Stephen Wilbers, *The Iowa Writers' Workshop* (Iowa City: University of Iowa Press, 1980), p. 49; emphasis added.

4. WS to Stephen Wilbers, February 26, 1976.

5. WS, *Sound of Mountain Water*, p. 205.

6. WS, "The Iowa Years," in *Communications Research—A Half Century Appraisal*, ed. Daniel Lerner and Lyle M. Nelson (Honolulu: University Press of Honolulu, 1977), p. 309.

7. Ibid., p. 305.

8. WS, *Where the Bluebird Sings*, p. 17.

9. Milton (Red) Cowan, interview by Jackson Benson, August 4, 1986.

10. Robin White and Ed McClanahan, "An Interview with Wallace Stegner," *Per/Se*, Fall 1968, p. 31.

11. WS, jottings in unlabeled notebook, n.d.

12. Milton (Red) Cowan, interview by Jackson Benson, August 4, 1986; Anne Riordan, personal communication.

13. WS to Jack Irvine, n.d.

14. Milton (Red) Cowan, interview by Jackson Benson, August 4, 1986.

15. Anne Riordan, personal communication.

16. WS to Mary Page, June 2, 1934.

17. WS to Sara Barnard, dated Thursday.

18. "Wallace Stegner," in *Contemporary Authors*, 9:264.

19. WS, *Where the Bluebird Sings*, p. 33.

20. WS to Sara Barnard, February 19, 1934.

21. WS to Mary Page, March 31, 1934.

22. WS to Sara Barnard, June 23, 1934.

23. Rev. P. O. Bersell to WS, July 16, 1934; WS to Mary Page, July 11, 1934. Fifty years later an English instructor at Augustana asked permission to use a portion of *Wolf Willow* in a college reader.

24. WS to Mary Page, July 15, 1934.

25. "Wallace Stegner," in *Contemporary Authors*, 9:264.

26. WS, "Game of Definitions," red notebook, n.d.

27. WS, interview by Jackson Benson, January 27, 1988; Mary Stegner, interview by Jackson Benson, November 18, 1988.

28. Mary Stegner, interview by Jackson Benson, January 20, 1989.

29. Peter S. Beagle, personal communication.

30. WS to Carol Brandt, May 8, 1984.

31. WS, "Strange Encounter," *California Living*, October 7, 1984.

32. WS to Phil and Peg Gray, July 15, 1956. There are frequent mentions of Mary's different ailments in the letters to the Grays; WS to Rachel Stegner, July 29, 1979.

33. WS, *Where the Bluebird Sings*, dedication.

34. Virginia Bennion Buchanan, personal communication.

35. Dr. Richard P. Wheat to WS, March 24, 1983.

36. WS, "Notes for an essay," n.d.

TALENTED TEACHER

Back to Utah and Forward to Wisconsin

1. Afterword by Mary Stegner, in WS, *Remembering Laughter* (New York: Penguin Books, 1996), p. 151.

2. "Wallace Stegner," in *Contemporary Authors*, p. 9:264.

3. WS, "Can Teachers Be Writers?" *Intermountain Review*, January 1, 1937.

4. Lynn Stegner, foreword to *On Teaching and Writing Fiction*, by WS (New York: Penguin Books, 2002), p. xiii. Stegner's Dartmouth lectures were first published as *Wallace Stegner on the Teaching of Creative Writing: Responses to a Series of Questions* (Hanover, N.H.: University Press of New England, 1988). There are currently more than three hundred MFA writing programs in the United States.

5. WS, "Literary by Accident," p. 15.

6. George Thomas to WS, November 2, 1937. Stegner also noted the Mormons' and Brigham Young's amazing fertility in the book.

7. S. B. Neff to George Thomas, March 1, 1937; George Thomas to S. B. Neff, April 13, 1937.

8. WS to George Thomas, May 9, 1937; Estella K. W. Shields to George Thomas, May 21, 1937; George Thomas to Estella K. W. Shields, May 22, 1937.

9. WS to Phil Gray, November 16, 1944.

10. WS, diary of 1937 trip to Europe, n.d.

11. "Wallace Stegner," in *Contemporary Authors*, 9:264–65.

12. WS to Syd Angleman, January 19, 1938.

13. WS, "Accomplishments," n.d. This document, which serves as a chronology of Stegner's early writing life, seems to have been part of his curriculum vitae.

14. Carl D. Brandt, personal communication.

15. Matthew J. Bruccoli, *James Gould Cozzens: A Life Apart* (New York: Harcourt Brace Jovanovich, 1983), pp. 83, 290–91. In his biography of Cozzens, Bruccoli devotes one chapter and an appendix to Baumgarten, whom he describes as "small, efficient, intelligent, determined, and an excellent judge of writing."

16. Cozzens acquired a reputation as a bigot. The critic Joseph Epstein attempted to demolish that perception by writing in *Commentary* ("Cozzens Repossessed," Sep-

tember 1983, pp. 68–69) that Cozzens's wife, who was his best and only friend and "the one critic whose advice he valued," was a Jew.

17. Bernice Baumgarten to WS, December 9, 1941.

18. Katharine White to Bernice Baumgarten, June 14, 1956.

19. WS, interview by Jackson Benson, January 27, 1988.

20. WS, *Crossing to Safety*, p. 132. *PMLA* (the journal of the Modern Language Association) is favored by academics.

The New England Years

1. Wilbur Schramm to WS, June 1, 1938.

2. WS, "The Iowa Years," pp. 309–10.

3. WS, *The Uneasy Chair: A Biography of Bernard DeVoto* (Salt Lake City: Gibbs Smith, 1988), p. 125.

4. Mary Stegner to Peg and Phil Gray, August 1938.

5. WS to Peg and Phil Gray, August 20, 1938.

6. Jay Parini, *Robert Frost: A Life* (New York: Henry Holt, 1999), pp. 303, 447.

7. WS and Etulain, *Conversations*, p. 171.

8. WS, *The Uneasy Chair*, p. 132.

9. "Bread Loaf Writer's Conference," Thirteenth Annual Session, August 17–31, 1938, p. 1.

10. WS, *The Uneasy Chair*, pp. 203–4.

11. For a full account of Frost's behavior see ibid., pp. 204–9.

12. WS, red notebook, n.d.

13. WS, *The Uneasy Chair*, p. 124.

14. Virginia Spencer Carr, *The Lonely Hunter: A Biography of Carson McCullers* (Garden City, N.Y.: Doubleday, 1975), pp. 107–8, 113.

15. WS, interview by Jackson Benson, November 5, 1987.

16. George Stegner referred to his financial situation and made pleas for money in seven handwritten letters he sent to WS between November 9, 1938, and April 17, 1939.

17. WS to George Stegner, May 17, 1939.

18. "Wallace Stegner," in *Contemporary Authors*, 9:265.

19. WS, *Big Rock Candy Mountain*, p. 551.

20. WS and Etulain, *Conversations*, p. 42. The location of the Stegner cemetery plot is the same in the novel as it is in reality.

21. Mortan and Phyllis Keller, *Making Harvard Modern: The Rise of America's University* (New York: Oxford University Press, 2001), p. 74.

22. David W. Johnson, "A Pleasant Lunch in the Country," *Harvard Magazine*, September/October 1984, pp. 79–80.

23. Both Stegner and Rideout recalled in separate interviews that Norman Mailer was in that first class. Mailer said he was never a student of Wally's. Dixie Brown, "Wallace Stegner: A Writer's Writer," *Peninsula*, January/February 1980; Walter Rideout, interview by Jackson Benson, April 10, 1987; Norman Mailer, two personal communications.

24. WS to Sharon Butala, October 27, 1992.

25. WS to Phil and Peg Gray, October 5, 1939.

26. Norman Foerster to WS, May 6, 1940.

27. WS to Howard Mumford Jones, September 22, 1947.

28. Alfred A. Knopf, the publisher of this book, is now an entity of the worldwide publishing conglomerate Bertelsmann.

29. WS to Phil and Peg Gray, October 5, 1939.

30. Mary Stegner to Peg Gray, April 20, 1942.

31. WS to Phil and Peg Gray, April 8, 1942.

32. WS expressed these sentiments in a number of letters to Phil and Peg Gray from April 8, 1942, to April 1944.

33. WS and Etulain, *Conversations*, pp. 116–17.

34. WS, *Mormon Country*, p. 30.

35. WS, "Plans for Work," typewritten note, 1942.

36. Ibid.; WS, ms. of foreword to *The Big Rock Candy Mountain*, Franklin Library Edition (Franklin Center, Penn., 1978), August 1976.

37. WS to Mark Schorer, December 10, 1942.

38. WS to Ted Morrison, November 22, 1942.

39. Mary Stegner to Peg and Phil Gray, June 12, 1942.

40. Mary Stegner to Peg Gray, December 5, 1942.

41. WS, "The Winter of Our Content," *Life*, February 1991.

42. WS and Etulain, *Conversations*, p. 19; WS, interview by Jackson Benson, November 4, 1987.

43. Robinson and Robinson, "An Interview," p. 62.

44. WS and Etulain, *Conversations*, pp. 127, 159.

45. The reviews are reprinted in Anthony Arthur, ed., *Critical Essays on Wallace Stegner* (Boston: G. K. Hall, 1982), pp. 17, 19.

46. Forrest G. Robinson and Margaret G. Robinson, "Wallace Stegner," *Quarry* (University of California, Santa Cruz) 4 (1974): 75–76.

47. WS to Phil and Peg Gray, April 23, 1944.

48. WS had favorably reviewed *No Day of Triumph* by the African American author J. Saunders Redding, calling attention to "the ineffectualism of segregated Negro education, drawing the color line, and practicing arrogant paternalism." WS, "How Serious Is Our Race Problem? An Unsparing, Fair-Minded Survey by an American Negro," *Atlantic*, December 1942, p. 130.

49. WS and Etulain, *Conversations*, p. 40.

50. WS to Richard Scowcroft, December 1, 1944; WS to Phil Gray, September 18, 1944.

51. WS and Etulain, *Conversations*, p. 65; WS to Phil Gray, August 23, 1945.

52. Elizabeth Cook-Lynn, *Why I Can't Read Wallace Stegner and Other Essays: A Tribal Voice* (Madison: University of Wisconsin Press, 1996), pp. xii–xiv, 29–40.

53. James R. Hepworth, "Wallace Stegner's Practice of the Wild," in *Wallace Stegner and the Continental Vision: Essays on Literature, History, and Landscape*, ed. Curt Meine (Washington, D.C.: Island Press, 1997), pp. 227–28; WS, "Out Where the Sense of Place Is a Sense of Motion," *Los Angeles Times Book Review*, June 3, 1990.

54. Beth LaDow, "The Unexpected Blossoming of Wallace Stegner's Boyhood Shit Fights" (Saskatchewan Centennial Lecture, University of Saskatchewan, March 8, 2004).

55. Patricia Nelson Limerick, "Precedents to Wisdom," in *The Geography of Hope*, ed. Page Stegner and Mary Stegner (San Francisco: Sierra Club Books, 1996), pp. 24–25.

56. WS to Ted Morrison, January 3, 1945.

57. Lynn White Jr. to WS, May 18, 1944, October 3, 1944.

58. WS to Ted Morrison, January 3, 1945.

59. "Wallace Stegner," in *Contemporary Authors*, 9:266; WS, "Literary by Accident," pp. 9–10.

The Stanford Years

1. WS to Phil and Peg Gray, July 6, 1945.

2. WS to Tom Heggen, August 5, 1945; WS to Dorothy Hillyer, August 5, 1945; Tom Heggen to WS, September 3, 1945.

3. Heggen drowned in sixteen inches of bathwater. Sleeping pills were scattered around the floor. The coroner ruled it an accidental death. The tabloids played up the suicide angle.

4. Juanita Brooks to WS, November 18, 1948.

5. WS to Juanita Brooks, August 1, 1949.

6. Boris Ilyin, interview by Jackson Benson, December 28, 1986.

7. Alvin C. Eurich, interview, October 4 and 7, 1980, Stanford University Oral History Project.

8. The ten 2006 Stegner Fellows, five in fiction and five in poetry, received $22,000 for living expenses for the school year. Four were from New York City and the others were from Baton Rouge, La.; Austin, Tex.; Tucson, Ariz.; Coos Bay, Ore.; San Francisco; and Melbourne, Australia.

9. WS to Richard Scowcroft, October 28, 1945.

10. WS to Ted Morrison, August 18 (1945?).

11. WS to Richard Scowcroft, April 21, 1947, May 5, 1947.

12. Nancy Packer, personal communication.

13. Richard Scowcroft, interview by William McPheron, June 16, 2000, Stanford University Oral History Project, pp. 14–16.

14. WS to Witter Bynner, March 28, 1946.

15. WS to Jackson Benson, January 28, 1988.

16. WS, quoted in Sherrard Gray, "A Remembrance of Wallace Stegner," n.d.

17. Lewis Hill to WS, November 30, 1947.

18. "Esther Kesselman, 1891–1983," *Hazen Road Dispatch*, Summer 1983.

19. WS to Robert Canzoneri, September 24, 1989.

20. WS to Lovell Thompson, February 3, 1948.

21. WS to Richard Scowcroft, September 9, 1945.

22. Robert Vitalis, "Wallace Stegner's Arabian Discovery: The Imperial Entailments of a Continental Vision" (working paper 8, International Center for Advanced Study, New York University, 2003), pp. 4, 33. The ideas in the paper would be incorporated into Vitalis's *America's Kingdom: Mythmaking on the Saudi Oil Frontier* (Palo Alto, Calif.: Stanford University Press, 2007).

23. WS, *Discovery! The Search for Arabian Oil* (Beirut, Lebanon: Middle East Export Press, 1971), p. 190.

24. WS, "Autobiography"; "Wallace Stegner," in *Contemporary Authors*, 9:267.

25. WS to Richard Scowcroft, August 6, 1967.

26. WS to Wilbur Schramm, November 23, 1948.

27. Page Stegner, personal communication.

28. WS to Page Stegner Jr. and Rachel Stegner Sheedy, various letters, and personal communications with both.

29. WS, interview by Jackson Benson, January 27, 1988.

30. WS to Richard Scowcroft, January 9, 1961.

31. Associated Students of Stanford University, "Stanford Scratch Sheet," Spring/Fall 1963.

32. Ed McClanahan, *My Vita, If You Will* (Washington, D.C.: Counterpoint, 1998), p. 8.

33. James D. Houston, personal communications.

34. WS, in *Twenty Years of Stanford Short Stories*, ed. WS and Richard Scowcroft (Palo Alto, Calif.: Stanford University Press, 1966), p. ix.

35. WS, *On Teaching and Writing Fiction*, pp. 35, 43, 60.

36. Wendell Berry, personal communication.

37. WS, *On Teaching and Writing Fiction*, pp. 6, 17, 56–57, 60.

38. WS to David Packard, May 1959.

39. WS, in *This I Believe*, ed. Edward R. Murrow (New York: Simon & Schuster, 1952), pp. 173–74.

40. WS, interview by Jackson Benson, June 12, 1989.

41. Don Moser to WS, March 6, 1978.

42. Edward Abbey, "The Sound of Mountain Water," *New York Times Book Review*, June 8, 1969.

43. Edward Abbey to WS, September 30, 1977.

44. WS, quoted in James Bishop Jr., *Epitaph for a Desert Anarchist: The Life and Legacy of Edward Abbey* (New York: Atheneum, 1994), pp. 198–99.

45. Wendell Berry to WS, May 23, 1989.

46. Richard Scowcroft, interview by Jackson Benson, November 5, 1987; WS, interview by Jackson Benson, January 26, 1988.

47. Ken Kesey, quoted in Elizabeth Tallent, "The Big X: Unraveling Mysteries in a Workshop for Fine Writing," *Stanford Today*, March/April 1996, p. 40.

48. Stephen L. Tanner, *Ken Kesey* (Boston: Twayne, 1983), pp. 11, 21.

49. Malcolm Cowley, "Ken Kesey at Stanford," in *Kesey*, ed. Michael Strelow (Eugene, Ore.: Northwest Review Books, 1977), p. 3.

50. Ken Kesey, quoted in Peter Joseph, *Good Times: An Oral History* (New York: Charterhouse, 1973), p. 382.

51. Malcolm Cowley to WS, August 16, 1961.

52. Gordon Lish, "What the Hell You Looking in Here For, Daisy Mae?" (interview with Ken Kesey), *Genesis West* 2, no. 5 (1963).

53. WS to Marshall Best, October 24, 1966.

54. WS to Wendell Berry, April 10, 1973; Wendell Berry, "Kentucky River Junction," dedicated to Ken Kesey and Ken Babbs, in *Collected Poems* (New York: North Point Press, 1999), pp. 149–50.

55. T. H. Watkins to WS, November 13, 1991.

56. Barry Lopez, transcript of 1993 memorial service for WS in Portland, Ore.; Ken Kesey, remarks at Claremont McKenna College, Claremont, Calif., September 17, 1993. Stegner deleted three pages of negative comments about Kesey in the transcript of the interviews by Richard Etulain, stating, "I've been much too critical." Richard W. Etulain, personal communication.

57. "Writer with a Talent," *Time*, November 28, 1960; WS to Mitchell J. Strucinski, November 25, 1960; Mitchell J. Strucinski to WS, November 28, 1960.

58. Mitchell J. Strucinski to WS, May 6, 1964.

59. WS, "Professor O'Connor at Stanford," in *Michael/Frank: Studies on Frank O'Connor*, ed. Maurice Sheehy (New York: Alfred A. Knopf, 1969), p. 98.

60. Ibid., pp. 96, 101.

61. WS to Richard Scowcroft, June 9, 1960.

62. Peter S. Beagle, personal communication.

63. James D. Houston, personal communication.

64. Larry McMurtry to WS, in *First Drafts, Last Drafts: Forty Years of the Creative Writing Program at Stanford*, ed. William McPheron (Palo Alto, Calif.: Stanford University Libraries, 1989), p. 57.

65. Cowley, "Ken Kesey at Stanford," p. 1.

66. Peter S. Beagle, personal communication.

67. WS and Etulain, *Conversations*, p. 135.

68. Robert Stone to WS, n.d. (probably 1967).

69. Robert Stone, quoted in Paul Perry, *On the Bus: The Complete Guide to the Legendary Trip of Ken Kesey and the Merry Pranksters and the Birth of the Counterculture* (New York: Thunder's Mouth Press, 1990), pp. 17–18.

70. Robert Stone, quoted ibid., pp. 21, 25.

71. Ibid., p. 29.

72. WS, "Hard Experience Talking," *Saturday Review*, August 19, 1967, p. 25; WS, *Interview with Wallace Stegner*, conducted by Kay Bonetti (Columbia, Mo.: American Audio Prose Library, 1987); Mary Stegner, interview by Jackson Benson, September 24, 1994.

73. Wendell Berry and Ed McClanahan, interview by Jackson Benson, n.d.

74. WS to Bev Chaney Jr., March 31, 1991.

Stone recounted his own version of the events in *Prime Green*, his 2007 memoir of the 1960s:

> When my pseudo-tumor pseudo-struck, occasioning medical bills that would have amounted to a year's income for Darius the Great, Stegner arranged to extend my fellowship so that I was covered by Stanford's health plan. (Wally's recollection of the circumstances under which he worked this out differed from mine. I had hoped to impress this old-time westerner with my cool courage. What he mostly recalled, good-naturedly but not quite so favorably impressed as I had hoped, was my *not* having the tumor I had been so enthusiastically promised by the goddamn team of blind eye doctors at Stanford Medical.)

Robert Stone, *Prime Green: Remembering the Sixties* (New York: HarperCollins, 2007), pp. 106–7. Stone drew from this account, as I had sent this portion of the manuscript to him to check for accuracy in 2006. He made clear in his account that he had never called Stegner "Wally" to his face.

75. WS, "Hard Experience Talking."

76. Robert Stone to WS, November 20, 1966.

77. Wendell Berry, "Wallace Stegner and the Great Community," *South Dakota Review*, Winter 1985, pp. 10–11, reprinted in Wendell Berry, *What Are People For?* (San Francisco: North Point Press, 1990).

78. Ernest Gaines, interview by Jackson Benson, June 5 and 15, 1990.

79. Nancy Packer, speech at Los Altos History Museum, Los Altos, Calif., February 10, 2005.

80. Berry, "Wallace Stegner and the Great Community," pp. 12–14.

81. Wendell Berry, "The Momentum of Clarity," in Stegner and Stegner, *Geography of Hope*, p. 73.

82. Wendell Berry to WS, October 4, 1963.

83. Wendell Berry to WS, Thanksgiving 1970.

84. WS to Gerald Freund, February 14, 1981.

85. Gerald Freund to WS, March 10, 1981.

86. WS, "A Letter to Wendell Berry," in *Wendell Berry*, ed. Paul Merchant (Lewiston, Idaho: Confluence Press, 1991), p. 51.

87. Ibid., p. 50.

88. WS, *Where the Bluebird Sings*, p. 207; Wendell Berry to WS, November 24, 1991.

89. Whit Hobbs to WS, September 10, 1990; Harry H. Crosby to WS, February 9, 1992.

90. Blanche McCrary Boyd to WS, February 28, 1977.

91. Shirley W. Hentzel to WS, April 4, 1979, August 7, 1992.

92. Harold Gilliam to WS, April 2, 1991.

93. Barry Lopez, "In Memoriam," in Stegner and Stegner, in *Geography of Hope*, pp. 117–20; Barry Lopez to WS, June 10, 1990.

94. Barry Lopez to WS, April 26, 1986.

95. WS to Barry Lopez, May 4, 1986.

96. WS to Barry Lopez, October 19, 1986, April 4, 1988.

97. Barry Lopez to WS, May 21, 1991; WS to Barry Lopez, May 30, 1991.

98. Ivan Doig, quoted in Stegner and Stegner, *Geography of Hope*, p. 125; WS to Marcia Magill, September 24, 1980.

99. Ivan Doig, "Under the Great Wide Sky," *Los Angeles Times Sunday Book Review*, April 12, 1992.

100. William Kittredge to WS, February 23, 1988.

101. Harriet Doerr to WS, February 15, 1984.

102. Terry Tempest Williams to WS, December 18, 1989, Christmas 1991; WS to Carl D. Brandt and Dan Frank, July 9, 1991.

103. Gretel Ehrlich, in Stegner and Stegner, *Geography of Hope*, p. 122; Rick Bass, "On Wilderness and Wallace Stegner," *Amicus Journal*, Spring 1997, pp. 23–27.

104. WS to Richard Scowcroft, October 27, 1959, September 15, 1965.

105. Robert Justice, Robert Hass, and Robert Pinsky, in McPheron, *First Drafts, Last Drafts*, pp. 37, 41, 68.

106. Edward Loomis, "Wallace Stegner and Yvor Winters as Teachers," *South Dakota Review*, Winter 1985, pp. 19–24.

107. WS, interview by Jackson Benson, January 28, 1988; Mary Stegner, interview by Jackson Benson, January 20, 1989.

108. WS to Boris Ilyin, January 23, 1968.

109. Richard Scowcroft, interview by William McPheron, June 22, 2000, Stanford University Oral History Project, p. 39.

110. "Albert Joseph Guérard, English Professor, Literary Icon, Dies," *Stanford Report*, November 13, 2000.

111. WS, quoted by Robert Hass, personal communication; WS, in WS and Scowcroft, *Twenty Years of Stanford Short Stories*, p. xvii.

112. Robert Pinsky, quoted in McPheron, *First Drafts, Last Drafts*, pp. 37, 68.

113. David Levin, *Exemplary Elders* (Athens: University of Georgia Press, 1990), pp. 129–34.

114. Richard Scowcroft, interview by Jackson Benson, November 5, 1987.

115. There is an echo of this concept in Carey McWilliams's earlier book *California: The Great Exception* (New York: Current Books, 1949).

116. WS, "California: The Experimental Society," *Saturday Review*, September 23, 1967. That same year WS followed up on the ahistorical theme and the shortsightedness of the hippie culture, stating, "For what matters in California is Now; it has no past tense." WS, "A Matter of Continuity," *American West Review*, December 1, 1967, p. 12.

117. WS, "The Experimental Society."

118. Gary Snyder to WS, November 24, 1967.

119. WS to Gary Snyder, January 27, 1968.

120. Gary Snyder to WS, February 1, 1968; WS to Gary Snyder, February 22, 1968.

121. WS, in Meine, *Stegner and the Continental Vision*, pp. 225–26.

122. Gary Snyder, personal communication.

123. WS to Wendell Berry, October 1, 1975.

124. Gary Snyder to WS, May 8, 1992; Mary Stegner to Gary Snyder, November 28, 1995.

125. Robert Hass, personal communication.

126. WS to William Styron, March 19, 1963.

127. James D. Houston, personal communication; Wendell Berry and Ed McClanahan, interviews by Jackson Benson, n.d.

128. WS to Richard Scowcroft, September 6, 1968.

129. WS to Jay Miller, February 12, 1972; WS, interview by Jackson Benson, January 27, 1988.

130. Wendell Berry, quoted in Mark Hunter, "In the Company of Wallace Stegner," *San Francisco*, July 1981, p. 43; Wendell Berry, interview by Jackson Benson, n.d.

131. WS, interview by Jackson Benson, January 27, 1988.

132. WS, in WS and Scowcroft, *Twenty Years of Stanford Short Stories*, p. xvii.

133. Robert Hass, personal communication; McClanahan, *My Vita*, p. 52.

134. Boris Ilyin, interview by Jackson Benson, December 28, 1986.

135. WS and Etulain, *Conversations*, pp. 74–76; Al Young, interview by Jackson Benson, June 12, 1990.

136. T. H. Watkins to WS, December 8, 1982.

137. WS to Malcolm Cowley, March 8, 1968.

138. WS to Howard Mumford Jones, April 2, 1970, December 30, 1970. Stegner dated the beginning of his teaching career to 1929, when he was twenty and corrected papers at the University of Utah. He taught at Augustana, his first unsupervised teaching job outside the university he was attending, in 1934.

139. Scott Turow, personal communication.

140. Joseph Kanon, " 'Ordinary Heroes': The Greatest Generation Gap," *New York Times Book Review*, November 6, 2005.

141. WS to Phil Gray, November 16, 1975; Ken Fields, personal communication.

RELUCTANT CONSERVATIONIST

Of National Parks and Arid Lands

1. T. H. Watkins, "Typewritten on Both Sides," *Audubon*, September 1987, pp. 92, 100.

2. WS, "Wallace Stegner: The Artist as Environmental Advocate," interview by Ann Lage, Regional Oral History Office, Bancroft Library, University of California, Berkeley, 1982, p. 34.

3. Ibid., pp. 2–3.

John Wesley Powell Rising

1. WS, *Beyond the Hundredth Meridian* (New York: Penguin Books, 1992), p. 161.

2. WS to William Culp Darrah, January 15, 1952.

3. WS, *Clarence Edward Dutton: An Appraisal* (Salt Lake City: University of Utah Press, 1935); this booklet was reprinted by the University of Utah Press in 2006.

4. WS, quoted in *Utah Chronicle*, January 7, 1937; WS, foreword to *Tertiary History of the Grand Cañon District*, by Clarence E. Dutton (Salt Lake City: Peregrine Smith Books, 1977). See also WS, "The Scientist as Artist: Clarence E. Dutton and the Tertiary History of the Grand Canon District," *American West*, May/June 1978.

5. WS, foreword to Dutton, *Tertiary History*, pp. viii–ix.

6. WS, "The Artist as Environmental Advocate," p. 4.

7. Corle quotes a 1942 letter from WS in his review of *Beyond the Hundredth Meridian*. Edwin Corle, *New York Herald Tribune Book Review*, September 19, 1954.

8. Juanita Brooks to WS, February 4, 1943.

9. WS to Bernard DeVoto, October 29, 1947.

10. William Culp Darrah, *Powell of the Colorado* (Princeton, N.J.: Princeton University Press, 1951).

11. WS to William Culp Darrah, January 12, 1948.

12. Darrah, *Powell of the Colorado*, p. 299; WS, *Beyond the Hundredth Meridian*, p. 299.

13. WS to David Brower, September 2, 1953.

14. WS, "San Juan and Glen Canyon," in *The Sound of Mountain Water*, pp. 102–21.

15. WS to Francis P. Farquhar, January 6, 1948.

16. WS to Phil Gray, August 8, 1948.

17. Alfred A. Knopf to WS, October 17, 1949.

18. WS to Lovell Thompson, March 21, 1951.

19. WS to Bernice Baumgarten, September 17, 1951.

20. WS, ed., *The Letters of Bernard DeVoto* (Garden City, N.Y.: Doubleday, 1975), pp. 322–26.

21. WS to Lovell Thompson, January 9, 1952.

22. Craig Wylie to WS, April 10, 1953, April 22, 1953.

23. WS to Paul Brooks, April 27, 1953; Craig Wylie to WS, April 30, 1953.

24. WS to Paul Brooks, October 18, 1953.

25. "Books of the Times," *The New York Times*, September 11, 1954; Thomas G. Manning, "Beyond the Hundredth Meridian," *American Historical Review*, January 1955, pp. 389–90.

26. Donald Worster, personal communication; Donald Worster, *A River Running West: The Life of John Wesley Powell* (New York: Oxford University Press, 2001), p. xii; Donald Worster, *An Unsettled Country: Changing Landscapes of the American West* (Albuquerque: University of New Mexico Press, 1994), p. 25.

27. Richard White, "Nature or Justice," *New Republic*, June 11, 2001, pp. 47–52; Karl Jacoby, "A River Running West," *Journal of American History*, June 2002.

28. WS, *Beyond the Hundredth Meridian*, pp. viii, 9, 15, 20, 21.

29. Ibid., p. 88.

30. Ibid., pp. 152–53.

31. WS, ed., *Report on the Lands of the Arid Region of the United States, with a More Detailed Account of the Lands of Utah*, by John Wesley Powell (Cambridge, Mass.: Belknap Press/Harvard University Press, 1962), p. xi. One can almost hear the current buzzword *sustainable* being applied today to Powell's concepts.

32. Worster, *A River Running West*, p. 360. Actually, DeVoto had used the raider metaphor in his "Easy Chair" columns for *Harper's*, and Stegner latched on to it.

33. WS, *Beyond the Hundredth Meridian*, p. 251.

34. Ibid., p. 338.

From Words to Deeds

1. WS to Bernice Baumgarten, January 7, 1953.

2. WS, "One-Fourth of a Nation—Public Lands and Itching Fingers," *Reporter*, May 12, 1953. It was a seminal article for Stegner.

3. Olaus J. Murie to Max Ascoli, May 6, 1953; David Brower to Ruth M. Davis, June 5, 1953.

4. David R. Brower to WS, August 26, 1953.

5. WS to David Brower, September 2, 1953.

6. WS, "The Artist as Environmental Advocate," p. 23.

7. WS to David R. Brower, September 2, 1953.

8. More properly known as the Advisory Board on National Parks, Historic Sites, Buildings, and Monuments.

9. Alfred A. Knopf to WS, November 19, 1954, February 8, 1955.

10. WS, "The Artist as Environmental Advocate," p. 2.

11. Alfred A. Knopf to WS, November 19, 1954; WS to Alfred A. Knopf, January 26, 1955.

12. Alfred A. Knopf to WS, November 26, 1954; WS to Alfred A. Knopf, November 30, 1954; Alfred A. Knopf to WS, December 13, 1954.

13. David R. Brower, notes on a conversation with Howard Zahniser, February 2, 1955.

14. WS, "The Marks of Human Passage," in *This Is Dinosaur: Echo Park Country and Its Magic Rivers*, ed. WS (New York: Alfred A. Knopf, 1955), pp. 3–17.

15. WS, *This Is Dinosaur*, p. 96.

16. David R. Brower to Malcolm B. Ellington, February 7, 1955.

17. David Brower to WS, September 18, 1962.

18. David Brower, *For Earth's Sake: The Life and Times of David Brower* (Salt Lake City: Peregrine Smith Books, 1990), p. 342.

19. WS, "Lake Powell," *Holiday*, May 1966. See also WS, *The Sound of Mountain Water*, pp. 121–36.

20. WS, brown California Tomorrow notebook, n.d. These sentiments are contained in a later magazine article: WS, "Myths of the Western Dam," *Saturday Review*, October 23, 1965.

21. Floyd Dominy to WS, April 20, 1966; WS to David R. Brower, May 23, 1966.

22. Mark W. T. Harvey, *A Symbol of Wilderness: Echo Park and the American Conservation Movement* (Albuquerque: University of New Mexico Press, 1994), pp. 258, 294.

The Next Lone Ranger

1. Roderick Nash, *Wilderness and the American Mind* (New Haven, Conn.: Yale University Press, 1982), p. 261; Dan Flores, "Citizen of a Larger Country: Wallace Stegner, the Environment, and the West," in *Wallace Stegner: Man & Writer*, ed. Charles E. Rankin (Albuquerque: University of New Mexico Press, 1996), p. 81.

2. David E. Pesonen to WS, June 15, 1960.

3. Scholars have traced the phrase "geography of despair" to Dante and the Renaissance, from whence the widely read Stegner may have plucked it and turned it around. The letter has been reproduced in countless forms, one being a limited boxed edition bound between cottonwood boards that sells for $3,500. The letter can be found in WS, *The Sound of Mountain Water*, pp. 145–53.

4. Wildlands Research Center, University of California, Berkeley, *Wilderness and Recreation: A Report on Resources, Values, and Problems* (Washington, D.C., 1962), pp. 34–36; Outdoor Recreation Resources Review Commission, *Outdoor Recreation for America* (Washington, D.C., 1962), pp. 131–32.

5. WS, "The Artist as Environmental Advocate," p. 12.

6. David Brower, ed., *Wilderness: America's Living Heritage* (San Francisco: Sierra Club Books, 1961), p. 96.

Closer to Home

1. Richard A. Walker, "Silicon City: The Urbanization of the Electronic Mecca" (unpublished ms., 2002), pp. 175, 185, 195.

2. WS, speech to open-space conference, Loma Prieta Chapter, Sierra Club, April 26, 1956.

3. WS, text for Voice of America broadcast, n.d.; WS, "East Palo Alto," *Saturday Review*, August 1, 1970.

4. WS, "The Peninsula," in *20-20 Vision: In Celebration of the Peninsula Hills*, ed. Phyllis Filiberti Butler (Palo Alto, Calif.: Green Foothills Foundation, 1982), p. 16.

5. WS, *All the Little Live Things* (New York: Penguin Books, 1991), pp. 16–17.

6. Ibid., pp. 53–54.

7. WS, in *Green Footnotes*, newsletter of the Committee for Green Foothills, September 1962.

8. Ruth Spangenberg, "The Founding of the Committee for Green Foothills," interview by Richard A. Walker, Regional Oral History Office, Bancroft Library, University of California, Berkeley, August 16, 2001, pp. 4, 5, 36; Mary Davey, interview by Richard A. Walker, University of California, Berkeley, August 29, 2001, p. 5.

9. WS, "The Artist as Environmental Advocate," p. 9.

10. WS, "The Peninsula," p. 25.

11. WS, "The Artist as an Environmental Advocate," p. 10.

12. WS, "The Peninsula," pp. 12, 14.

13. WS and Chekhov, quoted in Yvonne Jacobson, *Passing Farms: Enduring Values* (Los Altos, Calif.: William Kaufmann, 1984), p. x.

A National Agenda

1. Stewart L. Udall to WS, May 22, 1961.

2. Stewart L. Udall to WS, May 23, 1961.

3. Stewart L. Udall to WS, June 11, 1961.

4. WS, "The Artist as Environmental Advocate," p. 14.

5. WS to Stewart L. Udall, September 22, 1961, September 25, 1961.

6. WS to Phil Gray, October 7, 1961.

7. WS to Mrs. Kenneth Brown, October 26, 1961.

8. Don Moser to WS, February 13, 1962.

9. In the acknowledgments, Udall credited "my friend" Stegner for the outline and the two special assistants, Moser and Gilliam, for their help with the text. Another special assistant, the author Alvin M. Josephy Jr., selected the illustrations. Stewart L. Udall, *The Quiet Crisis* (New York: Holt, Rinehart & Winston, 1963).

10. WS to George Stewart, November 1, 1961.

11. WS, "The Artist as Environmental Advocate," pp. 12–15.

12. Ibid.

13. Ansel Adams to WS, in *Ansel Adams: Letters, 1916–1984*, ed. Mary Street Alinder and Andrea Gray Sullivan (Boston: Little, Brown, 1988), pp. 284–86. The Golden Gate National Recreation Area, in and around San Francisco, was created in 1972.

14. T. H. Watkins to WS, October 27, 1989.

15. WS, trip notes, October 8–16, 1961.

16. Ibid.

17. WS, "Building a Conservation Backfire in Utah," memo to Stewart L. Udall, October 23, 1961.

18. WS to Stewart L. Udall, November 7, 1961.

19. Ibid.; Gary O. Larson, *The Reluctant Patron: The United States Government and the Arts, 1943–1965* (Philadelphia: University of Pennsylvania Press, 1983), p. 155.

20. WS to Stewart L. Udall, December 30, 1961.

21. When he became chairman of the advisory board, Stegner had to disclose his financial interests. He and his wife owned small amounts of stock in a company that ran the concessions in Yosemite National Park, a lumber company that operated in redwood country, a science magazine, a Virginia public utility, Bay Area electronics firms, a pharmaceutical company, a paper company, and a copper-mining firm.

22. WS to Stewart L. Udall, December 9, 1962.

23. WS to Robert G. Sproul and Melville B. Grosvenor, December 26, 1964.

24. Minutes, meeting of Advisory Board on National Parks, Historic Sites, Buildings, and Monuments, October 5–14, 1964.

25. WS to Stewart L. Udall, October 7, 1965.

26. WS, "The Artist as Environmental Advocate," pp. 18–22. The Lyndon B. Johnson National Historic Site was created near Johnson City, Texas, in 1969. It was upgraded to a national historical park in 1980, six years after Johnson died.

27. Advisory Board on National Parks, Historic Sites, Buildings, and Monuments, minutes, August 8, 1965.

28. Stewart L. Udall to WS, August 22, 1966.

29. Stegner's defense of Udall appeared in two articles: WS, "Quiet Crisis or Lost Cause," *Saturday Review*, September 19, 1964; and WS, "To Save the Grand Canyon," *Saturday Review*, August 20, 1966. In the first article, the magazine did not identify Stegner as Udall's former special assistant.

30. WS to Stewart L. Udall, April 21, 1968.

The Sierra Club Years

1. WS to William E. Siri, July 25, 1964.

2. WS, "The Artist as Environmental Advocate," p. 26.

3. Ibid., p. 30.

4. Ibid., pp. 24–26; Watkins, "Typewritten on Both Sides," p. 100.

5. Ansel Adams to WS, November 8, 1968.

6. WS, "The Artist as Environmental Advocate," pp. 26–27.

7. WS, "Bitten by Worm of Power: Views of Brower Foes in Sierra Club," *Palo Alto Times*, February 11, 1969.

8. WS, "The Artist as Environmental Advocate," p. 27; WS to David Brower, May 16, 1990.

9. WS to Stewart L. Udall, October 23, 1974.

PROMINENT AUTHOR

Angle of Unrest

1. David Kipen, "Acute 'Angle' Wins Reader Poll," *San Francisco Chronicle*, November 11, 1999.

2. WS to James Hepworth, July 2, 1985.

3. WS, interview by representative of the American Name Society for publication in *Names*, January 13, 1957.

4. WS, " 'Truth' and 'Faking' in Fiction," *Writer*, February 1940; WS, "Fiction: A Lens on Life," *Saturday Review of Literature*, April 22, 1950.

5. WS to Phil Gray, July 24, 1947.

6. WS, *Joe Hill: A Biographical Novel* (New York: Penguin Books, 1990), p. 13.

7. WS to Mac (no last name), n.d. (possibly 1961).

8. WS, jottings in "On Biography and Fiction," notebook, April 29 (year unknown).

9. Robert Canzoneri, "Wallace Stegner: Trial by Existence," *Southern Review* 9, nos. 3–4 (1973).

10. WS, in David Dillon, "Time's Prisoners: An Interview with Wallace Stegner," in Arthur, *Critical Essays on Wallace Stegner*, p. 53.

11. WS, interview by Jackson Benson, November 5, 1987.

12. WS, "To: An Unidentified Query Concerning the Writing of *Angle of Repose*," draft for an article that would be published in the Literary Guild magazine.

13. WS to James Hepworth, August 15, 1985.

14. WS and Etulain, *Conversations*, p. 48.

15. Robert Canzoneri, personal communication. It was Canzoneri, a Stanford graduate student at the time, who discovered Foerster and told Stegner about him. WS, interview by Jackson Benson, January 27, 1988.

16. The immediate coverage of the Stephen Ambrose, Doris Kearns Goodwin, and Kaavya Viswanathan affairs and of Dan Brown and J. K. Rowling, whose cases had no merit, come immediately to mind. For the more reflective assessments, see Charles Isherwood, "The P. Word: Her Life, His Art, Your Call," *New York Times*, December 3, 2006; Jonathan Lethem, "The Ecstasy of Influence: A Plagiarism," *Harper's*, February 2007; and Richard A. Posner, *The Little Book of Plagiarism* (New York: Pantheon, 2007). An insightful review of Posner's book by Jonathan Kirsch, an author and lawyer specializing in publishing law, ran in the *Los Angeles Times Book Review* on January 28, 2007. What Posner's book achieved, Kirsch wrote, was "a healthy corrective to the public pillorying of accused plagiarists that has become something of a spectator sport." William Shakespeare, T. S. Eliot, Vladimir Nabokov, and Martin Luther King Jr. are most frequently cited as adding value to prior works. Of Shakespeare, Posner wrote: "Thousands of lines in his plays are verbatim copies or close paraphrases from various sources, along with titles and plot details, all without acknowledgment."

17. WS, "Western Record and Romance," in *Literary History of the United States*, ed. Robert E. Spiller et al. (New York: Macmillan, 1948), 2:868–69.

18. George H. McMurry to Arthur B. Foote, February 12, 1954.

19. WS to Janet Micoleau, January 17, 1955.

20. WS, ed., *Selected American Prose, 1841–1900: The Realistic Movement* (New York: Rinehart, 1958), p. 18.

21. McMurry, who was concentrating only on Foote's California years, surrendered the topic to Stegner. "You speak of my 'priority,' " wrote McMurry. "I've always felt yours is co-equal—or have you forgotten the ecstasy my face must have reflected the day I rushed up after the class in which you mentioned the whereabouts of the MHF letters?" George H. McMurry to WS, September 25, 1967.

22. WS to Janet (Mrs. Tyler) Micoleau, August 11, 1967.

23. Janet Micoleau to WS, September 5, 1967.

24. WS to Janet Micoleau, September 9, 1967.

25. There were two other granddaughters, Marian Foote Conway and Evelyn Foote Gardiner. Micoleau was in telephone contact with them.

26. Helena married Foote's most supportive editor, Richard Watson Gilder, who was the assistant editor of *Scribner's Monthly* and, later, the editor of *Century* magazine. The Gilders were one of the celebrity couples of the eastern literary establishment at the time.

27. WS to Rosamond Gilder, October 11, 1967; WS, interview by Jackson Benson, January 24, 1991.

28. Charles E. Rankin of the University of Oklahoma Press, personal communication; Carl D. Brandt of Brandt & Hochman, personal communication; Kathryn Court of Penguin Books, personal communication.

29. WS to Janet Micoleau, February 27, 1968.

30. WS to Carol Brandt, October 12, 1978.

31. Carl D. Brandt represented me on some earlier titles. The idea for the biography was mine. I was not represented by an agent at the time that I conceived it. I interested Ashbel Green of Knopf in the subject, he offered a contract, and then I contacted Carl and asked him to represent me again.

32. Carol Brandt to Michael Thomas, February 1, 1974; WS to Carol Brandt, May 2, 1972.

33. WS to Carol Brandt, September 12, 1980, October 7, 1981.

34. Mary Stegner, interview by Jackson Benson, January 20, 1989; WS, interview by Jackson Benson, January 27, 1988.

35. WS to Carol Brandt, February 20, 1968, February 26, 1968.

36. WS to Carol Brandt, February 26, 1968, March 14, 1968; WS to Malcolm Cowley, April 14, 1968.

37. Ken McCormick to WS, May 14, 1968.

38. WS, typewritten edited ms., titled "First, Second, and Third Tries at a Beginning," May 1968.

39. WS, *Angle of Repose* (New York: Penguin Books, 1992), p. 15.

40. WS, in Dan Tooker and Roger Hofheins, *Fiction! Interviews with Northern California Novelists* (New York: Harcourt Brace Jovanovich, 1976), p. 173.

41. WS, scraps of paper, box 95, folder 1, Wallace Earle Stegner Papers, Marriott Library, University of Utah.

42. Ibid.

43. WS to Carol Brandt, August 20, 1968, November 5, 1968.

44. WS to Carol Brandt, March 15, 1969.

45. WS to Janet Micoleau, March 3, 1970.

46. Rodman W. Paul to WS, March 20, 1970. The memoir would be Mary Hallock Foote, *A Victorian Gentlewoman in the Far West: The Reminiscences of Mary Hallock Foote*, ed. Rodman W. Paul (San Marino, Calif.: Huntington Library, 1972).

47. WS to Janet Micoleau, March 3, 1970.

48. Ibid.

49. Janet Micoleau to WS, April 12, 1970.

50. Janet Micoleau to WS, June 10, 1970.

51. Carol Brandt to WS, March 31, 1971.

52. WS to Carol Brandt, May 8, 1970.

53. WS to Howard Mumford Jones, April 2, 1970.

54. Carol Brandt to WS, May 11, 1970; Carol Brandt to Ken McCormick, June 5, 1970.

55. WS to Carol Brandt, June 22, 1970.

56. WS to Carol Brandt, June 27, 1970.

57. Carol Brandt to WS, September 20, 1970.

58. Ken McCormick to WS, November 25, 1970; Stewart Richardson to WS, December 21, 1970.

59. Stewart Richardson to WS, August 20, 1971.

60. Janet Micoleau to WS, n.d., but it seems to be from the same month as a letter from Tyler Micoleau to WS dated March 23, 1971.

61. WS to Page Stegner, October 1, 1971.

62. William Abrahams, "The Real Thing," *Atlantic Monthly*, April 1971, p. 96.

63. John Leonard, personal communication.

64. Thomas Lask, "El Dorado on the Horizon," *New York Times*, March 24, 1971; WS to Carol Brandt, June 26, 1971. I mentioned to Stegner that my book *A River No More*, which he had reviewed extremely favorably for *The New Republic*, had not been reviewed in *The New York Times Book Review*. I thought he replied that none of his books had been reviewed in that publication; but, of course, some had been reviewed. He may have forgotten, wanted to make a point, or misspoke because he was still angry—as is most likely, given what I now know about his character. Also, I may not have heard him correctly. Alfred Knopf was a great booster of my river book. When I mentioned the lack of a review in the *NYTBR*, he wrote me: "The failure of the Times Book Review, or of the paper for that matter, to review your book in any way is a splendid example of the negative power which that paper possesses. My own quarrel with the Book Review began as far back as 1919 when I was able to talk to old Adolph Ochs himself, who took the cheerful attitude, I remember, at one talk we had that what really mattered were not the reviews but the publishers' advertisements." Alfred A. Knopf to Philip L. Fradkin, November 13, 1981.

65. WS to Carol Brandt, June 26, 1971.

66. Malcolm Cowley to WS, August 21, 1971.

67. William DuBois, "The Last Word: The Well-Made Novel," *New York Times Book Review*, August 29, 1971.

68. Malcolm Cowley to WS, August 29, 1971.

69. WS to Stewart Richardson, September 3, 1971.

70. WS to Carol Brandt, May 2, 1972.

71. Wendell Berry to WS, July 20, 1971.

72. WS to Phil Gray, May 6, 1972.

73. John Leonard, "The Pulitzer Prizes: Fail-Safe Again," *New York Times Book Review*, May 14, 1972. No fiction prize was awarded in 1971.

74. Momaday had been appointed to the Stanford faculty the day before the Pulitzer Prizes were announced.

75. WS and Etulain, *Conversations*, p. 96.

76. Stewart Richardson to WS, May 22, 1972.

77. John Leonard, personal communication.

78. WS to Ken McCormick, October 29, 1972.

79. Stegner's next two novels, *The Spectator Bird* and *Recapitulation*, would be advertised in the *Times Book Review*.

80. WS, "Breaking a New York Monopoly on Books," *Palo Alto Weekly*, September 25, 1980.

81. WS and Etulain, *Conversations*, pp. 77–78.

82. WS, interview by Jackson Benson, November 4, 1987.

83. WS to Janet Micoleau, March 16, 1971.

84. WS, *Angle of Repose*, p. 509.

85. James D. Houston, personal communication; Linda K. Karrell, *Writing Together, Writing Apart: Collaboration in Western American Literature* (Lincoln: University of Nebraska Press, 2002), p. 179.

86. WS, in Tooker and Hofheins, *Fiction!*, p. 175.

87. WS, *Angle of Repose*, pp. 561, 563, 568.

88. Paul, in Foote, *A Victorian Gentlewoman*, pp. 402–3.

89. Stegner went to one rehearsal and concluded that "the libretto is pretty pro-

saic and the music maybe inaccessible." Following its fifth and final performance, he said, "The music listens better." WS to Carol Brandt, April 14, 1976, November 27, 1976.

90. Janet Micoleau to WS, September 11, 1976; Blake Green, "The Genteel Western Lady Behind This Season's New Opera," *San Francisco Chronicle*, September 8, 1976.

91. Janet Micoleau to WS, September 11, 1976.

92. Mary Ellen Williams Walsh, "*Angle of Repose* and the Writings of Mary Hallock Foote: A Source Study," in Arthur, *Critical Essays on Wallace Stegner*, p. 208.

93. Blake Green to WS, September 10, 1976.

94. WS to Blake Green, September 16, 1976.

95. Mary Ellen Williams Walsh, personal communication.

96. Marian Conway to Mary Ellen Williams [Walsh], January 11, 1980; Mary Ellen Williams Walsh to Marian Conway, April 8, 1980.

97. Mary Ellen Williams Walsh to Marian F. Conway, April 8, 1980; Walsh, "*Angle of Repose* and the Writings of Mary Hallock Foote," p. 185.

98. WS and Etulain, *Conversations*, p. 87. An interesting observation that a number of perceptive readers have made is that the present, as represented in *Angle of Repose* by Lyman Ward and other contemporary characters, is less convincing than Foote/Ward's past. "The Present seems less real than the Past. The narrator's situation is at once more comic and more grievous than his grandparents'. His wife has run away with the surgeon who took off his leg, and he cannot get both feet back on the ground." Merrill Lewis and Lorene Lewis, *Wallace Stegner*, Boise State College Western Writers Series 4 (Boise, Idaho: Boise State College, 1972), p. 37.

99. Mary Ellen Williams Walsh to Marian Conway, April 8, 1980.

100. Mary Ellen Williams Walsh to Marian Conway, April 23, 1980. The permissions are contained in the Micoleau correspondence that is in the Wallace Earle Stegner Papers at the University of Utah. The papers became available after Walsh wrote her essay but before most other critics voiced their objections to Stegner's use of the Foote material.

101. Anthony Arthur, personal communication.

102. Actually, that permission was for Stegner, not a member of the Foote family, to give.

103. Mary Ellen Williams Walsh to Marian Conway, May 23, 1980. This was exactly the predicament that Stegner found himself in.

104. Mary Ellen Williams Walsh to Marian Conway, May 23, 1980.

105. The book had a limited circulation: one thousand copies were printed. Anthony Arthur, personal communication.

106. Mary Ellen Williams Walsh, personal communication.

107. Anthony Arthur, personal communication.

108. Mary Ellen Williams Walsh, personal communication.

109. Jackson J. Benson, *Wallace Stegner: His Life and Work* (New York: Viking Press, 1996), p. 354.

110. Walsh, "*Angle of Repose* and the Writings of Mary Hallock Foote," p. 209.

111. For a discussion of what has come to be known as a homosocial relationship, meaning a close, nonsexual friendship between men or between women, see Carroll Smith-Rosenberg, "The Female World of Love and Ritual: Relations Between Women in Nineteenth-Century America," *Signs*, Autumn 1975, pp. 1–29.

112. WS, *Angle of Repose*, p. 57.

113. Walsh, "*Angle of Repose* and the Writings of Mary Hallock Foote," pp. 205–6, 208, 209.

114. WS and Etulain, *Conversations*, pp. 86–87, 163.

115. WS to James Hepworth, June 5, 1985, July 2, 1985, July 30, 1988. In the June 5 letter, Stegner cautioned Hepworth: "Do what you want. But be very careful how you quote me. It's bad enough to be injured by the ill will of enemies; I'd hate to be injured by the good will of a friend."

116. Evelyn Foote Gardiner, interview by Jackson Benson, August 3, 1993.

117. David Lavender, "The Tyranny of Facts," in *Old Southwest, New Southwest: Essays on a Region and Its Literature*, ed. Judy Nolte Lensink (Tucson, Ariz.: Tucson Public Library, 1987), pp. 63–73.

118. James Hepworth, "Wallace Stegner's *Angle of Repose:* One Reader's Response" (Ph.D. thesis, University of Arizona, 1989), p. 39; Hepworth, "Wallace Stegner's Practice of the Wild," p. 227. Elizabeth Cook-Lynn wrote the previously mentioned *Why I Can't Read Wallace Stegner and Other Essays*.

119. Benson, *Wallace Stegner*, p. 355.

120. When Benson first approached him with the idea of a biography, Stegner warned: "I am a private person, and my personal life seems to me the business of nobody but me and my family, and seeing it exploited or spread out—becoming the major character in a psychodrama—would give me nothing but a pain in the tail." WS to Jackson Benson, January 14, 1986. After Wally died, Mary Stegner carefully read Benson's drafts and asked for and received a number of revisions. Benson became exasperated, but he needed her permission to quote from Stegner's works. "I hope that you find this to be [a] good, well written book that is very flattering to your husband overall. . . . But, again, I would appreciate it if you can refrain as much as possible from objecting to items that might possibly be seen as in some possible way as negative. The book is so overwhelmingly positive, the reviewers are likely to doubt that I have been truthful, and if truthful, whether this is really a human being I am talking about." Jackson Benson to Mary Stegner, November 25, 1994. Besides correcting factual matters, Mary objected to Wally's not being portrayed as a widely read author of national stature, his being depicted as stuffy, and the mention of students whose work Wally did not admire. She asked Benson to delete four pages dealing with a novel that Wally considered one of his minor works.

121. Jackson Benson, introduction to *Angle of Repose*, by WS (New York: Penguin Classics, 2000), pp. xx–xxi.

122. Melody Graulich, "Book Learning: *Angle of Repose* as Literary History," in Rankin, *Wallace Stegner*, pp. 233, 241, 244, 246–47, 251.

123. Melody Graulich, personal communication.

124. WS and Etulain's *Conversations* was Karrell's only source for Stegner's defense; Micoleau's letters are not cited or mentioned in her text. Karrell, *Writing Together, Writing Apart*, pp. 157, 175, 198.

125. Sands Hall, *Fair Use* (Nevada City, Calif., 2005), pp. 8–9.

126. Linda K. Karrell, "The Postmodern Author on Stage: *Fair Use* and Wallace Stegner," *American Drama*, Summer 2005, pp. 70–89.

127. Susan Salter Reynolds, "Tangle of Repose," *Los Angeles Times Magazine*, March 23, 2003.

128. Christine Hill Smith, *Reading* A Victorian Gentlewoman in the Far West: The Reminiscences of Mary Hallock Foote, Boise State University Western Writers Series 154 (Boise, Idaho: Boise State University, 2002), pp. 35–39, 43.

129. Krista Comer, *Landscapes of the New West: Gender and Geography in Contemporary Women's Writing* (Chapel Hill: University of North Carolina Press, 1999), pp. 39, 43, 55.

130. Richard A. Posner, "On Plagiarism," *Atlantic Monthly*, April 2002, p. 23.

131. Richard A. Posner, *The Little Book of Plagiarism* (New York: Pantheon, 2007), p. 106.

132. Ibid., pp. 46, 108.

133. Malcolm Gladwell, "Something Borrowed," *New Yorker*, November 22, 2004.

134. Jonathan Kirsch, a Los Angeles writer, book critic, and literary property rights lawyer, commented: "I think Stegner's crucial error was not acknowledging that he quoted directly from his sources. His copyright page notice acknowledges only the use of 'facts from their real lives' but it is nowhere disclosed that he also used text from real letters [and the memoir]. Any theoretical and retroactive fair use defense—and, in a looser sense, the case against a finding of plagiarism—would have been much stronger had he done so." Jonathan Kirsch, personal communication.

The Coup de Grâce by the Times

1. WS to Avis DeVoto, February 9, 1974.
2. WS to Fawn Brodie, November 5, 1970.
3. WS to Avis DeVoto, May 3, 1971.
4. Fawn Brodie to WS, January 7, 1971.
5. Fawn Brodie to WS, March 31, 1975.
6. WS to Fawn Brodie, January 26, 1975.
7. Stegner seems to be saying that it is personal ties that count. He invented a private life for the Footes with whom he had no personal relationship, dealt only with the public DeVoto, would not have published *Crossing to Safety* if any of the Gray children had objected to it, and told his biographer, Jackson Benson, to stay away from his private life. He did offer the Foote family the opportunity to read the manuscript of *Angle of Repose* before publication. There is no way of knowing what their reaction would have been had they done so, or how Stegner would have dealt with it. WS to Fawn Brodie, March 15, 1974.
8. WS to Howard Mumford Jones, July 5, 1974.
9. WS to Carol Brandt, June 29, 1976.
10. WS to Carol Brandt, March 24, 1977.
11. Ken McCormick to Carol Brandt, March 24, 1977.
12. WS and Etulain, *Conversations*, p. 97.
13. Herbert Mitgang, "Howe Gets History Book Award," *New York Times*, April 12, 1977.
14. Herbert Mitgang, "Book Awards: Are the Judges Too Old?" *New York Times*, April 13, 1977.
15. Virginia Caldwell to WS, June 1983.
16. Orville Prescott to WS, May 23, 1977.
17. Berry, "Wallace Stegner and the Great Community," pp. 16–18; Ivan Doig, "West of the Hudson, Pronounced 'Wallace,' " in Stegner and Stegner, *Geography of Hope*, pp. 125–26.
18. Larry McMurtry, *New York Review of Books*, October 4, 2001.
19. Russell Martin, "Writers of the Purple Sage: Voices in Western Literature," *New York Times Magazine*, December 27, 1981. That consummate easterner John Updike wrote of the difficulty of being recognized in the West: "To the American literary establishment, the West Coast is out of sight and mind." He was referring to the Nobel laureate Czeslaw Milosz, a poet who lived in Berkeley. John Updike, *New Yorker*, December 31, 2001.

Taking Leave

1. Walker, "Silicon City," p. 635.

2. WS, "How to Be an Accessory Before the Fact," *Palo Alto Times*, January 8, 1977.

3. WS, "The Peninsula," p. 20.

4. WS, typewritten comments at the twenty-fifth anniversary of the founding of the Committee for Green Foothills, May 9, 1987.

5. John L'Heureux, personal communication.

6. Robert Polhemus, personal communication.

7. John L'Heureux to WS, July 21, 1982; WS to John L'Heureux, July 24, 1982.

8. Nancy Packer, personal communication.

9. David C. Weber to WS, September 22, 1976.

10. WS to Nancy Colberg, May 24, 1985.

11. Alexander Laurence, "Gilbert Sorrentino Interview," 1994, www.altx.com.

12. WS to Jackson Benson, June 26, 1989.

13. WS to Jack Shoemaker, September 13, 1982.

14. WS to Carol Brandt, May 8, 1984.

15. WS to Carl D. Brandt, May 4, 1986; Nancy Gray Keyes, interview by Jackson Benson, July 3, 1990; Nancy Gray Keyes to WS, July 14, 1986.

16. Samuel S. Vaughan to WS, October 2, 1986.

17. Doris Grumbach, "The Grace of Old Lovers," *New York Times Book Review*, September 20, 1987.

18. WS, typed notes for talk to the Intermountain Booksellers Association, Salt Lake City, September 12, 1987.

19. WS to James Hepworth, January 30, 1987.

20. WS to Charles Schlessiger, February 11, 1988.

21. WS to Carl D. Brandt, March 29, 1985.

22. Carl D. Brandt to Willis G. Regier, April 4, 1991.

23. Dan Frank to WS, July 1, 1985. Frank subsequently moved to Pantheon, where he published books by authors who had known or been influenced by Stegner, such as Gretel Ehrlich, Marc Reisner, and Terry Tempest Williams. Personal communication, Dan Frank.

24. Samuel S. Vaughan to WS, February 28, 1991. *Crossing* was nominated for a National Book Critics Circle Award in 1987 and *Bluebird* in 1992.

25. WS, untitled notes, n.d. It is not clear where Stegner gave the talk or if he actually gave it. The typewritten, carefully edited eight pages of notes indicate that it was aimed at an audience, was written after the publication of the fiction collection, and was not a frivolous exercise. Even if he didn't give the talk, the notes still represent his thinking on the subject.

26. WS to Carol Brandt, November 27, 1976.

27. WS, transcript of tape recording of a speech at the Herbst Theatre, San Francisco, n.d., but shortly after publication of *Crossing to Safety*.

28. WS to Carl D. Brandt, October 7, 1988, October 13, 1988.

29. WS to John Daniel, October 22, 1992.

30. Brett J. Olsen, "Wallace Stegner and the Environmental Ethic: Environmentalism as a Rejection of Western Myth," *Western American Literature*, Summer 1994, p. 139; WS, *Bluebird*, p. xxi.

31. WS, typewritten draft of an introduction to the Wilderness Letter for the Wilderness Society chapbook, *The Geography of Hope: A Wilderness Letter* 1992.

32. WS, "The Real Line," n.d. Fisher said the summary was written "a year or so" before Stegner died. Stephen Fisher, personal communication.

33. Allison Stegner is in the Stanford class of 2010.

34. Stegner was also nominated for the Nobel by the Western Literature Association. Richard W. Etulain, personal communication.

35. Watkins's numerous letters to Stegner in the Wallace Earle Stegner Papers at the University of Utah hint at fascinating replies from Wally. Watkins's widow, Joan, who now uses the name Ellen, is virtually incommunicado. She finally replied to my numerous queries in 2005, saying that Wally's letters were not "accessible."

36. *High Country News* and *The Bloomsbury Review*, both based in Colorado, have limited circulations and means. The *Los Angeles Times*, which once had the means, and the *San Francisco Chronicle* are now retrenching. *The San Francisco Review of Books* is defunct.

37. Barry Lopez to WS, June 10, 1990.

38. Notably absent from this list was Thomas McGuane, a Montana novelist and former Stegner Fellow. WS to William Kittredge, February 11, 1988.

39. Richard Etulain and James Hepworth also considered writing biographies but were discouraged by Mary Stegner. Page Stegner and Jo Ann Rogers, personal communications.

40. Charles F. Wilkinson to Dan Frank, June 11, 1993; WS to Charles F. Wilkinson, November 19, 1986.

41. Patricia Nelson Limerick to WS, November 11, 1989; WS to Charles F. Wilkinson, October 8, 1988.

42. David McCullough to WS, May 16, 1990.

43. WS, "Stegner: Leland Stanford's Dream Has Proven Durability," *Campus Report*, March 14, 1991.

44. WS to Sharon Butala, December 30, 1992.

45. WS to Carol Brandt, April 5, 1982.

46. WS, acceptance speech on receiving the lifetime achievement award of PEN USA in 1990, reprinted as WS, "Out Where the Sense of Place Is a Sense of Motion," *Los Angeles Times Book Review*, June 3, 1990.

47. Ibid.

48. WS, "The Sense of Place," *Harrowsmith Country Life*, September/October 1992, p. 42.

49. WS and Page Stegner, *American Places* (Moscow: University of Idaho Press, 1983), p. 49.

50. WS, *Interview*, conducted by Bonetti.

51. Two of the awards' finalists, William Kittredge and Charles Wilkinson, had been mentored by Stegner.

52. A wag in the Department of English at Stanford said, "Wallace Stegner died because he failed to yield." Ken Fields, personal communication.

53. Mary Stegner, interview by Jackson Benson, September 24, 1994; "Wallace Stegner—Acclaimed Writer of American West," *San Francisco Chronicle*, April 15, 1993.

54. Butala, the author of fifteen works of fiction and nonfiction, has been short-listed for a number of provincial and national literary awards in Canada.

55. Donald Kennedy, "Former President Pays Tribute to Stegner," *Stanford Daily*, April 15, 1993.

56. Sharon Butala, "The Night Wallace Stegner Died," *Brick*, Summer 1993, p. 25.

57. William H. Honan, "Wallace Stegner Is Dead at 84: Pulitzer Prize–Winning Author," *New York Times*, April 15, 1993.

58. "Western Heroes," *New Yorker*, May 10, 1993.

59. Robin Patterson to WS, April 16, 1993 (with a copy to Carl D. Brandt, July 21, 1993). Patterson had been a student at Stanford and was associated with the Aspen Center for Environmental Studies.

EPILOGUE

Saskatchewan

1. WS, *Wolf Willow*, p. 9.
2. WS to Sharon Butala, March 13, 1990, June 19, 1987.
3. Sharon Butala, *Perfection of the Morning: A Woman's Awakening in Nature* (St. Paul, Minn.: Hungry Mind Press, 1994), p. 174.
4. WS, *Wolf Willow*, p. 282.
5. WS to Sharon Butala, June 19, 1987.
6. "Eastend's Dinocountry," www.dinocountry.com.
7. WS to Sharon Butala, December 18, 1991.
8. Bea Tasche, personal communication.

Utah

1. Anne Riordan, personal communication.
2. WS, handwritten notes for "Glen Canyon Submersus," in *The Sound of Mountain Water*.
3. WS, "Glen Canyon Submersus," in *The Sound of Mountain Water*, p. 128.
4. Ibid., p. 133.

California

1. Foote, *A Victorian Gentlewoman*, p. 395.

Vermont

1. Jessamyn Smyth, personal communication.
2. William Kittredge, "Taking Our Turn, or Responsibilities," in Stegner and Stegner, *Geography of Hope*, p. 114.
3. William Kittredge, *Who Owns the West* (San Francisco: Mercury House, 1996), p. 71.
4. Ron Carlson, personal communication.
5. Julie Kirgo, "The Healing Country," *Vermont Magazine*, January/February 1993, pp. 57–61.
6. WS, response during a panel discussion, "Range of Visions: Wallace Stegner and the West," California Studies Conference, February 5, 1993.

INDEX

A NOTE ABOUT THE AUTHOR

PHILIP L. FRADKIN has written ten books about Alaska, California, and the interior West. *A River No More: The Colorado River and the West* is considered the classic study of that subject. He shared in a Pulitzer Prize at the *Los Angeles Times*, was western editor of *Audubon* magazine, and has taught at the University of California at Berkeley, Stanford University, and Williams College. He lives on the Pacific Coast just north of San Francisco.

A NOTE ON THE TYPE

THIS BOOK was set in Janson, a typeface long thought to have been made by the Dutchman Anton Janson, who was a practicing typefounder in Leipzig during the years 1668–1687. However, it has been conclusively demonstrated that these types are actually the work of Nicholas Kis (1650–1702), a Hungarian, who most probably learned his trade from the master Dutch typefounder Dirk Voskens. The type is an excellent example of the influential and sturdy Dutch types that prevailed in England up to the time William Caslon (1692–1766) developed his own incomparable designs from them.

Composed by North Market Street Graphics
Lancaster, Pennsylvania
Printed and bound by Berryville Graphics
Berryville, Virginia
Designed by Virginia Tan